AF474803

INFORMATION TECHNOLOGY
Selected Tutorials

IFIP – The International Federation for Information Processing

IFIP was founded in 1960 under the auspices of UNESCO, following the First World Computer Congress held in Paris the previous year. An umbrella organization for societies working in information processing, IFIP's aim is two-fold: to support information processing within its member countries and to encourage technology transfer to developing nations. As its mission statement clearly states,

> *IFIP's mission is to be the leading, truly international, apolitical organization which encourages and assists in the development, exploitation and application of information technology for the benefit of all people.*

IFIP is a non-profit making organization, run almost solely by 2500 volunteers. It operates through a number of technical committees, which organize events and publications. IFIP's events range from an international congress to local seminars, but the most important are:

- The IFIP World Computer Congress, held every second year;
- Open conferences;
- Working conferences.

The flagship event is the IFIP World Computer Congress, at which both invited and contributed papers are presented. Contributed papers are rigorously refereed and the rejection rate is high.

As with the Congress, participation in the open conferences is open to all and papers may be invited or submitted. Again, submitted papers are stringently refereed.

The working conferences are structured differently. They are usually run by a working group and attendance is small and by invitation only. Their purpose is to create an atmosphere conducive to innovation and development. Refereeing is less rigorous and papers are subjected to extensive group discussion.

Publications arising from IFIP events vary. The papers presented at the IFIP World Computer Congress and at open conferences are published as conference proceedings, while the results of the working conferences are often published as collections of selected and edited papers.

Any national society whose primary activity is in information may apply to become a full member of IFIP, although full membership is restricted to one society per country. Full members are entitled to vote at the annual General Assembly, National societies preferring a less committed involvement may apply for associate or corresponding membership. Associate members enjoy the same benefits as full members, but without voting rights. Corresponding members are not represented in IFIP bodies. Affiliated membership is open to non-national societies, and individual and honorary membership schemes are also offered.

INFORMATION TECHNOLOGY

Selected Tutorials

IFIP 18th World Computer Congress
Tutorials
22–27 August 2004
Toulouse, France

Edited by

Ricardo Reis
Universidade Federal do Rio Grande do Sul
Brazil

SPRINGER SCIENCE+BUSINESS MEDIA, LLC

Electronic Services <http://www.wkap.nl>

Library of Congress Cataloging-in-Publication Data

A C.I.P. Catalogue record for this book is available from the Library of Congress.

Information Technology: Selected Tutorials
Edited by Ricardo Reis

DOI 10.1007/978-1-4020-8159-0

Printed on acid-free paper.
www.springer.com/mycopy

Contents

Preface

This book contains a selection of tutorials on hot topics in information technology, which were presented at the IFIP 18th World Computer Congress. WCC2004 took place at the *Centre de Congrès Pierre Baudis*, in Toulouse, France, from 22 to 27 August 2004.

The 11 chapters included in the book were chosen from tutorials proposals submitted to WCC2004. These papers report on several important and state-of-the-art topics on information technology such as:

- Quality of Service in Information Networks
- Risk-Driven Development of Security-Critical Systems Using UMLsec
- Developing Portable Software
- Formal Reasoning About Systems, Software and Hardware Using Functionals, Predicates and Relations
- The Problematic of Distributed Systems Supervision
- Software Rejuvenation - Modeling and Analysis
- Test and Design-for-Test of Mixed-Signal Integrated Circuits
- Web Services
- Applications of Multi-Agent Systems
- Discrete Event Simulation
- Human-Centered Automation

We hereby would like to thank IFIP and more specifically WCC2004 Tutorials Committee and the authors for their contribution. We also would like to thank the congress organizers who have done a great job.

Ricardo Reis
Editor

QUALITY OF SERVICE IN INFORMATION NETWORKS

Augusto Casaca
IST/INESC, R. Alves Redol, 1000-029, Lisboa, Portugal.

Abstract: This article introduces the problems concerned with the provision of end-to-end quality of service in IP networks, which are the basis of information networks, describes the existing solutions for that provision and presents some of the current research items on the subject.

Key words: Information networks, IP networks, Integrated Services, Differentiated Services, Multiprotocol Label Switching, UMTS.

1. QUALITY OF SERVICE IN IP NETWORKS

Information networks transport, in an integrated way, different types of traffic, from classical data traffic, which has flexible Quality of Service (QoS) requirements, to real-time interactive traffic, which requires QoS guarantees from the network.

Most of the solutions for the transport of information in this type of networks assume that the networks run the Internet Protocol (IP), which provides a best-effort service. The best-effort service does not provide any guarantees on the end-to-end values of the QoS parameters, i.e. delay, jitter and packet loss. However, the best-effort concept results into a simple network structure and, therefore, not expensive.

The best-effort service is adequate for the transport of classical bursty data traffic, whose main objective is to guarantee that all the packets, sooner or later, reach the destination without errors. This is achieved by running the Transmission Control Protocol (TCP) over IP. Services like e-mail and file transfer are good examples of this case. The problem occurs when real-time interactive services, such as voice and video, run over IP. In this case, the achievement of an end-to-end delay and jitter smaller than a certain value is key to achieve a good QoS. This means that the best-effort paradigm needs to evolve within IP networks, so that new network models capable of efficiently transporting all the types of traffic can be deployed.

The end-to-end QoS in a network results from the concatenation of the distinct QoS values in each of the network domains. In reality, these QoS values depend on the QoS characteristics of the different routers and links, which form the network. The QoS is basically characterised by the transfer delay, jitter and probability of packet loss, all relative to the traffic traversing the network.

The end-to-end delay is caused by the store-and-forward mechanism in the routers and by the propagation delay in the links. Jitter, which is defined as the end-to-end delay variation for the distinct packets, is caused by the different time that each packet remains in the router buffers. Packet loss basically results from congestion in routers, which implies the discard of packets.

The evolution of the best-effort paradigm to improve the end-to-end QoS in an IP network can be achieved by doing resource allocation at the router level, by intervening in the routing mechanism and by traffic engineering in the network. All these actions can be performed simultaneously in a network or, alternatively, only some of them can be implemented, depending on the QoS objectives. In the following text we will analyse these different mechanisms.

The router structure in traditional best-effort networks, which is shown in figure 1, is very simple.

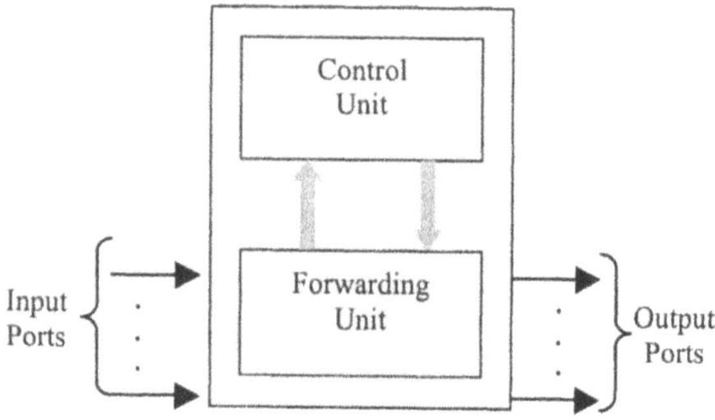

Figure 1. Best-effort router

The input ports accept packets coming from other routers and the output ports forward packets to other routers along the established routes. The forwarding unit sends each packet to the appropriate output port based on the IP destination address of the packet. For this purpose there is a routing table, which maps the destination address into the output port. The control unit is in charge of managing the forwarding unit. The routing protocol runs in the control unit.

To improve the QoS capabilities of the router, different mechanisms need to be implemented, which will result into a more complex structure for the router. These mechanisms are the following: classification, policing, marking, management of queues and scheduling [1].

Each traffic class, which requires bounded values for the end-to-end delay, jitter and packet loss, independent of the remaining traffic, needs a separate queue in the router. When a packet arrives at the router it needs to be classified and inserted into the respective queue. Also, after classifying a packet, it must be decided if there are enough resources in the queue to accept the packet. The policing mechanism is in charge of this action. A decision can also be taken in order to accept the packet conditionally, i.e. to mark the packet and discard it later in case of necessity. Each queue must have its own policy for packet discard depending on the characteristics of the traffic served by the queue. This is done by the queue management mechanism. Finally, a scheduling mechanism is required to decide on the frequency of insertion of packets into the output port that serves several queues.

Each of the referred mechanisms results into a new functional block in the router. QoS-capable routers are definitely more complex than best-effort routers, but must be able to inter-operate with them, because according to the Internet philosophy, incremental changes in one part of the network should be done without impact in the remaining parts of the network.

These QoS-capable routers are required for the new IP network models, namely Integrated Services (IntServ) and Differentiated Services (DiffServ), which need to allocate resources in the network routers for the distinct types of traffic classes. These network models will be explained later in this article.

The Internet routing is based on the shortest-path algorithm. Based on the IP address of the destination, this algorithm establishes a route between source and destination by using the shortest-path according to a well defined metric, for example, the number of routers to be traversed or the cost of the different routes. The algorithm is very simple, but it might cause an over-utilization of certain routes, leaving others free, when the network is highly loaded. This over-utilization results in extra delays and, in some cases, packet losses. An alternative is to use QoS-based routing, which originates multiple routing trees, in which each tree uses different combinations of parameters as the metric. This allows having different routes for the same source-destination pair according to the characteristics of the traffic. For example, one route could have delay as the metric and other route could have cost. The first one would be more appropriate for interactive traffic and the second one for bursty data traffic.

Finally, traffic engineering allows the network operator to explicitly indicate the use of certain routes in the network, also with the aim of achieving route diversification for the different traffic classes. Although traffic engineering uses techniques, which are different from the ones employed by QoS-based routing, if used in a network, can achieve by itself some of the objectives of QoS-based routing.

2. RESOURCE ALLOCATION MECHANISMS IN ROUTERS

As seen in the previous chapter, QoS-capable routers require the implementation of a number of additional mechanisms besides the ones provided in best-effort routers, namely classification, policing, marking, management of queues and scheduling.

2.1 Classification of packets

The selection of the input queue where to insert a packet arriving to a router depends on the packet class. The classification of the packet is based on n bits existing in the packet header. These n bits constitute the classification key and, therefore, up to 2^n classes can be defined.

Some complex classification schemes can consider several fields in the packet header to perform the classification, e.g. source address, destination address and TCP/UDP ports. However, the normal case only considers a single field in the header. In IP version 4 (IPv4) it is the TOS byte [2], in IP version 6 (IPv6) it is the TC byte [3]. To further simplify the classification scheme the semantics adopted for both versions of IP follows the one defined for the IP Differentiated Services (DiffServ) model [4]. This is one of the new models for IP networks having in view an improvement of the best-effort model as it will be studied in chapter 4. In the DiffServ model, the field equivalent to the TOS (IPv4) and TC (IPv6) is called the DiffServ field. It is one byte long and its structure is indicated in figure 2.

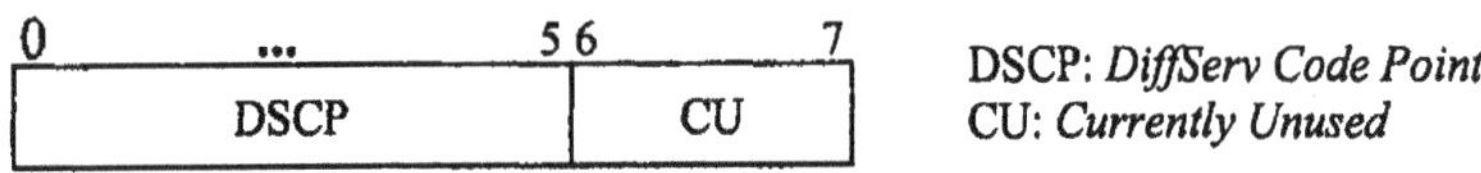

Figure 2. The DiffServ field

The 6 bits of the DSCP permit to define up to 64 different classes.

2.2 Policing and marking

Every class puts some limits on the timing characteristics of packet arrival. This consists on limiting the maximum allowed arrival rate and the maximum number of packets that can arrive within a certain time interval. The router polices the arrival of packets and can do one of two actions for the packets that do not respect the timing limits (out-of-profile packets), either eliminates all the out-of-profile packets, or marks them and lets them go into one of the router queues. The marking of packets allows that, in case of being necessary to drop packets in the queue, the marked ones might be selected to be the first ones to be discarded. The marking indication is given by a bit in the packet header.

The action of policing requires that the router is able to measure the timing characteristics of packet arrival so that it can decide whether the packets are in-profile or out-of-profile. These measurements are usually done by using the *token bucket* technique.

The best way to explain the *token bucket* technique is to symbolically consider that we have a bucket and tokens that are inserted or extracted from the bucket. The tokens are inserted into the bucket at the rate of x tokens/s and a token is removed from the bucket whenever a packet arrives at the router. The bucket has a capacity of k tokens. When a packet arrives, if there is at least one token to be extracted from the bucket, the packet is considered to be in-profile, but if the bucket is empty, the packet is considered out-of-profile. This technique allows the acceptance of bursty traffic up to a certain limit on the duration of the burst. The policing action can be followed by marking or not, this depending on the router implementation and also on the classification of the packet.

2.3 Management of queues

The router queue manager is responsible for the establishment and maintenance of the queues in the router.

The functions of the queue manager are: i) to insert a packet into the queue related to the packet class if the queue is not full; ii) to discard the packet if the queue is full; iii) to extract a packet from the queue when requested by the scheduler; iv) optionally, to perform an active management of the queue by monitoring the queue filling level and try to keep that filling level within acceptable limits, either by discarding or by marking packets.

An active management of the queues, although optional, is a recommended practice, as it allows accepting some traffic bursts without losing packets and can also diminish the packet delay in the router. There are several techniques to actively manage the router queues. We will mention some of the most relevant ones, namely, *Random Early Detection (RED), Weighted RED (WRED)* and *Adaptive RED (ARED)*.

It is known that the best solution to control the filling level of a queue shared by different flows of packets is to statistically generate feedback signals, whose intensity is a function of the average filling level of the queue [5].

The RED technique [6] utilizes the average filling level of the queue, as a parameter for a random function, which decides whether the mechanisms that avoid the queue overload must be activated. For a queue occupancy up to a certain threshold (*min*), all the packets remain in the queue. For a filling level above *min*, the probability of discarding packets rises linearly until a maximum filling level (*max*). Above *max* all the packets are discarded. The average filling level is recalculated whenever a packet arrives.

The WRED technique uses an algorithm that is an evolution of RED by "weighting" packets differently according to their marking. The RED algorithm still applies, but now the values of *min* and *max* depend on the packet being marked or not. For marked packets the values of *min* and *max* are lower than for unmarked ones, therefore, there is a more aggressive discard policy for the marked packets.

Finally, the ARED technique is also based on an algorithm derived from RED. In this case, the RED parameters are modified based on the history of occupancy of the queue. ARED adjusts the aggressiveness of the probability of packet dropping based on the more recent values of the average filling level of the queue. This provides a more controlled environment for the management of the queue occupancy.

2.4 Scheduling

Scheduling is the mechanism that decides when packets are extracted from the queues to be sent to a router output port. There are different degrees of complexity for the implementation of schedulers. The simplest ones have the only objective of serving queues in a certain sequence, without caring about the output rate of each queue. The more complex schedulers have the objective of guaranteeing a minimum rate for certain queues and continuously adapt its serving sequence for this purpose.

The simplest schedulers are the *Strict Priority* schedulers. The queues are ordered by decreasing priority and a queue with a certain priority is only served if the queues with higher priority are empty. To avoid that the queues with less priority are never served, the upstream routers must have mechanisms of policing to assure that the higher priority queues are never working at full capacity. If the scheduler is busy and a packet arrives at a higher priority queue, the scheduler completes the present transmission and only then serves the higher priority queue. This a useful mechanism for services that require a low delay. The maximum delay value depends on the output link speed and on the maximum length of the packet.

Another simple scheduling mechanism is the *Round Robin*. The scheduler serves the queues in a cyclic order, transmitting one packet before serving the next one. It jumps over empty queues. In *Round Robin* it is difficult to define limits for delays, but it assures that all the queues are served within a certain time.

The *Strict Priority* and *Round Robin* mechanisms do not take into consideration the number of bits transmitted each time a queue is served. As the packets have variable length, these two mechanisms cannot be used to control average rates for the different traffic classes. The control of the rates requires that the service discipline of the scheduler adapts dynamically to the number of bits transmitted from each queue.

The *Deficit Round Robin (DRR)* scheduling mechanism [7] is a variant of the *Round Robin*. It considers the number of bytes transmitted from a certain queue, compares that number with the number of bytes that should have been transmitted (to achieve a certain rate) and takes that difference as a deficit. This deficit is used to modify the service duration of the queue the next time it is served.

Weighted Fair Queueing (WFQ) [8] is also a variant of *Round Robin*. It continuously recalculates the scheduling sequence to determine the queue that has more urgency in being served to meet its rate target. It also gives different weights to each queue. In WFQ and DRR the average rates are only achieved after the transmission of many packets.

3. THE INTEGRATED SERVICES MODEL

The Integrated Services (IntServ) model was the first network model to be considered to improve the IP best-effort network towards the support of real-time services. This model is defined in [9]. Integrated Services is explicitly defined as an Internet service model that includes best-effort service, real-time service and controlled link sharing. Link sharing means to divide the traffic into different classes and assign to each of them a minimum percentage of the link bandwidth under conditions of overload, while allowing unused bandwidth to be available at other times.

Besides the best-effort service, there are two other classes of service supported: Guaranteed Service [10] and Controlled Load Service [11]. The Guaranteed Service (GS) is for real-time applications with strict requirements for bandwidth and delay. The Controlled Load (CL) service is for applications that require a performance equivalent to the one offered by a best-effort network with a low traffic load.

The IntServ model requires the processing of the traffic in every router along an end-to-end path and also requires a signalling protocol to indicate the requests from each flow. A flow is defined as a set of packets from a source to one or more receivers for which a common QoS is required. This might apply to packets that have the same source/ destination addresses and port numbers.

The IntServ model consists of a sequence of network elements (hosts, links and routers) that, altogether, supply a transit service of IP packets between a traffic source and its receivers. If there is a network element without QoS control it will not contribute to the IntServ. Before sending a new flow of packets into the network, there must be an admission control process in every network element along the end-to-end path. The flow admission is based on the characterisation of the traffic made by the source.

The IntServ applications are classified in real-time tolerant, real-time intolerant and elastic. As suggested by the name, tolerant real-time applications do not require strict network guarantees concerning delay and jitter. In elastic applications the packet delay and jitter in the network are not so important.

The GS service provides firm bounds on end-to-end delays and it is appropriate for intolerant real-time applications. An application indicates its expected traffic profile to the network, which evaluates the end-to-end maximum delay value that can guarantee and gives that indication to the application. The application decides whether that delay value is adequate and, in the affirmative case, proceeds by sending the flow of packets.

The CL service is defined by the IETF as a service similar to the best-effort service in a lightly loaded network. This service is adequate for real-time tolerant and elastic applications. Of course, many of the elastic applications can also be adequately served by the best-effort service.

The signalling protocol is a key element in the IntServ model, as it is used for doing resource reservation in the network routers. The signalling protocol makes resource reservation in two steps. The first one is admission control and the second one is configuration of the network elements to support the characteristics of the flow. The Resource Reservation protocol (RSVP) [12] has been selected as the signalling protocol for IntServ.

As schematically shown in figure 3, sources emit PATH messages to the receivers. Each PATH message contains two objects, *Sender_Tspec* and *Adspec*, respectively. The first object is the traffic descriptor and the second one describes the properties of the data path, including the availability of specific QoS control characteristics. The *Adspec* object can be modified in each router to reflect the network characteristics. The receivers reply with RESV messages to the source. A RESV message carries the object *Flowspec*, which contains the QoS expected by the receiver and to be applied to the source traffic.

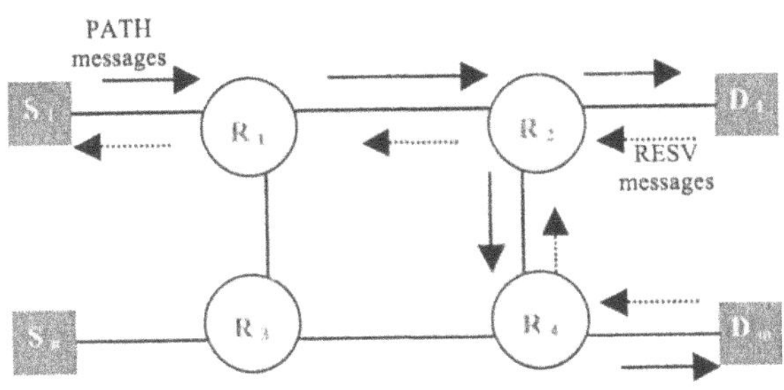

Figure 3. RSVP operation

To start a reservation, the source of the flow defines the *Sender_Tspec* and *Adspec* parameters and inserts them in a PATH message. At the receivers, *Sender_Tspec* and *Adspec* are used to determine the parameters to send back in the *Flowspec* object. In *Flowspec* it is indicated whether CL or GS is selected and it also carries the parameters required by the routers along the path, so that they can determine whether the request can be accepted. RSVP is appropriate for multicast operation.

All the routers along the path must do local measurements, followed by policing, so that the agreed bounds can be achieved. The resource reservation mechanism is independent of the routing algorithm. The RSVP messages circulate along the routes previously established by the routing algorithm.

4. THE DIFFERENTIATED SERVICES MODEL

The IntServ model is conceptually a good model to support both the real-time and non-real-time services in the Internet. However, in practice, this model is not scalable for the Internet. Its deployment would require to keep states in the routers for every flow and also to process these flows individually, which is very difficult to achieve. This was the main reason for the definition of another IP network model, the Differentiated Services (DiffServ) model [13]. DiffServ represents an incremental improvement of the best-effort service. It is a minimalist solution compared to IntServ, but it is scalable.

The DiffServ network structure is shown in figure 4. A network has edge and core routers. The edge routers map the customer's traffic into the core routers, whose main function is to transport packets to other routers until the egress edge router. The egress edge router communicates with the customer's terminal.

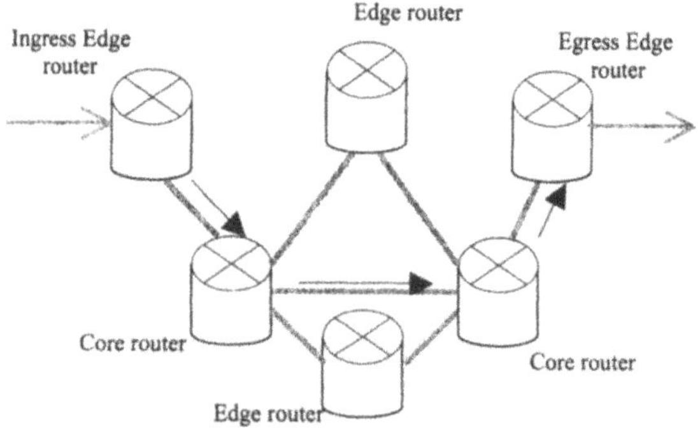

Figure 4. The DiffServ network model

The edge routers classify and police the customer's traffic before sending it to the network. The edge routers can refuse requests, therefore, transitory overloads can be solved. The more complex decisions are taken in the edge routers, simplifying the structure of the core routers, which implies that we can have faster core routers. Also we will have a smaller number of states than in IntServ as the packet context is established only from the DSCP field (see figure 2). The classification done in the edge routers allows that a large variety of traffic can be mapped into a small set of behaviours in the core network. In the DiffServ terminology, a collection of packets with the same DSCP is called DiffServ Behaviour Aggregate.

DiffServ introduces the concept of Per Hop Behaviour (PHB). Basically the PHB is the specific behaviour of the queue management and scheduling mechanisms in a network element. The concatenation of the different PHBs between an ingress and an egress edge router in the network defines the expected behaviour of the network and permits to define a Service Level Agreement with the customers.

DiffServ supports two distinct classes of PHBs besides best-effort. They are named Expedited Forwarding (EF) [14] and Assured Forwarding (AF) [15]. They are distinguished by the different coding values of the DSCP field. All bits with the value 0 in DSCP means a best-effort PHB.

EF PHB is defined by the code 101110 in the DSCP. This PHB is the most stringent one in DiffServ and is used for services that require low delay, low jitter and small packet loss. EF PHB requires co-ordination among the mechanisms of policing and scheduling along the path to be used by the EF packets. This service is sometimes also known as Premium service.

The AF PHB is less stringent than EF and is specified in terms of relative availability of bandwidth and characteristics of packet loss. It is adequate to support bursty traffic. In AF there are two types of context encoded in the DSCP: service class of the packet and precedence for the packet loss. The service class of the packet defines the router queue where it will be inserted. The loss precedence influences the weight allocated to the queue management algorithm, making this algorithm more or less aggressive towards packet discarding.

The first three bits of DSCP define the service class and the next two bits define the loss precedence. The sixth bit is fixed at 0. The standard defines four service classes and three loss precedence levels as shown in table 1. More classes and precedence levels can be defined for local use.

	Class 1	Class 2	Class 3	Class 4
Precedence 1 (low)	001 010	010 010	011 010	100 010
Precedence 2 (medium)	001 100	010 100	011 100	100 100
Precedence 3 (high)	001 110	010 110	011 110	100 110

Table 1. DiffServ classes and loss precedence levels

As the AF PHB is the one advised for the support of data applications, it is important to understand the interaction of this mechanism with TCP. Some authors claim that some improvements need to be done at the DiffServ level in order that TCP performance is not diminished [16]. This is a subject that requires further study.

The DiffServ model is simple and, therefore, attractive for deployment in the Internet. However, the mapping of a large number of flows into a limited number of PHBs requires techniques that are very dependent on the network topology and QoS characteristics of the routers, namely the classification, queue management and scheduling mechanisms.

5. INTEGRATED SERVICES OVER DIFFSERV NETWORKS

The IntServ model supports the delivery of end-to-end QoS to applications in an IP network. An important factor, however, has not allowed a large deployment of IntServ in the Internet. It has to do with the requirement for per-flow state and per-flow processing, which raises scalability problems.

On the other hand, the IntServ model is supported over different network elements. A DiffServ network can be viewed as one of these network elements, which exist in the end-to-end path between IntServ customers. As we know, the main benefit of DiffServ is to eliminate the need of per-flow state and per-flow processing and, therefore, making it a scalable model. In this context, IntServ and DiffServ can be used together to create a global end-to-end solution. In this global solution it is possible to have IntServ signalling between the hosts and the ingress router to the DiffServ network so that the router can indicate to the host whether there is enough network capacity to transport the packets related to the service. This capacity is provisioned during the configuration of the DiffServ network. The state information is only treated at the IntServ level.

The IntServ/DiffServ network configuration is shown in figure 5 [17].

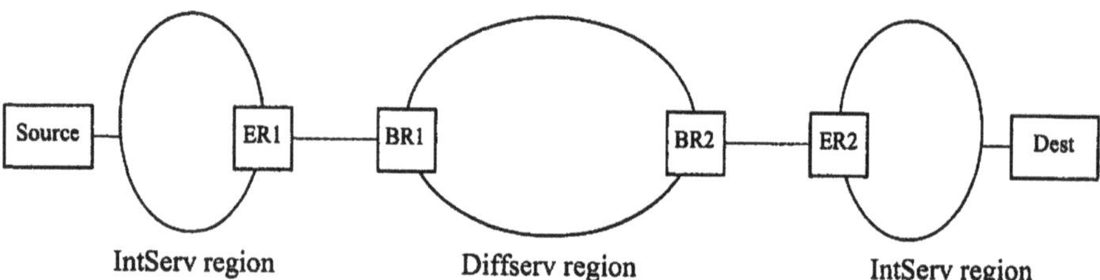

Figure 5. Reference IntServ/DiffServ configuration

The model distinguishes between edge routers (ER) and border routers (BR). Edge routers are egress/ ingress routers in the IntServ regions. Border routers are ingress/ egress routers in the DiffServ regions. The border routers are the ones that map the DiffServ ingress traffic into the network core routers (not represented in the figure). The RSVP signalling generated by the hosts is carried across the DiffServ regions. The signalling messages may be processed or not by the DiffServ routers. If the DiffServ region is RSVP-unaware, the border routers act as simple DiffServ routers, doing no processing of the RSVP messages. Edge routers do the admission control to the DiffServ region. If the DiffServ region is RSVP-aware, the border routers participate in RSVP signalling and do admission control for the DiffServ region.

This model to support QoS in an IP network is an attractive compromise, but some additional work still needs to be done, mainly concerned with the mapping of IntServ services to the services provided by the DiffServ regions, with the need for the deployment of equipments, named bandwidth brokers, that can provide resources in a DiffServ region in a dynamic and efficient way and for the support of multicast sessions with this network model [18].

6. MULTIPROTOCOL LABEL SWITCHING

Multiprotocol Label Switching (MPLS) provides traffic control and connection-oriented support to IP networks. These capabilities allow the provision of a basic connection-oriented mechanism to support QoS, ease the provision of traffic engineering in the network and also support the provision of Virtual Private Networks at the IP level [19].

MPLS must be clearly distinguished from the IP network models (IntServ, DiffServ) previously defined. The IntServ and DiffServ models are defined at the IP level, whereas the MPLS protocol runs below the IP level. MPLS configures the network to transport IP packets in an efficient way.

MPLS was preceded by other technologies, namely IP Switching from Ipsilon, ARIS from IBM, Tag Switching from Cisco and CSR from Toshiba. These different technologies had aims similar to MPLS and now they have been superseded by the MPLS standard defined at IETF [20].

IP packets are partitioned into a set of the so-called Forwarding Equivalent Classes (FEC). As defined in the standard, a particular router will consider two packets to be in the same FEC if there is some address prefix X in that router's routing tables such that X is the longest match for each packet's destination address. All packets which belong to a certain FEC and which travel from a particular node will follow the same path in the network. In MPLS, the assignment of a certain packet to a FEC is done at the network entry. The FEC is encoded as a label, which is appended to the packet header. This label is used in the network to switch the packets in the different routers which are MPLS-capable. These MPLS-capable routers are named Label Switching Routers (LSR) and have switching tables that operate using the packet label as an index to a table entry, which determines the next hop and a new label. MPLS simplifies the forwarding of packets in the network and allows explicitly sending a packet along a certain existing route. This latter technique is known as traffic engineering.

The MPLS label is a 32-bit field as shown in figure 6. The first 20 bits define the label value, which is defined at the network entry depending on the FEC to which the packet belongs. The label value has only local significance. It is changed by the LSRs in the switching process. The experimental bits are reserved for local use, the stack bit is used when labels are stacked and the Time to Live (TTL) field establishes a limit for the number of hops. The TTL field is important because the usual TTL function is encoded in the IP header, but the LSR only examines the MPLS label and not the IP header. By inserting TTL bits in the label, the TTL function can be supported in MPLS. If MPLS runs over a connection-oriented layer 2 technology, such as ATM or Frame Relay, the label value is inserted in the VPI/VCI field of ATM or in the DLCI field of Frame Relay.

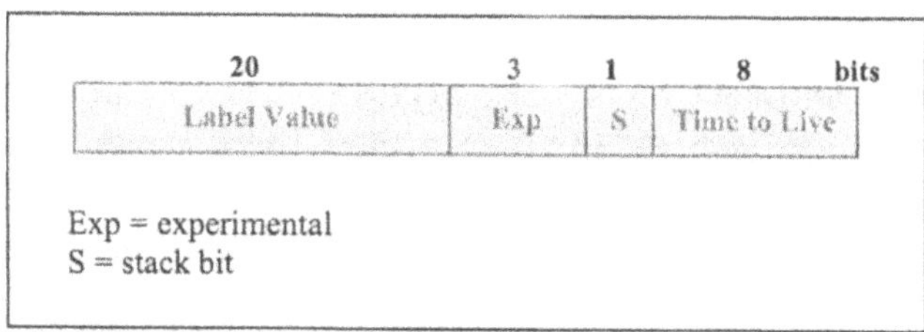

Figure 6. MPLS label format

The operation of MPLS can be described as follows. Initially, a path must be established in the network to send the packets of a given FEC. This path is known as Label Switched Path (LSP). The establishment of the LSP can take into consideration the resource allocation to be done in the network routers having in view the support for QoS provision. To establish this path, two protocols are used. The first one is the routing protocol, typically OSPF, which is used to exchange reachability and routing information. The second one is used to determine which route to use and which label values must be utilised in adjacent LSRs. This latter protocol can be the Label Distribution Protocol (LDP) or an enhanced version of RSVP (RSVP-TE). Alternatively, instead of using LDP or RSVP-TE, an explicit route can be provisioned by a network operator, which will assign the adequate label values.

When a packet enters the MPLS domain, the LSR assigns the packet to a certain FEC, and implicitly to an LSP, and inserts the MPLS label into the packet. The next action is to forward the packet. Within the MPLS domain, when an LSR receives a packet, the switching table is accessed, the label is substituted by a new one and the packet is forwarded to the next hop. Finally the egress LSR removes the label, examines the IP header and forwards the packet to the destination.

MPLS can be used to efficiently support the transport of packets in a DiffServ network [21]. At the ingress of a DiffServ network the IP packets are classified and marked with a DSCP, which corresponds to their Behaviour Aggregate. At each router the DSCP is used to select the respective PHB. RFC 3270 specifies how to support the DiffServ Behaviour Aggregates whose corresponding PHBs are currently defined over an MPLS network. It specifies the support of DiffServ for both IPv4 and IPv6 traffic, but only for unicast operations. The support of multicast operations is currently under study.

7. QUALITY OF SERVICE IN THIRD GENERATION WIRELESS NETWORKS

Third Generation wireless networks, also known in Europe as Universal Mobile Telecommunications System (UMTS), are a good example of information networks. Whereas second generation wireless networks were optimized for the communication of voice, third generation networks focus on the communication of information, including all the types of services. This requirement to transmit information in all its forms implies that the circuit switched based network architecture of second generation networks has to include also a packet switched part in its evolution towards a third generation network architecture.

The UMTS network architecture has been defined by 3GPP (Third Generation Partnership Project). 3GPP has planned the evolution of the network according to a series of releases. The first one to be implemented is known as Release 99 [22]. A simplified view of the UMTS architecture, according to Release 99, is shown in figure 7.

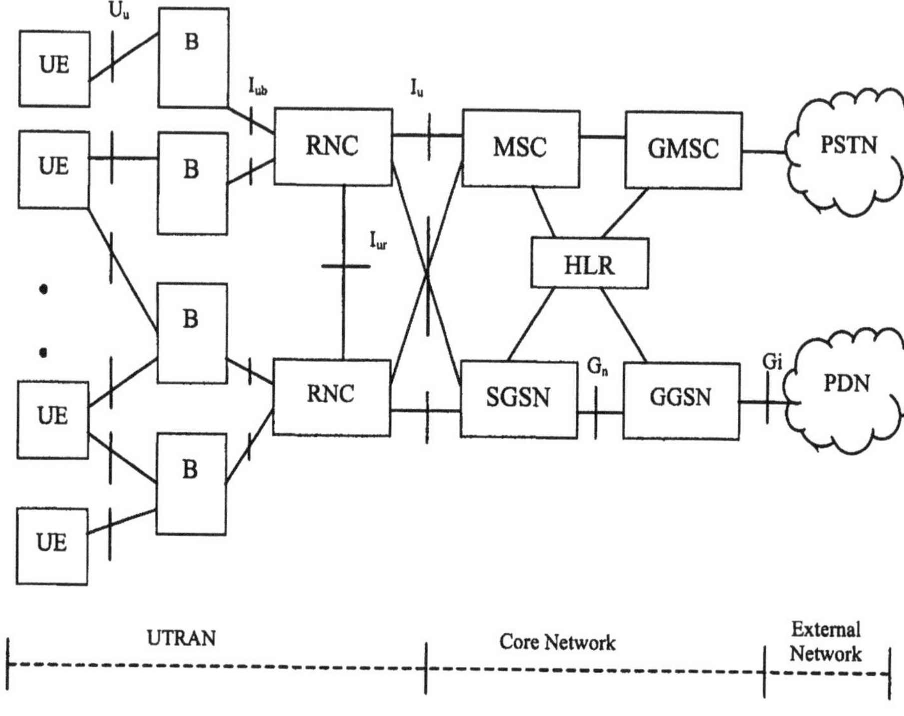

Figure 7. UMTS network architecture

The structure of a UMTS network consists of two main levels: radio access network and core network. They are separated by the Iu interface.

The Universal Terrestrial Radio Access Network (UTRAN) consists of a set of Base stations, known as nodes B, and a set of Radio Network Controllers (RNC). Each RNC controls a number of nodes B. Iub is the interface between a node B and an RNC. The RNCs may communicate between themselves via the Iur interface. The radio access part is comprised between the User Equipment (UE) and the nodes B (interface Uu). The RNC is the switching and control element of the UTRAN. Each RNC is respectively connected, via the Iu interface, to the Mobile services Switching Centre (MSC) and Serving GPRS Support Node (SGSN), which are two elements of the Core network.

The Core network consists of a circuit switched domain and a packet switched domain. The main elements in the circuit switched domain are the MSC and the Gateway MSC (GMSC). The MSC is responsible for the circuit switched connection management activities. The GMSC takes care of the connections to other PSTN networks. In the packet switched part, there are also two main elements, the SGSN and the Gateway GPRS Support

Node (GGSN), separated by the Gn interface. The SGSN supports packet communication towards the access network and is responsible for mobility management related issues. The GGSN maintains the connections towards other packet data networks, such as the Internet, via the Gi interface. The Home Location Register (HLR) contains the addressing and identity information for both the circuit and packet switched domains of the core network.

The problem of QoS provision in UMTS is particularly relevant for mobile packet switched based services, which constitute the main novelty introduced in UMTS networks compared to the previous generation of circuit switched wireless networks. The Core network circuit switched domain uses signalling protocols inherited from GSM. The Core network packet switched domain can be seen as an IP backbone internal to the operator network.

The end-to-end services are carried over the network using bearers. A bearer is a service providing QoS between two defined points. As the radio access network and core network have their own QoS properties, the QoS needs to be treated separately in each of these levels. The end-to-end QoS is the global result, which takes into account the distinct levels of the network.

In UMTS a specific medium access control protocol is used on the radio bearers, which link the UEs to the base stations. From the base stations to the core network, the transport of packets is done over ATM. In the core network, the information is encapsulated in IP; here, the QoS is treated according to the DiffServ model. The layer 2 protocols in the core network, which will transport the IP packets, are not standardized, although, in practice, ATM might be one of the main choices of network operators for this purpose.

In UMTS there is one additional feature, which consists in the UEs having the ability to negotiate the QoS parameters for a radio bearer. The negotiation is always initiated by the application in the UE and the network checks whether it can provide the required resources or if it rejects the request.

After the deployment of release'99, new releases are foreseen to upgrade UMTS networks in the future [23] [24]. The upgrade of the UMTS network aims, in a first phase, to evolve the whole core network into a packet switched architecture based on IP. This means that we will have voice over IP in the core network after the first phase of evolution is accomplished. The final aim is to have an "All-IP" network including the radio part. Therefore, we would have an end-to-end IP network to support the applications. Of course, this network would need to consider all the aspects covered in the previous chapters of the paper to achieve a satisfactory QoS for all types of services. Although this is the aim, it might still take some time to achieve it, due to the characteristics of the air interface, where the bandwidth availability is at a premium, which requires optimization of the mechanisms to provide QoS.

8. CONCLUSIONS

The problem of provisioning QoS in information networks is not completely solved yet. As seen in the previous chapters, the evolution of an IP best-effort network into a network that can provide QoS guarantees is not an easy task. Some significant steps have already been given, but research continues active in this field. As described next, the use of signalling protocols, the evolution towards IPv6 and the convergence of IP with existing networks are good examples of current research work in this area.

As we know, resource allocation in the network elements is required to comply with bounds in the values of the different QoS parameters. Resource allocation can be done by provisioning the network, but provisioning is neither flexible nor dynamic. Network operation would be more effective if a dynamic and flexible solution based on signalling could be implemented. One of the protocols that is often referred for this purpose is RSVP. Some extensions have been proposed to RSVP to provide additional features, namely security, more scalability and new interfaces. One well-known extension is the so-called RSVP-TE, which is used in MPLS to establish explicitly routed LSPs. Other protocols have also been proposed, such as YESSIR and Boomerang [25]. All these signalling protocols apply to the intra-domain level. If we wish to consider also inter-domain signalling, which is the global scenario, other signalling protocols need to be considered. BGRP is a signalling protocol for inter-domain aggregated resource reservation for unicast traffic [26]. Other inter-domain protocols under study are SICAP [27] and DARIS [28]. The comparative efficiency of all these protocols to serve the different types of services is under evaluation [29].

Currently, IP networks use IPv4. A new version of the protocol (IPv6) is ready since about ten years ago. Although the main new feature of IPv6 is a larger IP addressing space (128 bits instead of 32 bits), there are also new fields in the IP header that can be used to facilitate the QoS support. However, the introduction of IPv6 in the existing networks has not been done yet at a large scale. The best strategy of introducing IPv6 in the running networks is still under discussion as well as the best way of taking advantage of its new features [30] [31].

The support of the convergence of IP networks with other networks, such as the PSTN, is key to the success of information networks. This is an issue that has been under study in standardization bodies, namely at the ITU-T [32]. There is a need to coordinate the sharing of resources, which are done with different signalling protocols, in distinct operating domains.

Many other items related to the evolution of IP-based information networks are currently under study in several research projects, e.g. [33] and in standardization bodies, namely the IETF [34]. This study has a broad spectrum and extends from routing and transport to security issues in IP-based networks.

REFERENCES

[1] G. Armitage, Quality of Service in IP Networks, Macmillan Technical Publishing, 2000.

[2] P. Almquist, Type of Service in the Internet Protocol Suite, RFC 1349, IETF, July 1992.

[3] S. Dearing and R. Hinden, Internet Protocol Version 6 Specification, RFC 2460, IETF, December 1998.

[4] K. Nichols et al, Definition of the Differentiated Services Field in the IPv4 and IPv6 Headers, RFC 2474, IETF, December 1998.

[5] B. Braden et al, Recommendations on Queue Management and Congestion Avoidance in the Internet, RFC 2309, IETF, April 1998.

[6] S. Floyd and V. Jacobson, Random Early Detection Gateways for Congestion Avoidance, IEEE/ACM Transactions on Networking, no. 4, August 1993.

[7] M. Shreedar and G. Varghese, Efficient Fair Queueing Using Deficit Round Robin, ACM Sigcomm 95, October 1995.

[8] A. Demers et al, Analysis and Simulation of a Fair Queueing Algorithm, ACM Sigcomm89, September 1989.

[9] R. Braden et al, Integrated Services in the Internet Architecture: an Overview, RFC 1633, IETF, June 1994.

[10] S. Shenker et al, Specification of Guaranteed Quality of Service, RFC 2212, IETF, September 1997

[11] J. Wroclawski, Specification of the Controlled Load Service, RFC 2211, IETF, September 1997.

[12] J. Wroclawski, The Use of RSVP with IETF Integrated Services, RFC 2210, IETF, September 1997.

[13] S. Blake et al, An Architecture for Differentiated Services, RFC 2475, IETF, December 1998.

[14] V. Jacobson et al, An Expedited Forwarding PHB, RFC 2598, IETF, June 1999.

[15] J. Heinanen et al, Assured Forwarding PHB Group, RFC 2597, IETF, June 1999.

[16] P. Giacomazzi, L. Musumeci and G. Verticale, Transport of TCP/IP Traffic over Assured Forwarding IP-Differentiated Services, IEEE Network Magazine, Vol. 17, No.5, September/ October 2003.
[17] Y. Bernet et al, A Framework for Integrated Services Operation over Diffserv Networks, RFC 2998, IETF, November 2000.
[18] K Nichols et al, A two bit Differentiated Services Architecture for the Internet, RFC 2638, IETF, July 1999.
[19] William Stallings, MPLS, The Internet Protocol Journal, Volume 4, Number 3, September 2001.
[20] E. Rosen et al, Multiprotocol Label Switching, RFC 3031, IETF, January 2001.
[21] F. Le Faucheur et al, MPLS Support of Differentiated Services, RFC 3270, IETF, May 2002.
[22] 3GPP TS 23.002 V3.4.0, Network Architecture (Release 1999), December 2000.
[23] 3GPP TS 23.107, QoS Concept and Architecture (Release 4), June 2001.
[24] 3GPP TS 23.207, End-to-end QoS Concept and Architecture (Release 5), June 2001.
[25] J. Manner, Analysis of Existing Quality of Service Signalling Protocols, Internet-Draft, IETF, October 2003.
[26] P. Pan et al, BGRP: A Tree-Based Aggregation Protocol for Inter-domain Reservations, Journal of Communications and Networks, Vol. 2, No. 2, June 2000
[27] R. Sofia, R. Guerin, and P. Veiga. SICAP, A Shared-segment Inter-domain Control Aggregation Protocol, High Performance Switching and Routing Conference, Turin, Italy, June 2003.
[28] R. Bless, Dynamic Aggregation of Reservations for Internet Services, Proceedings of the Tenth International Conference on Telecommunication Systems - Modelling and Analysis, Volume One, Monterey, USA, October 2002.
[29] R. Sofia, R. Guerin, and P. Veiga. An Investigation of Inter-Domain Control Aggregation Procedures, International Conference on Networking Protocols, Paris, France, November 2002.
[30] M. Tatipamula, P. Grossetete and H. Esaki, IPv6 Integration and Coexistence Strategies for Next-Generation Networks, IEEE Communications Magazine, Vol. 42, No. 1, January 2004.
[31] Y. Adam et al, Deployment and Test of IPv6 Services in the VTHD Network, IEEE Communications Magazine, Vol. 42, No. 1, January 2004.
[32] N. Seitz, ITU-T QoS Standards for IP-Based Networks, IEEE Communications Magazine, Vol. 41, No. 6, June 2003.
[33] Euro NGI Network of Excelence, Design and Engineering of the Next Generation Internet; http://www.eurongi.org
[34] Internet Engineering Task Force; http://www.ietf.org/

RISK-DRIVEN DEVELOPMENT OF SECURITY-CRITICAL SYSTEMS USING UMLSEC

Jan Jürjens
Software & Systems Engineering, Dep. of Informatics, TU München, Germany
http://www.jurjens.de/jan – juerjens@in.tum.de

Siv Hilde Houmb
Department of Computer and Information Science, NTNU, Norway
http://www.idi.ntnu.no/ sivhoumb – sivhoumb@idi.ntnu.no

Abstract Despite a growing awareness of security issues in distributed computing systems, most development processes used today still do not take security aspects into account. To address this problem we make use of a risk-driven approach to develop security-critical systems based on UMLsec, the extension of the Unified Modeling Language (UML) for secure systems development, the safety standard ICE 61508, and the concept of model-based risk assessment (MBRA). Security requirements are handled as an integrated part of the development and derived from enterprize information such as security policies, business goals, law and regulation as well as project specific security demands. These are then updated and refined in each iteration of the process and finally refined to security requirements at a technical level, which can be expressed using UMLsec, and analyzed mechanically using the tool-support for UMLsec by referring to a precise semantics of the used fragment of UML.

Keywords: Critical systems development, risk-driven development (RDD), model-based risk assessment (MBRA), model-driven development (MDD)

1. Introduction

Traditionally, in software development projects the focus is put on meeting the end-users' needs in terms of functionality. This has lead to rapidly developed systems with none or little attention to security, and many security-critical systems developed in practise turn out to be insecure. Part of the reason is that most often, security is not an integrated part of the system development process. While functional requirements are carefully analyzed during system development, non-functional requirements, such as security requirements, are often considered only after the fact. In addition, in practice one has to worry about cost issues and try to achieve an adequate level of security under given time limits and financial constraints.

Lifecycle models and development processes are useful means of describing the various phases of a development project, from the conception of a system to its eventual decommissioning [Lev95]. Several standards exist to guide the development of critical systems, e.g. IEC 61508 [IEC] and the MIL-STD-882B standard [DoD84]. The Australian/New Zealand standard AS/NZS 4360:1999 Risk management [43699] is a general standard targeting risk management. The IST-project CORAS [COR02] is based on the concept of model based risk assessment (MBRA) and has developed an integrated system development and risk management process aiming at security-critical systems. The process is based on AS/NZS 4360, Rational Unified Process (RUP) [Kru99], and the Reference Model for Open Distributed Processes (RM-ODP) [Put00]. The focus is on handling security issues throughout the development process.

In our work we have adapted part of the lifecycle model of IEC 61508 and combined it with the risk management process of AS/NZS4360. Further, we base ourselves on the integrated process of CORAS to support specification of security requirements at an enterprize level, while we use a UML extension for secure systems development, UMLsec [Jür02; Jür03b], to specify security requirements at a technical level, which is then analyzed using tool-support for UMLsec.

This chapter is organized as following. Section 2 presents related work and put the work into context. Section 3 discusses distributed system security, while Section 4 provide a brief description of UMLsec. In Section 5 we discuss security evaluation of UML diagrams and presents the tool supporting security evaluation using UMLsec. Section 6 deals with risk-driven development and provide a brief description of IEC 61508, AS/NZS4360, and the integrated process of CORAS. In Section 7 we present the MBRA development process for security-critical systems, while Section 8 provides an example of how to specify and refine security requirements through the development using the MBRA process. In Section 9, we summarize the main contributions of the chapter.

2. Related Work

There exist a number of specialized risk assessment methodologies for the security domain. Within the domain of health care information systems the British Government's Central Computer and Telecommunication Agency (CCTA) has developed CRAMM [BD92], CCTA risk analysis and management methodology. CRAMM aims at providing a structured and consistent approach to computer management of all systems. The UK National Health Service considers CRAMM to be the standard for risk analysis within systems supporting health care. However, CRAMM is intended for risk analysis of computerized systems in general.

Reactive System Design Support (RSDS) [LAC00] and Surety Analysis [WCF99] are methodologies integrating modelling and risk analysis methods. RSDS is an integrated modelling and risk analysis tool-supported methodology developed by King's College London and B-Core UK, ltd, while Surety Analysis is a method developed in Sandia National Laboratories, a governmental research organization in the U.S. and aims at the modelling and risk analysis of critical and complex systems. These approaches do not however put particular focus on specification, allocation, and verification of security requirements.

E.B. Fernandez and J.C. Hawkins present in [FH97] an extension of use cases and interaction diagrams to develop distributed system architecture requirements. Among other non-functional requirements they introduce questions for requirements elaboration, like system communication load, fault tolerance, safety, real-time deadlines, and security. However, this work is mainly focused on application examples for use cases in security-critical systems, not on giving a methodology for their development or a concept for their integration with domain models. More generally, there are further approaches to a rigorous development of critical systems based on UML, including [PO01; GFR02] (and other articles in [JCF$^+$02]).

3. Distributed System Security

We explain a few important recurring security requirements of distributed object-oriented systems which are encapsulated in UML stereotypes and tags in the UMLsec profile by associating formalizations of these requirements (referring to the formal semantics) as constraints with the stereotypes. The formalizations are obtained following standard approaches to formal security analysis.

Fair exchange When trading goods electronically, the requirement fair exchange postulates that the trade is performed in a way that prevents both parties from cheating. If for example the buyer has to make a prepayment, he should be able to prove having made the payment and to reclaim the money if that good is subsequently not delivered.

Non-repudiation One way of providing fair exchange is by using the security requirement of *non-repudiation* of some action, which means that this action cannot subsequently be denied successfully. That is, the action is *provable*, usually wrt. some trusted third party.

Secure logging For fraud prevention in electronic business transactions, and in particular to ensure non-repudiation, one often makes use of auditing. Here the relevant security requirement represents that the auditing data is, at each point during the transaction of the system, consistent with the actual state of the transaction (to avoid the possibility of fraud by interrupting the transaction).

Guarded access One of the main security mechanisms is access control, which ensures that only legitimate parties have access to a security-relevant part of the system. Sometimes access control is enforced by *guards.*

Secure information flow Where trusted parts of a system interact with untrusted parts, one has to ensure that there is no indirect leakage of sensitive information from a trusted to an untrusted parties. The relevant formal security requirement on the flow of information in the system is called secure information flow. Trusted parts of a system are often marked as "high", untrusted parts as "low".

Secrecy and Integrity Two of the main data security requirements are *secrecy* (or *confidentiality*; meaning that some information can be *read* only by legitimate parties) and *integrity* (some information can be *modified* only by legitimate parties).

Secure communication link Sensitive communication between different parts of a system needs to be protected. The relevant requirement of a *secure communication link* is here assumed to provide secrecy and integrity for the data in transit.

For UMLsec, we give validation rules that evaluate a model with respect to listed security requirements. Many security requirements target the behavior of a system in interaction with its environment and potential adversaries. To verify these requirements, we use the formal semantics defined in Section 5.

4. UMLsec

We recall the fragment of UMLsec needed in our context. More details can be found in [Jür02; Jür03b]. UMLsec allows one to express security-

Stereotype	Base Class	Tags	Constraints	Description
secrecy	dependency			assumes secrecy
integrity	dependency			assumes integrity
critical	object, subsystem	secrecy, integrity		critical object
secure links	subsystem		dependency security matched by links	enforces secure communication links
secure dependency	subsystem		<<**call**>>,<<**send**>> respect data security	structural interaction data security
data security	subsystem		provides data sec.	basic datasec requirements
fair exchange	subsystem	start,stop	after start eventually reach stop	enforce fair exchange

Figure 1. Some UMLsec stereotypes

related information within the diagrams in a UML system specification. The extension is given in form of a UML profile using the standard UML extension mechanisms. *Stereotypes* are used together with *tags* to formulate security requirements and assumptions on the system environment; *constraints* give criteria that determine whether the requirements are met by the system design.

Stereotypes define new types of modelling elements extending the semantics of existing types or classes in the UML metamodel. Their notation consists of the name of the stereotype written in double angle brackets « », attached to the extended model element. This model element is then interpreted according to the meaning ascribed to the stereotype.

One way of explicitly defining a property is by attaching a *tagged value* to a model element. A tagged value is a name-value pair, where the name is referred to as the *tag*. The corresponding notation is {*tag*=*value*} with the tag name tag and a corresponding *value* to be assigned to the tag.

Another way of adding information to a model element is by attaching *Constraints* to refine its semantics. Stereotypes can be used to attach tagged values and constraints as pseudo-attributes of the stereotyped model elements.

In Figure 1 we give the relevant fragment of the list of stereotypes from UMLsec, together with their tags and constraints.

We shortly explain the use of the stereotypes and tags given in Figure 1. More information can be found in [Jür02; Jür03b].

critical This stereotype labels objects that are critical in some way, which is specified in more detail using the corresponding tags. The tags are **{secrecy}** and **{integrity}**. The values of the first two are the names of expressions or variables (that is, attributes or message arguments) of the current object the secrecy (resp. integrity) of which is supposed to be protected.

secure links This stereotype on subsystems containing deployment diagrams is used to ensure that security requirements on the communication are met by the physical layer.

secure dependency This stereotype on subsystems containing static structure diagrams ensures that the «call» and «send» dependencies between objects or subsystems respect the security requirements on the data that may be communicated across them, as given by the tags {secrecy} and {integrity} of the stereotype «critical».

fair exchange This stereotype of (instances of) subsystems has associated tags *start* and *stop* taking names of states as values. The associated constraint requires that, whenever a *start* state in the contained activity diagram is reached, then eventually a *stop* state will be reached.

5. Security evaluation of UML diagrams using formal semantics

For some of the constraints used to define the UMLsec extensions we need to refer to a precisely defined semantics of behavioral aspects, because verifying whether they hold for a given UML model may be mathematically non-trivial. Firstly, the semantics is used to define these constraints in a mathematically precise way. Secondly, in ongoing work, we are developing mechanical tool support for analyzing UML specifications (for example in [Sha03; Men], and a few other student projects). For this, a precise definition of the meaning of the specifications is necessary, and it is useful to formulate this as a formal model for future reference before coding it up. For security analysis, the security-relevant information from the security-oriented stereotypes is then incorporated.

Note that because of the complexities of the UML, it would take up too much space to recall our formal semantics here completely. Instead, we just define precisely and explain the interfaces of the semantics that we need here to define the UMLsec profile. More details on the formal semantics can be found in [Jür03b]. Our formal semantics of a simplified fragment of UML using Abstract State Machines (ASMs) includes the following kinds of diagrams:

Class diagrams define the static class structure of the system: classes with attributes, operations, and signals and relationships between classes. On the instance level, the corresponding diagrams are called *object diagrams*.

Statechart diagrams (or *state diagrams*) give the dynamic behavior of an individual object or component: events may cause a change in state or an execution of actions.

Sequence diagrams describe interaction between objects or system components via message exchange.

Activity diagrams specify the control flow between several components within the system, usually at a higher degree of abstraction than statecharts and sequence diagrams. They can be used to put objects or components in the context of overall system behavior or to explain use cases in more detail.

Deployment diagrams describe the physical layer on which the system is to be implemented.

Subsystems (a certain kind of *packages*) integrate the information between the different kinds of diagrams and between different parts of the system specification.

There is another kind of diagrams, the use case diagrams, which describe typical interactions between a user and a computer system. They are often used in an informal way for negotiation with a customer before a system is designed. We will not use it in the following. Additionally to sequence diagrams, there are *collaboration diagrams*, which present similar information. Also, there are *component diagrams*, presenting part of the information contained in deployment diagrams.

The used fragment of UML is simplified significantly to keep a formal treatment that is necessary for some of the more subtle security requirements feasible and to allow model-checking of UML specifications. Note also that in our approach we identify system objects with UML objects, which is suitable for our purposes. Also, as with practical all analysis methods, also in the real-time setting [Wat02], we are mainly concerned with instance-based models.

Although simplified, our choice of a subset of UML is reasonable for our needs, as we have demonstrated in several industrial case-studies (some of which are documented in [Jür03b]).

The formal semantics for subsystems incorporates the formal semantics of the diagrams contained in a subsystem. Although restricted in several ways (see [Jür03b]) any one time an object's behavior is represented by only one diagram in the formal semantics

- models actions and internal activities explicitly (rather than treating them as atomic given events), in particular the operations and the parameters employed in them,

- provides passing of messages with their parameters between objects or components specified in different diagrams, including a dispatching mechanism for events and the handling of actions, and thus
- allow in principle whole specification documents to be based on a formal foundation.

In particular, we can compose subsystems by including them into other subsystems. It prepares the ground for the tool-support based on this precise semantics.

Objects, and more generally system components, can communicate by exchanging messages. These consist of the message name, and possibly arguments to the message, which will be assumed to be elements of the set. Message names may be prefixed with object or subsystem instance names. Each object or component may receive messages received in an input queue and release messages to an output queue.

In our model, every object or subsystem instance O has associated multi-sets inQu_O and outQu_O (*event queues*). Then our formal semantics models sending a message $msg = op(exp_1, \ldots, exp_n) \in \mathbf{Events}$ from an object or subsystem instance S to an object or subsystem instance R as follows:

(1) S places the message $R.msg$ into its multi-set outQu_S.

(2) A scheduler distributes the messages from out-queues to the intended in-queues (while removing the message head); in particular, $R.msg$ is removed from outQu_S and msg added to inQu_R.

(3) R removes msg from its in-queue and processes its content.

In the case of operation calls, we also need to keep track of the sender to allow sending return signals. This way of modelling communication allows for a very flexible treatment; for example, we can modify the behavior of the scheduler to take account of knowledge on the underlying communication layer.

At the level of single objects, behavior is modelled using statecharts, or (in special cases such as protocols) possibly as using sequence diagrams. The internal activities contained at states of these statecharts can again be defined each as a statechart, or alternatively, they can be defined directly using ASMs.

Using subsystems, one can then define the behavior of a system component C by including the behavior of each of the objects or components directly contained in C, and by including an activity diagram that coordinates the respective activities of the various components and objects.

Thus for each object or component C of a given system, our semantics defines a function $[\![C]\!]()$ which

- takes a multi-set I of input messages and a component state S and
- outputs a set $[\![C]\!](I, S)$ of pairs (O, T) where O is a multi-set of output messages and T the new component state (it is a *set* of pairs because of the non-determinism that may arise)

together with an *initial state* S_0 of the component.

Specifically, the behavioral semantics $[\![D]\!]()$ of a statechart diagram D models the run-to-completion semantics of UML statecharts. As a special case, this gives us the semantics for activity diagrams. Any sequence diagram $\mathcal{S}$ gives us the behavior $[\![\mathcal{S}.C]\!]()$ of each contained component C.

Subsystems group together diagrams describing different parts of a system: a system component $\mathcal{C}$ given by a subsystem $\mathcal{S}$ may contain subcomponents $\mathcal{C}_1, \ldots, \mathcal{C}_n$. The behavioral interpretation $[\![\mathcal{S}]\!]()$ of $\mathcal{S}$ is defined as follows:

(1) It takes a multi-set of input events.

(2) The events are distributed from the input multi-set and the link queues connecting the subcomponents and given as arguments to the functions defining the behavior of the intended recipients in $\mathcal{S}$.

(3) The output messages from these functions are distributed to the link queues of the links connecting the sender of a message to the receiver, or given as the output from $[\![\mathcal{S}]\!]()$ when the receiver is not part of $\mathcal{S}$.

When performing security analysis, after the last step, the adversary model may modify the contents of the link queues in a certain way, which is explained in the next section.

5.1. Security analysis of UML diagrams

Our modular UML semantics allows a rather natural modelling of potential adversary behavior. We can model specific types of adversaries that can attack different parts of the system in a specified way. For example, an attacker of type *insider* may be able to intercept the communication links in a company-wide local area network. We model the actual behavior of the adversary by defining a class of ASMs that can access the communication links of the system in a specified way. To evaluate the security of the system with respect to the given type of adversary, we consider the joint execution of the system with any ASM in this class. This way of reasoning allows an intuitive formulation of many security properties. Since the actual verification is rather indirect this way, we also give alternative intrinsic ways of defining security properties below, which are more manageable, and show that they are equivalent to the earlier ones.

Thus for a security analysis of a given UMLsec subsystem specification $\mathcal{S}$, we need to model potential adversary behavior. We model specific types of adversaries that can attack different parts of the system in a specified way. For this we assume a function $\mathsf{Threats}_A(s)$ which takes an *adversary type* A and a stereotype s and returns a subset of $\{\mathsf{delete}, \mathsf{read}, \mathsf{insert}, \mathsf{access}\}$ (*abstract threats*). These functions arise from the specification of the physical layer of the system under consideration using deployment diagrams, as explained in Sect. 4. For a link l in a deployment diagram in $\mathcal{S}$, we then define the set $\mathsf{threats}_A^{\mathcal{S}}(l)$ of *concrete threats* to be the smallest set satisfying the following conditions:

If each node n that l is contained in[1] carries a stereotype s_n with $\mathsf{access} \in \mathsf{Threats}_A(s_n)$ then:

- If l carries a stereotype s with $\mathsf{delete} \in \mathsf{Threats}_A(s)$ then $\mathsf{delete} \in \mathsf{threats}_A^{\mathcal{S}}(l)$.
- If l carries a stereotype s with $\mathsf{insert} \in \mathsf{Threats}_A(s)$ then $\mathsf{insert} \in \mathsf{threats}_A^{\mathcal{S}}(l)$.
- If l carries a stereotype s with $\mathsf{read} \in \mathsf{Threats}_A(s)$ then $\mathsf{read} \in \mathsf{threats}_A^{\mathcal{S}}(l)$.
- If l is connected to a node that carries a stereotype t with $\mathsf{access} \in \mathsf{Threats}_A(t)$ then $\{\mathsf{delete}, \mathsf{insert}, \mathsf{read}\} \subseteq \mathsf{threats}_A^{\mathcal{S}}(l)$.

The idea is that $\mathsf{threats}_A^{\mathcal{A}}(x)$ specifies the *threat scenario* against a component or link x in the ASM system $\mathcal{A}$ that is associated with an adversary type A. On the one hand, the threat scenario determines, which data the adversary can obtain by *accessing* components, on the other hand, it determines, which actions the adversary is permitted by the threat scenario to apply to the concerned links. delete means that the adversary may delete the messages in the corresponding link queue, read allows him to read the messages in the link queue, and insert allows him to insert messages in the link queue.

Then we model the actual behavior of an adversary of type A as a *type A adversary machine*. This is a state machine which has the following data:

[1]Note that nodes and subsystems may be nested one in another.

- a control state control $\in$ State,
- a set of *current adversary knowledge* $\mathcal{K} \subseteq \mathbf{Exp}$, and
- for each possible control state $c \in$ State and set of knowledge $K \subseteq \mathbf{Exp}$, we have
  - a set $\mathsf{Delete}_{c,K}$ which may contain the name of any link l with delete $\in \mathsf{threats}_A^S(l)$
  - a set $\mathsf{Insert}_{c,K}$ which may contain any pair (l, E) where l is the name of a link with insert $\in \mathsf{threats}_A^S(l)$, and $E \in \mathcal{K}$, and
  - a set $\mathsf{newState}_{c,k} \subseteq$ State of states.

The machine is executed from a specified initial state control := $\mathsf{control}_0$ with a specified *initial knowledge* $\mathcal{K} := \mathcal{K}_0$ iteratively, where each iteration proceeds according to the following steps:

(1) The contents of all link queues belonging to a link l with read $\in \mathsf{threats}_A^S(l)$ are added to $\mathcal{K}$.

(2) The content of any link queue belonging to a link $l \in \mathsf{Delete}_{\mathsf{control},\mathcal{K}}$ is mapped to $\emptyset$, .

(3) The content of any link queue belonging to a link l is enlarged with all expressions E where $(l, E) \in \mathsf{Insert}_{\mathsf{control},\mathcal{K}}$.

(4) The next control state is chosen non-deterministically from the set $\mathsf{newState}_{\mathsf{control},\mathcal{K}}$.

The set $\mathcal{K}_0$ of initial knowledge contains all data values v given in the UML specification under consideration for which each node n containing v carries a stereotype s_n with access $\in \mathsf{Threats}_A(s_n)$. In a given situation, $\mathcal{K}_0$ may also be specified to contain additional data (for example, public encryption keys).

Note that an adversary A able to remove all values sent over the link l (that it, $\mathsf{delete}_l \in \mathsf{threats}_A^S(l)$) may not be able to selectively remove a value e with known meaning from l: For example, the messages sent over the Internet within a virtual private network are encrypted. Thus, an adversary who is unable to break the encryption may be able to delete all messages undiscrimatorily, but not a single message whose meaning would be known to him.

To evaluate the security of the system with respect to the given type of adversary, we then define the *execution of the subsystem $\mathcal{S}$ in presence of an adversary of type A* to be the function $[\![\mathcal{S}]\!]_A()$ defined from $[\![\mathcal{S}]\!]()$

by applying the modifications from the adversary machine to the link queues as a fourth step in the definition of $[\![S]\!]()$ as follows:

(4) The type A adversary machine is applied to the link queues as detailed above.

Thus after each iteration of the system execution, the adversary may non-deterministically change the contents of link queues in a way depending on the level of physical security as described in the deployment diagram (see Sect. 4).

There are results which simplify the analysis of the adversary behavior defined above, which are useful for developing mechanical tool support, for example to check whether the security properties secrecy and integrity (see below) are provided by a given specification. These are beyond the scope of the current paper and can be found in [Jür03b].

One possibility to specify security requirements is to define an idealized system model where the required security property evidently holds (for example, because all links and components are guaranteed to be secure by the physical layer specified in the deployment diagram), and to prove that the system model under consideration is behaviorally equivalent to the idealized one, using a notion of behavioral equivalence of UML models. This is explained in detail in [Jür03b].

In the following subsection, we consider alternative ways of specifying the important security properties secrecy and integrity which do not require one to explicitly construct such an idealized system and which are used in the remaining parts of this paper.

5.2. Important security properties

The formal definition of the two main security properties secrecy and integrity considered in this section follow the standard approach of [DY83] and are defined in an intuitive way by incorporating the attacker model.

Secrecy The formalization of secrecy used in the following relies on the idea that a process specification preserves the secrecy of a piece of data d if the process never sends out any information from which d could be derived, even in interaction with an adversary. More precisely, d is leaked if there is an adversary of the type arising from the given threat scenario that does not initially know d and an input sequence to the system such that after the execution of the system given the input in presence of the adversary, the adversary knows d (where "knowledge", "execution" etc. have to be formalized). Otherwise, d is said to be kept secret.

Thus we come to the following definition.

Definition 1 *We say that a subsystem S* preserves the secrecy *of an expression E from adversaries of type A if E never appears in the knowledge set $\mathcal{K}$ of A during execution of* $[\![S]\!]_A()$.

This definition is especially convenient to verify if one can give an upper bound for the set of knowledge $\mathcal{K}$, which is often possible when the security-relevant part of the specification of the system S is given as a sequence of command schemata of the form *await event e – check condition g – output event e'* (for example when using UML sequence diagrams or statecharts for specifying security protocols, see Sect. 4).

Examples.

- The system that sends the expression $\{m\}_K :: K \in \mathbf{Exp}$ over an unprotected Internet link does not preserve the secrecy of m or K against attackers eavesdropping on the Internet, but the system that sends $\{m\}_K$ (and nothing else) does, assuming that it preserves the secrecy of K against attackers eavesdropping on the Internet.

- The system that receives a key K encrypted with its public key over a dedicated communication link and sends back $\{m\}_K$ over the link does not preserve the secrecy of m against attackers eavesdropping on and inserting messages on the link, but does so against attackers that cannot insert messages on the link.

Integrity The property integrity can be formalized similarly: If during the execution of the considered system, a system variable gets assigned a value initially only known to the adversary, then the adversary must have caused this variable to contain the value. In that sense the integrity of the variable is violated. (Note that with this definition, integrity is also viewed as violated if the adversary as an honest participant in the interaction is able to change the value, so the definition may have to be adapted in certain circumstances; this is, however, typical for formalizations of security properties.) Thus we say that a system preserves the integrity of a variable v if there is no adversary A such that at some point during the execution of the system with A, v has a value i_0 that is initially known only to A.

Definition 2 *We say that a subsystem S* preserves the integrity *of an attribute a from adversaries of type A with initial knowledge $\mathcal{K}_0$ if during* *execution of* $[\![S]\!]_A()$*, the attribute* a *never takes on a value appearing in* $\mathcal{K}_0$ *but not in the specification* S.

The idea of this definition is that S preserves the integrity of a if no adversary can make a take on a value initially only known to him, in interaction with $\mathcal{A}$. Intuitively, it is the "opposite" of secrecy, in the sense that secrecy prevents the flow of information from protected sources to untrusted recipients, while integrity prevents the flow of information in the other direction. Again, it is a relatively simple definition, which may however not prevent implicit flows of information.

5.3. Tool support

Security validation in our approach is performed through mechanical analysis that validates the fulfilment of the constraints of the security requirements, as those associated with the stereotypes defined in Section 4. A first version has been demonstrated at [Jür03a]. The tool works with UML 1.4 models, which can be stored in a XMI 1.2 (XML Metadata Interchange) format by a number of existing UML design tools. To avoid processing UML models directly on the XMI level, the MDR (MetaData Repository, http://mdr.netbeans.org) is used, which allows one to operate directly on the UML concept level (as used by e.g. the UML CASE tool Poseidon, http://www.gentleware.com). The MDR library implements repository for any model described by a modelling language compliant to the MOF (Meta Object Facility).

Figure 2 illustrates the functionality of the tool. The developer creates a model and stores it in the UML 1.4 / XMI 1.2 file format. The file is imported by the tool into the internal MDR repository. The tool accesses the model through the JMI interfaces generated by the MDR library. The checker parses the model and checks the constraints associated with the stereotype. The results are delivered as a text report for the developer describing found problems, and a modified UML model, where the stereotypes whose constraints are violated are highlighted.

6. Risk-Driven Development

In the following, we give a brief introduction to the lifecycle of IEC 61508, the principle of AS/NZS4360, and the work of CORAS which we base our MBRA development approach on. Risk-driven development is risk-driven in that it focusses on assessing risks and proposing treatments throughout a set of activities. We assume that functional requirements are handled as part of the development and focus on security requirements and the allocation of security requirements in this section.

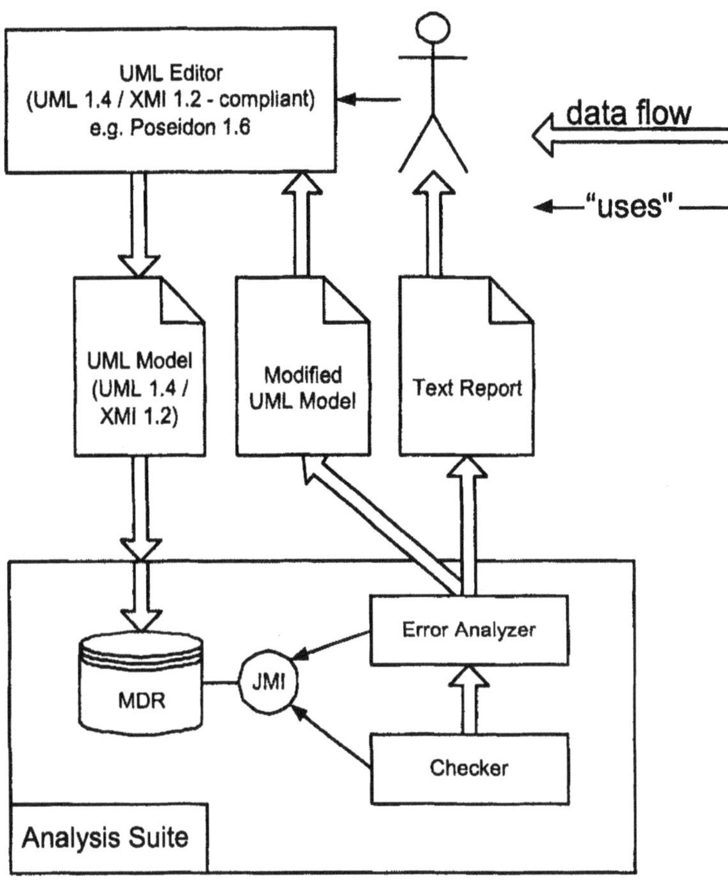

Figure 2. The UMLsec analysis tool

6.1. IEC 61508

The IEC standard IEC 61508 (Functional safety of electrical/electronic/ programmable electronic safety-related systems) [IEC] covers important aspects that need to be addressed when electrical, electronic, and programmable devices are used in connection with safety functions. The strategy of the standard is to derive safety requirements from a hazard and risk analysis and to design the system to meet those safety requirements, taking all possible causes of failure into account. The essence is that all activities relating to functional safety are managed in a planned and methodical way, with each phase having defined inputs and outputs [Bro00]. The standard considers all phases in a safety lifecycle, from initial concept, through design, implementation, operation and maintenance to decommissioning. Figure 3 depicts the lifecycle model of IEC 61508.

IEC 61508 applies to any safety-related software in which is implemented as the aforesaid solutions. This includes: (a) software that is part of a safety-related system; (b) software that is used to develop a safety-related system; and (c) the operating system, system software, communication software, human computer interface (HCI) functions, utilities, and software engineering tools used with (a) or (b).

The process consists of the following phases:

(1) **Concept:** An understanding of the system and its environment is developed.

(2) **Overall scope definition:** The boundaries of the system and its environment are determined, and the scope of the hazard and risk analysis is specified.

(3) **Hazard and risk analysis:** Hazards and hazardous events of the system, the event sequences leading to the hazardous events, and the risks associated with the hazardous events are determined.

(4) **Overall safety requirements:** The specification for the overall safety requirements is developed in order to achieve the required functional safety.

(5) **Safety requirements allocation:** The safety functions contained in the overall safety requirements specification are allocated to the safety-related system, and a safety integrity level is allocated to each safety function.

(6) **Overall operation and maintenance planning:** A plan is developed for operating and maintaining the system, and the required

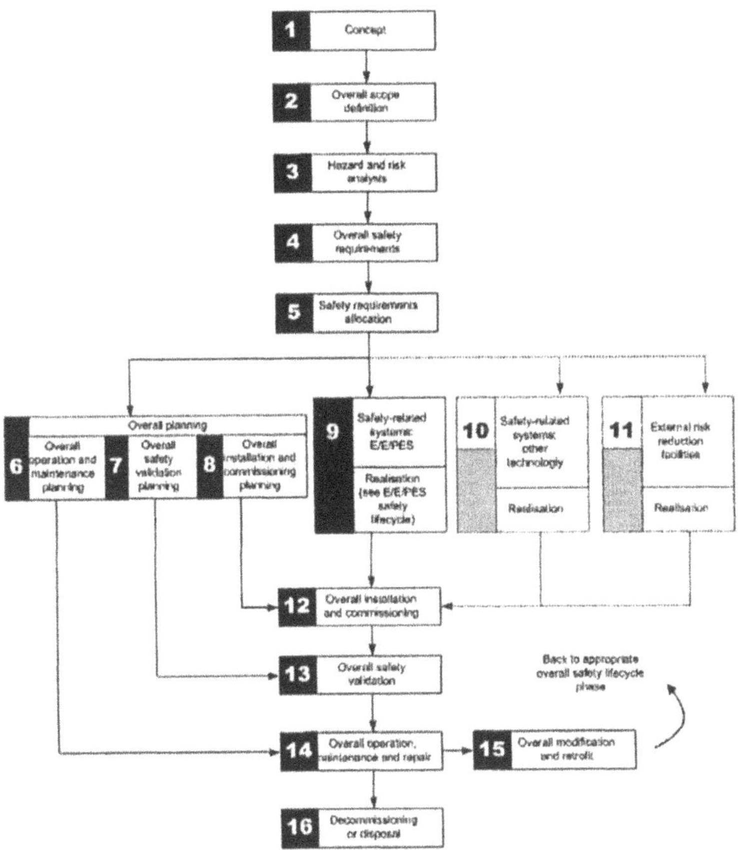

Figure 3. Overall safety lifecycle of IEC 61508

functional safety is ensured to be maintained during operation and maintenance.

(7) **Overall safety validation planning:** A plan for the overall safety validation of the system is developed.

(8) **Overall installation and commissioning planning:** Plans, ensuring that the required functional safety are achieved, are developed for the installation and commissioning of the system.

(9) **Safety-related systems:** The Electrical, Electronic and Programmable Electronic Systems (E/E/PES) safety-related system is created conforming to the safety requirements specification.

(10) **Safety-related systems (other technology):** Safety-related systems based on other technology are created to meet the requirements specified for such systems (outside scope of the standard).

(11) **External risk reduction facilities:** External risk reduction facilities are created to meet the requirements specified for such facilities (outside scope of the standard).

(12) **Overall installation and commissioning:** The Electrical, Electronic and Programmable Electronic Systems (E/E/PES) safety-related system is installed and commissioned.

(13) **Overall safety validation:** The Electrical, Electronic and Programmable Electronic Systems (E/E/PES) safety-related system is validated to meet the overall safety requirements specification.

(14) **Overall operation, maintenance and repair:** The system is operated, maintained and repaired in order to ensure that the required functional safety is maintained.

(15) **Overall modification and retrofit:** The functional safety of the system is ensured to be appropriate both during and after modification and retrofit.

(16) **Decommissioning or disposal:** The functional safety of the system is ensured to be appropriate during and after decommissioning or disposing of the system.

6.2. Model-based risk assessment: The CORAS approach

Model-based risk assessment (MBRA) has been a research topic since the early 80-ies [KM87; GO84] and builds on the concept of applying system modelling when specifying and describing the systems to be assessed as an integrated part of the risk assessment. The CORAS framework is based on the concept of MBRA and employs modelling methodology for three main purposes: (1) To describe the target of evaluation at the right level of abstraction, (2) As a medium for communication and interaction between different groups of stakeholders involved in a risk assessment, and (3) To document risk assessment results and the assumptions on which these results depend.

Figure 4 outlines the sub-processes and activities contained in the CORAS risk management process, which is a refinement of AS/NZS 4360:1999. Further information on the CORAS risk management process can be found in [HdBLS02].

Sub-process 1: Identify Context
- Activity 1.1: Identify areas of relevance
- Activity 1.2: Identify and value assets
- Activity 1.3: Identify policies and evaluation criteria
- Activity 1.4: Approval

Sub-process 2: Identify Risks
- Activity 2.1: Identify threats to assets
- Activity 2.2: Identify vulnerabilities of assets
- Activity 2.3: Document unwanted incidents

Sub-process 3: Analyse Risks
- Activity 3.1: Consequence evaluation
- Activity 3.2: Frequency evaluation

Sub-process 4: Risk Evaluation
- Activity 4.1: Determine level of risk
- Activity 4.2: Prioritise risks
- Activity 4.3: Categorise risks
- Activity 4.4: Determine interrelationships among risk themes
- Activity 4.5: Prioritise the resulting risk themes and risks

Sub-process 5: Risk Treatment
- Activity 5.1: Identify treatment options
- Activity 5.2: Assess alternative treatment approaches

Figure 4. Sub-processes and activities in the CORAS risk management process [HdBLS02]

The integrated system development and risk management process of CORAS is based on the CORAS risk management process, the Reference Model - Open Distributed Processing (RM-ODP), and the Rational Unified Process (RUP). RUP structures system development according to four phases: (1) Inception, (2) Elaboration, (3) Construction, and (4) Transition. As illustrated in Figure 5, these two processes are combined in order to address security throughout the development. In each iteration in the development one assesses a particular part of the system or the whole system at a particular viewpoint according to RM-ODP. For each of the iterations, treatments are evaluated and proposed according to a cost-benefit strategy.

7. MBRA Development Process for Security-Critical Systems

In system development, one usually distinguishes between three levels of abstractions: the requirement specification, the design specification, and the implementation. The design specification is thus a refinement of the requirement specification, and the implementation is a refinement of the design specification.

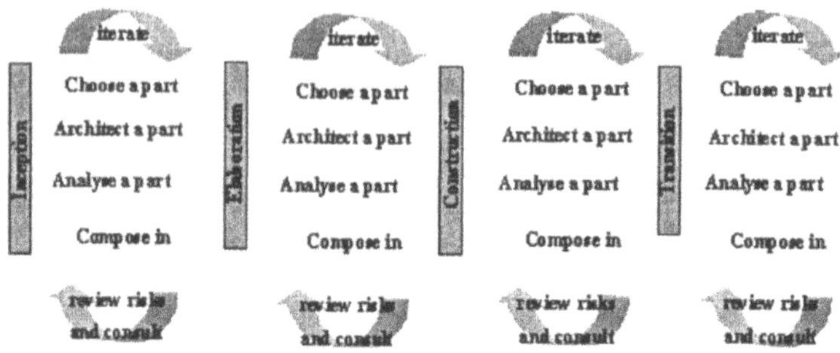

Figure 5. The integrated system development and risk management process

In the MBRA development process for security-critical systems (see Figure 6), we make use of the engineering and technical experience gained when developing safety critical systems within the process industry. The development process is based on the concept of handling safety requirements in IEC 61508 and the idea of using models both to document the system and as input to risk management from the CORAS integrated risk management and system development process. The process is both stepwise iterative and incremental. For each iteration more information is added and increasingly detailed versions of the system are constructed through subsequent iterations.

The first two phases concern the specification of concepts and overall scope definition of the system. A system description and a functional requirements proposition are the results of these two phases. This information is further used as input to the preliminary hazard analysis (PHA). By performing a PHA early in the development process, the most obvious and conspicuous potential hazards can be identified and handled more easily and at a lower cost. Furthermore, the PHA aids in the elicitation of security requirements for the system, which is the fourth phase in the development process. Based on the security policy for the involved organizations, security requirements are specified first on the enterprize level and then refined into more technical specifications using UMLsec. Phase 4 targets the identification of security threats using e.g. Security-HazOp [Vog01]. Security threats are then analyzed in terms of finding the frequency of occurrence and potential impacts of the threats. Based on the results from risk analysis, risks are evaluated and either accepted or not accepted. Unacceptable risks are treated by refining or by specifying new security requirements or by introducing safeguards before the risk management step is iterated until no unacceptable risks remain. When the required security level is achieved, the system is implemented and tested. If the implemented version is not approved, the process is reiterated from the risk management step. The whole process is iterated from phase 1 whenever updating the system description or the functional requirements.

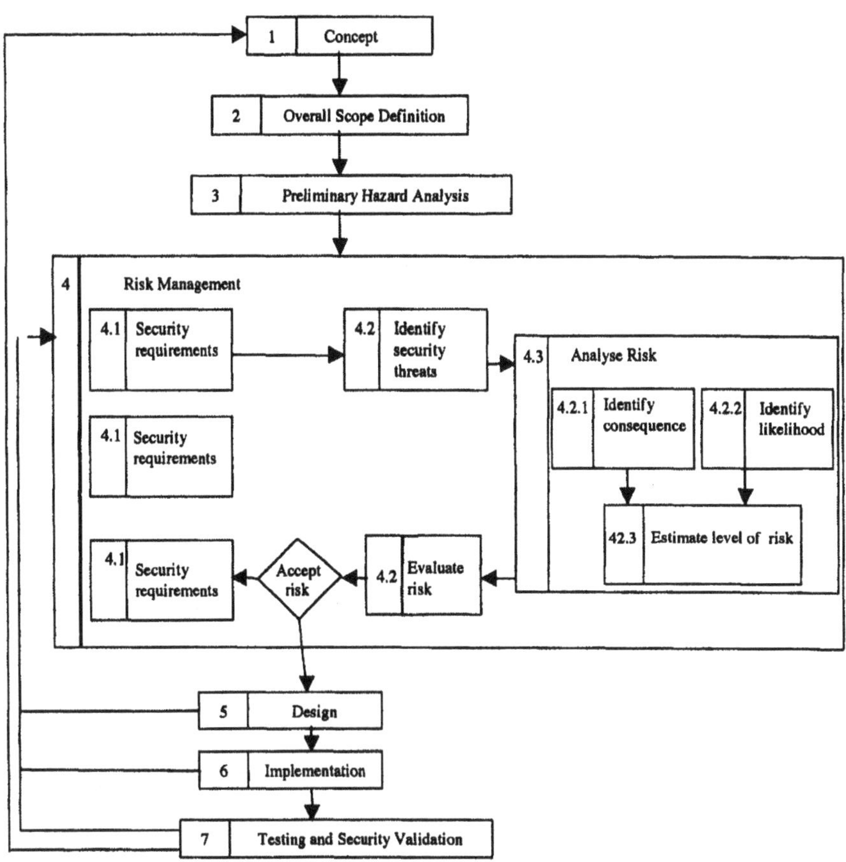

Figure 6. Development process for security-critical systems

8. Development of a AIBO-Lego Mindstorm Prototype Using the Approach

In this Section, we will illustrate the use and applicability of the risk-driven development process for security-critical systems using a AIBO-Lego Mindstorm prototype system. The system is used as a medium of teaching the effect of handling security and safety as an integrated part of development and to test the applicability of techniques and ap-

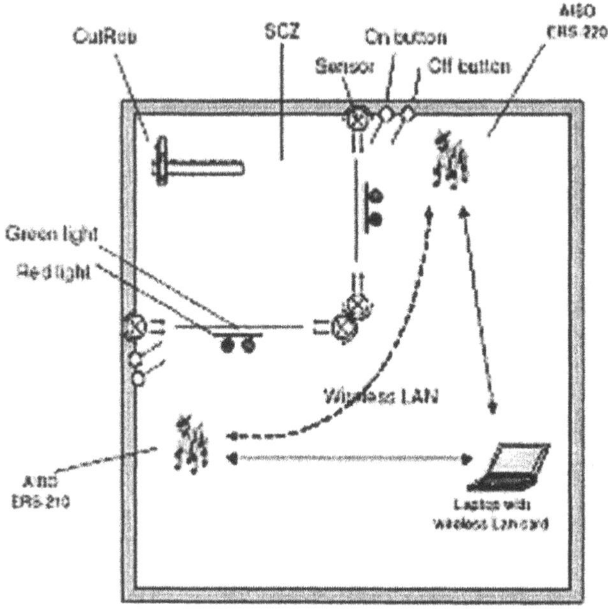

Figure 7. Illustration of the prototype system

proaches for development of security-critical systems at the Norwegian University of Science and Technology (NTNU), Norway. The prototype was developed as part of a Master Thesis at NTNU [Sør02] and consists of an prototypical industrial robot and a computerized control and monitoring system. The control system is implemented using Lego Mindstorm and the monitoring system is implemented using Sony AIBO robots as the monitoring system and a PC-controller (portable computer with software) representing the control system. AIBO and PC-controller communicate using WLAN and TCP/IP as depicted in Figure 7.

8.1. Concept and overall scope definition

Concept and overall scope definition constitute the first two phases of the process. The main objective of these two phases is to define the main objective and purpose of the system. The main objective of the Lego-AIBO system is to develop a prototype to investigate the relationship between security threats and safety consequences in a safety critical system that make use of computerized monitoring and control systems. However, in this context we will only look into the security aspects of the computerized monitoring and control system. The main objective

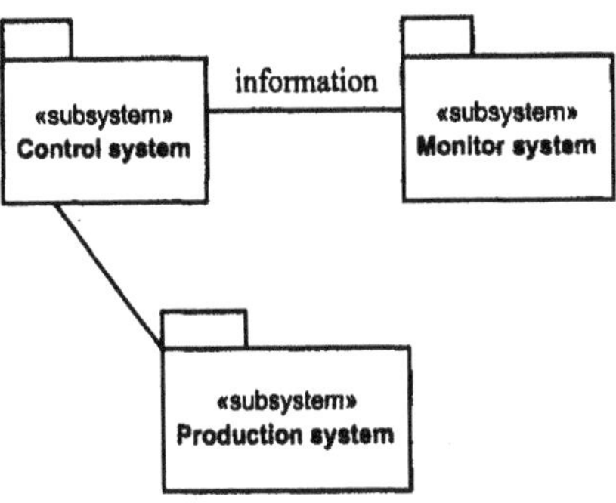

Figure 8. The main components of the AIBO-Lego prototype

of these two systems is to monitor all access to the safety zone of the system and prevent unauthorized access to the zone.

The AIBO-Lego prototype system consists of three components, the monitoring system, the control system, and the production system as depicted in Figure 8. The control system receives information from the AIBO (monitoring system), processes this information, and sends instructions to the production system based on the information provided by the AIBO. The main functionality of the interface between the monitoring and the control system, represented by the AIBO and the PC-controller, is to send and receive information as illustrated in Figure 9.

8.2. Preliminary hazard analysis (PHA)

When the purpose and scope of the system has been established, a preliminary hazard analysis is performed. In this phase, we use Security-HazOp as described in [GWJ01] to identify overall security threats to the system. However, due to space restrictions we will only focus on security threats related to the communication between the monitoring

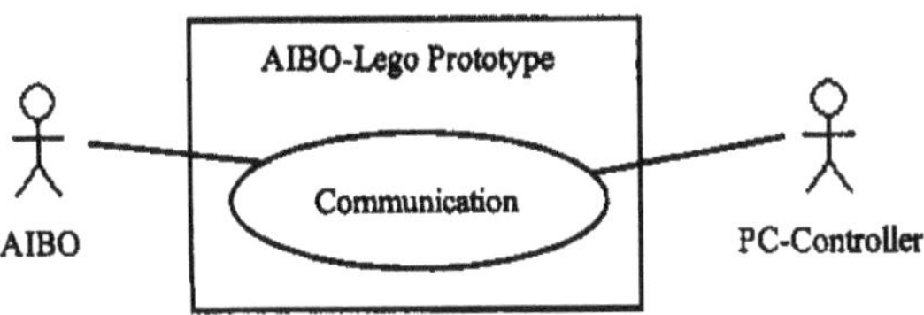

Figure 9. Overview of the main functionality between the AIBO and PC-controller

Pre-Guideword	Attribute	Components	Post-Guideword
Deliberate Unintentional	Disclosure Manipulation Denial Fabrication Delay	AIBO PC-controller Communication	Insider Outsider Technical failure Virus Physical blocking

Figure 10. Combination of guidewords used for PHA

and control system. The reader is referred to Chapter 9 in [Sør02] for more information on the result of the PHA.

Security-HazOp is an adaptation of the safety analysis method HazOp (Hazard and Operability Analysis) for Security-Critical systems. Security-HazOp make use of the negation of the security attributes as part of the guidewords. Guidewords, in HazOp, is used to guide the brainstorming process when identifying security threats. The reader is referred to [Lev95] for more information on HazOp. Security-HazOp is performed as a brainstorming session using different combinations of sentences of the form:

Pre-Guideword Attribute *of* **Component** *due to* **Post-Guideword.**

Figure 10 depicts the combination of guidewords used for PHA. Pre-guideword denotes whether the attack is intentional or not, while attribute is the negation of the security attributes secrecy, integrity, and availability. Components denotes the components that are analyzed and the post-guideword relate to the threat agent who is responsible for the attack.

As input to PHA in a risk-driven development, we use UML diagrams describing the main functionality of the system. These diagrams are called PHA input diagrams. Figure 11 provide an example of a PHA input diagram. PHA input diagrams could be any type of UML diagram, however, since we are mainly concerned with information flow and behavior in Security-Critical systems, one usually uses one or several of the UML behavioral diagrams. Figure 11 depicts a PHA input diagram modelled as a UML sequence diagram. The diagram specifies the main interface between the control and monitoring system in the AIBO-Lego prototype.

When using UML models as input to PHA or other risk analysis methods one goes through each diagram using a set of guidelines. These guidelines specify two things: Firstly, the information provided by the specific UML diagram that should be used as input, and secondly, how to use the information as input to risk analysis methods. The risk analysis methods supported are HazOp (Hazard and Operability analysis), FME(C)A (Failure Mode, Effect, and Criticality Analysis, and FTA (Fault Three Analysis). Currently, all UML 1.4 diagrams are supported by the guidelines (will be updated to support UML 2.0 when finalized). As an example we will describe the guideline for using UML sequence diagrams as input to HazOp. The reader is referred to [GSD+03] for more information on the guidelines.

HazOp is organized as structured brainstorming using a group of experts. The brainstorming meetings consist of a set of experts, a risk analysis leader, and a risk analysis secretary. The risk analysis leader goes through the set of guidelines as already explained, while the secretary records the result from the brainstorming during the meeting. The result from the brainstorming is recorded in a HazOp table, as illustrated in Figure 12. The columns *Pre-Guideword*, *Attribute*, and *Post-Guideword* are the same as described in Figure 10. The column *ID* is used to assign a unique id to the threat scenario, while the column *Asset* denotes the information from the UML diagram being analyzed. For the guideline for use of UML sequence diagrams as input to HazOp, assets are represented as either messages or objects. Generally, an asset is something of value to one or more stakeholders and can be anything from a particular piece of information to a physical computer or other equipment. Assets are typically derived from requirement specifications. For more information on how to identify assets, see [GSD+03]. The column *Component* denotes the part of the system the asset is part of or connected to. In the case of the example, we are looking at the communication between the AIBO and the PC-Controller. The column *Threat* describes the event that may happen. In the example, the threat is derived from combining pre-guideword, attribute, asset, and components,

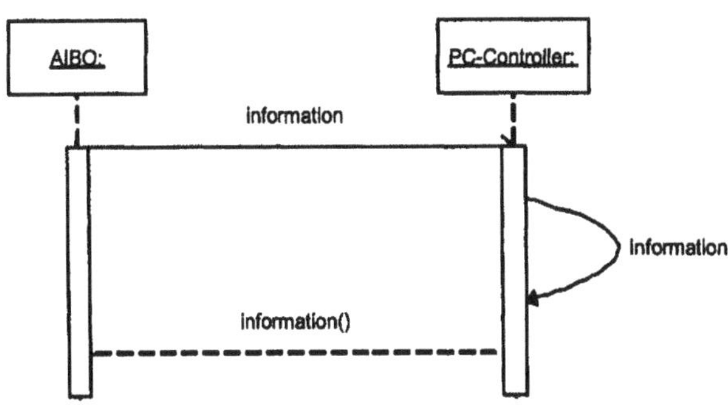

Figure 11. PHA input diagram as UML sequence diagram

for example *deliberate manipulation of information on communication channel*, which gives the threat *Incorrect, but valid information.* The column *Threat scenario* describes who or what causes the threat to occur and the column *Unwanted incident* describes what happens if the threat occurs. In the example death or severe damage to personnel is the unwanted incident of the threat that incorrect, but valid information is sent on the communication channel because an outsider has altered the information.

We use the UML sequence diagram in Figure 11 as the PHA input diagram. PHA input diagrams specify both the structural and behavioral aspects of a system, and one typically makes use of a set of UML diagrams as PHA input diagrams in order to cover both aspects during risk analysis. Sequence diagrams describe the behavior of the system.

Figure 12 provides an example of a PHA with Figure 11 as PHA input diagram.

ID	Pre-Guideword	Asset	Attribute	Component	Post-Guideword	Threat	Threat scenario	Unwanted incident
1a	Deliberate	Information	Manipulation	Communication	Outsider	Incorrect, but valid information	Outsider alters information	Death or severe damage to personnel

Figure 12. Example of use of guideline for use of UML sequence diagram as input to Security-HazOp

The main result from PHA is a list of security threats which are then used as input to a security requirement specification and allocation, which is the next phase in the development process. In this context, we focus on the security attribute integrity and the security threats related to breach of integrity. We look into the communication between the AIBO robot and the PC controller where any alteration, being either accidental or intentional, may lead to unauthorized access to the system, which might lead to death or serious damage to either unauthorized or authorized personnel. Since we are dealing with a distributed object–oriented system we need to make use of secure communication link between the monitoring and control system (see Section 3) to ensure integrity for information in transit. This can be ensured by encrypting the communication link, which is WLAN using TCP/IP as the communication protocol, between the AIBO and the PC controller.

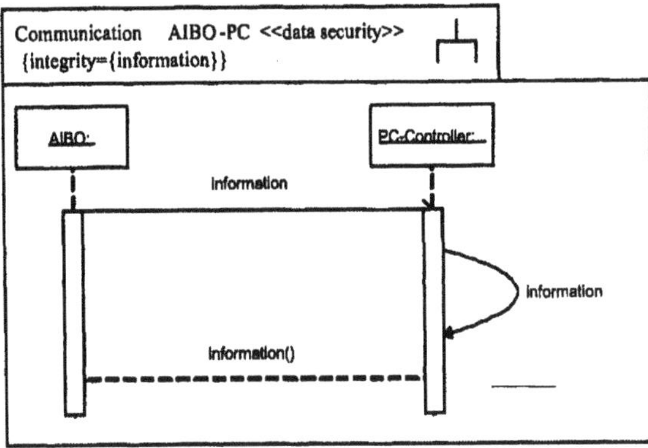

Figure 13. Security requirement for integrity preservation of the communication between AIBO and PC-controller

The treatment option is transformed into security requirements in the next phase of the development process, which is the risk management and specification of security requirements phase.

8.3. Risk management and specification of security requirements

Risk management concerns the following activities:

- specifying security requirements addressing security threats from PHA,
- performing risk identification to reveal unsolved security issues, and
- analyzing and proposing treatments for the unsolved issues evaluated as not acceptable.

In our example, the PHA sketched in the previous section identified the need to preserve the integrity of the communication between AIBO and the PC-controller. In this phase in the development, we specify the security requirements using UMLsec. We make use of the UMLsec stereotype «data security» and the {integrity} as defined in Section 4 to fulfill the demand on preserving integrity of data in transit. Figure 13 depict the specification of the security requirement integrity preservation specifying the communication as «data security» and specifying the data in need of protection using the {integrity}.

As defined in Sect. 4 and Sect. 5, for an adversary type A and a stereotype s, we have $\mathsf{Threats}_A(s) \in \{\mathsf{delete}, \mathsf{read}, \mathsf{insert}, \mathsf{access}\}$, which are the actions that adversaries are capable of with respect to physical links or nodes stereotyped with s. Specifying the security requirement for preservation of integrity is done using the UMLsec stereotype «data security» in connection with the {integrity} on the transport layer of the model, and the stereotype «secure links» on the physical layer. The constraint on the communication links between AIBO and PC-controller is that for each dependency d with stereotype «integrity» between components on nodes $n \neq m$, we have a communication link l between n and m with stereotype t such that $\mathsf{insert} \notin \mathsf{Threats}_A(s)$.

In the next phase of the development process, the security requirements are addressed and allocated through treatment options. This is further implemented and validated during the testing and security validation phase of the development.

8.4. Design and implementation

Design in this context relates to the allocation of security requirements, while implementation relates to the actual implementation of the requirements according to the design specification.

During the PHA and the risk management and specification of security requirements, we identified the need to preserve the integrity of the communication between the AIBO, representing the monitoring system, and the PC-controller, representing the control system. The communication link between the AIBO and the PC-controller is a WLAN connection, which is not encrypted by default. We address this requirement by making use of encryption according to the encryption protocol depicted in Figure 14.

We thus decide to create a secure channel for the sensitive data that has to be sent over the untrusted networks, by making use of cryptography. As usual, we first exchange symmetric session keys for this purpose. Let us assume that, for technical reasons, we decide not to use a standard and well-examined protocol such as SSL but instead a customized key exchange protocol such as the one in Fig. 14. The goal is to exchange a secret session key K, using previously exchanged public keys K_C and K_S, which is then used to sign the data s which should satisfy integrity before transmission. Here $\{M\}_K$ is the encryption of the message M with the key K, $Sign_K(M)$ is the signature of the message M with K, and :: denotes concatenation.

One can now again use stereotypes to include important security requirements on the data that is involved. Here, the stereotype «critical data» labels classes containing sensitive data and has the associated tags {secrecy}, {integrity}, and {fresh} to denote the respec-

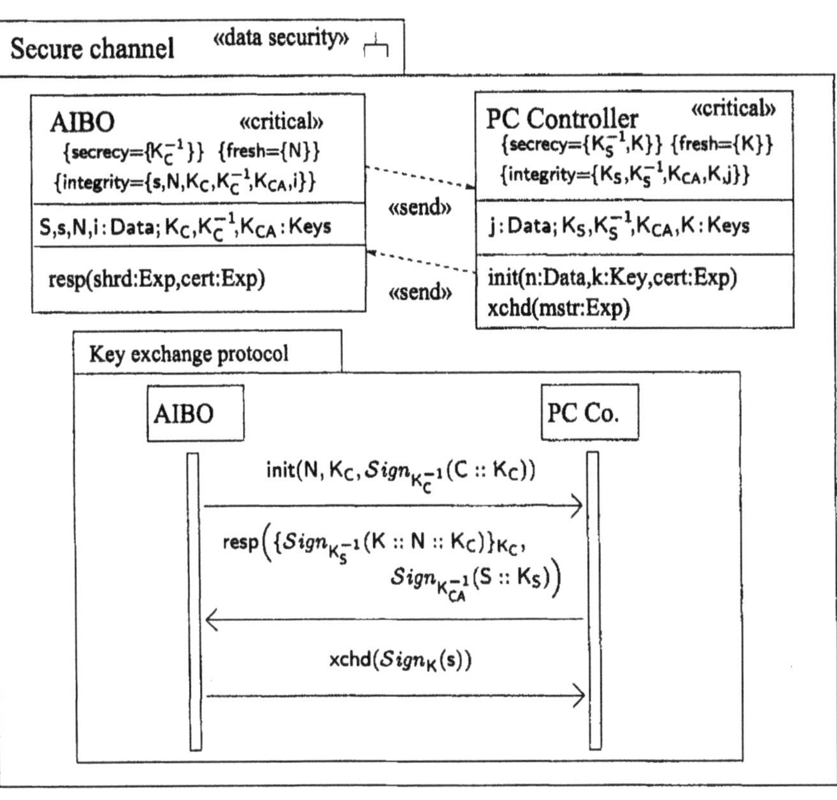

Figure 14. Key exchange protocol

tive security requirements on the data. The constraint associated with «data security» then requires that these requirements are met relative to the given adversary model. We assume that the standard adversary is not able to break the encryption used in the protocol, but can exploit any design flaws that may exist in the protocol, for example by attempting so-called "man-in-the-middle" attacks (this is made precise for a universal adversary model in Sect. 5.1). Technically, the constraint then enforces that there are no successful attacks of that kind. Note that it is highly non-trivial to see whether the constraint holds for a given protocol. However, using well-established concepts from formal methods applied to computer security in the context of UMLsec, it is possible to verify this automatically.

We refer to [Sør02] for further details on these two phases in the development process.

8.5. Testing and security validation

Testing and security validation target both the testing of functional requirements and the validation of the fulfillment of security requirement. In this context, we refer to other sources for testing strategies such as [Pat00] and will only discuss and illustrate how to perform the security validation.

Security requirements are specified using UMLsec and the security validation is performed using the tool support for UMLsec as described in Section 5.3.

9. Conclusion

Traditionally, software development processes do not offer particular support for handling security requirements. In most cases, security issues are only considered after the fact, which is both costly and resource demanding. Security should therefore be handled as an integrated part of system development. The focus is on providing an adequate level of security given resource bounds on time and money.

We have presented a MBRA development process for security-critical systems based on the safety standard IEC 61508 and integrated system development and risk management process of CORAS. The process consists of seven phases:

(1) Concept,

(2) Scope definition,

(3) Preliminary Hazard Analysis,

(4) Risk Management,

(5) Design,

(6) Implementation, and

(7) Testing and security validation.

The main aim is to use models not only to specify and document the system, but also as input into the PHA and risk management.

In our approach, models are used for five purposes:

(1) precise specification of non-functional requirements,

(2) as a medium to communicate non-functional requirements,

(3) to describe the target of assessment,

(4) as a medium to communicate risk assessment results, and

(5) to document risk assessment results.

Furthermore, models are also used for security validation using tool support for UMLsec. The main purpose of this is to validate that the implementation fulfills the security requirements.

The process is illustrated using an AIBO-Lego Mindstorm prototype system, where the focus is on the computerized part of the system and how security threats may affect the safety of the system. However, the process is designed for security-critical system in general and target both small web applications as well as large scale production systems.

Acknowledgments

The work is based on the results from the IST-project CORAS and the work done by the 11 partners in this project and the Master Thesis of Karine Sorby, NTNU, Norway.

References

AS/NZS 4360:1999. Risk management. Standards Australia, Strathfield, 1999.

B. Barber and J. Davey. The use of the ccta risk analysis and management methodology cramm in health information systems. In K.C. Lun, P. Degoulet, T.E. Piemme, and O. Rienhoff, editors, *MEDINFO 92*, pages 1589–1593, Amsterdam, 1992. North Holland Publishing Co.

S. Brown. Overview of iec 61508: design of electrical/electronic/programmable electronic safety-related systems. *Computing Control Engineering Journal*, 11:6–12, February 2000.

CORAS, The CORAS Intregrated Platform. Poster at the CORAS public workshop during ICT-2002, 2002.

DoD. Military standard: System safety program requirements. Standard MIL-STD-882B, Department of Defense, Washington DC 20301, USA, 30 March 1984.

D. Dolev and A. Yao. On the security of public key protocols. *IEEE Transactions on Information Theory*, 29(2):198–208, 1983.

E.B. Fernandez and J.C. Hawkins. Determining role rights from use cases. In *Workshop on Role-Based Access Control*, pages 121–125. ACM, 1997.

G. Georg, R. France, and I. Ray. An aspect-based approach to modeling security concerns. In Jürjens et al. [JCF+02].

S.B. Guarro and D. Okrent. The logic flowgraph: A new approach to process failure modeling and diagnonsis for disturbance analysis applications. *Nuclear Technology*, page 67, 1984.

B.A. Gran, N. Stathiakis, G. Dahll, R. Fredriksen, A. P-J.Thunem, E. Henriksen, E. Skipenes, M.S. Lund, K. Stlen, S.H. Houmb, E.M. Knudsen, and E. Wislff. The coras methodology for model-based risk assessment. Technical report, IST Technical Report, http://sourceforge.coras.org/, 2003.

B.A. Gran, R. Winther, and O-A. Johnsen. Security assessments for safety critical systems using hazops. In *In Proceeding of Safecomp 2001*, 2001.

S.-H. Houmb, F. den Braber, M. Soldal Lund, and K. Stolen. Towards a UML profile for model-based risk assessment. In Jürjens et al. [JCF+02].

IEC 61508: 2000 Functional Safety of Electrical/Electronic/Programmable Electronic (E/E/PE) Safety-Related Systems".

J. Jürjens, V. Cengarle, E. Fernandez, B. Rumpe, and R. Sandner, editors. *Critical Systems Development with UML*, number TUM-I0208 in TUM technical report, 2002. UML'02 satellite workshop proceedings.

J. Jürjens. UMLsec: Extending UML for secure systems development. In J.-M. Jézéquel, H. Hussmann, and S. Cook, editors, *UML 2002 – The Unified Modeling Language*, volume 2460 of *LNCS*, pages 412–425, Dresden, Sept. 30 – Oct. 4 2002. Springer.

J. Jürjens. Developing Security-Critical Systems with UML, 2003. Series of tutorials at international conferences including OMG DOCsec 2002, IFIP SEC 2002, APPLIED INFORMATICS 2003, ETAPS 2003, OMG Workshop On UML for Enterprise Applications 2003, Formal Methods Symposium 2003. Download of material at http://www4.in.tum.de/~juerjens/csdumltut .

J. Jürjens. *Secure Systems Development with UML*. Springer, 2003. In preparation.

I.S. Kim and M. Modarres. Application of Goal Tree-Success Tree Model as the Knowledge-Base of Operator Advisory System. *Nuclear Engineering & Design J.*, 104:67–81, 1987.

P. Krutchten. *The Rational Unified Process, An Introduction*. Readings, MA. Addison-Wesley, 1999.

K. Lano, K. Androutsopoulos, and D. Clark. Structuring and Design of Reactive Systems using RSDS and B. In *FASE 2000*, LNCS. Springer-Verlag, 2000.

N. G. Leveson. *Safeware: System safety and computers*. Addison-Wesley, 1995. ISBN: 0-201-11972-2.

S. Meng. Secure database design with UML. Bachelor's thesis, Munich University of Technology. In preparation.

R. Patton. *Software Testing*. SAMS, 2000.

R.F. Paige and J.S. Ostroff. A proposal for a lightweight rigorous UML-based development method for reliable systems. In *Workshop on Practical UML-Based Rigorous Development Methods*, Lecture Notes in Informatics, pages 192–207. German Computer Society (GI), 2001. UML 2001 satellite workshop.

J.R. Putman. *Architecting with RM-ODP*. Prentice-Hall, 2000.

M. Shaw. Writing good software engineering research papers. In *25th International Conference on Software Engineering*, page 726, Portland, Oregon, May 03 - 10 2003.

K. Sørby. Relationship between security and safety in a security-safety critical system: Safety consequences of security threats. Master's thesis, Norwegian University of Science and Technology, 2002.

Udo Voges, editor. *Security Assessments of Safety Critical Systems Using HAZOPs*, volume 2187 of *Lecture Notes in Computer Science*. Springer, 2001. ISBN: 3-540-42607-8.

B. Watson. The Real-time UML standard. In *Real-Time and Embedded Distributed Object Computing Workshop*. OMG, July 15-18 2002.

G. Wyss, R. Craft, and D. Funkhouser. *The Use of Object-Oriented Analysis Methods in Surety Analysis*. Sandia National Laboratories Report, 1999.

DEVELOPING PORTABLE SOFTWARE

James D. Mooney
Lane Department of Computer Science and Electrical Engineering, West Virginia University, PO Box 6109, Morgantown, WV 26506 USA

Abstract: Software portability is often cited as desirable, but rarely receives systematic attention in the software development process. With the growing diversity of computing platforms, it is increasingly likely that software of all types may need to migrate to a variety of environments and platforms over its lifetime. This tutorial is intended to show the reader how to design portability into software projects, and how to port software when required.

Key words: software engineering; software portability

1. INTRODUCTION

Most software developers agree that portability is a desirable attribute for their software projects. The useful life of an application, for example, is likely to be extended, and its user base increased, if it can be migrated to various platforms over its lifetime. In spite of the recognized importance of portability, there is little guidance for the systematic inclusion of portability considerations in the development process.

There is a fairly large body of literature on aspects of portability. A comprehensive bibliography is provided by Deshpande (1997). However, most of this literature is based on anecdotes and case studies (e.g. Blackham (1988), Ross (1994)). A few seminal books and papers on portability appeared in the 1970s (e.g. Brown (1977), Poole (1975), Tanenbaum (1978)). Several books on software portability were published in the 1980s (Wallis (1982), Dahlstrand (1984), Henderson (1988), LeCarme (1989)). None of these publications provide a systematic, up-to-date presentation of portability techniques for present-day software. This tutorial offers one approach to reducing this void.

Well-known strategies for achieving portability include use of standard languages, system interface standards, portable libraries and compilers, etc. These tools are important, but they are not a substitute for a consistent portability strategy during the development process. The problems are compounded considerably by the more demanding requirements of much present-day software, including timing constraints, distribution, and sophisticated (or miniaturized) user interfaces.

This tutorial introduces a broad framework of portability issues, but concentrates on practical techniques for bringing portability considerations to the software development process. The presentation is addressed both to individual software designers and to those participating in an organized development process.

It is not possible in a paper of this length to provide a detailed and thorough treatment of all of the issues and approaches for software portability. We will offer an introduction designed to increase awareness of the issues to be considered.

2. THE WHAT AND WHY OF PORTABILITY

In this section we will examine what we mean by portability, consider some related concepts, and discuss why porting may be desirable.

2.1 What is Portability?

The concept of software portability has different meanings to different people. To some, software is portable only if the executable files can be run on a new platform without change. Others may feel that a significant amount of restructuring at the source level is still consistent with portability.

The definition we will use for this study leans toward the latter view and includes seven key concepts. This definition originally appeared in Mooney (1990):

> A *software unit* is portable (exhibits portability) across a *class of environments* to the *degree* that the *cost* to *transport and adapt* it to a new environment in the class is less than the *cost* of *redevelopment.*

Let's examine the key concepts in this definition.

- *Software Unit.* Although we will often discuss portability in the context of traditional applications, most ideas may also apply to other types of software units, ranging from components to large software systems.

- *Environment.* This term refers to the complete collection of external elements with which a software unit interacts. These may include other software, operating systems, hardware, remote systems, documents, and people. The term is more general than platform, which usually refers only to the operating system and computer hardware.
- *Class of Environments.* We use this term to emphasize that we seek portability not only to a set of specific environments, which are known a priori, but to all environments meeting some criteria, even those not yet developed.
- *Degree of Portability.* Portability is not a binary attribute. We consider that each software unit has a quantifiable degree of portability to a particular environment or class of environments, based on the cost of porting. Note that the degree of portability is not an absolute; it has meaning only with respect to a specific environment or class.
- *Costs and Benefits.* There are both costs and benefits associated with developing software in a portable manner. These costs and benefits take a variety of forms.
- *Phases of Porting.* We distinguish two major phases of the porting process: *transportation* and *adaptation.* Adaptation includes most of the modifications that need to be made to the original software, including automated retranslation. Transportation refers to the physical movement of the software and associated artifacts, but also includes some low level issues of data representation.
- *Porting vs. Redevelopment.* The alternative to porting software to a new environment is redeveloping it based on the original specifications. We need to compare these two approaches to determine which is more desirable. Porting is not always a good idea!

Note that while we concentrate on the porting of software, there may be other elements for which portability should be considered. These include related software such as libraries and tools, as well as data, documentation, and human experience.

2.2 Why should we Port?

Before we make the effort to make software portable, it is reasonable to ask why this may be a good idea. Here are a few possible reasons:

- There are many hardware and software platforms; it is not only a Windows world.
- Users who move to different environments want familiar software.

- We want easier migration to new system versions and to totally new environments.
- Developers want to spend more time on new development and less on redevelopment.
- More users for the same product means lower software costs.

The advantages of portability may appear differently to those having different roles. Here are some of the key stakeholders in software development and their possible interests in portability:

- *Users* may benefit from portable software because it should be cheaper, and should work in a wider range of environments.
- *Developers* should benefit from portable software because implementations in multiple environments are often desired over the lifetime of a successful product, and these should be easier to develop and easier to maintain.
- *Vendors* should find software portability desirable because ported implementations of the same product for multiple environments should be easier to support, and should increase customer loyalty.
- *Managers* should find advantages in portable software since it is likely to lead to reduced maintenance costs and increased product lifetime, and to simplify product enhancement when multiple implementations exist. However, managers must be convinced that the cost to get the first implementation out the door may not be the only cost that matters!

2.3 Why shouldn't we Port?

Portability is not desirable in all situations. Here are some reasons we may not want to invest in portability:

- Sometimes even a small extra cost or delay in getting the product out the door is not considered tolerable.
- Sometimes even a small reduction in performance or storage efficiency cannot be accepted.
- Sometimes a software unit is so tightly bound to a specialized environment that a change is extremely unlikely.
- Sometimes source files or documentation are unavailable. This may be because developers or vendors are protective of intellectual property rights.

2.4 Levels of Porting

A software unit goes through multiple representations, generally moving from high to low level, between its initial creation and actual execution. Each of these representations may be considered for adaptation, giving rise to multiple levels of porting:

- *Source Portability.* This is the most common level; the software is adapted in its source-level, human-readable form, then recompiled for the new target environment.
- *Binary Portability.* This term refers to porting software directly in its executable form. Usually little adaptation is possible. This is the most convenient situation, but possible only for very similar environments.
- *Intermediate-Level Portability.* In some cases it may be possible to adapt and port a software representation that falls between source and binary.

2.5 Portability Myths

The portability problem is often affected by the "silver bullet" syndrome. A wide variety of innovations have all promised to provide universal portability. These include:

- Standard languages (e.g., FORTRAN, COBOL, Ada, C, C++, Java)
- Universal operating systems (e.g., Unix, MS-DOS, Windows, JavaOS)
- Universal platforms (e.g., IBM-PC, SPARC, JavaVM, .NET)
- Open systems and POSIX
- OOP and distributed object models (e.g., OLE, CORBA)
- Software patterns, architectures, and UML
- The World Wide Web

All of these have helped, but none have provided a complete solution. We will examine both the value and the limitations of these technologies.

3. INTERFACES AND MODELS

A software unit interacts with its environment through a collection of *interfaces*. If we can make these interfaces appear the same across a range of environments, much of the problem of portability has been solved. The first step in controlling these interfaces is to identify and understand them. We will make use of *interface models* to establish a framework for discussion.

A number of interface models have been defined and used by industry and governments. Examples include the U.S. Department of Defense Technical Reference Model, The Open Group Architectural Framework, and the CTRON model. Most of these are quite complex, identifying a large number of interface types classified along multiple dimensions.

A very simple but useful model was developed as part of the POSIX effort to create a framework for *open systems*. Open systems are defined as environments that are largely based on non-proprietary industry standards, and so are more consistent with portability goals. The model defined by the POSIX committees is the Open Systems Environment Reference Model (OSE/RM) (ISO/IEC 1996).

This model is illustrated in Figure 1. It defines two distinct interfaces: the interface between an application and a platform (the Application Program Interface, or API) and the interface between a platform and the external environment (the External Environment Interface, or EEI).

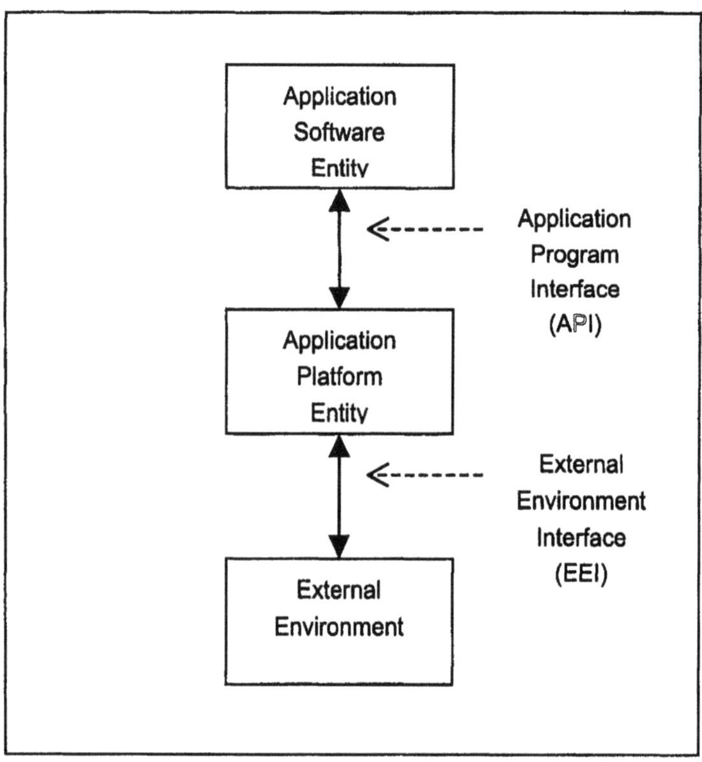

Figure 1. The POSIX Open Systems Environment Reference Model

The OSE/RM does not provide much detail by itself, but it forms the foundation for many of the other models.

The interface model that will form the basis for our study is the *Static Interface Model (SIM)*, originally proposed by the author (Mooney, 1990). This model assumes that the software to be ported is an application program, although other software units would lead to a similar form. The application is in the upper left corner, and the interfaces with which it interacts are shown below and to the right.

The model identifies three *direct interfaces* with which the application is assumed to interact through no (significant) intermediary. These are:

- The *Processor/Memory Interface*, also called the *Architecture Interface*, which handles all operations at the machine instruction level.
- The *Operating System Interface*, responsible for all services provided to an application by the operating system.
- The *Library Interface*, which represents all services provided by external libraries.

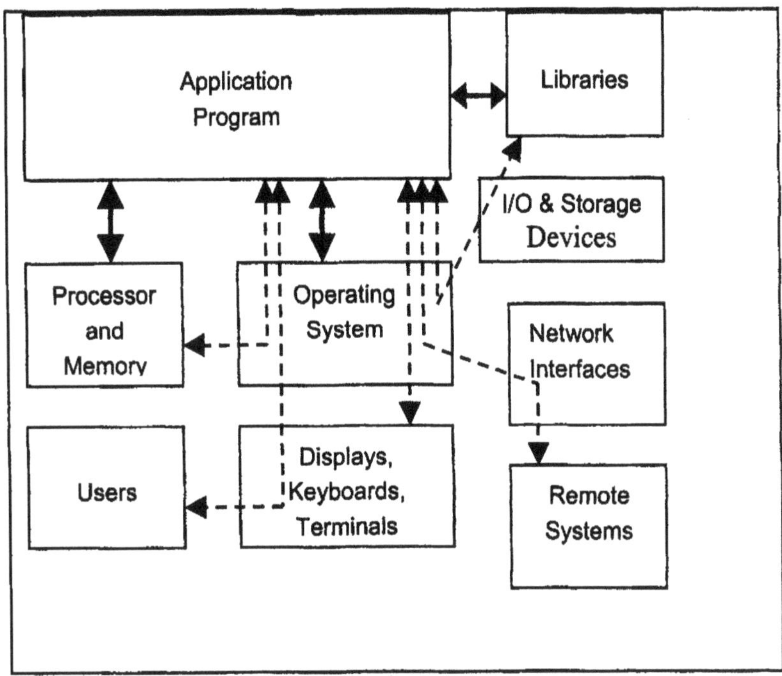

Figure 2. The Static Interface Model

The model further identifies a number of *indirect interfaces*, which are composed of multiple direct interfaces connecting other entities. For example, the user interface involves a chain of interfaces between the application, the operating system, the terminal device, and the user.

Note that the model only identifies interfaces between the application and other entities. Also note that the Operating System Interface could, strictly speaking, be called indirect, since a library is usually involved. However, it is useful to treat this as a direct case.

The value of these models lies in using them to identify and focus on specific interfaces that may be amenable to a particular portability strategy. The SIM provides a useful level of detail for this purpose. As we will see in Section 5, we can identify distinct and useful strategies for each of the direct interfaces of this model.

The interface models considered here are *static models*; they represent a snapshot of the state of a computing system, typically during execution. *Dynamic models* are also used to identify the various representations which may exist for a software unit (and its interfaces) and the translation steps that occur between representations. In the usual case, software ready for porting to a specific environment exists in the form of a *source program* in a common "high-level" programming language. This program may originally have been derived from still higher-level representations. This source program is translated into one or more *intermediate forms,* and a final translation produces the *executable form* to be loaded into memory and executed. Each of these representations offers a different opportunity to bridge interface differences through manual or automated modification.

Other models that may be useful include models of the porting process itself. These are beyond the scope of this paper.

4. THE ROLE OF STANDARDS

A standard is a commonly accepted specification for a procedure or for required characteristics of an object. It is well known that standards can play a crucial role in achieving portability. If a standard can be followed for a particular interface, chances are greatly increased that different environments can be made to look the same. However, standards evolve slowly, so many important interface types are not standardized. Also, standards have many limitations, and only a small number of the vast array of standards in existence can be considered a reliable solution to the problem.

Here we will briefly discuss some issues in the use of standards to help solve the software portability problem. We are interested in *software interface standards*: those that define an interface between multiple entities, at least one of which is software. A very large collection of computer-related standards fits this description.

A software interface standard will aid in the development of portable software if it:

1. provides a clear, complete and unambiguous specification for a significant interface or subset, in a form suitable for the software to be developed;
2. Has implementations that are widely available or may be easily developed for likely target environments.

Unfortunately, many standards fall short of these requirements. They may be expressed in an obscure notation that is hard to understand, or in natural language that is inherently imprecise. There are often many contradictions and omissions. A standard will only become widely implemented if there is already a high demand for it; often a major barrier is the cost of the standard itself.

Standards come into being in three principal ways, each with their own advantages and disadvantages.

- *Formal standards* are developed over an extended time by widely recognized standards organizations such as ISO. They represent a broad and clear consensus, but they may take many years to develop, and are often obsolete by the time they are approved. Some very successful formal standards include the ASCII standard for character codes, the IEEE binary floating point standard, the POSIX standard for the UNIX API, and the C language standard.
- *Defacto standards* are specifications developed by a single organization and followed by others because of that organization's dominance. These are popular by definition but subject to unpredictable change, often for limited commercial interests. Examples include the IBM-PC architecture, the VT-100 terminal model, and the Java language.
- *Consortium standards* are a more recent compromise. They are developed in an open but accelerated process by a reasonably broad-based group, often formed for the specific purpose of maintaining certain types of standards. Example standards in this class include Unicode, OpenGL, and the Single Unix Specification.

Standards will play a critical role in the strategies to be discussed, but they are only a starting point.

5. STRATEGIES FOR PORTABILITY

If software is to be made portable, it must be designed to minimize the effort required to adapt it to new environments. However, despite good portable design, some adaptation will usually be necessary. This section is concerned with identifying strategies that may be used during development to reduce the anticipated level of adaptation, and during porting to carry out the required adaptation most effectively.

5.1 Three Key Principles

There are many approaches and techniques for achieving greater portability for a given software unit. These techniques may be effectively guided by three **key principles**.

5.1.1 Control the Interfaces

As noted in previous sections, the major problems of portability can be overcome by establishing a common set of interfaces between a software entity and all elements of its environment. This set may include many different interfaces of various types and levels.

These interfaces may take many forms: a programming language, an API for system services, a set of control codes for an output device.

Commonality of the interfaces requires that each interface be made to look the same from the viewpoint of the software being developed, in spite of variations in the components on the other side. This goal may be achieved by many different strategies. Some of these strategies may successfully establish a common interface during initial development, while others will require further effort during porting.

5.1.2 Isolate Dependencies

In a realistic software project there will be elements that must be dependent on their environment, because variations are too great or critical to be hidden by a single common interface. These elements must be confined to a small portion of the software, since this is the portion that may require modification during porting.

For example, software that manages memory dynamically in a specialized way may be dependent on the underlying memory model of the architecture or operating system; graphics algorithms may depend on the output models supported; high-performance parallel algorithms may need to vary depending on the architectural class of the machine.

Notice that this is also an interface issue, since the dependent portions of the software need to be isolated behind a limited set of interfaces.

5.1.3 Think Portable

This final principle is simply an admonition to be conscious of the portability goal during all design decisions and development activities. Many portability problems arise not because there was no way to avoid them, but because portability wasn't considered when the choice was made.

5.2 Classifying the Strategies

The strategies to be studied are concerned with controlling particular interfaces. They can be identified and classified by considering the various interface models of Section 2. Static models such as the SIM or the OSE/RM allow us to identify the principal interfaces with which a typical application interacts. We have seen that the primary low-level interfaces can be classified as *architecture* interfaces (including processor, memory, and direct I/O), *operating system* interfaces (including APIs), and *library* interfaces (including support packages).

We are most interested in achieving commonality for these low-level interfaces. These interfaces in turn mediate access to higher-level interfaces such as the user interface, file systems, network resources, and numerous domain-specific abstractions. Controlling these interfaces can be viewed as special cases of controlling the underlying interfaces to the architecture, operating system, and libraries.

The first and most essential strategy for portable software development is the use of a suitable programming language. Portable programming in an appropriate language will generally provide a common model for most (but not all) of the elements of each of the three main interface classes. The remaining elements must be dealt with by considering the interfaces more directly.

There are thus four main classes of strategies that are most important to consider:

1. Language-based strategies
2. Library strategies
3. Operating system strategies
4. Architecture strategies

three main types. We examine these types in the next subsection. We will then discuss strategies of each type that apply to each of the four classes.

5.3 Three Types of Strategies

The object of an interface strategy is to enable a software unit at one side of the interface to adapt to multiple environments at the other side. If we can arrange for the software unit to have the same predictable view of the interface for all environments, the problem has been solved. This can occur if there is a well-known common form that most environments will follow, or if the element on the other side of the interface can be kept the same in each environment.

If there is no common model known when the software unit is designed, then interface differences are likely to exist when porting is to be done. In this case, a translation may be possible to avoid more extensive modifications to the software.

These considerations lead us to identify three fundamental types of strategies. All of the more specific strategies we will consider can be placed into one (or occasionally more) of these types.

5.3.1 Standardize the Interface

If an existing standard can be identified which meets the needs of the software unit and is likely to be supported by most target environments, the software can be designed to follow this standard. For example, if most environments provide a C compiler, which adequately implements the C standard, it may be advantageous to write our programs in standard C.

This strategy must be followed in the initial development of the software. It relies on the expectation that the standard will truly be supported in (nearly) identical form in the target environments. Figure 5 depicts the general form of this strategy.

5.3.2 Port the Other Side

If the component on the other side of the interface can be ported or reimplemented in each target environment, it will consistently present the same interface. For example, porting a library of scientific subroutines ensures that they will be available consistently in the same form.

This strategy may be chosen during initial development, or selected for a specific implementation. Note that in this case we are actually "extending the boundaries" of the ported software, and trading some interfaces for others. The interfaces between the extra ported components and their environment which is not ported, must be handled by other strategies.

5.3.3 Translate the Interface

If the interfaces do not match, elements on one side may be converted into the equivalent elements on the other. This may be done by an overall translation process when porting, or by providing extra software that interprets one interface in terms of the other during execution.

An example of the first variation is the usual compiling process. The common representation for the architecture interface of a program (in the source language) is translated to the specific architecture of the target. The second variation is illustrated by a library that converts one set of graphics functions to a different set provided in the target environment.

This strategy may be planned during development but must be carried out in the context of a specific implementation.

There is one alternative to all these approaches; that is to redesign the software to fit the interface of the target environment. This is not a portability strategy, but an alternative to porting. Sometimes this is the best alternative, and we must know how to make a choice. This issue will be discussed later.

We now are prepared for a look at the various strategies associated with each of the main classes: language, library, operating system, and architecture.

5.4 Language Based Strategies

Effective approaches to portable design start with the choice and disciplined use of a suitable programming language. If the language allows a single expression of a program to be understood identically in all target environments, then portability will be achieved.

In practice, it is very often possible to express many of a program's requirements in a common language, but not all of them. If the language includes no representation for certain concepts, they must be handled by other strategy classes.

Sometimes the language in which the program is currently expressed is not supported for the target environment. In this case it becomes necessary to translate the software from one language to another.

The source language representation of a software unit is the most convenient starting point for both manual adaptation (e.g. editing) and automated adaptation (e.g. compiling) to prepare it for use in a given target environment. Therefore language-based strategies are the single most essential class in our collection.

Language strategies for portability may be classified according to the three types identified in the previous section: standardize, port, translate.

5.4.1 Standard Languages

Programming languages were among the first types of computer-related specifications to be formally standardized. Today formal standards exist for over a dozen popular general-purpose languages, including FORTRAN, COBOL, Ada, Pascal, C, and C++ (note that standardization for Java is not yet achieved).

Writing a program in a standard language is an essential step in achieving portability. However, it is only a starting point. The language must be one that is actually available in most expected target environments. No standard is clear, complete and unambiguous in every detail, so the programmer must follow a discipline (think portable!) that avoids use of language features which may have differing interpretations. No language covers all of the facilities and resources that particular programs may require, so portability in some areas must be achieved by other means.

Effective use of standard languages is crucial to achieving portability. Each of the most widely-used languages presents a somewhat different set of opportunities and problems for effective portable programming. For example, C does not fully define the range of integers; many Java features continue to vary as the language evolves. Standard language strategies, and the issues raised by specific languages, are often the subject of books and are beyond the scope of this paper.

5.4.2 Porting the Compiler

One of the potential problems of the use of standard languages is the fact that different compilers may use different interpretations in areas where the standard is not completely clear. If the same compiler is used for each target environment, then its interpretation of a software unit will not vary, even if it is non-standard!

To exploit this situation, we may choose to write a program for a specific compiler, then "port the compiler" to each new environment. Porting the compiler, of course, may be a daunting task, but it needs to be done only once to make all software for that compiler usable on the new target. Thus the payoff may be great, and if we are lucky, someone has already done it for us.

It is actually misleading to speak of *porting* the compiler; the essential requirement is to *retarget* the compiler. The compiler's "back end" must be modified to generate code for the new machine. Many compilers are designed to make this type of adaptation relatively easy. The retargeted compiler *may* also be ported to the new environment, but it does not actually matter on which system it runs.

In some cases the compiler is a commercial product, not designed to allow adaptation by its users. In this case we must rely on the vendor to do the retargeting, or else this strategy is unavailable. Many open source compilers, such as the GNU compilers, are designed for easy retargeting.

5.4.3 Language Translation

A compiler translates software from a human-oriented language to a language suitable for execution by machine. It is also possible to translate programs from one human-oriented language to another. If we are faced with a program written in a language for which we have no compiler for the target, and no prospect of obtaining one, then "source-to-source translation" may be the best porting strategy available.

Translating software from Pascal to FORTRAN or C to Java is considerably more challenging than compiling, though not as difficult as natural language translation. Several tools are available which perform reasonable translations among selected languages. Usually these tools can do only an imperfect job; translation must be regarded as a semi-automated process, in which a significant amount of manual effort may be required.

Translation can also be used as a development strategy, when compiler variations are anticipated. Software may be originally written in a "higher-level" language that can be translated into multiple languages or, more likely, language dialects, using a preprocessor. This is more likely to be a strategy that can be fully automated.

5.5 Library Strategies

No programming language directly defines all of the resources and facilities required by a realistic program. Facilities that are neither defined within the language nor implemented by the program itself must be accessed explicitly through the environment. This access may take the form of procedure or function calls, method invocations, messages, program-generated statements or commands, etc. Whatever the mechanism, the aim is to obtain services or information from software and physical resources available in the environment.

These resources are organized into packages, collections, or subsystems that we may view uniformly as *libraries*. Examples may include language-based libraries such as C standard functions, scientific computation libraries, graphic libraries, domain-specific classes and templates, mail server processes, network interfaces, or database management systems.

These libraries provide a class of interfaces, and programs that rely on them will be most portable if they are able to access these facilities in a common form. When this is not possible, adaptation will be required.

We must assume, of course, that the target systems are capable of supporting the services and facilities to which the libraries provide access. No portability strategy can enable a program that plays music to run on a system that has no hardware support for sound!

Once again we can identify three classes of library strategies according to our three principal types: standardize, port, translate. We will overview these strategies in the following subsections

5.5.1 Standard Libraries

Many types of library facilities are defined by formal or defacto standards. This group is led by libraries that are incorporated into specific language standards, such as the C standard function library, Ada standard packages, standard procedures and functions of Pascal, standard templates for C++, etc. Software written in these languages should use the standard facilities as far as possible, taking care to distinguish what is actually standard and what has been added by a particular language implementation.

Additional standard library facilities are not bound to a specific language but are widely implemented in many environments. This is especially likely for libraries providing services of broad usefulness. Some examples here include GKS libraries for low-level graphics functions, MPI for message passing, CORBA for distributed object access, or SQL for database access. Portable software may rely on such libraries if they are expected to be widely available, but must make use of an alternate strategy when they are not.

If the absence of a library supporting an important standard is a major drawback for the target environment, it may be worthwhile to consider implementing such a library. This is likely to be a major effort but could significantly improve the target environment as well as aiding the immediate porting project.

5.5.2 Portable Libraries

Instead of relying on the wide availability of library implementations which conform to a common standard, we may rely on a single implementation, not necessarily standardized (although it creates a de facto standard), which is or can be ported to a wide variety of environments.

A few examples include the mathematical libraries of the Numerical Algorithms Group (NAG) and the linear algebra library LINPACK for high-performance computing.

If the library is non-proprietary and its source code is available, then we may rely on porting the library ourselves when faced with an environment which does not support it. Again, this may be a large task, perhaps larger than porting the rest of the software, but the benefits may apply to many projects. If the library is proprietary, the only hope is to appeal to the vendor.

5.5.3 Interface Translation

In some cases the target environment will provide a library with the necessary functionality, but not in the expected form. In this case an additional library must be created to "bridge" the difference. This library becomes a part of the porting effort, and must present the required services in the form expected by the program, using the facilities provided by the native library. The effort to create such a bridge library can range from minimal to extensive, depending on the extent of the difference between the two interfaces. Once created it may provide benefits for multiple projects, as though the library itself had been ported.

5.6 Operating System Strategies

Many of the services which a program accesses from its environment are provided or mediated by the operating system (OS). As can be seen from the Static Interface Model, the OS may directly provide services such as process management, memory management, file access, timing services, security services, etc. It is also a key mediator in the user interface, and in interfaces to networks and I/O devices.

Some of these services, such as simple file access, may be defined directly by the programming language. Others may be defined by standard libraries such as the C library. However, a variety of services may be obtainable only by direct request to the OS. This is especially true of many newly important services such as thread management, multimedia, or

Internet access for which higher-level standards are still evolving. The OS interface is thus a key issue for portability in a large number of programs.

Since portability is most commonly considered as a proper expectation of application programs (more than specialized system programs), the operating system interface is referred to as the Application Program Interface, or **API.** It would perhaps be more accurate to speak of the "OSAPI", identifying the entity on both sides of the interface, but this term has not caught on.

Most OSs support a number of programming languages and must make their services available in a uniform language-independent form. This creates the need for two representations of the API: a language-independent form, as presented by the OS, and a representation in terms of the particular programming language used, called a *language binding*. A small library is needed to provide services in the form specified by the language binding and convert them to the form provided by the underlying operating system. In this discussion we will ignore this extra layer and focus our strategies on the language-independent API.

As before, we can consider three main classes of strategies: standardize, port, or translate.

5.6.1 Standard APIs

As recently as the early 1980s there was no such thing as a "standard" API. Each specific OS presented its services in its own way. Even when the services were equivalent, there was no effort to represent them by a common model.

A great deal of variation often existed (and still does) even within versions of the "same" OS. Many subtle differences in UNIX APIs have made portability a problem even from one UNIX to another. This created a strong motivation for the POSIX project. Similar problems across versions of proprietary OSs led vendors to create their own internal standards.

Today there are a variety of established and developing standards for APIs, both formal and defacto. Important examples include the POSIX system interface for "UNIX-like" environments, and the Win-32 API for Microsoft Windows systems.

Unfortunately, there are few standard APIs which span distinctly different types of operating systems, such as UNIX *and* Windows *and* z/OS *and* Palm OS, etc. In some cases standard APIs can be implemented (less naturally and efficiently, of course) by libraries on top of a different type of OS. The POSIX API, in particular, has been implemented for a wide variety of environments which are not actually similar to UNIX.

If the set of target systems anticipated for porting, or a significant subset, is covered by a standard API, then that standard should probably be followed. If not, we must continue with other strategies.

5.6.2 Porting the Operating System

The idea of porting an operating system may seem completely unreasonable. The purpose of the OS is to manage resources, including hardware resources, so its design must be tied closely to the machine architecture. Because of the need for efficiency and compactness, many OSs have been written in assembly language. The OS is designed from the ground up to suit a particular machine; moving it to another just doesn't make sense.

In spite of this, a number of operating systems have been successfully ported, and some have been designed to be portable. A few early research systems in this category include OS/6, MUSS, and THOTH. These systems were designed in ways that allowed hardware access but remained somewhat architecture-independent, often using the generic architecture strategy discussed below. They were programmed in medium-level "system implementation languages" such as BCPL. As a result, they were successfully ported to multiple hardware environments.

The quintessential example of a portable OS today is UNIX. UNIX has been ported to, or reimplemented for, almost every known hardware environment suited for general-purpose computing. UNIX and all of its related programs are written in C, so porting is greatly facilitated by the creation of a C compiler. The various implementations represent many slight variations, but they all share a common core of UNIX concepts.

Porting a compiler is a project that is likely to have high costs but also high benefits. This is true to a much greater degree for OS porting. The effort required may be enormous, but the result is the ability to support a whole new collection of software in the new environment.

Unfortunately, though, most environments can only run one OS at a time for all users. Porting a new OS means removing the old one. This will have a very strong impact on users; we do not recommend that you change the OS on a system that is used by many people unless there is broad agreement that this is a good idea!

5.6.3 Interface Translation

If it is not possible to ensure that the API for which the program is designed will be supported in the target environment, then a translation library may be necessary. This library can range from trivial to highly complex, depending on the differences in the resource models expected by the program and those supported on the target platform. For example, the Windows interface is implemented on UNIX systems, and POSIX libraries are available for environments as diverse as OpenVMS and MVS.

5.7 Architecture Strategies

The first and most fundamental of the three main direct interfaces is the interface to the machine architecture. At its lowest level this is manifest as a set of machine instructions together with other hardware resources such as registers and a memory model.

It is generally expected that the programming language will hide the details of the architecture; this is after all its primary purpose. However, there are often architectural details that are not encapsulated in programming languages, such as the precision of floating point operations, or the organization of special memory models. Some languages include structures biased toward a particular architectural model, such as C with its orientation toward Digital PDP-11 and VAX architectures. Even if the language can hide the architecture completely, providing one or a few common architecture interfaces can greatly simplify compiler design. In the extreme, identical architectures across platforms can eliminate the need for recompilation, allowing for binary portability.

For all of these reasons, we may want to consider strategies that provide greater standardization of the lower-level architectural interface.

As usual we consider the three principal strategies of standardization, porting, and translation. Here we run into a problem. It is clear what is meant by standardizing an architecture, but how do we "port the machine?" Architecture translation may also seem impractical, but there are two different types of strategies that fit this description.

In the end we can identify three distinct types of strategies at the architecture level. However, their relation to the three primary categories is a little more complicated.

5.7.1 Standard Architectures

The straightforward concept of a standard architecture is that a large collection of computers should have the same "machine-level" architecture (i.e., instruction set, registers, data types, memory model, etc.) even though they are produced by various companies. The clearest example of this concept is the de facto standard IBM-PC architecture, which is copied precisely by numerous "clones" made by companies other than IBM. Because the architecture is identical (except perhaps for a few details related only to maintenance) all of the same software can be run. There have been clones of systems as diverse as the IBM S/360, the Intel 8080 processor chip, and the Macintosh.

A few formal architecture standards have also been developed. Japan's TRON project defined a microprocessor architecture which has actually been implemented by over a dozen companies. The Sun SPARC architecture has been approved as a formal standard, although it is not yet implemented outside of Sun.

Today few users care greatly about the architecture of their computers, as long as they run the desired software and achieve good performance. However, companies that sell computers must be able to point to unique advantages of their product, which necessarily means differences. Makers of IBM clones try to meet this need by higher performance, lower cost, or better I/O devices. Other implementors may add extended features such as better memory management, but programs that rely on these features lose the benefits of portability.

Occasionally success can be achieved by standardizing a limited part of the architecture. The IEEE binary floating point standard is now almost universally used in floating point hardware, and has greatly relieved a major portability problem for numerical software.

5.7.2 Generic Architectures

As an alternative to a standard architecture that is to be implemented by computing hardware directly, a common architecture may be defined which is intended to be "easily translated" into the physical architecture of a variety of computers. A common compiler can produce code for the generic architecture, and a machine-dependent translation converts this code into native instructions for each specific system. This may be an attractive approach if the translation step is simple and if the final performance of the software is not greatly reduced.

The generic representation of the program may be viewed as a low-level intermediate form in the translation process. It may be translated to native machine code before execution, or it may be interpreted "on the fly." Microprogrammed architectures may have the option of interpreting the generic machine code by a special microprogram. This option has become less common since the advent of RISC processors, which are usually not microprogrammed.

5.7.3 Binary Translation

In previous discussions we have noted that significant adaptation is generally not practical for a program in "binary" (executable) form. In spite of this, there are times when it becomes essential to convert software already compiled for one architecture into a form that can be used on a very different architecture. Two well-known examples of this approach have arisen as major computer vendors migrated to newer, RISC-class architectures:

- The change in Digital systems from the VAX to the Alpha
- The change in Macintosh systems from the 68000 to the PowerPC

In these situations a great deal of application software, already in executable form for the older environments, must be made to work in the newer one. To meet this need, strategies have evolved for effective binary translation as a transitional strategy. Typically, this approach uses a combination of translation before execution where possible, and run-time emulation otherwise. The success of the approach may rely on strong assumptions, such as the assumption that the program being translated is a well-behaved client of a particular operating system.

6. THE SOFTWARE DEVELOPMENT PROCESS

The previous section has identified a wide range of strategies for increasing portability by controlling the interfaces of a software unit. To put these strategies to work we must see how portability concerns fit into the software development process.

The discussion in this section is focused on incorporating portability in a large-scale software development process. However, most of the recommendations may be applied to small projects as well.

6.1.1 The Software Lifecycle

A number of models of the software lifecycle are used both to understand the lifecycle and to guide the overall development strategy. These are surveyed in many software engineering texts, such as Sommerville (2000). Most widely known is the waterfall model, in which activities progress more or less sequentially through specification, design, implementation, and maintenance. Recently popular alternatives include rapid prototyping and the spiral model, with frequent iterations of the principal activities. Testing (and debugging) and documentation may be viewed as distinct activities, but are usually expected to be ongoing throughout the process.

Each of the principal activities of the lifecycle is associated with some distinct portability issues. However, the sequencing and interleaving of these activities, which distinguishes the models, does not substantially affect these issues. Thus our discussion is applicable across the usual models, but will focus primarily on the individual activities.

6.1.2 Specification

The purpose of a specification is to identify the functionality and other properties expected in the software to be developed. There are many proposed structures for such a specification, ranging from informal to fully formal, mathematical notations. Formal notations in current use express the *functional* requirements of a software product, but are not designed to express non-functional requirements such as reliability, performance, or portability. If such requirements exist they must be expressed by less formal means.

We offer three guidelines for the specification activity to maximize portability, regardless of the form chosen for the specifications:

1. *Avoid portability barriers.* It is important that a specification should not contain statements and phrases that arbitrarily restrict the target environment, unless those restrictions are conscious and intentional. For example, "the program shall prompt the user for an integer value" is better than "the program shall display a 2 by 3 inch text box in the center of the screen".
2. *State constraints explicitly.* It is important to know, for example, if the application must process a database with one million records or must maintain a timing accuracy of 5 milliseconds. This can be used in part to determine which target environments are reasonable.
3. *Identify target classes of environments.* After consideration of the constraints and necessary portability barriers, the specification should identify the broadest possible class of target environments that may make sense as candidates for future porting.
4. *Specify portability goals explicitly.* If the form permits, it is desirable to identify portability as a goal, and the tradeoffs that can be made to achieve it. An example might be "the program shall be developed to be easily ported to any interactive workstation environment, supporting at least thousands of colors, provided that development costs do not increase by more than 10% and performance does not decrease by more than 2% compared to non-portable development."

6.1.3 Design

Design is the heart of software development. Here our understanding of what the software is to do, embodied in the specification, directs the development of a software architecture to meet these requirements. At this stage the developer must select the approach to portability, and choose appropriate strategies.

A large software project may require several levels of design, from the overall system architecture to the algorithms and data structures of individual modules. A systematic design method may be used, such as Structured Design, SADT, JSD, OOD, etc. The various methods have widely differing philosophies, and may lead to very different designs. However, they share a common objective: to identify a collection of elements (procedures, data structures, objects, etc.) to be used in implementing the software, and to define a suitable partitioning of these elements into modules.

The resulting design (perhaps at various levels) has the form of a collection of interacting modules that communicate through interfaces. It is well understood that clear and careful interface design is a crucial element of good software design.

Ideally, a software design is independent of any implementation and so is perfectly portable by definition. In practice, the choice of design will have a major impact on portability.

Portability issues in design are focused on partitioning. We identify four guidelines:

1. *Choose a suitable methodology*. Some design methods may be more favorable to portable design. For example, object-oriented design provides a natural framework for encapsulating external resources.
2. *Identify external interfaces*. A systematic review of the functionality required by the software unit from its environment should lead to a catalog of external interfaces to be controlled.
3. *Identify and design to suitable standards*. Standards should be identified that address interfaces in the catalog, and that are likely to be supported in the target environments. The design should organize these interfaces, as far as possible, in accordance with these standards.
4. *Isolate system-dependent interfaces*. By considering the interfaces with no clear standard or other obvious strategy, and the intended class of target environments for porting, the developer can make reasonable predictions that these interfaces will need system-specific adaptation. These interfaces then become strong candidates for isolation.

6.1.4 Implementation

Implementation is concerned with transforming a design into a working software product. If good design practice has been followed, the design in most cases should not be platform-specific, even if it is not explicitly portable.

In most cases, the implementation targets one specific environment. Occasionally, versions for multiple environments are implemented simultaneously. During portable development, it is also possible to envision an implementation that has no specific target, but is ready for porting to many environments.

Developers who strive for portability most frequently concentrate their attention on the implementation phase, so the issues here are fairly well understood. We offer three guidelines:

1. *Choose a portable language.* If the language or languages to be used were not determined by the design phase, thy must be chosen now. Many factors go into good language choice, including programmer experience, availability of tools, suitability for the application domain, etc. An additional factor should be considered: is the language well standardized, widely implemented, and thus a good choice for portability?
2. *Follow a portability discipline.* It is not enough to select a good language; the language should be used in a disciplined way. Every language has features that are likely to be portability problems. Any compiler features that check for portability should be enabled.
3. *Understand and follow the standards.* The design phase and language choice have identified standards for use. The programmer must study and understand those standards, to be sure that the implementation actually matches what the standard says, and what will be expected on the other side of the interface.

6.1.5 Testing and Debugging

Testing is an essential activity for any type of software development. Many projects also make use of formal verification, to demonstrate a high likelihood of correctness by logical reasoning. However, this does not remove the need for testing.

The goal of testing is to verify correct behavior by observation in a suitable collection of specific test cases. It is not possible to test all cases, but there are well-known techniques to generate sets of test cases that can cover most expected situations and lead to a reasonably high confidence level in the correct operation of the software.

Guidelines for the testing activity are:

1. *Develop a reusable test plan.* A written test plan is always important. For portable software the test plan should be designed to be reused for new ported implementations. Based on design choices and experience to date, the plan should cleanly separate tests of system-dependent modules from tests of the modules that are common to all (or many) implementations. It should be anticipated that after porting, the same tests will be applicable to the common modules (and should produce the same results!).
2. *Document and learn from errors.* A record should be kept, as usual, of all errors found, and the debugging strategies used to correct them. Again these records should be divided between common and system-dependent parts. Errors that have been corrected in common modules should not usually recur after a port.
3. *Don't ignore compiler warnings.* Warnings from a compiler are often taken lightly, since they generally indicate a construct that is questionable but not considered a fatal error. If the program seems to work, the warning may be ignored. It is highly likely, though, that the problem identified by warnings means an increased likelihood of failure when running in a different environment. An unitialized variable may be harmless in one implementation, but cause incorrect behavior in the next.
4. *Test portability itself.* If portability has been identified as an intended attribute in the specifications, it is necessary to test if this goalhas been achieved. This may require the use of portability metrics, discussed briefly below.

6.1.6 Documentation

Many types of documents are associated with a well-managed software process. Portability will have an impact on the documentation activity as well as the other development phases.

Portability guidelines for documentation are:

1. *Develop portable documentation.* The documentation phase offers an opportunity to take advantage of the commonality of portions of a software unit across multiple implementations. Technical documentation can be separated between the common part and the system-specific part. The common part will not change for new implementations. The same is true for user documentation, but with a caution: Users should be

presented with documentation that is specific for their environment, and avoids references to alternate environments.

2. *Document the porting process.* The technical documentation should explain the aspects of the design that were provided for the sake of portability, and provide instructions for those who will actually port the software.

6.1.7 Maintenance

The maintenance phase is the payoff for portable development. Each requirement to produce an implementation in a new environment should be greatly facilitated by the efforts to achieve portability during original development. Other maintenance activities, such as error correction and feature enhancement, will not be impeded by portable design and may possibly be helped.

The only complicating factor is the need to maintain multiple versions. Where possible, clearly, common code should be maintained via a single source, if the versions are under the control of a common maintainer. Issues of multiversion maintenance are widely discussed in the literature and will not be repeated here.

6.1.8 Measuring Success

An important management concern is to demonstrate with facts and figures that making software portable is a good idea, as well as to show that this goal has been achieved. Metrics are required to evaluate portability in this way. One useful metric is the degree of portability, defined as:

DP = 1 – (cost of porting) / (cost of redevelopment)

This metric may be estimated before beginning a porting project by comparing the estimated cost of porting with that of redevelopment, using standard cost estimation techniques. Note that the elements of the cost must be considered in the context of a specific target environment or class of environments. Degree of portability has no meaning without this context.

The main difference between the two cost alternatives is that porting begins with adaptation, while redevelopment begins with redesign and reimplementation.

If DP < 0, porting is more costly and should be avoided. If DP >= 0, then it will range between 0 and 1. In this case porting is the preferred solution, and the vale of DP is proportional to the expected cost of porting.

This metric may be estimated before initial development, to determine if portable development is worthwhile. It may also be estimated after initial development to characterize the portability that has been achieved.

7. OTHER ISSUES

This section briefly overviews two additional areas of concern that need to be considered for a more complete understanding of the software portability problem.

7.1.1 Transportation and Data Portability

We have identified two major phases of porting: adaptation and transportation. So far we have focused on adaptation issues. Transportation addresses problems of physical movement of software and associated artifacts, whether by means of transportable media or a network. This phase also must contend with a number of problems of data representation.

Transportation issues can be identified in several categories:

- *Media Compatibility.* There may be no common media format between the source and target environments. Even if both accept floppy disks, for example, there are different sizes, densities, and formats. The physical drive must accept the media from a different system, and it must further understand the information that is on it.
- *Network compatibility.* A similar problem can occur if two systems are connected by a network. In this case differences in network protocols can present effective communication.
- *Naming and file systems.* The problem is more complex if the data to be transported represents a set of files for which names and relationships must be maintained. There are dozens of file system types, and no standard format for data transport. Each environment understands only a limited number of "foreign" file systems, and may have different rules about file naming.
- *Data compatibility.* Low level data issues may occur due to differences in character codes supported, different strategies for indicating line endings, different rules on byte order for multibyte integers, etc. The problems are more complex if data is to be transported in formats such as floating point or structures or arrays.

7.1.2 Cultural Adaptation

It is not always desirable that ported software behave in exactly the same way as the original. There are many reasons why different behavior may be wanted. Many though not all of these are related to the user interface. We define the process of meeting the varying behavioral needs of each environment as *cultural adaptation*. This may take several forms:

1. *Adapting to user experience.* The type of user interface preferred by a travel agent for booking airline flights is very different than that preferred by a casual user. In the same way, a user experienced with Macintosh systems will not want a new application to behave like a Windows program, *unless* they are even more familiar with the Windows version of that application.
2. *Adapting to human cultures.* This involves many processes identified under the heading of internationalization and localization. It may be necessary to translate all text, including labels, etc., to different languages with very different structure from the original. In addition, issues as diverse as the sort order for databases or the use of color to convey certain meanings must be reconsidered.
3. *Adapting to environment capabilities and constraints.* One example of this is the need to use different computational algorithms for different high-performance parallel computers. Another is the problem of *economic portability* (Murray-Lasso 1990). Many users in schools, non-profit agencies, or less developed countries continue to work with computers much less capable than today's state-of-the-art. To avoid leaving these users behind, software should be adaptable to these older environments, even if its performance and functionality are reduced.

8. CONCLUSION

This paper has surveyed a broad range of issues to be considered in the development of portable software. A range of strategies has been proposed for addressing the problems. We have also examined ways in which portability may be incorporated into the software development process.

We have only been able, however, to explore the surface of the problem. Some of the issues that have not been discussed are:

- Tools for developing portable software
- Analysis of costs and benefits
- The porting process itself
- Portability for special domains, such as parallel and real-time software
- The relationship between portability and reuse

Portability vs. reuse is discussed by Mooney (1995). Most of these issues are examined in a course taught by the author at West Virginia University (Mooney 1992). More information is available on the course website (Mooney 2004).

REFERENCES

Blackham, G. Building software for portability. 1988, *Dr. Dobb's Journal,* **13**(12):18-26.

Brown, P.J.,(ed), 1977, *Software Portability,* Cambridge University Press, Cambridge, U.K.

Dahlstrand, I., 1984, *Software Portability and Standards,* Ellis Horwood, Chichester, U.K.

Deshpande, G., Pearse, T., and Omar, P., 1997, Software portability annotated bibliography, *ACM SIGPLAN Not.*, **32**(2):45-53

Henderson, J., 1988, *Software Portability*, Gower Technical Press., Aldershot, U.K..

ISO/IEC, 1996, *Guide to the POSIX Open System Environment,* TR 14252

Lecarme, O., Gart, M. P., and Gart, M., 1989, *Software Portability With Microcomputer Issues*, Expanded Edition, McGraw-Hill, New York.

Mooney, J. D., 1990, Strategies for supporting application portability, *IEEE Computer,* **23**(11):59-70.

Mooney, J. D. 1992, A course in software portability, in *Proc. 23rd SIGCSE Tech. Symp.*, ACM Press, New York, pp. 163-167.

Mooney, J. D., 1995, Portability and reusability: common issues and differences, *Proc. ACM Comp. Sci. Conf.*, ACM Press, New York, pp. 150-156.

Mooney, J. D.. 2004, CS 533 (Developing Portable Software) course website, West Virginia University, Morgantown, WV, http://csee.wvu.edu/~jdm/classes/cs533

Murray-Lasso, M., 1990, Cultural and social constraints on portability, *ISTE J. of Research on Computing in Education,* **23**(2):253-271.

Poole, P .C. and Waite, W. M., 1975, Portability and adaptability, in *Software Engineering: An Advanced Course*. F. L. Bauer, ed., Springer-Verlag, Berlin.

Ross, M., 1994, Portability by design, *Dr. Dobb's Journal*, **19**(4):41 ff.

Sommerville, I. 2000, *Software Engineering,* 6th ed, Addison-Wesley, Reading, Mass.

Tanenbaum, A. S., Klint, P., and Bohm, W., 1978, Guidelines for software portability, *Software -- Practice and Experience,* **8**(6):681-698.

Wallis, P. J. L., 1982, *Portable Programming,* John Wiley & Sons, New York.

FORMAL REASONING ABOUT SYSTEMS, SOFTWARE AND HARDWARE

Using Functionals, Predicates and Relations

Raymond Boute
INTEC, Ghent University
boute@intec.UGent.be

Abstract Formal reasoning in the sense of "letting the symbols do the work" was Leibniz's dream, but making it possible and convenient for everyday practice irrespective of the availability of automated tools is due to the calculational approach that emerged from Computing Science.

This tutorial provides an initiation in a formal calculational approach that covers not only the discrete world of software and digital hardware, but also the "continuous" world of analog systems and circuits. The formalism (*Funmath*) is free of the defects of traditional notation that hamper formal calculation, yet, by the unified way it captures the conventions from applied mathematics, it is readily adoptable by engineers.

The fundamental part formalizes the equational calculation style found so convenient ever since the first exposure to high school algebra, followed by concepts supporting expression with variables (pointwise) and without (point-free). Calculation rules are derived for (i) proposition calculus, including a few techniques for fast "head" calculation; (ii) sets; (iii) functions, with a basic library of generic functionals that are useful throughout continuous and discrete mathematics; (iv) predicate calculus, making formal calculation with quantifiers as "routine" as with derivatives and integrals in engineering mathematics. Pointwise and point-free forms are covered. Uniform principles for designing convenient operators in diverse areas of discourse are presented. Mathematical induction is formalized in a way that avoids typical errors associated with informal use. Illustrative examples are provided throughout.

The applications part shows how to use the formalism in computing science, including data type definition, systems specification, imperative and functional programming, formal semantics, deriving theories of programming, and also in continuous mathematics relevant to engineering.

Keywords: Analysis, calculational reasoning, data types, functional predicate calculus, Funmath, generic functionals, programming theories, quantifiers

Introduction: motivation and overview

Motivation. Parnas [26] notes that professional engineers can be distinguished from other designers by their ability to use mathematics. In classical (electrical, mechanical) engineering this ability is *de facto* well-integrated. In computing it is still a remote ideal or very fragmented at best; hence the many urgings to integrate formal methods throughout all topics [15, 32]. According to Gopalakrishnan [15], the separate appellation "formal methods" would be redundant if mathematics was practiced in computing as matter-of-factly as in other branches of engineering.

Still, computing needs a more formal mathematical style than classical engineering, as stressed by Lamport [23]. Following Dijkstra [14] and Gries [16], "formal" is taken in the usual mathematical sense of manipulating expressions on the basis of their *form* (syntax) rather than some *interpretation* (semantics). The crucial benefit is the guidance provided by calculation rules, as nicely captured by the maxim *"Ut faciant opus signa"* of the Mathematics of Program Construction conferences [5].

In applied mathematics and engineering, calculation with derivatives and integrals is essentially formal. Readers who enjoyed physics will recall the excitement when calculation pointed the way in case semantic intuition was clueless, showing the value of parallel syntactic intuition. Algebra and analysis tools (Maple, Mathematica etc.) are readily adopted because they stem from formalisms meant for human use (hand calculation), have a unified basis and cover a wide application spectrum.

Comparatively, typical *logical* arguments in theory development are informal, even in computing. Symbolism is often just *syncopation* [29], i.e., using logic symbols as mere shorthands for natural language, such as $\forall$ and $\exists$ abbreviating "for all" and "there exists". This leaves formal logic unexploited as a *reasoning aid* for everyday mathematical practice.

Logic suffers from the historical accident of having had no chance to evolve into a proper calculus for humans [14, 18] before attention shifted to mechanization (even before the computer era). Current logic tools are not readily adopted and need expert users. Arguably this is because they are not based on formalisms suited for human use (which includes "back-of-an-envelope" symbolic calculation). Leading researchers [27] warn that using symbolic tools before mental insight and proficiency in logic is acquired obscures elements that are crucial to understanding.

This tutorial bridges the essential gaps. In particular, it provides a formalism (*Funmath*) by which engineers can calculate with predicates and quantifiers as smoothly as with derivatives and integrals. In addition to direct applicability in everyday mathematical practice whatever the application, it yields superior insight for comparing and using tools.

Overview. Sections 1–3 cover preliminaries and the basis of the formalism: functional predicate calculus and generic functionals. Sections 4–6 show applications in diverse areas of computing and "continuous" mathematics. Due to page limitations, this is more like an extended syllabus, but a full 250-page course text [10] is available from the author.

1. Calculating with expressions and propositions

A *formalism* is a *language* (*notation*) plus formal *calculation rules*. Our formalism needs only four language constructs. Two of these (similar to [17]) are covered here, the other two appear in later sections.

1.1 Expressions, substitution and equality

Syntax conventions. The syntax of *simple expressions* is defined by the following BNF grammar. Underscores designate terminal symbols.

$$\begin{array}{lcl} \mathit{expression} & ::= & \mathit{variable} \mid \mathit{constant}_0 \mid \mathit{application} \\ \mathit{application} & ::= & \underline{(}\mathit{cop}_1\ \mathit{expression}\underline{)} \mid \underline{(}\mathit{expression}\ \mathit{cop}_2\ \mathit{expression}\underline{)} \end{array}$$

Here *variable*, $\mathit{constant}_0$, cop_1 en cop_2 are domain-dependent. Example: with $\mathit{variable} ::= \underline{x} \mid \underline{y} \mid \underline{z}$ and $\mathit{constant}_0 ::= \underline{a} \mid \underline{b} \mid \underline{c}$ and operators defined by $\mathit{cop}_1 ::= \underline{\mathit{succ}} \mid \underline{\mathit{pred}}$ and $\mathit{cop}_2 ::= \underline{+} \mid \underline{\cdot}$, we obtain expressions like 'a' 'x' '$(\mathit{succ}\, y)$' '$(a+y)$' '$((a \cdot (\mathit{succ}\, x)) + y)$'.

When clarity requires, we use quotes ' ' for strings of terminals, and $[\![\ ]\!]$ if metavariables may be present. Lowercase words (e.g., *expression*) designate a nonterminal, the first letter in uppercase (e.g., E) the corresponding syntactic category, i.e., set of symbol strings, and the first letter itself (e.g., e) is a metavariable for a string in that set. Example: let metavariables v, c, ϕ, $\star$ correspond to V, C_0, C_1, C_2, and e, e' to E; then $[\![v]\!]$, $[\![c]\!]$, $[\![(\phi\, e)]\!]$, $[\![(e \star e')]\!]$ represent all forms of simple expressions.

Parentheses can be made optional by the usual conventions. We define *formulas* by $\mathit{formula} ::= \mathit{expression} \underline{=} \mathit{expression}$, as in $x \cdot y = y \cdot x$.

Substitution. Replacing every occurrence of variable v in expression e by expression d is written $e[v := d]$ and formalized recursively by

Sv:	$w[v := d] = (v = w)\,?\,d \mid w$	for variable v in V
S0:	$c[v := d] = c$	for constant c in C_0
S1:	$(\phi\, e)[v := d] = (\phi\, e[v := d])$	for ϕ in C_1 and e in E
S2:	$(e \star e')[v := d] = (e[v := d] \star e'[v := d])$	for $\star$ in C_2; e, e' in E

All equalities here are purely syntactic (not part of formulas). Expressions like $c\,?\,b \mid a$ (as in **Sv**) are understood as "if c then b, else a". Example: for $(a \cdot \mathit{succ}\, x + y)[x := z \cdot a]$ the rules yield '$a \cdot \mathit{succ}\,(z \cdot a) + y$'.

Multiple (parallel) substitution is a straightforward generalization.

Deduction and equational reasoning Later on we shall see formulas other than equality. Generally, an *inference rule* is a little "table"

$$\frac{Prems}{q}$$

where *Prems* is a set of formulas called *premisses* and q a formula called the *conclusion*. Inference rules are used as follows.

A *consequence* of a set *Hyps* of formulas (called *hypotheses*) is either one of the hypotheses or the conclusion of an inference rule whose premisses are consequences of *Hyps*. A *deduction* is a record of these correspondences. We write $Hyps \vdash q$ if q is a consequence of *Hyps*.

Axioms are selected hypotheses (application-dependent). *Theorems* are consequences of axioms, and *proofs* are deductions of theorems.

The main inference rules are *instantiation* and the *rules for equality*.

a. *Instantiation* (strict): $\dfrac{p}{p[v := e]}$

b. *Leibniz's principle* (not strict): $\dfrac{d = d'}{e[v := d'] = e[v := d'']}$

c. *Symmetry* of equality (not strict): $\dfrac{e'' = e'}{e' = e''}$

d. *Transitivity* of equality (not strict): $\dfrac{e = e', e' = e''}{e = e''}$

A *strict* inference rule requires that its premisses are *theorems*.

In the *equational style*, deductions are recorded in the format

$$\begin{array}{lll} e & =\langle\text{justification}\rangle & e' \\ & =\langle\text{justification}\rangle & e'' \quad \text{etc.} \end{array} \tag{1}$$

The inference rules are fitted into this format as follows.

a. *Instantiation* In equational reasoning, premiss p is a theorem of the form $d' = d''$, hence the conclusion $p[v := e]$ is $(d' = d'')[v := e]$ which has the form $e' = e''$. Example: $(a + b) \cdot c \;\; =\langle x \cdot y = y \cdot x\rangle \;\; c \cdot (a + b)$.

b. *Leibniz* Premiss p is of the form $d' = d''$ and the conclusion is $e[v := d'] = e[v := d'']$, which has the form $e' = e''$. Example: with premiss $y = a \cdot x$ we may write $x + y \;\; =\langle y = a \cdot x\rangle \;\; x + a \cdot x$.

c. *Symmetry* Premiss p is of the form $e'' = e'$ and the conclusion is $e' = e''$. However, this simple step is usually taken tacitly.

d. *Transitivity* has two equalities for premisses. It is used implicitly to justify chaining $e = e'$ and $e' = e''$ as in (1) to conclude $e = e''$.

1.2 Pointwise and point-free styles of expression

One can specify functions *pointwise* by referring to points in the domain, as in $square\, x \;=\; x^2$, or *point-free* using functionals, as in $square = multiply \circ duplicate$ (comment needed nor given at this stage).

The respective archetypes of these styles are *lambda terms* and *combinator terms*, briefly discussed next to capture the essence of symbolic manipulation in both styles in an application-independent form.

Syntax of lambda terms. Bound and free occurrences. The syntax for *lambda terms* [2] is defined by the following BNF grammar.

$$\textit{term} \quad ::= \quad \textit{variable} \mid \underline{(}\textit{term term}\underline{)} \mid \underline{(\lambda}\textit{variable}\underline{.}\textit{term}\underline{)}. \tag{2}$$

Examples: x (xy) $(\lambda x.(((y(\lambda x.(\lambda y.((xz)(\lambda z.((xy)z))))))y)z))$

Naming convention Λ is the syntactic category and $L..R$ metavariables for terms; u, v, w metavariables for variables; x, y, z are typical variables, and symbols like **C**, **D**, **I**, **K**, **S** abbreviate often-used terms.

Terminology A term like (MN) is an *application*, $(\lambda v.M)$ is an *abstraction*: $\lambda v.$ is the *abstractor* and M (the *scope* of $\lambda v.$) the *abstrahend*.

Parentheses convention Outer parentheses are optional in (MN) and in $(\lambda v.M)$ if these terms stand alone or as an abstrahend. Hence the scope extends as far as parentheses permit. Application associates to the left, (LMN) standing for $((LM)N)$. Nested abstractions like $\lambda u.\lambda v.M$ are written $\lambda uv.M$. Example: $\lambda x.y(\lambda xy.xz(\lambda z.xyz))yz$ stands for $(\lambda x.(((y(\lambda x.(\lambda y.((xz)(\lambda z.((xy)z))))))y)z))$, saving 18 parentheses.

Bound and free occurrences Every occurrence of v in $\lambda v.M$ is *bound*. Occurrences that are not bound are *free*. Example: numbering variable occurrences in $\lambda x.y(\lambda xy.xz(\lambda z.xyz))yz$ from 0 tot 11, the only free ones are those of y and z at places 1, 5, 10 and 11. We write $\varphi\, M$ for the set of variables with free occurrences in M, for instance $\varphi\,`\lambda z.xyz' = \{\underline{x}, \underline{y}\}$.

Substitution and calculation rules (lambda-conversion). Substituting L for w in M, written $M[w := L]$ or $M[^w_L$, is defined recursively:

$$\begin{array}{rrcll} \textbf{Svar:} & v[^w_L & = & (v = w)\,?\,L \dagger [\![v]\!] & \\ \textbf{Sapp:} & (MN)[^w_L & = & (M[^w_L\, N[^w_L) & \\ \textbf{Sabs:} & (\lambda v.M)[^w_L & = & (\lambda u.M[^v_u[^w_L) & \quad \text{for fresh } u \end{array}$$

The fresh variable u in **Sabs** prevents free variables in L becoming bound by $\lambda v.$, as in the *erroneous* elaboration $(\lambda x.xy)[^y_x = \lambda x.xx$, which should have been $(\lambda x.xy)[^y_x = \lambda z.zx$.

The *calculation rules* firstly are those for equality: *symmetry*, *transitivity* and *Leibniz's principle*, i.e., $\frac{M=N}{L[v:=M]=L[v:=N]}$. Proper axioms are:

$$\begin{array}{ll} \alpha\textbf{-conversion:} & (\lambda v.M) = (\lambda w.M[^v_w) \quad \text{provided } w \notin \varphi\, M \\ \beta\textbf{-conversion:} & (\lambda v.M)N = M[^v_N \end{array}$$

For instance, $(\lambda xy.xy) =_\alpha \lambda xz.xz$ and $(\lambda xy.xy)y =_\beta \lambda z.yz$.

Additional axioms yield variants. Examples are: *rule* ξ: $\frac{M=N}{\lambda v.M=\lambda v.N}$, *rule* η (or η**-conversion**): $(\lambda v.Mv) = M$ (provided $v \notin \varphi M$) and *rule* ζ (*extensionality*): $\frac{Mv=Nv}{M=N}$ provided $v \notin \varphi(M, N)$. As an additional axiom (assuming α and β), rule ζ is equivalent to ξ and η combined.

Henceforth we assume α, β and extensionality, i.e., "everything". Examples of η-conversion are $(\lambda x.yzx) =_\eta yz$ and $\lambda xy.xy =_\eta \lambda x.x$.

Redexes, normal forms and closed terms. A term like $(\lambda v.M)N$ is a *β-redex* and $\lambda v.Mv$ (with $v \notin \varphi M$) is a *η-redex*. A *$\beta\eta$-normal form* (or just "normal form") is a term not containing a β- or η-redex. A term "has a normal form" if it can be reduced to a normal form. According to the *Church-Rosser theorem*, a term has at most one normal form. The term $(\lambda x.xx)(\lambda x.xx)$ even has none.

Closed terms or (lambda-)*combinators* are terms without free variables. Beta-conversion can be encapsulated by properties expressed using metavariables. For instance $\mathbf{S}$, standing for $\lambda xyz.xz(yz)$, has property $\mathbf{S}PQR = PR(QR)$ by β-conversion.

Expressions without variables: combinator terms. Syntax:

$$term \ ::= \ \underline{\boldsymbol{K}} \mid \underline{\boldsymbol{S}} \mid \underline{(}term\ term\underline{)} \tag{3}$$

where $\boldsymbol{K}$ and $\boldsymbol{S}$ are *constants* (using different font to avoid confusion with lambda-combinators). As before, LMN stands for $((LM)N)$.

The calculation rules firstly are those for equality. By lack of variables, Leibniz's principle is $\frac{M=N}{LM=LN}$ and $\frac{M=N}{ML=NL}$. The proper axioms are

$$\boldsymbol{K}LM = L \quad \text{and} \quad \boldsymbol{S}PQR = PR(QR)$$

and *extensionality*: if M en N satisfy $ML = NL$ for any L, then $M = N$.

E.g., $\boldsymbol{SK}MN = \langle \boldsymbol{S}PQR = PR(QR)\rangle\ \boldsymbol{K}N(MN) = \langle \boldsymbol{K}LM = L\rangle\ N$. Hence, defining $\boldsymbol{I}$ as $\boldsymbol{SKK}$ yields an identity operator: $\boldsymbol{I}N = N$.

Converting combinator terms into (extensionally) equal lambda combinators is trivial. For the reverse, define for every w an operator $[w]$:

For variables w:	$[w]w = \boldsymbol{I}$	(Rule I)
For variables v ($\neq w$):	$[w]v = \boldsymbol{K}v$	(Rule K')
For constants c:	$[w]c = \boldsymbol{K}c$	(Rule K")
For applications:	$[w](MN) = \boldsymbol{S}([w]M)([w]N)$	(Rule S)
For abstractions:	$[w](\lambda v.M) = [w]([v]M)$	(Rule *abs*)

The crucial property of this operator is $\lambda w.M = [w]M$.

There are two important shortcuts: provided $w \notin \varphi M$, we can use $[w](Mw) = M$ (Rule η) and $[w]M = \boldsymbol{K}M$ (Rule K), the latter being a more efficient replacement for both (K') and (K"). Example: $\lambda xyz.xzy$ $=\langle \lambda w.M = [w]M\rangle\ [x]([y]([z]xzy))\ =\langle \text{rules}\rangle\ \boldsymbol{S}(\boldsymbol{S}(\boldsymbol{KS})(\boldsymbol{S}(\boldsymbol{KK})\boldsymbol{S}))(\boldsymbol{KK})$.

1.3 Calculational proposition logic

The syntax is that of simple expressions, now with propositional operators. The generic inference rule is *instantiation*. Equality is postponed. We introduce the propositional operators one by one, each with its corresponding axioms and (for $\Rightarrow$ only) its inference rule.

0. Implication ($\underline{\Rightarrow}$). Inference rule: *Modus Ponens:* $\frac{p,\, p \Rightarrow q}{q}$ (MP).

Axioms:	*Weakening:*	$x \Rightarrow y \Rightarrow x$
	Distributivity:	$(x \Rightarrow y \Rightarrow z) \Rightarrow (x \Rightarrow y) \Rightarrow (x \Rightarrow z)$

Convention: $p \Rightarrow q \Rightarrow r$ stands for $p \Rightarrow (q \Rightarrow r)$, not for $(p \Rightarrow q) \Rightarrow r$. Each stage yields a collection of properties (theorems), e.g., at stage **0**:

Idempotency of $\Rightarrow$:	$x \Rightarrow x$
Right isotony of $\Rightarrow$:	$(x \Rightarrow y) \Rightarrow (z \Rightarrow x) \Rightarrow (z \Rightarrow y)$
MP as a formula:	$x \Rightarrow (x \Rightarrow y) \Rightarrow y$
Shunting with $\Rightarrow$:	$(x \Rightarrow y \Rightarrow z) \Rightarrow y \Rightarrow x \Rightarrow z$
Left antitony of $\Rightarrow$:	$(x \Rightarrow y) \Rightarrow (y \Rightarrow z) \Rightarrow (x \Rightarrow z)$
Absorption for $\Rightarrow$:	$(x \Rightarrow x \Rightarrow y) \Rightarrow x \Rightarrow y$

Naming properties is very convenient for invoking them as calculation rules. The properties allow chaining calculation steps by $\Rightarrow$ as in (1).

Very convenient is the *deduction theorem*: if $p \vdash q$ then $\vdash (p \Rightarrow q)$. It allows proving $p \Rightarrow q$ by assuming p as hypothesis (even if p is not a theorem, but then it may not be instantiated) and deducing q.

Henceforth Leibniz's principle will be written $d' = d'' \Rightarrow e[^v_{d'} = e[^v_{d''}$.

1. Negation ($\underline{\neg}$). Axiom: *Contrapositivity:* $(\neg x \Rightarrow \neg y) \Rightarrow y \Rightarrow x$. We write $\neg^n$ for n-fold negation: $\neg^0 p = p$ and $\neg^{n+1} p = \neg(\neg^n p)$.

This stage yields the following main properties.

Contradictory antecedents:	$\neg x \Rightarrow x \Rightarrow y$
Skew idempotency of $\Rightarrow$:	$(\neg x \Rightarrow x) \Rightarrow x$
Double negation:	$\neg^2 x \Rightarrow x$ and $x \Rightarrow \neg^2 x$
Reverse contrapositive:	$(x \Rightarrow y) \Rightarrow \neg y \Rightarrow \neg x$
Strengthened contrapositive:	$(\neg x \Rightarrow \neg y) \Rightarrow (\neg x \Rightarrow y) \Rightarrow x$
Dilemma:	$(x \Rightarrow y) \Rightarrow (\neg x \Rightarrow y) \Rightarrow y$

Note: $\Rightarrow$ and $\neg$ form a complete logic; all further stages are just luxury.

2. Truth constant ($\underline{1}$) with axiom: 1; **falsehood constant ($\underline{0}$)** with axiom: $\neg 0$. Typical properties:

Left identity and *right zero* of $\Rightarrow$:	$(1 \Rightarrow x) \Rightarrow x$ and $(x \Rightarrow 1) \Rightarrow 1$
Corresponding laws for constant 0:	$(0 \Rightarrow x) \Rightarrow \neg x$ and $(0 \Rightarrow x) \Rightarrow 1$

The rules thus far are sufficient for proving the following

$$\text{Lemma}: \begin{array}{lll} \text{(a)} & \neg x \Rightarrow p[^{x}_{0} \Rightarrow p & \text{and} \quad \neg x \Rightarrow p \Rightarrow p[^{x}_{0}; \\ \text{(b)} & x \Rightarrow p[^{x}_{1} \Rightarrow p & \text{and} \quad x \Rightarrow p \Rightarrow p[^{x}_{1} \end{array}$$

The proof uses induction on the structure of p (a variable, a constant, an implication $q \Rightarrow r$, or a negation $\neg q$). An immediate consequence is

$$\text{Theorem, Case Analysis:}\quad p[^{x}_{0}, p[^{x}_{1} \vdash p.$$

This is the "battering ram" for quickly verifying any conjecture or proving any further theorem in propositional calculus, often by inspection.

3. Logical equivalence (equality) ($\equiv$). The axioms are:

Antisymmetry of $\Rightarrow$: $(x \Rightarrow y) \Rightarrow (y \Rightarrow x) \Rightarrow (x \equiv y)$
Weakening of $\equiv$: $(x \equiv y) \Rightarrow x \Rightarrow y$ and $(x \equiv y) \Rightarrow y \Rightarrow x$

One can prove that $\equiv$ is reflexive, symmetric, and transitive. Moreover,

$$\text{Theorem, Leibniz's principle for } \equiv:\quad (x \equiv y) \Rightarrow (p[^{v}_{x} \equiv p[^{v}_{y}).$$

Hence, formally $\equiv$ is the *equality* operator for propositional expressions. To minimize parentheses, we give $\equiv$ lower precedence than *any* other operator, just as $=$ has lower precedence than *arithmetic* operators.

Theorems for $\Rightarrow$ that have a converse can be reformulated as equalities. A few samples are: shunting $(x \Rightarrow y \Rightarrow z) \equiv (y \Rightarrow x \Rightarrow z)$, contrapositive $(x \Rightarrow y) \equiv (\neg y \Rightarrow \neg x)$, double negation $\neg^2 x \equiv x$.

Semidistributivity of $\neg$ *over* $\equiv$, namely, $\neg(x \equiv y) \equiv (\neg x \equiv y)$ and *associativity* of $\equiv$ (not shared with $=$) are other properties.

4. Logical inequality ($\not\equiv$) or, equivalently, **exclusive-OR ($\oplus$).** Axiom: $x \not\equiv y \equiv \neg(x \equiv y)$, i.e., the dual of $\equiv$, or $x \oplus y \equiv \neg(x \equiv y)$.

This operator is also associative, symmetric, and mutually associative and interchangeable with $\equiv$ as long as the parity of the number of appearances is preserved, e.g., $x \equiv z \not\equiv y \equiv y \not\equiv x \equiv z$.

The final stage introduces the usual logical OR and logical AND.

5. Disjunction ($\vee$). Axiom: $x \vee y \equiv \neg x \Rightarrow y$.
Conjunction ($\wedge$). Axiom: $x \wedge y \equiv \neg(x \Rightarrow \neg y)$.
Main properties are the *rules of De Morgan*: $\neg(x \wedge y) \equiv (\neg x \vee \neg y)$ and $\neg(x \vee y) \equiv (\neg x \wedge \neg y)$, and many rules relating the other operators, including not only the familiar rules of binary algebra or switching algebra, but also often-used rules in calculational logic [13, 17], such as

$$\textit{Shunting with } \wedge:\quad x \Rightarrow y \Rightarrow z \equiv x \wedge y \Rightarrow z$$

1.4 Binary algebra and conditional expressions

The preliminaries conclude with a "concrete" (non-axiomatic) proposition calculus, and calculation rules for conditional expressions.

Binary algebra. Binary algebra views propositional operators ($\Rightarrow$, $\neg$, $\wedge$ etc.) as functions on the set $\mathbb{B}$ of booleans. As explained in [6, 8], we define $\mathbb{B} := \{0, 1\}$ rather than using separate "truth values" like T, F. The main advantage is that this makes binary algebra a subalgebra of *minimax algebra*, namely, the algebra of the *least upper bound* ($\curlyvee$) and *greatest lower bound* ($\curlywedge$) operators over $\mathbb{R}' := \mathbb{R} \cup \{-\infty, +\infty\}$, defining

$$a \curlyvee b \leq c \equiv a \leq c \wedge b \leq c \quad \text{and} \quad c \leq a \curlywedge b \equiv c \leq a \wedge c \leq b. \tag{4}$$

A collection of algebraic laws is easily derived by high school algebra. In binary algebra, $\Rightarrow$, $\equiv$, $\vee$, $\wedge$ are restrictions to $\mathbb{B}$ of $\leq$, $=$, $\curlyvee$, $\curlywedge$ [8]. Laws of minimax algebra particularize to laws over $\mathbb{B}$, e.g., from (4):

$$a \vee b \Rightarrow c \equiv (a \Rightarrow c) \wedge (b \Rightarrow c) \quad \text{and} \quad c \Rightarrow a \wedge b \equiv (c \Rightarrow a) \wedge (c \Rightarrow b)$$

A variant sharing most (not all) properties is proposed by Hehner [20].

Conditional expressions. This very convenient formulation of conditional expressions is based on the combining the following 3 elements:
(i) Tuples as functions, defining $(a, b, c)\, 0 = a$ and $(a, b, c)\, 1 = b$ etc.
(ii) Binary algebra embedding propositional calculus in $\mathbb{B}$-arithmetic.
(iii) Generic functionals, in particular *function composition* ($\circ$) defined here by $(f \circ g)\, x = f\,(g\, x)$ and *transposition* (^{U}) with $f^{\mathsf{U}} y\, x = f\, x\, y$. The main properties for the current purpose are the distributivity laws

$$f \circ (x, y, z) = f\, x, f\, y, f\, z \quad \text{and} \quad (f, g, h)^{\mathsf{U}} x = f\, x, g\, x, h\, x.$$

For binary c and any a and b, we now *define* the conditional $c\,?\, b \nmid a$ by

$$c\,?\, b \nmid a \quad = \quad (a, b)\, c. \tag{5}$$

Simple calculation yields two distributivity laws for conditionals:

$$f\,(c\,?\, x \nmid y) = c\,?\, f\, x \nmid f\, y \quad \text{and} \quad (c\,?\, f \nmid g)\, x = c\,?\, f\, x \nmid g\, x. \tag{6}$$

In the particular case where a and b (and, of course, c) are all binary,

$$c\,?\, b \nmid a \quad \equiv \quad (c \Rightarrow b) \wedge (\neg c \Rightarrow a) \tag{7}$$

Finally, since predicates are functions and $z=$ is a predicate,

$$z = (c\,?\, x \nmid y) \quad \equiv \quad (c \Rightarrow z = x) \wedge (\neg c \Rightarrow z = y) \tag{8}$$

These laws are all one ever needs for working with conditionals!

2. Introduction to Generic Functionals

2.1 Sets, functions and predicates

Sets and set equality. We treat sets formally, with basic operator $\in$ and calculation rules directly defined or derived via proposition calculus, such as $e \in X \cap Y \equiv e \in X \wedge e \in Y$ and $e \in X \cup Y \equiv e \in X \vee e \in Y$. The Cartesian product has axiom $(d, e) \in X \times Y \equiv d \in X \wedge e \in Y$.

Leibniz's principle yields for set elements $d = e \Rightarrow (d \in X \equiv e \in X)$. In our (higher-order) formalism, we require it for sets as well:

$$\text{Leibniz (sets):} \quad X = Y \Rightarrow (e \in X \equiv e \in Y). \tag{9}$$

Equivalently, $(p \Rightarrow X = Y) \Rightarrow p \Rightarrow (e \in X \equiv e \in Y)$, for proposition p.

The converse is expressed as follows: for fresh variable (tuple) v,

$$\text{Set extensionality:} \quad \frac{p \Rightarrow (v \in X \equiv v \in Y)}{p \Rightarrow X = Y}. \tag{10}$$

Here p allows embedding extensionality in a calculation chain as

$$\begin{array}{lll} p & \Rightarrow\langle\text{Calculations deriving r.h.s.}\rangle & v \in X \equiv v \in Y \\ & \Rightarrow\langle\text{Set extensionality}\rangle & X = Y \end{array}$$

cautioning that this should *not* be read as $(v \in X \equiv v \in Y) \Rightarrow X = Y$.

The *empty* set $\emptyset$ has axiom $x \notin \emptyset$. A singleton set is written $\iota\, e$, with axiom $d \in \iota\, e \equiv d = e$. We reserve $\{\ \}$ for better purposes discussed later, one consequence being the rule $e \in \{v : X \mid p\} \equiv e \in X \wedge p[^v_e$.

Functions and predicates. A function f is *not* a set of pairs (which is the *graph* of the function), but a mathematical concept in its own right, fully specified by its *domain* $\mathcal{D}\, f$ and its *mapping*. This is axiomatized by a *domain axiom* and a *mapping axiom*, which are of (or can be rewritten in) the form $x \in \mathcal{D}\, f \equiv p$ and $x \in \mathcal{D}\, f \Rightarrow q$ respectively. Here q typically is a proposition with f and x, as illustrated in $n \in \mathbb{N} \Rightarrow \mathit{succ}\, n = n + 1$.

In declarative formalisms, types are sets. Notions from programming are too restrictive for mathematics [9, 25]. For instance, if we assume a function *fac* to be specified such that $\mathcal{D}\, \mathit{fac} = \mathbb{N}$, then instantiating

$$n > 0 \Rightarrow \mathit{fac}\, n = n \cdot \mathit{fac}\,(n - 1),$$

with $n := 0$ would be a type error in programming due to the application $\mathit{fac}\,(-1)$, although mathematically this is perfectly sensible.

Since mapping specifications have the form the form $x \in \mathcal{D}\, f \Rightarrow q$, the consequent q is irrelevant in case $x \notin \mathcal{D}\, f$. Expressions of this form (or $x \in \mathcal{D}\, f \wedge q$ etc.) are called *guarded* [9] and, if properly written, are seen to be "robust" with respect to out-of-domain applications.

A *predicate* P is a $\mathbb{B}$-valued function: $x \in \mathcal{D}\, P \Rightarrow P\, x \in \mathbb{B}$.

Bindings and abstraction. A *binding* has the general form $i : S \wedge p$ (the $\wedge p$ is optional). It denotes no object by itself, but *introduces* or *declares* a (tuple of) identifiers(s) i, at the same time specifying that $i \in S \wedge p$. For instance, $n : \mathbb{Z} \wedge n \geq 0$ is interchangeable with $n : \mathbb{N}$.

As explained elsewhere [10], the common practice of overloading the relational operator $\in$ with the role of binding, as in $\{x \in \mathbb{Z} \mid x < y\}$, can lead to ambiguities, which we avoid by always using : for binding.

Identifiers are *variables* if declared in an *abstraction* (of the form *binding . expression*), constants if declared in a *definition* **def** *binding*.

Our abstraction generalizes lambda abstraction by specifying domains:

$$\begin{array}{ll} \text{Domain axiom:} & d \in \mathcal{D}\,(v : X \wedge p \,.\, e) \equiv d \in X \wedge p[^v_d \\ \text{Mapping axiom:} & d \in \mathcal{D}\,(v : X \wedge p \,.\, e) \Rightarrow (v : X \wedge p \,.\, e)\, d = e[^v_d \end{array} \qquad (11)$$

We assume $v \notin \varphi X$. Abstraction is also the key to synthesizing familiar expressions such as $\{n : \mathbb{Z} \,.\, 2 \cdot n\}$, $\forall x : \mathbb{R} \,.\, x^2 \geq 0$ and $\sum i : 0 \,..\, n \,.\, x^i$.

Function equality. Leibniz's principle in guarded form for domain elements is $d = e \Rightarrow d \in \mathcal{D} f \wedge e \in \mathcal{D} f \Rightarrow f\, d = f\, e$. For functions:

$$\text{Leibniz (functions):} \quad \begin{array}{lll} f = g & \Rightarrow & \mathcal{D} f = \mathcal{D} g \\ & \wedge & (e \in \mathcal{D} f \cap \mathcal{D} g \Rightarrow f\, e = g\, e) \end{array} \qquad (12)$$

or $(p \Rightarrow f = g) \Rightarrow p \Rightarrow \mathcal{D} f = \mathcal{D} g \wedge (e \in \mathcal{D} f \cap \mathcal{D} g \Rightarrow f\, e = g\, e)$. Since this captures all that can be deduced from $f = g$, the converse is:

Function extensionality:

$$\frac{p \Rightarrow \mathcal{D} f = \mathcal{D} g \wedge (v \in \mathcal{D} f \cap \mathcal{D} g \Rightarrow f\, v = g\, v)}{p \Rightarrow f = g}. \qquad (13)$$

We use (13) in chaining calculation steps as shown for sets.

As an example, let $f := v : X \wedge q \,.\, d$ and $g := v : Y \wedge r \,.\, e$ (using v in both preserves generality by α-convertibility). Now (11) and (12) yield

$$\begin{array}{l} (v : X \wedge q \,.\, d) = (v : Y \wedge r \,.\, e) \\ \quad \Rightarrow \quad (v \in X \wedge q \equiv v \in Y \wedge r) \wedge (v \in X \cap Y \wedge q \wedge r \Rightarrow d = e) \end{array}$$

Constant functions. Constant functions are trivial but useful. We specify them using the *constant function definer* ($^\bullet$) defined by

$$X^\bullet e \quad = \quad v : X \,.\, e \quad \text{assuming } v \notin \varphi e. \qquad (14)$$

Equivalently, $x \in \mathcal{D}\,(X^\bullet e) \equiv x \in X$ and $x \in \mathcal{D}\,(X^\bullet e) \Rightarrow (X^\bullet e)\, x = e$.

Two often-used special forms deserve their own symbol. The *empty function* ε is defined by $\varepsilon = \emptyset^\bullet e$ (regardless of e since $\emptyset^\bullet e = \emptyset^\bullet e'$). The *one-point function definer* ($\text{—}\mapsto\text{—}$) is defined by $d \mapsto e = \iota\, d^\bullet e$ for any d and e, which is similar to *maplets* in Z [28].

2.2 Concrete generic functionals, first batch

Design principle. Generic functionals [11] support the point-free style but, unlike the untyped combinator terms from section 1.2, take into account function domains. One of them (filtering) is a generalization of $f = x : \mathcal{D} f \,.\, f\, x$ (η-conversion) to introduce or eliminate variables; the others can reshape expressions, e.g., to make filtering applicable.

The design principle can be explained by analogy with familiar functionals. For instance, function composition ($\circ$), with $(f \circ g)\, x = f\,(g\, x)$, traditionally requires $\mathcal{R}\, g \subseteq \mathcal{D}\, f$, in which case $\mathcal{D}\,(f \circ g) = \mathcal{D}\, g$. Instead of restricting the argument functions, we define the *domain of the result functions* to contain *exactly those points that do not cause out-of-domain applications* in the image definition. This makes the functionals applicable to all functions in continuous and discrete mathematics.

This first batch contains only functionals whose definition does not require quantification. For conciseness, we use abstraction in the definitions; separation into domain and mapping axioms is a useful exercise.

Function and set filtering ($\downarrow$). For any function f, predicate P,

$$f \downarrow P \quad = \quad x : \mathcal{D} f \cap \mathcal{D} P \mathrel{\wedge\!\!\!\!\cdot} P\, x \,.\, f\, x \tag{15}$$

This captures the usual *function restriction* ($\rceil$): for function f, set X,

$$f \rceil X \quad = \quad f \downarrow (X^{\bullet} 1). \tag{16}$$

Similarly, for any set X we define $x \in (X \downarrow P) \equiv x \in X \cap \mathcal{D} P \wedge P\, x$.

We write a_b for $a \downarrow b$. With partial application, this yields a formal basis and calculation rules for convenient shorthands like $f_{<n}$ and $\mathbb{Z}_{>0}$.

Function composition ($\circ$). For any functions f and g,

$$f \circ g \quad = \quad x : \mathcal{D} g \mathrel{\wedge\!\!\!\!\cdot} g\, x \in \mathcal{D} f \,.\, f\,(g\, x). \tag{17}$$

Dispatching (&) [24] and parallel ($\|$). For any functions f and g,

$$f \,\&\, g \quad = \quad x : \mathcal{D} f \cap \mathcal{D} g \,.\, f\, x, g\, x \tag{18}$$

$$f \,\|\, g \quad = \quad (x, y) : \mathcal{D} f \times \mathcal{D} g \,.\, f\, x, g\, y \tag{19}$$

(Duplex) direct extension ($\widehat{\ }$). For any functions $\star$ (infix), f, g,

$$f \mathbin{\widehat{\star}} g \quad = \quad x : \mathcal{D} f \cap \mathcal{D} g \mathrel{\wedge\!\!\!\!\cdot} (f\, x, g\, x) \in \mathcal{D}\,(\star) \,.\, f\, x \star g\, x \tag{20}$$

Sometimes we need *half direct extension*: for any function f, any x,

$$f \mathbin{\overleftarrow{\star}} x = f \mathbin{\widehat{\star}} (\mathcal{D} f^{\bullet} x) \quad \text{and} \quad x \mathbin{\overrightarrow{\star}} f = (\mathcal{D} f^{\bullet} x) \mathbin{\widehat{\star}} f. \tag{21}$$

Simplex direct extension ($\overline{\ }$) is defined by $\overline{f}\, g = f \circ g$.

Function override. For any functions f and g,

$$f \mathbin{\oslash} g \;=\; x : \mathcal{D} f \cup \mathcal{D} g \,.\, x \in \mathcal{D} f \;?\; f\,x \nmid g\,x \tag{22}$$

$$f \mathbin{\otimes} g \;=\; x : \mathcal{D} f \cup \mathcal{D} g \,.\, x \in \mathcal{D} g \;?\; g\,x \nmid f\,x \tag{23}$$

Function merge ($\uplus$). For any functions f and g,

$$f \uplus g \;=\; x : \mathcal{D} f \cup \mathcal{D} g \wedge (x \in \mathcal{D} f \cap \mathcal{D} g \Rightarrow f\,x = g\,x) \,.\, (f \mathbin{\oslash} g)\,x \tag{24}$$

Relational functionals: compatibility (©), subfunction ($\subseteq$).

$$f \circledcirc g \;\equiv\; f \rceil \mathcal{D} g = g \rceil \mathcal{D} f$$

$$f \subseteq g \;\equiv\; f = g \rceil \mathcal{D} f.$$

Remark on algebraic properties. The operators presented entail a rich collection of algebraic laws that can be expressed in point-free form, yet preserve the intricate domain refinements (as can be verified calculationally). Examples are: for composition, $f \circ (g \circ h) = (f \circ g) \circ h$ and $\overline{h \circ g} = \overline{h} \circ \overline{g}$; for extension, $(\widehat{\star}) = \overline{(\star)} \circ (\&)$. Elaboration is beyond the scope of this tutorial, giving priority to later application examples.

Elastic extensions for generic functionals. *Elastic operators* are functionals that, combined with function abstraction, unobtrusively replace the many ad hoc abstractors from common mathematics, such as $\forall x : X$ and $\sum_{i=m}^{n}$ and $\lim_{x \to a}$. If an elastic operator F and (infix) operator $\star$ satisfy $F\,(x, y) = x \star y$, then F is an *elastic extension* of $\star$. Such extensions are not unique, leaving room for judicious design, as illustrated here for some two-argument generic functionals.

Transposition. Noting that $(g \,\&\, h)\,x\,i = (g, h)\,i\,x$ for i in $\mathbb{B}$ suggests taking *transposition* (^{T}) for the elastic extension of &, in view of the argument swap in $f^T y\,x = f\,x\,y$. Making this generic requires deciding on the definition of $\mathcal{D} f^T$ for any function family f. For & we want $\mathcal{D} f^{\mathsf{T}} = \bigcap x : \mathcal{D} f \,.\, \mathcal{D}(f\,x)$ or, in point-free style, $\mathcal{D} f^{\mathsf{T}} = \bigcap (\mathcal{D} \circ f)$. For the most "liberal" design, union is the choice. Elaborating both yields

$$f^{\mathsf{T}} \;=\; y : \bigcap (\mathcal{D} \circ f) \,.\, x : \mathcal{D} f \,.\, f\,x\,y \tag{25}$$

$$f^{\mathsf{U}} \;=\; y : \bigcup (\mathcal{D} \circ f) \,.\, x : \mathcal{D} f \wedge (y \in \mathcal{D}\,(f\,x)) \,.\, f\,x\,y \tag{26}$$

Parallel ($\|$). For any function family F and function f,

$$\| F\,f \;=\; x : \mathcal{D} F \cap \mathcal{D} f \wedge f\,x \in \mathcal{D}\,(F\,x) \,.\, F\,x\,(f\,x) \tag{27}$$

This is a typed variant of the $\boldsymbol{S}$-combinator from section 1.2.

3. Functional Predicate Calculus

3.1 Axioms and basic calculation rules

Axioms. A *predicate* is a $\mathbb{B}$-valued function. We define the *quantifiers* $\forall$ and $\exists$ as predicates over predicates. For any predicate P:

$$\forall P \equiv P = \mathcal{D}\,P^{\bullet}1 \quad \text{and} \quad \exists P \equiv P \neq \mathcal{D}\,P^{\bullet}0 \tag{28}$$

The point-free style is chosen for clarity. The familiar forms $\forall\, x : X\,.\,p$ is obtained by taking for P a predicate $x : X\,.\,p$ where p is a proposition.

Most derived laws are equational. The proofs for the first few laws require separating $\equiv$ into $\Rightarrow$ and $\Leftarrow$, but the need to do so will diminish as laws accumulate, and vanishes by the time we reach applications.

Calculation example. Function equality (12, 13) as one equation.

THEOREM, Function equality: $f = g \equiv \mathcal{D}\,f = \mathcal{D}\,g \wedge \forall\,(f \mathrel{\widehat{=}} g)$ (29)

Proof: We show ($\Rightarrow$), the converse is similar.

$$\begin{array}{lll}
f = g & \Rightarrow\langle\text{Leibniz (12)}\rangle & \mathcal{D}\,f = \mathcal{D}\,g \wedge (x \in \mathcal{D}\,f \cap \mathcal{D}\,g \Rightarrow f\,x = g\,x) \\
 & \equiv\langle p \equiv (p \equiv 1)\rangle & \mathcal{D}\,f = \mathcal{D}\,g \wedge x \in \mathcal{D}\,f \cap \mathcal{D}\,g \Rightarrow (f\,x = g\,x) = 1 \\
 & \equiv\langle\text{Def. (20, 14)}\rangle & \mathcal{D}\,f = \mathcal{D}\,g \wedge \\
 & & x \in \mathcal{D}\,(f \mathrel{\widehat{=}} g) \Rightarrow (f \mathrel{\widehat{=}} g)\,x = (\mathcal{D}\,(f \mathrel{\widehat{=}} g)^{\bullet}1)\,x \\
 & \Rightarrow\langle\text{Extens. (13)}\rangle & \mathcal{D}\,f = \mathcal{D}\,g \wedge (f \mathrel{\widehat{=}} g) = \mathcal{D}\,(f \mathrel{\widehat{=}} g)^{\bullet}1 \\
 & \equiv\langle\text{Defin. } \forall \text{ (28)}\rangle & \mathcal{D}\,f = \mathcal{D}\,g \wedge \forall\,(f \mathrel{\widehat{=}} g)
\end{array}$$

Duality and other simple consequences of the axioms. By "head calculation", $\forall\,(X^{\bullet}1) \equiv 1$ and $\exists\,(X^{\bullet}0) \equiv 0$. Proof: (14), (28). In particular: $\forall\,\varepsilon \equiv 1$ and $\exists\,\varepsilon \equiv 0$ (proof: using $\varepsilon = \emptyset^{\bullet}1 = \emptyset^{\bullet}0$).

Illustrative of the algebraic style is the following theorem.

THEOREM, Duality (generalized De Morgan): $\forall\,(\overline{\neg}\,P) \equiv (\overline{\neg}\,\exists)\,P$ (30)

Proof:

$$\begin{array}{lll}
\forall\,(\overline{\neg}\,P) & \equiv\langle\text{Def. } \forall \text{ (28)}\rangle & \overline{\neg}\,P = \mathcal{D}\,(\overline{\neg}\,P)^{\bullet}1 \\
 & \equiv\langle\text{Lemma A (31)}\rangle & \overline{\neg}\,P = \mathcal{D}\,P^{\bullet}1 \\
 & \equiv\langle\text{Lemma B (31)}\rangle & P = \overline{\neg}\,(\mathcal{D}\,P^{\bullet}1) \\
 & \equiv\langle\text{Lemma C (31), } 1 \in \mathcal{D}\,\neg\rangle & P = \mathcal{D}\,P^{\bullet}(\neg\,1) \\
 & \equiv\langle\neg\,1 = 0, \text{ definit. } \exists \text{ (28)}\rangle & \neg\,(\exists\,P) \\
 & \equiv\langle\text{Defin. } \overline{\ } \text{ and } \exists\,P \in \mathcal{D}\,\neg\rangle & \overline{\neg}\,\exists\,P
\end{array}$$

The lemmata are stated below, leaving the proofs as exercises.

LEMMATA: (A) $\mathcal{D}\,(\overline{\neg}\,P) = \mathcal{D}\,P$ (B) $\overline{\neg}\,P = Q \equiv P = \overline{\neg}\,Q$ (31)
(C) $x \in \mathcal{D}\,g \Rightarrow \overline{g}\,(X^{\bullet}x) = X^{\bullet}(g\,x)$

Given the preceding two representative proofs, further calculation rules will be stated without proof. Here are some initial distributivity rules.

Collecting $\forall/\wedge$:	$\forall P \wedge \forall Q \Rightarrow \forall (P \mathbin{\widehat{\wedge}} Q)$
Splitting $\forall/\wedge$:	$\mathcal{D} P = \mathcal{D} Q \Rightarrow \forall (P \mathbin{\widehat{\wedge}} Q) \Rightarrow \forall P \wedge \forall Q$
Distributivity $\forall/\wedge$:	$\mathcal{D} P = \mathcal{D} Q \Rightarrow (\forall (P \mathbin{\widehat{\wedge}} Q) \equiv \forall P \wedge \forall Q)$
Collecting $\exists/\vee$:	$\mathcal{D} P = \mathcal{D} Q \Rightarrow \exists P \vee \exists Q \Rightarrow \exists (P \mathbin{\widehat{\vee}} Q)$
Splitting $\exists/\vee$:	$\exists (P \mathbin{\widehat{\vee}} Q) \Rightarrow \exists P \vee \exists Q$
Distributivity $\exists/\vee$:	$\mathcal{D} P = \mathcal{D} Q \Rightarrow (\exists (P \mathbin{\widehat{\vee}} Q) \equiv \exists P \vee \exists Q)$

Rules for equal predicates and isotony rules are the following.

Equal predicates under $\forall$:	$\mathcal{D} P = \mathcal{D} Q \;\Rightarrow\; \forall (P \mathbin{\widehat{\equiv}} Q) \Rightarrow (\forall P \equiv \forall Q)$
Equal predicates under $\exists$:	$\mathcal{D} P = \mathcal{D} Q \;\Rightarrow\; \forall (P \mathbin{\widehat{\equiv}} Q) \Rightarrow (\exists P \equiv \exists Q)$
Isotony of $\forall/\Rightarrow$:	$\mathcal{D} Q \subseteq \mathcal{D} P \;\Rightarrow\; \forall (P \mathbin{\widehat{\Rightarrow}} Q) \Rightarrow (\forall P \Rightarrow \forall Q)$
Isotony of $\exists/\Rightarrow$:	$\mathcal{D} P \subseteq \mathcal{D} Q \;\Rightarrow\; \forall (P \mathbin{\widehat{\Rightarrow}} Q) \Rightarrow (\exists P \Rightarrow \exists Q)$

The latter two help chaining proof steps: $\forall (P \mathbin{\widehat{\Rightarrow}} Q)$ justifies $\forall P \Rightarrow \forall Q$ or $\exists P \Rightarrow \exists Q$ if the stated set inclusion for the domains holds.

The following theorem generalizes $\forall (X^\bullet 1) \equiv 1$ and $\exists (X^\bullet 0) \equiv 0$.

THEOREM, Constant Predicates:

$$\forall (X^\bullet p) \equiv X = \emptyset \vee p \quad \text{and} \quad \exists (X^\bullet p) \equiv X \neq \emptyset \wedge p \qquad (32)$$

More distributivity laws. The main laws are the following.

Distributivity $\vee/\forall$:	$\forall (q \mathbin{\vec{\vee}} P) \equiv q \vee \forall P$
L(eft)-distrib. $\Rightarrow/\forall$:	$\forall (q \mathbin{\vec{\Rightarrow}} P) \equiv q \Rightarrow \forall P$
R(ight)-distr. $\Rightarrow/\exists$:	$\forall (P \mathbin{\overleftarrow{\Rightarrow}} q) \equiv \exists P \Rightarrow q$
P(seudo)-dist. $\wedge/\forall$:	$\forall (q \mathbin{\vec{\wedge}} P) \equiv (q \wedge \forall P) \vee \mathcal{D} P = \emptyset$

We present the same laws in pointwise form, assuming v not free in q.

Distributivity $\vee/\forall$:	$\forall (v : S \,.\, q \vee p) \equiv q \vee \forall v : S \,.\, p$
L(eft)-distrib. $\Rightarrow/\forall$:	$\forall (v : S \,.\, q \Rightarrow p) \equiv q \Rightarrow \forall v : S \,.\, p$
R(ight)-distr. $\Rightarrow/\exists$:	$\forall (v : S \,.\, p \Rightarrow q) \equiv \exists (v : S \,.\, p) \Rightarrow q$
P(seudo)-dist. $\wedge/\forall$:	$\forall (v : S \,.\, q \wedge p) \equiv (q \wedge \forall v : S \,.\, p) \vee S = \emptyset$

Here are the corresponding laws for $\exists$ (in point-free form only).

Distributivity $\wedge/\exists$:	$\exists (q \mathbin{\vec{\wedge}} P) \equiv q \wedge \exists P$
P(seudo)-dist. $\vee/\exists$:	$\exists (q \mathbin{\vec{\vee}} P) \equiv (q \vee \exists P) \wedge \mathcal{D} P \neq \emptyset$
L(eft)-P-distrib. $\Rightarrow/\exists$:	$\exists (q \mathbin{\vec{\Rightarrow}} P) \equiv (q \Rightarrow \exists P) \wedge \mathcal{D} P \neq \emptyset$
R(ight)-P-distr. $\Rightarrow/\forall$:	$\exists (P \mathbin{\overleftarrow{\Rightarrow}} q) \equiv (\forall P \Rightarrow q) \wedge \mathcal{D} P \neq \emptyset$

Instantiation and generalization. The following theorem replaces axioms of traditional formal logic. It is proven from (28) using (12, 13).

THEOREM, Instantiation: $\forall P \Rightarrow e \in \mathcal{D}\,P \Rightarrow P\,e$ (33)

Generalization: $p \Rightarrow v \in \mathcal{D}\,P \Rightarrow P\,v \vdash p \Rightarrow \forall P$ (34)

v being a fresh variable. Two typical proof techniques are captured by

METATHEOREM, $\forall$-introduction/removal: assuming fresh v,

$p \Rightarrow \forall P$ is a theorem iff $p \Rightarrow v \in \mathcal{D}\,P \Rightarrow P\,v$ is a theorem. (35)

METATHEOREM, Witness: assuming fresh v,

$\exists P \Rightarrow p$ is a theorem iff $v \in \mathcal{D}\,P \Rightarrow P\,v \Rightarrow p$ is a theorem. (36)

Significance: for $p = 1$, (35) reflects typical implicit use of generalization: to prove $\forall P$, prove $v \in \mathcal{D}\,P \Rightarrow P\,v$, or assume $v \in \mathcal{D}\,P$ and prove $P\,v$.

Also, (36) formalizes a well-known informal proof scheme: to prove $\exists P \Rightarrow p$, "take" a v in $\mathcal{D}\,P$ satisfying $P\,v$ (the "witness") and prove p.

As expected, we allow weaving (34) into a calculation chain in the following way, called *generalization of the consequent*: for fresh v,

$$\begin{array}{lll} p & \Rightarrow\langle\text{Calculation yielding } v \in \mathcal{D}\,P \Rightarrow P\,v\rangle & v \in \mathcal{D}\,P \Rightarrow P\,v \\ & \Rightarrow\langle\text{Generalization of the consequent}\rangle & \forall P. \end{array} \quad (37)$$

This convention (37) is used in the derivation of a few more basic calculation rules; it is rarely (if ever) appropriate beyond.

Trading. An example of using (37) is in the proof of the following.

THEOREM, Trading under $\forall$: $\forall P_Q \equiv \forall (Q \mathbin{\widehat{\Rightarrow}} P)$ (38)

Proof: We prove only $\Rightarrow$, the converse $\Leftarrow$ being similar.

$$\begin{array}{lll} \forall P_Q & \Rightarrow\langle\text{Instantiation (33)}\rangle & x \in \mathcal{D}\,(P_Q) \Rightarrow P_Q\,x \\ & \equiv\langle\text{Definition} \downarrow \text{(15)}\rangle & x \in \mathcal{D}\,P \cap \mathcal{D}\,Q \wedge Q\,x \Rightarrow P\,x \\ & \equiv\langle\text{Shunting } \wedge \text{ to } \Rightarrow\rangle & x \in \mathcal{D}\,P \cap \mathcal{D}\,Q \Rightarrow Q\,x \Rightarrow P\,x \\ & \equiv\langle\text{Axiom } \widehat{\ }, \text{ remark}\rangle & x \in \mathcal{D}\,(Q \mathbin{\widehat{\Rightarrow}} P) \Rightarrow (Q \mathbin{\widehat{\Rightarrow}} P)\,x \\ & \Rightarrow\langle\text{Gen. conseq. (37)}\rangle & \forall (Q \mathbin{\widehat{\Rightarrow}} P) \end{array}$$

From (38) and using duality (30), one can prove the $\exists$-counterpart.

THEOREM, Trading under $\exists$: $\exists P_Q \equiv \exists (Q \mathbin{\widehat{\wedge}} P)$ (39)

3.2 Expanding the toolkit of calculation rules

Building a full toolkit is beyond the scope of this tutorial and fits better in a textbook. Therefore, we just complement the preceding section with some guidelines and observations the reader will find sufficient for expanding the toolkit as needed.

Quantifiers applied to abstraction and tuples. With abstractions we synthesize or recover commonly used notations. For instance, letting $R := x : X . r$ and $P := x : X . p$ in the trading theorem (38) yields

$$\text{Trading (pointwise form):} \quad \begin{array}{lcl} \forall (x : X \wedge r . p) & \equiv & \forall (x : X . r \Rightarrow p) \\ \exists (x : X \wedge r . p) & \equiv & \exists (x : X . r \wedge p) \end{array} \qquad (40)$$

For a tuple p, q of booleans, $\forall (p, q) \equiv p \wedge q$ and $\exists (p, q) \equiv p \vee q$.

A few more selected rules for $\forall$. We express them in both styles.

(i) Algebraic style. Legend: let P and Q be *predicates*, R a family of predicates (i.e., $R\,x$ is a predicate for any x in $\mathcal{D}\,R$), and S a relation. The *currying* operator —^{C} maps a function f with domain $X \times Y$ into a higher-order function f^{C} defined by $f^{\mathsf{C}} = x : X . y : Y . f\,(x, y)$. The range operator $\mathcal{R}$ is defined by $y \in \mathcal{R}\,f \equiv \exists x : \mathcal{D}\,f . f\,x = y$.

Merge rule	$P \copyright Q \Rightarrow \forall (P \cup Q) = \forall P \wedge \forall Q$
Transposition	$\forall (\forall \circ R) = \forall (\forall \circ R^{\mathsf{T}})$
Nesting	$\forall S = \forall (\forall \circ S^{\mathsf{C}})$
Composition rule	$\forall P \equiv \forall (P \circ f)$ provided $\mathcal{D}\,P \subseteq \mathcal{R}\,f$ (proof later)
One-point rule	$\forall P_{=e} \equiv e \in \mathcal{D}\,P \Rightarrow P\,e$

(ii) Using dummies. Legend: let p, q and r be $\mathbb{B}$-valued *expressions*, and assume the usual restrictions on types and free occurrences.

Domain split	$\forall (x : X \cup Y . p) \equiv \forall (x : X . p) \wedge \forall (x : Y . p)$
Dummy swap	$\forall (x : X . \forall y : Y . p) \equiv \forall (y : Y . \forall x : X . p)$
Nesting	$\forall ((x, y) : X \times Y . p) \equiv \forall (x : X . \forall y : Y . p)$
Dummy change	$\forall (y : \mathcal{R}\,f . p) \equiv \forall (x : \mathcal{D}\,f . p[^{y}_{f\,x})$
One-point rule	$\forall (x : X \wedge x = e . p) \equiv e \in X \Rightarrow p[^{x}_{e}$

The one-point rule is found very important in applications. Being an equivalence, it is stronger than instantiation ($\forall P \Rightarrow e \in \mathcal{D}\,P \Rightarrow P\,e$).

A variant: the *half-pint rule*: $\forall (x : \mathcal{D}\,P . P\,x \Rightarrow x = e) \Rightarrow \exists P \Rightarrow P\,e$.

Swapping quantifiers and function comprehension. Dummy swap $\forall (x : X . \forall y : Y . p) \equiv \forall (y : Y . \forall x : X . p)$ and its dual for $\exists$ take care of "homogeneous" swapping. For mixed swapping in one direction,

THEOREM, Swap $\forall$ out: $\exists (y : Y . \forall x : X . p) \Rightarrow \forall (x : X . \exists y : Y . p)$ (41)

The converse does not hold, but the following is a "pseudo-converse". Axiom, *Function comprehension*: for any relation $\text{—}R\text{—} : Y \times X \to \mathbb{B}$,

$$\forall (x : X . \exists y : Y . y\,R\,x) \Rightarrow \exists f : X \to Y . \forall x : X . (f\,x)\,R\,x. \qquad (42)$$

This axiom (whose converse is easy to prove) is crucial for implicit function definitions.

4. Generic Applications

Most of applied mathematics and computing can be presented as applications of generic functionals and functional predicate calculus. This first batch of applications is generic and useful in any domain.

4.1 Applications to functions and functionals

Function range and applications. We define the range operator

$$\text{Function range } \mathcal{R}\text{:} \quad y \in \mathcal{R}\, f \equiv \exists\,(x : \mathcal{D}\, f \,.\, f\, x = e) \qquad (43)$$

In point-free style: $e \in \mathcal{R}\, f \equiv \exists\,(f \overset{\leftharpoondown}{=} e)$. Now we can prove the

$$\textsc{Theorem}, \text{Composition rule} \quad \begin{array}{l} \text{(i) } \forall P \Rightarrow \forall\,(P \circ f) \\ \text{(ii) } \mathcal{D}\, P \subseteq \mathcal{R}\, f \Rightarrow (\forall\,(P \circ f) \equiv \forall P) \end{array} \qquad (44)$$

We prove the common part; items (i) and (ii) follow in 1 more step each.

$$\begin{array}{lll} \forall\,(P \circ f) & \equiv \langle \text{Definition } \circ \rangle & \forall\, x : \mathcal{D}\, f \wedge f\, x \in \mathcal{D}\, P \,.\, P\,(f\, x) \\ & \equiv \langle \text{Trading sub } \forall \rangle & \forall\, x : \mathcal{D}\, f \,.\, f\, x \in \mathcal{D}\, P \Rightarrow P\,(f\, x) \\ & \equiv \langle \text{One-point rule} \rangle & \forall\, x : \mathcal{D}\, f \,.\, \forall\, y : \mathcal{D}\, P \,.\, y = f\, x \Rightarrow P\, y \\ & \equiv \langle \text{Swap under } \forall \rangle & \forall\, y : \mathcal{D}\, P \,.\, \forall\, x : \mathcal{D}\, f \,.\, y = f\, x \Rightarrow P\, y \\ & \equiv \langle \text{R-dstr. } \Rightarrow/\exists \rangle & \forall\, y : \mathcal{D}\, P \,.\, \exists\,(x : \mathcal{D}\, f \,.\, y = f\, x) \Rightarrow P\, y \\ & \equiv \langle \text{Definition } \mathcal{R} \rangle & \forall\, y : \mathcal{D}\, P \,.\, y \in \mathcal{R}\, f \Rightarrow P\, y \end{array}$$

The dual is $\exists\,(P \circ f) \Rightarrow \exists\, P$ and $\mathcal{D}\, P \subseteq \mathcal{R}\, f \Rightarrow \exists\,(P \circ f) \equiv \exists\, P$.

An important application is expressing *set comprehension*. Introducing $\{\text{—}\}$ as an operator *fully interchangeable* with $\mathcal{R}$, expressions like $\{2, 3, 5\}$ and $Even = \{m : \mathbb{Z} \,.\, 2 \cdot m\}$ have a familiar form and meaning.

Indeed, since tuples are functions, $\{e, e', e''\}$ denotes a set by listing its elements. Also, $k \in \{m : \mathbb{Z} \,.\, 2 \cdot m\} \equiv \exists\, m : \mathbb{Z} \,.\, k = 2 \cdot m$ by (43). To cover common forms (without their flaws), abstraction has two variants:

$$\begin{array}{rll} e \mid x : X & \text{stands for} & x : X \,.\, e \\ x : X \mid p & \text{stands for} & x : X \wedge p \,.\, x, \end{array}$$

which synthesizes expressions like $\{2 \cdot m \mid m : \mathbb{Z}\}$ and $\{m : \mathbb{N} \mid m < n\}$.

Now binding is always trouble-free, even in $\{n : \mathbb{Z} \mid n \in Even\} = \{n : Even \mid n \in \mathbb{Z}\}$ and $\{n \in \mathbb{Z} \mid n : Even\} \neq \{n \in Even \mid n : \mathbb{Z}\}$.

All desired calculation rules follow from predicate calculus by the axiom for $\mathcal{R}$. A repetitive pattern is captured by the following property.

$$\textsc{Theorem}, \text{Set comprehension:} \quad e \in \{x : X \mid p\} \equiv e \in X \wedge p[^x_e \qquad (45)$$

$$\text{Proof:} \quad \begin{array}{lll} e \in \{x : X \wedge p \,.\, x\} & \equiv \langle \text{Def. range (43)} \rangle & \exists\, x : X \wedge p \,.\, x = e \\ & \equiv \langle \text{Trading, twice} \rangle & \exists\, x : X \wedge x = e \,.\, p \\ & \equiv \langle \text{One-point rule} \rangle & e \in X \wedge p[^x_e \end{array}$$

A generic function inverse ($-^-$). For any function f,

$$\mathcal{D}\, f^- = \mathsf{Bran}\, f \quad \text{and} \quad y \in \mathcal{D}\, f^- \Rightarrow f\,(f^-\, y) = y. \tag{46}$$

with, for Bdom (*bijectivity domain*) and Bran (*bijectivity range*),

$$\begin{aligned} \mathsf{Bdom}\, f &= \{x : \mathcal{D}\, f \mid \forall\, x' : \mathcal{D}\, f \,.\, f\, x' = f\, x \Rightarrow x' = x\} && (47) \\ \mathsf{Bran}\, f &= \{f\, x \mid x : \mathsf{Bdom}\, f\}. && (48) \end{aligned}$$

Elastic extensions of generic functionals. *Elastic merge* ($\bigcup\!\!\!\cdot$) is defined in 2 parts to avoid clutter. For any function family f,

$$\begin{aligned} y \in \mathcal{D}\,(\textstyle\bigcup\!\!\!\cdot\, f) &\equiv && (49) \\ y \in \textstyle\bigcup(\mathcal{D} \circ f) \wedge \forall\,(x, x') : (\mathcal{D}\, f)^2 \,.\, y \in \mathcal{D}\,(f\, x) \cap \mathcal{D}\,(f\, x') &\Rightarrow f\, x\, y = f\, x'\, y \\ y \in \mathcal{D}\,(\textstyle\bigcup\!\!\!\cdot\, f) &\Rightarrow \forall\, x : \mathcal{D}\, f \,.\, y \in \mathcal{D}\,(f\, x) \Rightarrow \textstyle\bigcup\!\!\!\cdot\, f\, y = f\, x\, y && (50) \end{aligned}$$

$\mathcal{D}\, f$ need not be discrete. Any function g satisfies $g = \bigcup\!\!\!\cdot\, x : \mathcal{D}\, g \,.\, x \mapsto g\, x$ and $g^- = \bigcup\!\!\!\cdot\, x : \mathcal{D}\, g \,.\, g\, x \mapsto x$; especially the latter is remarkable.

Elastic compatibility (©) For any function family f

$$© f \;\equiv\; \forall\,(x, y) : (\mathcal{D}\, f)^2 \,.\, f\, x © f\, y \tag{51}$$

In general, $\cup\!\!\!\cdot$ is not associative, but $© \,(f, g, h) \Rightarrow (f \cup\!\!\!\cdot\, g) \cup\!\!\!\cdot\, h = f \cup\!\!\!\cdot\, (g \cup\!\!\!\cdot\, h)$.

A generic functional refining function types. The most common function typing operator is the *function arrow* ($\rightarrow$) defined by $f \in X \rightarrow Y \;\equiv\; \mathcal{D}\, f = X \wedge \mathcal{R}\, f \subseteq Y$, making $f\, x$ always of type Y. Similarly, $f \in X \not\rightarrow Y \equiv \mathcal{D}\, f \subseteq X \wedge \mathcal{R}\, f \subseteq Y$ defines the *partial arrow*.

More refined is the *tolerance* concept [11]: given a family T of sets, called the *tolerance function*, then a function f *meets* tolerance T iff $\mathcal{D}\, f = \mathcal{D}\, T$ and $x \in \mathcal{D}\, f \cap \mathcal{D}\, T \Rightarrow f\, x \in T\, x$. We define an operator $\times$:

$$f \in \times T \equiv \mathcal{D}\, f = \mathcal{D}\, T \wedge \forall\, x : \mathcal{D}\, f \cap \mathcal{D}\, T \,.\, f\, x \in T\, x \tag{52}$$

Equivalently, $\times T = \{f : \mathcal{D}\, T \rightarrow \bigcup T \mid \forall\,(f \mathbin{\widehat{\in}} T)\}$. The tolerance can be "exact": $f = g \equiv f \in \times\,(\iota \circ g)$ (exercise).

Since $\times\,(A, B) = A \times B$ (exercise), we call $\times$ the *generalized functional Cartesian product*. Another property is $A \rightarrow B = \times\,(A^\bullet B)$.

Clearly, $\times\,(a : A \,.\, B_a) = \{f : A \rightarrow \bigcup\, a : A \,.\, B_a \mid \forall\, a : A \,.\, f\, a \in B_a\}$. This point-wise form is a *dependent type* [19] or *product of sets* [30]. We write $A \ni a \rightarrow B_a$ as a shorthand for $\times\, a : A \,.\, B_a$, especially in chained dependencies: $A \ni a \rightarrow B_a \ni b \rightarrow C_{a,b} = \times\, a : A \,.\, \times\, b : B_a \,.\, C_{a,b}$. This is (intentionally) similar to, but *not* the same as, the function arrow.

Remarkable is the following simple explicit formula for the inverse: $\times^- S = x : \bigcap\,(f : S \,.\, \mathcal{D}\, f) \,.\, \{f\, x \mid f : S\}$ for any S in $\mathcal{D} \times^-$ (exercise).

4.2 Calculating with relations

Concepts. Given set X, we let $\mathsf{pred}_X := X \to \mathbb{B}$ and $\mathsf{rel}_X := X^2 \to \mathbb{B}$. We list some potential characteristics of relations R in rel_X, formalizing each property by a predicate $P : \mathsf{rel}_X \to \mathbb{B}$ and an expression for $P\,R$. Point-free forms as in [1] are left as an exercise.

Characteristic	P	Expression for $P\,R$ (pointwise)
Reflexivity	Refl	$\forall x : X \,.\, x\,R\,x$
Transitivity	Trns	$\forall (x,y,z) : X^3 \,.\, x\,R\,y \Rightarrow y\,R\,z \Rightarrow x\,R\,z$
Symmetry	Symm	$\forall (x,y) : X^2 \,.\, x\,R\,y \Rightarrow y\,R\,x$
Antisymmetry	Ants	$\forall (x,y) : X^2 \,.\, x\,R\,y \Rightarrow y\,R\,x \Rightarrow x = y$
Equivalence	EQ	$\mathsf{Refl}\,R \wedge \mathsf{Trns}\,R \wedge \mathsf{Symm}\,R$
Partial order	PO	$\mathsf{Refl}\,R \wedge \mathsf{Trns}\,R \wedge \mathsf{Ants}\,R$
Well-founded	WF	$\forall S : \mathcal{P}X \,.\, S \neq \emptyset \Rightarrow \exists x : X \,.\, x\; \mathit{ismin}_R\; S$

In the last line, $x\;\mathit{ismin}_{\prec}\;S \equiv x \in S \wedge \forall y : X \,.\, y \prec x \Rightarrow y \notin S$. We often write $\prec$ for R. Here *ismin* had type $\mathsf{rel}_X \to X \times \mathcal{P}X \to \mathbb{B}$, but predicate transformers of type $\mathsf{rel}_X \to \mathsf{pred}_X \to \mathsf{pred}_X$ are more elegant. Hence we use the latter in the following characterizations of extremal elements.

Characteristic	Symbol	Definition
Lower bound	lb	$\mathsf{lb}_{\prec}\,P\,x \equiv \forall y : X \,.\, P\,y \Rightarrow x \prec y$
Least	lst	$\mathsf{lst}_{\prec}\,P\,x \equiv P\,x \wedge \mathsf{lb}\,P\,x$
Minimal	min	$\mathsf{min}_{\prec}\,P\,x \equiv P\,x \wedge \forall y : X \,.\, y \prec x \Rightarrow \neg(P\,y)$
Upper bound	ub	$\mathsf{ub}_{\prec}\,P\,x \equiv \forall y : X \,.\, P\,y \Rightarrow y \prec x$
Greatest	gst	$\mathsf{gst}_{\prec}\,P\,x \equiv P\,x \wedge \mathsf{ub}\,P\,x$
Maximal	max	$\mathsf{max}_{\prec}\,P\,x \equiv P\,x \wedge \forall y : X \,.\, x \prec y \Rightarrow \neg(P\,y)$
Least u.b.	lub	$\mathsf{lub}_{\prec} = \mathsf{lst}_{\prec} \circ \mathsf{ub}_{\prec}$
Greatest l.b.	glb	$\mathsf{glb}_{\prec} = \mathsf{gst}_{\prec} \circ \mathsf{lb}_{\prec}$

Calculational reasoning about extremal elements. In this example, we derive some properties used later. A predicate $P : \mathsf{pred}_X$ is *isotonic* for a relation $\_\!\prec\!\_ : \mathsf{rel}_X$ iff $\forall (x,y) : X^2 \,.\, x \prec y \Rightarrow P\,x \Rightarrow P\,y$.

THEOREM: For any $\_\!\prec\!\_ : \mathsf{rel}_X$ and $P : \mathsf{pred}_X$, (53)

0. If $\prec$ is reflexive, then $\forall (y : X \,.\, x \prec y \Rightarrow P\,y) \Rightarrow P\,x$.
1. If $\prec$ is transitive, then $\mathsf{ub}_{\prec}\,P$ is isotonic w.r.t. $\prec$.
2. If P is isotonic for $\prec$, then $\mathsf{lst}_{\prec}\,P\,x \equiv P\,x \wedge \forall (y : X \,.\, P\,y \equiv x \prec y)$.
3. If $\mathsf{Refl} \prec$ and $\mathsf{Trns} \prec$, then $\mathsf{lub}_{\prec}\,P\,x \equiv \forall (y : X \,.\, \mathsf{ub}\,P\,y \equiv x \prec y)$.
4. If $\prec$ is antisymmetric, then $\mathsf{lst}_{\prec}\,P\,x \wedge \mathsf{lst}_{\prec}\,P\,y \Rightarrow x = y$.

Replacing lb by ub and so on yields complementary theorems.

Proofs. For part 0, instantiate with $y := x$. For part 1, we assume $\prec$ transitive and prove $x \prec y \Rightarrow \mathsf{ub}_\prec P\,x \Rightarrow \mathsf{ub}_\prec P\,y$ in shunted form.

$$
\begin{array}{lll}
\mathsf{ub}_\prec P\,x & \Rightarrow \langle p \Rightarrow q \Rightarrow p\rangle & x \prec y \Rightarrow \mathsf{ub}_\prec P\,x \\
 & \equiv \langle \text{Definition } \mathsf{ub}\rangle & x \prec y \Rightarrow \forall\, z : X \,.\, P\,z \Rightarrow z \prec x \wedge 1 \\
 & \equiv \langle p \Rightarrow e[^v_1] = e[^v_p]\rangle & x \prec y \Rightarrow \forall\, z : X \,.\, P\,z \Rightarrow z \prec x \wedge x \prec y \\
 & \Rightarrow \langle \text{Transitiv. } \prec\rangle & x \prec y \Rightarrow \forall\, z : X \,.\, P\,z \Rightarrow z \prec y \\
 & \equiv \langle \text{Definition } \mathsf{ub}\rangle & x \prec y \Rightarrow \mathsf{ub}_\prec P\,y
\end{array}
$$

For part 2, we assume P isotonic and calculate $\mathsf{lst}_\prec P\,x$

$$
\begin{array}{lll}
\mathsf{lst}_\prec P\,x & \equiv \langle \text{Defin. } \mathsf{lst}, \mathsf{lb}\rangle & P\,x \wedge \forall\, y : X \,.\, P\,y \Rightarrow x \prec y \\
 & \equiv \langle \text{Modus Pon.}\rangle & P\,x \wedge (P\,x \Rightarrow \forall\, y : X \,.\, P\,y \Rightarrow x \prec y) \\
 & \equiv \langle \text{L-dstr. } \Rightarrow/\forall\rangle & P\,x \wedge \forall\, y : X \,.\, P\,x \Rightarrow P\,y \Rightarrow x \prec y \\
 & \equiv \langle \text{Isotony of } P\rangle & P\,x \wedge \forall\, y : X \,.\, (P\,x \Rightarrow P\,y \Rightarrow x \prec y) \\
 & & \qquad \wedge\, (P\,x \Rightarrow x \prec y \Rightarrow P\,y) \\
 & \equiv \langle \text{L-dstr. } \Rightarrow/\wedge\rangle & P\,x \wedge \forall\, y : X \,.\, P\,x \Rightarrow (P\,y \Rightarrow x \prec y) \\
 & & \qquad \wedge\, (x \prec y \Rightarrow P\,y) \\
 & \equiv \langle \text{Mut. implic.}\rangle & P\,x \wedge \forall\, y : X \,.\, P\,x \Rightarrow (P\,y \equiv x \prec y) \\
 & \equiv \langle \text{L-dstr. } \Rightarrow/\forall\rangle & P\,x \wedge (P\,x \Rightarrow \forall\, y : X \,.\, P\,y \equiv x \prec y) \\
 & \equiv \langle \text{Modus Pon.}\rangle & P\,x \wedge \forall\, (y : X \,.\, P\,y \equiv x \prec y)
\end{array}
$$

Part 3 combines 0, 1, 2. Part 4 (uniqueness) is a simple exercise and justifies defining the usual glb (and lub) functionals $\bigsqcap$ (and $\bigsqcup$).

4.3 Induction principles

A relation $\prec\; : X^2 \to \mathbb{B}$ is said to *support induction* iff $\mathsf{SI}\,(\prec)$, where

$$\mathsf{SI}\,(\prec) \quad \equiv \quad \forall\, P : \mathsf{pred}_X \,.\, \forall\, (x : X \,.\, \forall\, (y : X_{\prec x} \,.\, P\,y) \Rightarrow P\,x) \Rightarrow \forall\, P$$

One can show $\mathsf{SI}\,(\prec) \equiv \mathsf{WF}\,(\prec)$; a calculational proof is given in [10].

Examples are the familiar strong and weak induction over $\mathbb{N}$. One of the axioms for natural numbers is: every nonempty subset of $\mathbb{N}$ has a *least* element under $\leq$ or, equivalently, a *minimal* element under $<$. Strong induction over $\mathbb{N}$ is obtained by taking $<$ for $\prec$, yielding

$$\forall\, P : \mathsf{pred}_{\mathbb{N}} \,.\, \forall\, (n : \mathbb{N} \,.\, \forall\, (m : \mathbb{N} \,.\, m < n \Rightarrow P\,m) \Rightarrow P\,n) \Rightarrow \forall\, P \qquad (54)$$

Weak induction over $\mathbb{N}$ can be obtained from (54) or as follows. Define $\prec$ by $m \prec n \equiv m + 1 = n$ and prove that $\mathsf{WF}\,(\prec)$. Hence, from (53),

$$\forall\, P : \mathsf{pred}_{\mathbb{N}} \,.\, P\,0 \wedge \forall\, (n : \mathbb{N} \,.\, P\,n \Rightarrow P\,(n+1)) \Rightarrow \forall\, P. \qquad (55)$$

Another example is structural induction over data structures (see later).

An important preparatory step to avoid errors in proofs by induction is always making the induction predicate P and all quantification explicit, and avoiding vague designations such as "induction over n". This is especially important in case other variables are involved.

5. Applications in Computing

5.1 Calculating with data structures

Unifying principle: data types as function spaces. Tuples, sequences and so on are ubiquitous in computing as well as mathematics, and derive most benefit from being defined as functions. This allows sharing the collection of generic functionals and their calculation rules.

Sequences. This term encompasses tuples, arrays, lists and so on. A *sequence* is function with domain $\square n$ for some $n : \mathbb{N} \cup \iota\,\infty$. We define (i) the *block* operator $\square : \mathbb{N} \cup \iota\,\infty \to \mathcal{P}\,\mathbb{N}$ with $\square n = \{m : \mathbb{N} \mid m < n\}$, as in $\square 2 = \mathbb{B}$, (ii) the *power* of a set by $A \uparrow n = \square n \to A = \times(\square n^{\bullet} A)$, also written A^n, (iii) the *length* operator (#) by $\# x = n \equiv \mathcal{D}\, x = \square n$. This also covers *arrays* in programming.

The set of *lists* over A, written A^*, is defined by $A^* = \bigcup n : \mathbb{N} . A^n$. Infinite lists are covered by $A^\infty = \mathbb{N} \to A$. *Tuples* are similarly defined as functions. *Tuple types* are then types of the form $\times S$ where S is any sequence of nonempty sets. Clearly $\times S \subseteq (\bigcup S)^{\# S} \subseteq (\bigcup S)^*$.

As in [7], we define the list operators *prefixing* (— >— —) and *concatenation* (— ++ —) for any a and any sequences x and y by

$$a \succ\!\!- x = i : \square(\# x + 1) . (i = 0) \mathbin{?} a \mid x\,(i - 1) \tag{56}$$

$$x +\!\!+ y = i : \square(\# x + \# y) . (i < \# x) \mathbin{?} x\, i \mid y\,(i - \# x) \tag{57}$$

The formulas $\varepsilon +\!\!+ y = y$ and $(a \succ\!\!- x) +\!\!+ y = a \succ\!\!- (x +\!\!+ y)$ can be seen as either theorems derived from (57) or a recursive definition replacing (57). The (weak) structural induction principle for finite lists over A is

$$\forall P : \mathsf{pred}_{A^*} . P\,\varepsilon \wedge \forall (x : A^* . P\,x \Rightarrow \forall a : A . P\,(a \succ\!\!- x)) \Rightarrow \forall P \tag{58}$$

The notation x, y, z is complemented by $\tau\, a = 0 \mapsto a$ covering length 1.

Records and other structures. *Records* as in PASCAL [21] are expressed via the funcart product $\times$ as *functions* whose domain is a set of field labels constituting an *enumeration type*. For instance, letting **name** and **age** be elements of an enumeration type,

$$Person := \times\,(\mathbf{name} \mapsto \mathbb{A}^* \mathbin{\dot\cup} \mathbf{age} \mapsto \mathbb{N})$$

defines a function type such that an identifier $person : Person$ satisfies $person\,\mathbf{name} \in \mathbb{A}^*$ and $person\,\mathbf{age} \in \mathbb{N}$. Obviuosly, by defining $\mathsf{record}\, F = \times\,(\dot\bigcup F)$, one can also write $Person := \mathsf{record}\,(\mathbf{name} \mapsto \mathbb{A}^*, \mathbf{age} \mapsto \mathbb{N})$.

Trees are functions whose domains are *branching structures*, i.e., sets of sequences describing the path from the root to a leaf in the obvious way (for any branch labeling). Other structures are covered similarly

Example: relational databases. The record type declaration **def** $CID := \mathsf{record}\,(\mathsf{code} \mapsto Code, \mathsf{name} \mapsto \mathbb{A}^*, \mathsf{inst} \mapsto Staff, \mathsf{prrq} \mapsto Code^*)$ specifies the type of tables of the form

Code	Name	Instructor	Prerequisites
CS100	Basic Mathematics for CS	R. Barns	none
MA115	Introduction to Probability	K. Jason	MA100
CS300	Formal Methods in Engineering	R. Barns	CS100, EE150
...	...	...	

All typical query-operators are subsumed by generic functionals:
The *selection*-operator (σ) is subsumed by $\sigma\,(S, P) = S \downarrow P$.
The *projection*-operator (π) is subsumed by $\pi\,(S, F) = \{r \rceil F \mid r : S\}$.
The *join*-operator ($\bowtie$) is subsumed by $S \bowtie T = S \otimes T$.
Here $\otimes$ is the generic *function type merge* operator, defined as in [11] by $S \otimes T = \{s \cup t \mid (s, t) : S \times T \wedge s \circledcirc t\}$. Its elastic extension (exercise) is the generic variant of Van den Beuken's function type merge [31]. Note that function type merge is associative, although function merge is not.

5.2 Systems specification and implementation

Abstract specification. An abstract specification should be free of implementation decisions. We consider *sorting* as an example.

Let A be a set with total order $\sqsubseteq$. Sorting means that the result is ordered and has the same contents. We formalize this by two functions: $ndesc : A^* \to \mathbb{B}$ ("nondescending") and $\S : A^* \to A \to \mathbb{N}$ ("inventory") such that $\S\, x\, a$ is the number of times a is present in x

$$\begin{aligned} ndesc\, x &\equiv \forall (i, j) : (\mathcal{D}\, x)^2 \,.\, i \leq j \Rightarrow x\, i \sqsubseteq x\, j \\ \S\, x\, a &= \textstyle\sum i : \mathcal{D}\, x \,.\, a = f\, i \end{aligned}$$

Our general definition of $\sum$ has 3 parts: $\sum \varepsilon = 0$ and $\sum\,(a \mapsto c) = c$ and $\sum\,(f \cup g) = \sum f + \sum g$ for any a, any numeric c and any number-valued functions f and g with finite nonintersecting domains. We specify

$$\textbf{spec}\ sort : A^* \to A^*\ \textbf{with}\ ndesc\,(sort\, x) \wedge \S\,(sort\, x) = \S\, x$$

The general form **spec** $v : X \wedge p$ introduces v with axiom $v \in X \wedge p$.

Implementation. A typical (functional) program implementation is

$$\begin{aligned} &\textbf{def}\ qsort : A^* \to A^*\ \textbf{with} \\ &\quad qsort\, \varepsilon = \varepsilon \wedge \\ &\quad qsort\,(a \succ\!\!- x) = qsort\, u \mathbin{+\!\!+} \tau\, a \mathbin{+\!\!+} qsort\, v\ \textbf{where}\ u, v := split\, a\, x \\ &\textbf{def}\ split : A \to A^* \to A^* \times A^*\ \textbf{with} \\ &\quad split\, a\, \varepsilon = \varepsilon, \varepsilon \wedge \\ &\quad split\, a\,(b \succ\!\!- x) = (a \sqsubseteq b)\, ?\, (u, b \succ\!\!- v) \mid (b \succ\!\!- u, v) \\ &\qquad\qquad\qquad\qquad\quad \textbf{where}\ u, v := split\, a\, x \end{aligned}$$

Verification. We must prove $asc\,(qsort\,x)$ and $\S\,(qsort\,x) = \S\,x$.

Here we give an outline only; more details are found in [8]. Based on problem analysis, we introduce functions *le* and *ge*, both of type $A \times A^* \to \mathbb{B}$, with $a\,le\,x \equiv \forall\, i : \mathcal{D}\,x\,.\,a \sqsubseteq x\,i$ and $a\,ge\,x \equiv \forall\, i : \mathcal{D}\,x\,.\,x\,i \sqsubseteq a$.

Properties most relevant here are expressed by two lemmata: for any x and y in A^* and a in A, and letting $u, v := split\,a\,x$, we can show:

	Split lemma	Concatenation lemma
(a)	$\S\,u \mathbin{\widehat{+}} \S\,v = \S\,x$	$\S\,(x \mathbin{+\!\!+} y) = \S\,x \mathbin{\widehat{+}} \S\,y$
(b)	$a\,ge\,u \wedge a\,le\,v$	$asc\,(x \mathbin{+\!\!+} \tau\,a \mathbin{+\!\!+} y) \equiv asc\,x \wedge asc\,y \wedge a\,ge\,x \wedge a\,le\,y$

Note that $\S\,(x \mathbin{+\!\!+} y) = \S\,x \mathbin{\widehat{+}} \S\,y$ together with $\S\,\varepsilon = A^\bullet\,0$ and $\S\,(\tau\,a) = (=a)\,\rceil\,A$ makes § into a *list homomorphism* as defined in [3].

The properties $asc\,\varepsilon \equiv 1$ and $asc\,(a \succ\!\!- x) \equiv a\,le\,x \wedge asc\,x$ and the mixed property $\S\,x = \S\,y \Rightarrow ge\,x = ge\,y \wedge le\,x = le\,y$ are the ingredients for making the proof of $asc\,(qsort\,x)$ and $\S\,(qsort\,x) = \S\,x$ simple exercise.

A hardware-flavored example. Here we consider a data flow example whose implementation style is typical for hardware but also for dataflow languages such as LabVIEW [4]. Let the specification be

$$\textbf{spec}\ f : \mathbb{N} \to A\ \textbf{with}\ f\,n = (n = 0)\,?\,a \nmid g\,(f\,(n-1)), \tag{59}$$

for a given set A, element a in A and function $g : A \to A$. By calculation,

$$\begin{aligned} f\,n &= \langle \text{Def. } f \rangle \quad (n = 0)\,?\,a \nmid g\,(f\,(n-1)) \\ &= \langle \text{Def. } \circ \rangle \quad (n = 0)\,?\,a \nmid (g \circ f)\,(n-1) \\ &= \langle \text{Def. D} \rangle \quad \mathrm{D}_a\,(g \circ f)\,n \\ &= \langle \text{Def. } \overline{\ } \rangle \quad \mathrm{D}_a\,(\overline{g}\,f)\,n \\ &= \langle \text{Def. } \circ \rangle \quad (\mathrm{D}_a \circ \overline{g})\,f\,n, \end{aligned}$$

yielding the *fixpoint equation* $f = (\mathrm{D}_a \circ \overline{g})\,f$ by extensionality. The function $\mathrm{D} : A \to A^* \to A^+$ is defined by $\mathrm{D}_a\,x\,n = (n = 0)\,?\,a \nmid x\,(n-1)$.

Let the variable n be associated with discrete time, then D is the *unit delay* element. The block diagram in Fig. 1 realizes $f = (\mathrm{D}_a \circ \overline{g})\,f$.

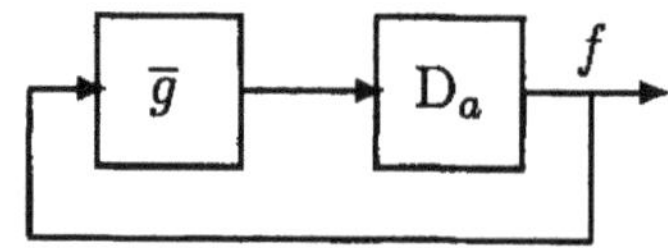

Figure 1. Signal flow realization of specification (59)

5.3 Formal semantics and programming theories

Abstract syntax. This example shows how generic functionals subsume existing ad hoc conventions as in [24]. For *aggregate constructs* and *list productions*, we use the $\times$-operator as embodied in the record and list types. For *choice productions* where a disjoint union is needed, we define a generic operator $|$ such that, for any family F of types,

$$|F = \bigcup x : \mathcal{D}\,F\,.\,\{x \mapsto y \mid y : F\,x\} \tag{60}$$

simply by analogy with $\bigcup F = \bigcup (x : \mathcal{D}\,F\,.\,F\,x) = \bigcup x : \mathcal{D}\,F\,.\,\{y \mid y : F\,x\}$. Typical examples are (with field labels from an enumeration type):

$\textbf{def}\ \mathit{Program} := \mathsf{record}\,(\mathit{declarations} \mapsto \mathit{Dlist}, \mathit{body} \mapsto \mathit{Instruction})$
$\textbf{def}\ \mathit{Dlist} := D^*$
$\textbf{def}\ D := \mathsf{record}\,(v \mapsto \mathit{Variable}, t \mapsto \mathit{Type})$
$\textbf{def}\ \mathit{Instruction} := \mathit{Skip} \cup \mathit{Assignment} \cup \mathit{Compound} \cup \text{etc.}$

For disjoint union one can write $\mathit{Skip} \mid \mathit{Assignment} \mid \mathit{Compound}$ etc.

Instances of programs, declarations, etc. can be defined as

$$\textbf{def}\ p : \mathit{Program}\ \textbf{with}\ p = \mathit{declarations} \mapsto \mathit{dl} \uplus \mathit{body} \mapsto \mathit{instr}$$

Static semantics. Subsuming [24], the *validity* of declaration lists (no double declarations) and the variable inventory are expressed by

$\textbf{def}\ \mathit{Vdcl} : \mathit{Dlist} \to \mathbb{B}\ \textbf{with}\ \mathit{Vdcl}\ \mathit{dl} = \mathsf{inj}\,(\mathit{dl}^{\mathsf{T}} v)$
$\textbf{def}\ \mathit{Var} : \mathit{Dlist} \to \mathcal{P}\ \mathit{Variable}\ \textbf{with}\ \mathit{Var}\ \mathit{dl} = \mathcal{R}\,(\mathit{dl}^{\mathsf{T}} v)$

The *type map* (from variables to types) [24] of a valid declaration list is

$$\begin{aligned}&\textbf{def}\ \mathit{typmap} : \mathit{Dlist}_{\mathit{Vdcl}} \ni \mathit{dl} \to \mathit{Var}\ \mathit{dl} \to \mathit{Tval}\ \textbf{with}\\ &\quad \mathit{typmap}\ \mathit{dl} = \mathit{tval} \circ (\mathit{dl}^{\mathsf{T}}\, t) \circ (\mathit{dl}^{\mathsf{T}}\, v)^{-}\end{aligned}$$

The function merge obviates case expressions. For instance, assume

$\textbf{def}\ \mathit{Expression} := \mathit{Constant} \cup \mathit{Variable} \cup \mathit{Applic}$
$\textbf{def}\ \mathit{Constant} := \mathit{IntCons} \cup \mathit{BoolCons}$
$\textbf{def}\ \mathit{Applic} := \mathsf{record}\,(\mathit{op} \mapsto \mathit{Operator}, \mathit{term} \mapsto \mathit{Expression},$
$\qquad\qquad\qquad\qquad \mathit{term}' \mapsto \mathit{Expression})$

Then, letting $\mathit{Tmap} := \bigcup \mathit{dl} : \mathit{Dlist}_{\mathit{Vdcl}}\,.\,\mathit{typmap}\ \mathit{dl}$ and $\mathit{Tval} := \{\mathit{it}, \mathit{bt}, \mathit{ut}\}$ (integer, boolean, undefined), the type of expressions is defined by

$$\begin{aligned}&\textbf{def}\ \mathit{Texp} : \mathit{Tmap} \to \mathit{Expression} \to \mathit{Tval}\ \textbf{with}\\ &\quad \mathit{Texp}\ \mathit{tm} \ = \ (c : \mathit{IntCons}\,.\,\mathit{it}) \uplus (c : \mathit{BoolCons}\,.\,\mathit{bt})\\ &\qquad\qquad\quad \uplus\ (v : \mathit{Variable}\,.\,\mathit{ut}) \otimes \mathit{tm}\\ &\qquad\qquad\quad \uplus\ (a : \mathit{Applic}\,.\,(a\ \mathit{op} \in \mathit{Arith\_op})\ ?\ \mathit{it} \nmid \mathit{bt})\end{aligned}$$

jointly with an "expression validity" function, left as an exercise [11].

Deriving programming theories. Functional predicate calculus subsumes special program logics by deriving their axioms as theorems.

Let the *state* s be the tuple made of the program variables (and perhaps auxiliary ones), and $\mathbf{S}$ its type. Variable reuse is made unambiguous by priming: $`s$ denotes the state before and s' the state after the execution of a command. We use $s \bullet e$ as shorthand for $s : \mathbf{S} \,.\, e$.

If C is the set of commands, $\mathsf{R} : C \to \mathbf{S}^2 \to \mathbb{B}$ and $\mathsf{T} : C \to \mathbf{S} \to \mathbb{B}$ are defined such that the effect of a command c can be described by two equations: $\mathsf{R}\, c\, (`s, s')$ for state change and $\mathsf{T}\, c\, `s$ for termination. For technical reasons, we sometimes we write $\mathsf{R}\, c\, (s, s')$ and $\mathsf{T}\, c\, s$ by α-conversion.

Here is an example for Dijkstra's *guarded command* language [13].

Syntax Command c	Behavior (program equations or equivalent program) State change $\mathsf{R}\, c\, (s, s')$	Termination $\mathsf{T}\, c\, s$
$v := e$	$s' = s[^v_e$	1
`skip`	$s' = s$	1
`abort`	0	0
$c' ; c''$	$\exists t \bullet \mathsf{R}\, c'\, (s, t) \wedge \mathsf{R}\, c''\, (t, s')$	$\mathsf{T}\, c'\, s \wedge \forall t \bullet \mathsf{R}\, c'\, (s, t) \Rightarrow \mathsf{T}\, c''\, t$
`if` $[\!]\, i : I \,.\, b_i$ `->` c'_i `fi`	$\exists i : I \,.\, b_i \wedge \mathsf{R}\, c'_i\, (s, s')$	$\exists b \wedge \forall i : I \,.\, b_i \Rightarrow \mathsf{T}\, c'_i\, s$
`do` b `->` c' `od`	`if` $\neg b$ `-> skip` $[\!]$ b `->` $(c' ; c)$ `fi`	

Let the state before and after executing c satisfy a (*antecondition*) and p (*postcondition*) respectively, then Hoare-semantics is captured by

$$\{a\}\; c\; \{p\} \equiv \forall `s \bullet \forall s' \bullet a[^s_{`s} \wedge \mathsf{R}\, c\, (`s, s') \Rightarrow p[^s_{s'} \qquad \text{“partial correctness”}$$
$$\mathit{Term}\, c\, a \equiv \forall `s \bullet a[^s_{`s} \Rightarrow \mathsf{T}\, c\, `s \qquad \text{“termination”}$$
$$[a]\; c\; [p] \equiv \{a\}\; c\; \{p\} \wedge \mathit{Term}\, c\, a \qquad \text{“total correctness”}$$

Now everything is reduced to functional predicate calculus. Calculating

$$\begin{aligned}
[a]\; c\; [p] &\equiv \langle \text{Definition} \rangle & \forall `s \bullet \forall s' \bullet a[^s_{`s} \Rightarrow (\mathsf{R}\, c\, (`s, s') \Rightarrow p[^s_{s'}) \wedge \mathsf{T}\, c\, `s \\
&\equiv \langle \text{Ldistr.} \Rightarrow/\forall \rangle & \forall `s \bullet a[^s_{`s} \Rightarrow \forall s' \bullet (\mathsf{R}\, c\, (`s, s') \Rightarrow p[^s_{s'}) \wedge \mathsf{T}\, c\, `s \\
&\equiv \langle \text{Pdistr.} \wedge/\forall \rangle & \forall `s \bullet a[^s_{`s} \Rightarrow \forall (s' \bullet \mathsf{R}\, c\, (`s, s') \Rightarrow p[^s_{s'}) \wedge \mathsf{T}\, c\, `s \\
&\equiv \langle \text{Change var} \rangle & \forall s \bullet a \Rightarrow \forall (s' \bullet \mathsf{R}\, c\, (s, s') \Rightarrow p[^s_{s'}) \wedge \mathsf{T}\, c\, s
\end{aligned}$$

and theorem (53) justifies capturing Dijkstra-style semantics [13] by

$$\mathsf{wla}\, c\, p \equiv \forall s' \bullet \mathsf{R}\, c\, (s, s') \Rightarrow p[^s_{s'} \qquad \text{“weakest liberal antecondition”}$$
$$\mathsf{wa}\, c\, p \equiv \mathsf{wla}\, c\, p \wedge \mathsf{T}\, c\, s \qquad \text{“weakest antecondition”}$$

From this, we obtain by calculation in functional predicate calculus [12]

$$\begin{aligned}
\mathsf{wa}\, [\![v := e]\!]\, p &\equiv p[^v_e \\
\mathsf{wa}\, [\![c' ; c'']\!]\, p &\equiv \mathsf{wa}\, c'\, (\mathsf{wa}\, c''\, p) \\
\mathsf{wa}\, [\![\texttt{if}\ [\!]\, i : I \,.\, b_i \texttt{ -> } c'_i\ \texttt{fi}]\!]\, p &\equiv \exists b \wedge \forall i : I \,.\, b_i \Rightarrow \mathsf{wa}\, c'_i\, p \\
\mathsf{wa}\, [\![\texttt{do}\ b \texttt{ -> } c'\ \texttt{od}]\!]\, p &\equiv \exists n : \mathbb{N} \,.\, w^n\, (\neg b \wedge p) \quad \text{defining } w \text{ by} \\
w\, q &\equiv (\neg b \wedge p) \vee (b \wedge \mathsf{wa}\, c'\, q) \quad .
\end{aligned}$$

6. Applications in continuous mathematics

6.1 An example in mathematical analysis

The topic is *adjacency* [22], here expressed by a predicate transformer since predicates were found to yield more elegant formulations than sets.

$$\textbf{def}\ \mathsf{ad} : \mathsf{pred}_{\mathbb{R}} \to \mathsf{pred}_{\mathbb{R}}\ \textbf{with}\ \mathsf{ad}\, P\, v \equiv \forall \epsilon : \mathbb{R}_{>0} . \exists x : \mathbb{R}_P . |x - v| < \epsilon$$

The concepts "open" and "closed" are similarly defined by predicates.

$$\begin{array}{l} \textbf{def}\ \mathsf{open} : \mathsf{pred}_{\mathbb{R}} \to \mathbb{B}\ \textbf{with} \\ \quad \mathsf{open}\, P \equiv \forall v : \mathbb{R}_P . \exists \epsilon : \mathbb{R}_{>0} . \forall x : \mathbb{R} . |x - v| < \epsilon \Rightarrow P\, x \\ \textbf{def}\ \mathsf{closed} : \mathsf{pred}_{\mathbb{R}} \to \mathbb{B}\ \textbf{with}\ \mathsf{closed}\, P \equiv \mathsf{open}\, (\overline{\neg} P) \end{array}$$

An exercise in [22] is proving the *closure property* $\mathsf{closed}\, P \equiv \mathsf{ad}\, P = P$. The calculation, assuming the (easily proven) lemma $P\, v \Rightarrow \mathsf{ad}\, P\, v$, is

$$\begin{array}{ll} \mathsf{closed}\, P & \\ \equiv\langle\text{Def. closed}\rangle & \mathsf{open}\, (\overline{\neg} P) \\ \equiv\langle\text{Def. open}\rangle & \forall v : \mathbb{R}_{\overline{\neg} P} . \exists \epsilon : \mathbb{R}_{>0} . \forall x : \mathbb{R} . |x - v| < \epsilon \Rightarrow \overline{\neg} P\, x \\ \equiv\langle\text{Trading } \forall\rangle & \forall v : \mathbb{R} . \overline{\neg} P\, v \Rightarrow \exists \epsilon : \mathbb{R}_{>0} . \forall x : \mathbb{R} . |x - v| < \epsilon \Rightarrow \overline{\neg} P\, x \\ \equiv\langle\text{Contrap.}\rangle & \forall v : \mathbb{R} . \neg \exists (\epsilon : \mathbb{R}_{>0} . \forall x : \mathbb{R} . P\, x \Rightarrow \neg (|x - v| < \epsilon)) \Rightarrow P\, v \\ \equiv\langle\text{Duality}\rangle & \forall v : \mathbb{R} . \forall (\epsilon : \mathbb{R}_{>0} . \exists x : \mathbb{R} . P\, x \wedge |x - v| < \epsilon) \Rightarrow P\, v \\ \equiv\langle\text{Def. ad}\rangle & \forall v : \mathbb{R} . \mathsf{ad}\, P\, v \Rightarrow P\, v \\ \equiv\langle\text{Lemma}\rangle & \forall v : \mathbb{R} . \mathsf{ad}\, P\, v \equiv P\, v \quad . \end{array}$$

6.2 An example about transform methods

This example formalizes Laplace transforms via Fourier transforms. In doing so, we pay attention to using functionals in a formally correct way. In particular, we avoid common abuses of notation like $\mathcal{F}\{f(t)\}$ and write $\mathcal{F}\, f\, \omega$ instead. As a consequence, in the definitions

$$\mathcal{F}\, f\, \omega = \int_{-\infty}^{+\infty} e^{-j \cdot \omega \cdot t} \cdot f\, t \cdot \mathrm{d}t \qquad \mathcal{F}'\, g\, t = \frac{1}{2 \cdot \pi} \cdot \int_{-\infty}^{+\infty} e^{j \cdot \omega \cdot t} \cdot g\, \omega \cdot \mathrm{d}\omega$$

the bindings are clear and unambiguous without contextual information. This is important in formal calculation. For what follows, we assume some familiarity with transforms via the usual informal treatments.

Given $\mathrm{l}_{-} : \mathbb{R} \to \mathbb{R} \to \mathbb{R}$ with $\mathrm{l}_\sigma\, t = (t < 0)\, ?\, 0 \nmid e^{-\sigma \cdot t}$ (conditioning functions), we define the Laplace-transform $\mathcal{L}$ of a given function f by:

$$\mathcal{L}\, f\, (\sigma + j \cdot \omega) \quad = \quad \mathcal{F}\, (\mathrm{l}_\sigma \mathbin{\widehat{\cdot}} f)\, \omega \tag{61}$$

for real σ and ω, with suitable conditions on σ to make $\mathrm{l}_\sigma \mathbin{\widehat{\cdot}} f$ Fourier transformable. With $s := \sigma + j \cdot \omega$ we obtain $\mathcal{L}\, f\, s = \int_0^{+\infty} f\, t \cdot e^{-s \cdot t} \cdot \mathrm{d}t$.

The converse $\mathcal{L}'$ is specified by $\mathcal{L}'(\mathcal{L}\,f)\,t = f\,t$ for all $t \geq 0$, weakened where $\mathrm{l}_\sigma \hat{\cdot} f$ is discontinuous: in these points information is lost by $\mathcal{F}$, and $\mathcal{F}' \circ \mathcal{F}$ reproduces a given function exactly in the continuous parts only. For these (nonnegative) t-values,

$$
\begin{aligned}
\mathcal{L}'(\mathcal{L}\,f)\,t &= \langle\text{Specification}\rangle\quad f\,t \\
&= \langle e^{\sigma \cdot t} \cdot \mathrm{l}_\sigma\, t = 1\rangle\quad e^{\sigma \cdot t} \cdot \mathrm{l}_\sigma\, t \cdot f\,t \\
&= \langle\text{Definition } \hat{\ }\rangle\quad e^{\sigma \cdot t} \cdot (\mathrm{l}_\sigma \hat{\cdot} f)\,t \\
&= \langle\text{Weakening}\rangle\quad e^{\sigma \cdot t} \cdot \mathcal{F}'(\mathcal{F}\,(\mathrm{l}_\sigma \hat{\cdot} f))\,t \\
&= \langle\text{Definition } \mathcal{F}'\rangle\quad e^{\sigma \cdot t} \cdot \tfrac{1}{2\cdot\pi} \cdot \int_{-\infty}^{+\infty} \mathcal{F}\,(\mathrm{l}_\sigma \hat{\cdot} f)\,\omega \cdot e^{j\cdot\omega\cdot t} \cdot \mathrm{d}\,\omega \\
&= \langle\text{Definition } \mathcal{L}\rangle\quad e^{\sigma \cdot t} \cdot \tfrac{1}{2\cdot\pi} \cdot \int_{-\infty}^{+\infty} \mathcal{L}\,f\,(\sigma + j \cdot \omega) \cdot e^{j\cdot\omega\cdot t} \cdot \mathrm{d}\,\omega \\
&= \langle\text{Factor } e^{\sigma \cdot t}\rangle\quad \tfrac{1}{2\cdot\pi} \cdot \int_{-\infty}^{+\infty} \mathcal{L}\,f\,(\sigma + j \cdot \omega) \cdot e^{(\sigma + j\cdot\omega)\cdot t} \cdot \mathrm{d}\,\omega \\
&= \langle s := \sigma + j\cdot\omega\rangle\quad \tfrac{1}{2\cdot\pi\cdot j} \cdot \int_{\sigma - j\cdot\infty}^{\sigma + j\cdot\infty} \mathcal{L}\,f\,s \cdot e^{s\cdot t} \cdot \mathrm{d}\,s
\end{aligned}
$$

For $t < 0$, of course $\mathcal{L}'(\mathcal{L}\,f)\,t = 0$. The calculation shows how to derive the inverse transform using functionals in a formally correct way.

7. Some final notes on the Funmath formalism

The formalism used in this tutorial is called *Funmath*, a contraction of *Fun*ctional *math*ematics. It is not “yet another computer language”, but an approach for designing formalisms by characterizing mathematical objects as functions whenever this is possible and useful. The latter is the case quite more often than common conventions suggest.

As we have seen, the language needs four constructs only:

0 *Identifier*: a constant or a variable, declared by a binding.

1 *Application*: a function with argument(s), as in $f\,x$ and $x \star y$.

2 *Tupling*, of the form e, e', e'', was briefly introduced in section 1.4.

3 *Abstraction*, of the form $v : X \wedge p\,.\,e$, was introduced in section 2.1.

The calculation rules and their application were the main topic of this tutorial. Only function application requires a few additional notes.

Identifiers denoting functions are called *operators* The standard affix convention is *prefix*, as in $f\,x$. Other affix conventions can be specified by dashes in the binding introducing the operator, e.g., $-\!\star\!-$ for infix. Parentheses restore the standard prefix convention, e.g., $(\star)(x, y) = x \star y$.

Partial application is the following convention for omitting arguments. Let $-\!\star\!- : X \times Y \to Z$. For any $x : X$ and $y : Y$ we have $(x\,\star) \in Y \to Z$ with $(x\,\star)\,y = x \star y$ and $(\star\,y) \in X \to Z$ with $(\star\,y)\,x = x \star y$.

Argument/operator alternations of the form $x{\star}y{\star}z$ are called *variadic application* and (in Funmath) are *always* defined via an elastic extension: $x \star y \star z = F\,(x, y, z)$. An example is $x \wedge y \wedge z = \forall\,(x, y, z)$. This is not restricted to associative or commutative operators. For instance, letting con and inj be the *constant* and *injective* predicates over functions, we define $x = y = z \equiv \mathsf{con}\,(x, y, z)$ and $x \neq y \neq z \equiv \mathsf{inj}\,(x, y, z)$. The latter gives $x \neq y \neq z$ the most useful meaning (x, y, z distinct).

From the material in this tutorial, it is clear the language and the calculation rules jointly constitute a very broad-spectrum formalism.

References

[1] Chritiene Aarts, Roland Backhouse, Paul Hoogendijk, Ed Voermans and Jaap van der Woude, *A relational theory of data types.* Lecture notes, Eindhoven University (December 1992)

[2] Henk P. Barendregt, *The Lambda Calculus — Its Syntax and Semantics*, North-Holland (1984)

[3] Richard Bird, *Introduction to Functional Programming using Haskell.* Prentice Hall International Series in Computer Science, London (1998)

[4] Robert H. Bishop, *LabVIEW Student Edition*, Prentice Hall, N.J. (2001)

[5] Eerke Boiten and Bernhard Möller, *Sixth International Conference on Mathematics of Program Construction* (Conference announcement), Dagstuhl (2002). `http://www.cs.kent.ac.uk/events/conf/2002/mpc2002`

[6] Raymond T. Boute, "A heretical view on type embedding", *ACM Sigplan Notices 25*, pp. 22–28 (Jan. 1990)

[7] Raymond T. Boute, "Declarative Languages — still a long way to go", in: Dominique Borrione and Ronald Waxman, eds., *Computer Hardware Description Languages and their Applications*, pp. 185–212, North-Holland (1991)

[8] Raymond T. Boute, *Funmath illustrated: A Declarative Formalism and Application Examples.* Declarative Systems Series No. 1, Computing Science Institute, University of Nijmegen (July 1993)

[9] Raymond T. Boute, "Supertotal Function Definition in Mathematics and Software Engineering", *IEEE Transactions on Software Engineering, Vol. 26*, No. 7, pp. 662–672 (July 2000)

[10] Raymond Boute, *Functional Mathematics: a Unifying Declarative and Calculational Approach to Systems, Circuits and Programs — Part I: Basic Mathematics.* Course text, Ghent University (2002)

[11] Raymond T. Boute, "Concrete Generic Functionals: Principles, Design and Applications", in: Jeremy Gibbons and Johan Jeuring, eds., *Generic Programming*, pp. 89–119, Kluwer (2003)

[12] Raymond T. Boute, "Calculational semantics: deriving programming theories from equations by functional predicate calculus", Technical note B2004/02, INTEC, Universiteit Gent (2004) (submitted for publication to *ACM TOPLAS*)

[13] Edsger W. Dijkstra and Carel S. Scholten, *Predicate Calculus and Program Semantics.* Springer-Verlag, Berlin (1990)

[14] Edsger W. Dijkstra, *Under the spell of Leibniz's dream.* EWD1298 (April 2000). `http://www.cs.utexas.edu/users/EWD/ewd12xx/EWD1298.pdf`

[15] Ganesh Gopalakrishnan, *Computation Engineering: Formal Specification and Verification Methods* (Aug. 2003). `http://www.cs.utah.edu/classes/cs6110/lectures/CH1/ch1.pdf`

[16] David Gries, "Improving the curriculum through the teaching of calculation and discrimination", *Communications of the ACM 34*, 3, pp. 45–55 (March 1991)

[17] David Gries and Fred B. Schneider, *A Logical Approach to Discrete Math*, Springer-Verlag, Berlin (1993)

[18] David Gries, "The need for education in useful formal logic", *IEEE Computer 29*, 4, pp. 29–30 (April 1996)

[19] Keith Hanna, Neil Daeche and Gareth Howells, "Implementation of the Veritas design logic", in: Victoria Stavridou and Tom F. Melham and Raymond T. Boute, eds., *Theorem Provers in Circuit Design*, pp. 77–84. North Holland (1992)

[20] Eric C. R. Hehner, *From Boolean Algebra to Unified Algebra.* Internal Report, University of Toronto (June 1997, revised 2003)

[21] Kathleen Jensen and Niklaus Wirth, *PASCAL User Manual and Report.* Springer-Verlag, Berlin (1978)

[22] Serge Lang, *Undergraduate Analysis.* Springer-Verlag, Berlin (1983)

[23] Leslie Lamport, *Specifying Systems: The TLA+ Language and Tools for Hardware and Software Engineers.* Pearson Education Inc. (2002)

[24] Bertrand Meyer, *Introduction to the Theory of Programming Languages.* Prentice Hall, New York (1991)

[25] David L. Parnas, "Education for Computing Professionals", *IEEE Computer 23*, 1, pp. 17–20 (January 1990)

[26] David L. Parnas, "Predicate Logic for Software Engineering", *IEEE Trans. SWE 19*, 9, pp. 856–862 (Sept. 1993)

[27] Raymond Ravaglia, Theodore Alper, Marianna Rozenfeld, Patrick Suppes, "Successful pedagogical applications of symbolic computation", in: N. Kajler, *Computer-Human Interaction in Symbolic Computation.* Springer, 1999. `http://www-epgy.stanford.edu/research/chapter4.pdf`

[28] J. Mike Spivey, *The Z notation: A Reference Manual.* Prentice-Hall (1989).

[29] Paul Taylor, *Practical Foundations of Mathematics* (second printing), No. 59 in *Cambridge Studies in Advanced Mathematics*, Cambridge University Press (2000); quotation from comment on chapter 1 in `http://www.dcs.qmul.ac.uk/~pt/Practical_Foundations/html/s10.html`

[30] Robert D. Tennent, *Semantics of Programming Languages.* Prentice-Hall (1991).

[31] Frank van den Beuken, *A Functional Approach to Syntax and Typing*, PhD thesis. School of Mathematics and Informatics, University of Nijmegen (1997)

[32] Jeannette M. Wing, "Weaving Formal Methods into the Undergraduate Curriculum", *Proceedings of the 8th International Conference on Algebraic Methodology and Software Technology (AMAST)* pp. 2–7 (May 2000) `http://www-2.cs.cmu.edu/afs/cs.cmu.edu/project/calder/www/amast00.html`

THE PROBLEMATIC OF DISTRIBUTED SYSTEMS SUPERVISION - AN EXAMPLE : GENESYS

Jean-Eric Bohdanowicz[1], Stefan Wesner[2], Laszlo Kovacs[3], Hendrik Heimer[4], Andrey Sadovykh[5]
[1]EADS SPACE Transportation, [2]HLRS - Stuttgart University, [3]MTA SZTAKI, [4]NAVUS GmbH, [5]LIP6

Abstract: This chapter presents the problematic of the distributed systems supervision through a comprehensive state-of-the-art. Issues are illustrated with a case study about an innovative and generic supervision tool, GeneSyS.

Key words: Supervision, distributed management, state-of-the-art, GeneSyS, intelligent agent, Web-Services.

1. INTRODUCTION

«Today, the performance of information systems directly governs company competitiveness », such is the report that can be pulled from the evolution of the information technologies.

The supervision of the computer infrastructure becomes therefore an element of vital importance for the whole set of companies. In a context where «business» is tangled closely with the information system to give birth to «e-business», it has been necessary to erase the border between technology and business in order to provide some indicators valuable for the company managers.

As a result, near the end of 1990's, the concept of «frameworks» has been considered like the solution for the supervision of distributed systems and applications.

These frameworks can be compared with ERP's although their respective domains of application are different : their ambition is to manage the whole information system through an integrated unique offer.

Since several months, many study groups like Gartner Group or Meta Groups grant to make a mitigated balance on the usage of these frameworks. The complexity of implementation of these platforms seems to have made indeed fail close to 3 projects on 4. Besides, the very elevated costs of licenses and deployment have limited such a solution perimeter to big companies.

Historically, the principles of network supervision are older than those governing the frameworks and mainly based upon the SNMP protocol (and its extensions). Numerous network monitoring offers are today available on the market. That's why the editors leaders of the sector, conscious of the competitive hazard that the frameworks represent, made their offer to evolve toward system and applications monitoring. However, network supervision platforms do not constitute the ideal basis for systems and application supervision.

Therefore, most users are today facing a spiny problem : there is no available pragmatic approach for the global network, systems and applications supervision and, with the international dimension of today's projects, this supervision of distributed systems is becoming necessary and primordial and it requires a wide panel of services :

- **Application management** including deployment, set-up, start, stop, hold/resume and configuration management (for instance, for redundancy management purpose),
- **Time synchronisation**,
- **Network management** including parameterisation and performances (e.g. dynamic control of bandwidth allocation) **and monitoring**,
- **Security**,
- **Archiving**.

These services requirements lead to have a set of independent software components designed in a distributed way using the following technologies :

- the *applications*, distributed on the remote sites,
- the *groupware*, allowing the collaborative working,
- the *middleware*, managing the distribution (like CORBA, HLA…),
- the *synchronisation*, giving the same time reference to all the sites such as NTP,

- the *security*, protecting the data transmission and access control to the resources,
- the *network management*, using mainly SNMP,
- the *network layer*, interconnecting the remote sites and the various equipment within a given site,
- the *hardware platforms*, implementing the distributed system services.

What is needed is a convergence of the different supervision offers. This has been observed toward a "single vision" consisting in an enterprise type approach. This new tendency is related to the will of, on one hand, the "systems supervision" solutions editors to open their products to the network and, on the other hand, the "network supervision" developers to integrate in their solutions a system monitoring.

But today, none of these available solutions was specifically designed to fulfil its principal task: the global supervision with an "enterprise" point of view. Historically, these solutions are mainly proprietary, most of the time made of a pool of offers acquired by the mean of external growth and aimed at covering a large functional scale.

Today, the supervision of distributed systems is mainly done on a case by case basis and also mainly at independent technical services levels. The distributed applications used on these systems are supervised in a very limited way. Furthermore, the user-interface is often questionable as it requires expert people and suffers from a lack of automation and user friendliness.

The main purpose of this chapter is to present :

- in a first part, a state-of-the-art of the existing technologies, features, standards, protocols, tools involved in the distributed systems supervision world,
- in a second part, a new, innovative, open and generic approach which is detailed through the description of the GeneSyS project.

2. STATE OF THE ART

The state of the art section intends to give an overview of some of the main standards, protocols and tools used in the distributed systems supervision field. This section is also providing a list of current supervision frameworks and related research projects.

2.1 Standards in Distributed Management

This paragraph describes two of the most known standards: SNMP and JMX. In addition, DMTF general use standards are listed at the end of this section.

2.1.1 SMTP

The network management technologies have been developed during the whole history of networks. The most known of them are High-level Entity Management System (HEMS), Simple Gateway Monitoring Protocol (SGMP) and Common Management Information Protocol (CMIP). These technologies highly contributed to the Simple Network Management Protocol (SNMP).

SNMP is the most widely used protocol for the management of IP based networks. Its concept also allows management of end systems and applications using specific Agents and Management Information Bases (MIB). Although SNMP version 3, covering security issues, was already released, the version 1, due to its robustness, is still widely used.

SNMP is an application level protocol on top of UDP. SNMP managed network consists of three major components (Figure 1): managed devices, agents and Network Management Systems (NMS). The managed devices can be hosts, network interfaces, routers, bridges, hubs and etc. The agents are the program components running in the managed devices. Agents collect an information about managed devices and make it available for NMS by the mean of SNMP. The NMS executes the management applications to monitor and control the managed devices.

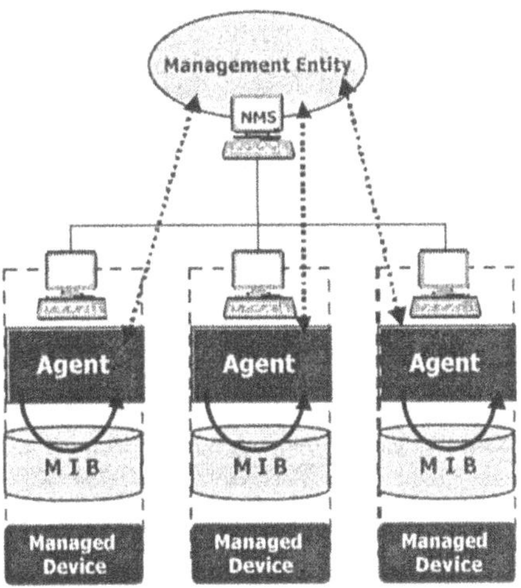

Figure 1. SNMP Managed Network

The management capability of the devices can be quite poor due to, for example, slow CPU or memory limitations. That is why the agent should minimise its impact on the managed device. Moreover, all calculation and monitoring data processing is centralised in Network Management System which, in addition, implements graphical user interface (GUI).

Communication between Agents and NMS is assured by the Network Management Framework protocol. This protocol supports the Query/Response mechanism when Agents send parameters values upon request of the NMS, as well as the Subscribe mechanism, which deals with asynchronous messages sent by Agent to NMS when a particular event happens.

The Managed Devices are monitored and controlled using four basic SNMP commands: read, write, trap, and traversal operations.

- The read command is used by an NMS to monitor managed devices. The NMS examines different variables that are maintained by managed devices.
- The write command is used by an NMS to control managed devices. The NMS changes the values of variables stored within managed devices.
- The trap command is used by managed devices to asynchronously report events to the NMS. When certain types of events occur, a managed device sends a trap to the NMS.
- Traversal operations are used by the NMS to determine which variables a managed device supports and to sequentially gather information in variable tables, such as a routing table.

SNMP lacks any authentication capabilities, which results in vulnerability to a variety of security threats. These include masquerading occurrences, modification of information, message sequence and timing modifications, and disclosure. Masquerading consists of an unauthorised entity attempting to perform management operations by assuming the identity of an authorised management entity. Modification of information involves an unauthorised entity attempting to alter a message generated by an authorised entity so that the message results in unauthorised accounting management or configuration management operations. Message sequence and timing modifications occur when an unauthorised entity reorders, delays, or copies and later replays a message generated by an authorised entity. Disclosure results when an unauthorised entity extracts values stored in managed objects, or learns of noticeable events by monitoring exchanges between managers and agents. Because SNMP does not implement authentication, many vendors do not implement Set operations, thereby reducing SNMP to a monitoring facility.

2.1.2 JMX

The Java Management eXtensions (JMX) is a SUN specification describing the design patterns of smart Java agents for application and network management. The specification includes the architecture, the design patterns, APIs and core services. The JMX provides Java developers with means to instrument Java code and create smart Java agents and management applications. The JMX components also provide means for extension of existing Java based management middleware. It is already planned to integrate JMX into such systems as:

- WBEM (JSR-000048 WBEM Services Specification for CIM/WBEM manager and provider APIs)[1]
- SNMP Manager API (currently reviewed by the Java Community Process)

The JMX propose a three layers architecture comprising:

- Instrumental level (interfaces to manageable resources),
- Agent level (Server),
- Distributed Services level (External Applications).

The following figure is clarifying the relations between these levels and their components.

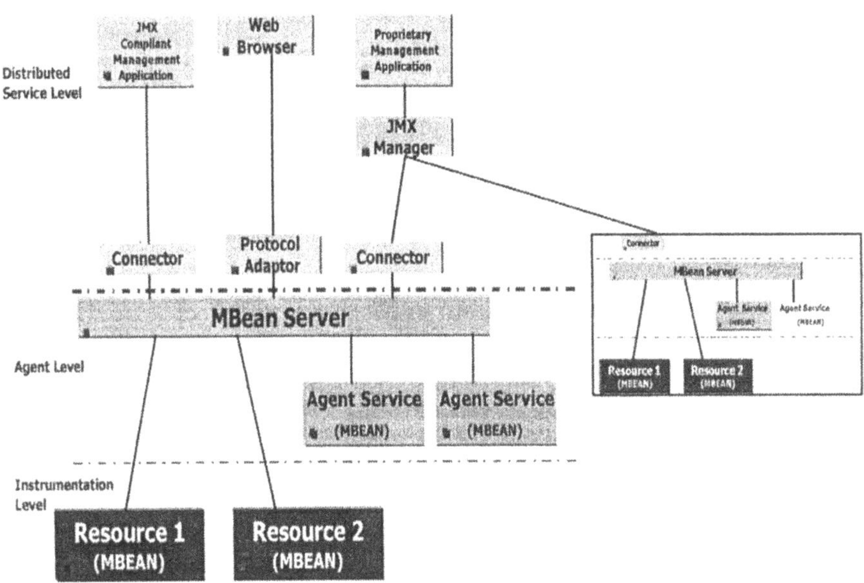

Figure 2. Relationship between components of the JMX architecture

Instrumentation Level: This level deals with components to be managed. A JMX manageable component can be an application, a service, a device, a user and etc. An instrumentation can be done through a Java interface or thin Java wrapper by means of implementation of Manageable Beans (MBeans). An MBean is a special Java Bean that should be implemented with stricter design pattern than a common Java Bean. The main aim of the instrumentation is to provide services to the agent level (to a Mbean Server). This server manage all communications between the MBeans.

Moreover, the instrumentation level supports publish/subscribe communication model (notification mechanism) which is a standard for Java Beans, this mechanism is used to propagate the notifications events to the upper levels.

JMX is a quite portable system, since it requires that resource is compatible only with JDK 1.1.x, EmbeddedJava, PersonalJava or Java2. It means that wide rage of resources can be managed. Besides, JMX ensures high level of automation of management for such instrumented resources.

Agent Level: This level deals with the management agents. The Agents can directly access the instrumented resources to control them and to publish them to Management applications on upper level.

The JMX agent consists of an MBean Server and a set of services for handling MBeans. Due to this separation, the agent and instrumented resources can be placed on different hosts. Similar to the approach at the instrumentation level, the JMX agent is designed to be independent regarding the Management application that is using the agent.

Distributed Services Level: The blue blocs on Figure 2 represent the Distributed Services level which deals with Management applications. However, this level is not yet well defined in the JMX specification. This level defines the interfaces needed for the implementation of JMX managers that are purposed to integrate managed resources seamless to their environment. In addition, the components named Connector and Protocol Adapter are used to provide information to different clients.

2.1.3 Distributed Management Task Forces Standards

The Distributed Management Task Forces (DMTF) released several specifications widely used in modern supervision frameworks, like OpenView and Unicenter. The most relevant are:

Common Information Model <http://www.dmtf.org/standards/cim> (CIM) - a common data model of an implementation-neutral schema for describing overall management information in a network/enterprise environment.

Web-Based Enterprise Management <http://www.dmtf.org/standards/wbem> (WBEM) - a set of management and Internet standard technologies developed to unify the management of enterprise computing environments.

2.2 Supervision Frameworks

This section gives an outline of the current frameworks in the supervision domain focusing on the 3 main frameworks : Tivoli, Unicenter and HP Openview. A short overview of other existing frameworks is also provided.

2.2.1 Tivoli (IBM) (http://www.tivoli.com)

The Tivoli framework is built on a CORBA compliant middleware, it is more dedicated to distributed system administration : software distribution, remote configuration, remote control, remote monitoring. Its design is proprietary, thus it does not support standard protocols (like SNMP) but it can be interfaced with the IBM's network analysis product Netview in order to enhance the field of operations.

2.2.1.1 Overview

The ***Tivoli Management Environment*** (TME) is a product line whose base component is the Tivoli Management Environment ***Framework***. Using the Tivoli Framework and a combination of TME applications, it is possible to manage large distributed networks with multiple operating systems, various network services, diverse system tasks and constantly changing nodes and users.

The TME Framework provides a set of common services or features that are used by the TME applications installed on the Framework. Examples of services provided by the Framework are:

- The DHCP service.
- The Task library through which tasks can be created and executed on multiple TME resources.
- A scheduler that makes it possible to schedule all TME operations including the execution of tasks created in the TME Task library.
- The RDBMS interface module (RIM) that enables some TME applications to write application specific information to relational databases.
- The query facility that allows search and retrieval of information from a relational database.

TME applications installed on the TME Framework are enabled to use the services provided by the Framework.

TME provides centralised control of a distributed environment, which can include mainframes, UNIX or NT workstations, and PCs. A single system administrator can perform the following task for bunches of networked systems:

- Manage user and group accounts
- Deploy new or upgrade existing software
- Inventory existing system configuration
- Monitor the resources of systems either inside or outside the TME environment
- Manage internet and intranet access and control
- Manage third-party applications.

2.2.1.2 TME Management Services

The TME Framework enables installation and creation of several management services such as:

- **TMR Server** – It includes the libraries, binaries, data files, and graphical user interface needed to install and manage a TME environment. TMR servers maintain the TMR server database and co-ordinate all communications with the TME managed nodes.
- **Managed Node** – A TME Managed Node runs the same software that runs on a TMR Server. Managed nodes maintain their own databases, which can be accessed by the TMR server. When managed nodes communicate directly with other managed nodes, they perform the same communication or security operations performed by the TMR Server. The primary difference between a TMR server and a managed node is the size of the database.
- **Endpoint gateway** – An endpoint gateway controls all communications with and operations on TME endpoints. A single gateway can support communications with thousands of endpoints. A gateway can launch method on an endpoint or run methods on the endpoint's behalf. Created on an existing managed node, the gateway is a proxy managed node that provides access to the endpoint methods and provides the communications with the TMR server that the endpoint occasionally require.
- **Endpoint** – An endpoint is any system that runs an endpoint service (daemon). Typically, an endpoint is installed on a machine that is not used for daily management operations. Endpoints run a very small amount of software and do not maintain a database. The majority of systems in most TME installations are endpoints.

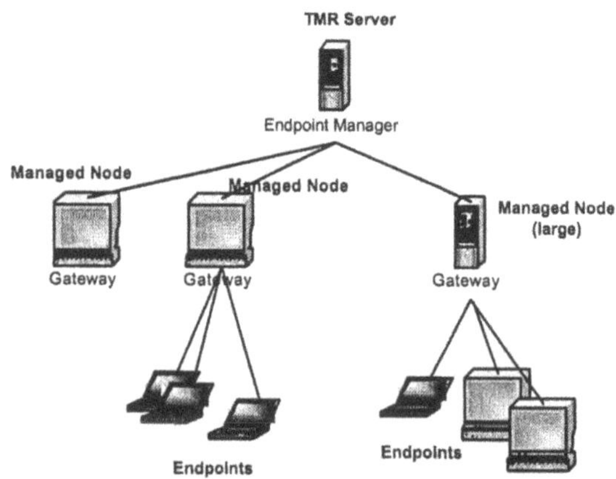

Figure3. TME Framework Nodes

Every TME framework installation begins with a TMR Server, which is just a special case of a managed node with some additional responsibilities, such as locating objects within the TME distributed database and performing authentication for method invocations. For every method invocation, the TMR server must be contacted to locate the object and authenticate the method invocation. In addition, the TMR server is the point at which much of the inter-TMR communication takes place.

2.2.1.3 Communications and networks

TME provides a distributed environment on top of which system management application run. This environment consists of one or more machines that perform operations in a distributed and parallel fashion. Each machine in a TMR has a long-running service, or daemon, called the **oserv** that communicates with other TME services, or daemons, on other machines in a peer-to-peer based manner. An operation initiated on one machine may start multiple operations on machines across the network, all running in parallel to complete their portion of the overall task.

The configuration of TMRs and the location of file servers have a significant impact on the performance of the TME installation. For example, if two sites are connected through a slow line over which TME requests and operations are run, each site should then be a TMR and have a local file server with the appropriate TME binaries. In this manner, the only traffic that passes over the slow line between the sites are management requests, not large amounts of data or requests for information from a remote TME server.

Due to the distributed architecture, it is important that the communications and network function efficiently. The TME server speeds up error and timeout scenarios as well as ensures reliable and accurate error handling and recovery (e.g. it can track machines that are temporarily unavailable due to network problems).

TME provides a service called **Multiplexed Distribution** (Mdist) service, to enable synchronous distributions of large amounts of data to multiple targets in an enterprise. The Mdist service is used by a number of TME applications, such as TME Software Distribution, to maximise data throughput across large, complex networks.

During a distribution of data to multiple targets, Mdist sets up a distribution tree of communication channels from the source host to targets through repeaters. Mdist limits its own use of the network, as configured through repeater parameters, to help prevent intense network activity that can stress network bandwidth for periods of time.

There are fundamentally two types of network communication services available in TME – all other communications that use the TME Framework are built on top of these two communications services:

- Inter-Object Messaging (IOM)
- Inter-dispatcher communication (objcall service)

IOM represents the direct communication between object implementations. Once two object implementations are running, they can establish an IOM channel between them for the purpose of bulk data transfers. This channel is preferred from bulk data transfers, since sending large amounts of data as arguments to methods (via dispatcher) is slow and inefficient. An IOM channel usually only lasts as long as it takes to transfer the data it was created to accommodate.

Examples of IOM usage are: software, profiles and tasks distribution, file transfers between managed node files, TME database backups, TME desktop (GUI) communications.

As the primary type of communication in TME, the objcall service is used by all method invocations. When two dispatchers communicate, inter-dispatcher connections are sustained: the connection isn't broken unless the network breaks it, or unless one of the dispatchers is restarted.

An example of inter-dispatcher communication is illustrated in the following figure, which shows communications between two dispatchers and two object implementations.

2.2.2 Unicenter (Computer Associates) (http://www.cai.com)

The Unicenter framework is based on a central object repository containing all devices managed by the platform. Its implementation is more open than Tivoli's, it admits use of various protocols and let developers adding some extension modules.

2.2.2.1 Unicenter architecture

Unicenter architecture consists of the following:

- ***Real Work Interface*** – graphical user interface driven by a "Common Object Repository".

  Unicenter TNG's Real World Interface allows management applications to identify the business resources they manage, as well as the relationships among those resources. It draws on the

Common Object Repository to generate management maps dynamically.

- ***Common Object Repository*** (CORE) – central storage mechanism for all components of Unicenter TNG, accessible by management functions and third-party applications.

  The CORE is the location where all Unicenter TNG management functions store information about managed resources, their properties and relationships. Third-party applications and all Unicenter TNG components access CORE. The CORE is an object-based repository, which is database independent and designed for multi-user and multi-system operations.
- ***Managers and agents*** – core management facilities that provide resource management throughout an enterprise and agents means to monitor and control all aspects of the business enterprise.

  To manage varieties of hardware and software, widely dispersed across a network and distributed across multiple disparate platforms, Unicenter TNG proposes an infrastructure comprised of agents and managers. Agents reside on or near the managed resources, gather data about the resources and filter the data to identify and report the most important information to managers.

  Managers may be located anywhere in the network. They analyse the information sent to them by agents, correlate the various pieces of information in the environment to discover trends and patterns and determine how to best control the managed resources in the context of management policies.

2.2.2.2 Unicenter TNG's distributed management approach

In Unicenter TNG's manager/agent architecture, the functions that use management information, control management actions and delegate management authority are architecturally separate from the functions that produce management data and act on behalf of managers. Many managers can monitor a single agent and vice versa. GUI can use the Common Object Repository and multiple managers can update that repository.

Manager's role - A manager is one of many software bosses in the enterprise management system. Managers issue requests to agents for data and then perform analyses and correlations on the data received about their management environment.

Unicenter TNG has for example the following managers: a workload manager, storage manager, asset manager, problem manager, software distribution manager, configuration manager, file manager, calendar manager, report manager, user/security manager...

There is also a special manager called Distributed State Machine (DSM), which manage groups of agents that instrument resources. This manager is essential to integration of third-party agents.

Agent's role - Agents monitor information about one or more resources and relay that information to a manager under specific circumstances or criteria. Agents can periodically report to their managers or be asked (polled) for information by managers.

Unicenter TNG offers several agents right out of the box: DB2 agent, DCE agent, Informix agent, Ingres II agent, MVS agent, Netware agent, OpenEdition agent, OpenVMS agent, Oracle agent, OS/2 agent, OS/390 System agent, SQL Server agent, Sybase agent, Tandem NSK agent, Unix agent, Windows 3.1 agent, Windows 95 agent, Windows NT agent…

2.2.2.3 Unicenter TNG agent technology and integration

Unicenter TNG agent technology makes it possible to instrument practically any resource in an IT infrastructure. It provides facilities for creating custom agents. The open architecture supports agents created by other software vendors who have followed the Unicenter TNG agent specifications.

Unicenter TNG provides a SDK, which helps third parties to integrate their solutions into Unicenter TNG. The SDK consists of API organised as the following:

- WorldView (GUI) API
- Enterprise Management API
- Agent Factory

The ***Worldview API*** is comprised of the Real World Interface and the Common Object Repository. It provides utilities for customising the GUI without impacting the behaviour of the management applications.

The ***Enterprise Management API*** controls all the management functions and common services provided in Unicenter TNG and provides them for cross-application integration. It provides multi-platform management facilities for security, help desk, event management… Third-party management applications can share policies, request services from, and provide services to other management functions.

The ***Agent Factory API*** allows third parties to construct multi-platform, scalable manager/agent applications. These agents may also be deployed over the Internet and Intranets. It is a complete development environment for building agents that communicate with management applications using

SNMP. Within Unicenter TNG architecture, those management applications include WorldView and third-party applications at the Enterprise Management level.

2.2.2.4 Unicenter TNG's Agent Factory environment

The Agent Factory allows building a SNMP agent with minimum effort: only the code that is specific to the resources needs to be written. The functions that are common to any agent, such as encoding and decoding SNMP protocol data units and routing requests, are provided by a set of ***common services*** and a ***Distributed Services Bus***. Agents in Unicenter TNG run within the Agent Factory environment, supported by the common service and the distributed Service Bus.

The Agent Factory provides the API libraries, executable code for the common services and Distributed Services Bus, utilities to configure and test agents. The common services consist of the executable code for three objects that perform the functions common to all agents: SNMP Gateway, SNMP Administrator, Object Store.

The ***Object Store*** consists of disk storage and the process that reads from and writes to that storage area. Object Store is designed to handle all incoming get and set requests by default. The API functions can be used to code a task that periodically calculates attribute values and send them to Object Store, where they are available whenever the SNMP Administrator receives a get or get-next request. Besides acting as a repository for current attribute values, Object Store also holds other critical agent data.

2.2.3 Openview (HP) (http://www.hp.com)

Since the begining dedicated to network supervision, the Openview environement has been augmented with many functionalities linked to systems and applications. Its implementation is based on SNMP and its design is closer to a software suite than a framework like IBM's or CA's.

2.2.3.1 Overview

HP Openview IT/Operations (ITO) is a software application that provides central operations and problem management for multi-vendor distributed systems.

ITO consists of a central management server in the form of a manager, which interacts with intelligent software-agents installed on the managed systems (called nodes). Management status information, messages, and monitoring values are collected from such sources as system or application log files, SNMP traps, SNMP variables. Filters and thresholds are applied and the information is then converted into a standard format for presentation to the central management server. Once the information is retrieved, ITO can immediately initiate corrective actions and provide individual guidance for problem identification and further problem resolutions.

All management information and associated records needed for future analysis and audit are stored in a central repository called the History Database. It allows the automation of certain problem resolution processes.

2.2.3.2 ITO functioning

ITO monitors, controls and maintains systems in heterogeneous environments, by managing events, messages and actions. ITO uses events, messages, and actions to observe and control status, formulate and provide information, react to and correct problems.

When an event occurs, a message is generated as a result of that event. ITO performs event correlation on messages rather than on events: messages are copied rather than diverted to the correlation engine so that critical messages may avoid the possibility of being delayed or even lost in the correlation process. Messages are structured pieces of information, created by events. ITO intercepts and collects messages, and thereby is informed of events.

ITO message management can combine messages into logically related groups, bringing together messages from lots of related sources, providing status information about a class of managed objects or services. Other message management operations can classify and filter messages to ensure that important information is clearly displayed.

When an event occurs on a managed object, a message is created as a result. The ITO Agent on that managed node receives the message and filters it. It can then forward it and/or log it locally. If the message satisfies the filter, it is converted into ITO message format and forwarded to the management server. If a local action on the message is configured, it will be started. The management server can perform the following actions: assign the message to another message group, start non-local automatic actions configured for the message on the specified node, forward the message to external notification interfaces and trouble ticket service, escalate the message to another pre-configured management server. The active message is stored in the database and displayed in a Message Browser window in one or more ITO display stations. When the message is acknowledged, it is removed from the active Browser and put in the history database.

2.2.3.3 ITO architecture

ITO architecture is comprised of the following:

- The management server.
- Managed nodes.

ITO software is divided into two basic components:

- Agents and sub-agents
- Managers.

The agent and sub-agent are located on the managed nodes and are responsible for generating messages, collecting and forwarding information, monitoring parameters.

The management software is located on the management server and communicates with, controls and directs the agents. It stores the central database and runs the graphical user interfaces.

The management server performs the central role of ITO. It collects data from managed nodes, managed and re-groups messages, calls the appropriate agent to start actions or initiate sessions on managed nodes, controls the history database for messages and performed actions, forwards messages, installs ITO agent software on managed nodes, intercepts SNMP traps.

2.2.3.4 Integration of applications into ITO

Existing applications can be integrated into ITO, at different levels, through various interfaces, to provide diverse capabilities and advantages:

- Application Desktop integration – applications are registered within ITO and represented by symbols in the application desktop window. Operators use these symbols daily to start applications and resolve problems.
- Event Integrations – applications can write messages to logfiles, use ITO API or send SNMP traps in order to manage events through ITO
- Action Integration – application start-ups can be incorporated into an automatic, or operator initiated action.
- Monitor Integration – monitoring applications such as scripts, programs, MIB variable based programs can be started by ITO and use API to return values. The monitored values can then be compared to threshold limits.

2.2.4 Other frameworks

Openmaster (Evidian-Bull) (http://www.evidian.com)
Openmaster was designed like a universal platform supporting a large field of protocols : SNMP, CMIS, CMIP ... Network oriented, Evidian's Openmaster strategy seems today to focus on security purposes.

Nagios (OpenSource)
Nagios is an OpenSource framework that provides a flexible approach for centralised system monitoring. The core component is a Linux application that runs periodically a set of shell scripts. These scripts monitors different parameters (ping, system resource load, motherboard temperature, etc.) on local and remote hosts. A user-friendly GUI is secured by a web front-end.

2.3 Related Projects

This paragraph intends to present a list of related research project and organisations that are of interest when entering in the distributed systems supervision world.

Projects

ANDROID - The Active Distributed Open Infrastructure Development project provides a manageable programmable network infrastructure. The communication mechanism uses XML-based protocol. A genetic algorithm is used for intelligent policies based server management.

AgentScape - Scalable Resource Management for Multi-Agent Systems

MANTRIP - The Management Testing and Reconfiguration of IP based networks project is an example of Mobile Agent Technology (MAT) in the context of Network Management.

SHUFFLE - this project proposes an agent based approach to control resources in UMTS networks.

OPENDREAMS - The Open Distributed Reliable Environment architecture and Middleware for Supervision project was to satisfy the needs of advanced Supervision and Control Systems (SCSs) for the management of large equipment infrastructures such as telecommunication networks, electricity and water distribution networks, large buildings, etc. A Corba implementation was used as backbone assuring the interoperability and openness of the platform architecture.

web services architecture and technology to manage distributed resources. The work is ongoing.

Agents management related projects:

AgentLight - Platform for Lightweight Agents project is dedicated to development of agent-based middleware for mobile devices using J2ME and FIPA compatible API.

AgentCities - This project is purposed to set up a world-wide network of always running FIPA test-bed platforms.

LEAP - The Lightweight Extensible Agent Platform is another project addressing the needs of mobile enterprises. The proposed architecture is based on JADE (Java FIPA implementation)

SAFIRA - The support Affective Interactions for Real-time Applications project provides a framework to enrich interactions and applications using a real-time multi-agent middleware.

Intelligent agents related projects:

Agent Academy - this project is concentrated on a data-mining framework for training intelligent agent. The project uses standards from FIPA and OMG, like FIPA ACL and KQML for agents' communication and OMG XMI and CWM MOF for data-mining.

PISA - The Privacy Incorporated Software Agent project deals with development of security software agents for the Internet and E-commerce.

RACING -The Rational Agent Coalitions for Intelligent Mediation of Information Retrieval on the Net is another example of agent-based data mining.

2.4 Intelligent Supervision

This section describes an innovative feature that needs to be implemented in the new supervision solution : the intelligent supervision.

Systems that leverage from simple monitoring system towards autonomous systems extend the basic components of data monitoring and potentially higher level components that analyse and interpret this basic data into higher layer information with elements that have the ability to react without further human intervention on a detected critical or failure situation. Such "intelligent" components need either pre-recorded knowledge or have to analyse a system.

We have identified three major elements of such a system:

- Case-Database solutions based on historical data and/or expert knowledge
- Topology Analysis for identifying root causes of failures
- System Behaviour Prediction

The following sections describe these elements in more details and provide an overview on the current state of the art in this area.

2.4.1 Case Database Approach

The Case Database approach for the management of distributed applications (as described in [2], [3]) is based on a set of cases containing specific symptom-cause pairs in a database. If a monitored situation fits or is similar to a symptom stored in the case database, the prepared solutions for such a case can be executed. The major problem to be solved in this kind of systems is finding appropriate metrics for evaluating the level of similarity between the monitored symptoms and the one stored in the database. Another critical point is the size and quality of the case database. Very often, historical data for example from a trouble ticket system are used to feed such databases (see[4]). Another approach correlates basic events to higher-level events that allow reacting either a system administrator or potentially an intelligent component correctly. This is either realised using programming language constructs (see [5]) or the system to be monitored is modelled with its event behaviour (cf. [6]).

2.4.2 Topology Analysis

Distributed applications consist out of interdependent components on different levels ranging from network, middleware, up to the application layer. In order to define good policies on how to detect and to react on problems in the operation of a distributed applications, knowledge on the topology and the dependencies of the different components is necessary. In [7], an event correlator based on dependency graphs is introduced. Using this dependency graph, it is possible to identify which components of a distributed system will be affected if an error occurs. The advantage of this approach is that it is not limited to react on situations that have been discovered in the past. As the errors are tracked down to single components, the mechanisms to solve a discovered problem are likely less complex and the complicated part of case database oriented systems matching the current problem situation with a stored solution does not apply.

2.4.3 Prediction Systems

Another component needed for autonomous supervision is an intelligent element using historical monitored data as the basis for predicting the behaviour of the system in the near future in order to allow supervision components to react in a proactive way. Significant work in this area exists for prediction of network behaviour e.g. the Network Weather Service (NWS) (see [8]) or the Remos System (see [9]). The common feature in these toolkits is to collect data on the supervised network and use this historical information in order to predict the load of the network in the near future. However they are almost limited to the network layer with a small part of monitoring of the system status.

3. INTRODUCTION TO GENESYS

The following sections are intended to present an innovative solution for distributed systems supervision. Through this example, the reader will be able to understand the real and practical issues of designing, specifying, implementing a generic, open and comprehensive supervision solution.

3.1 What is GeneSyS ?

GeneSyS (Generic System Supervision) is a European Union project (IST-2001-34162) co-funded by the Commission of the European Communities (5th Framework). EADS SPACE Transportation (France) is the project Co-ordinator, with University of Stuttgart (Germany), MTA SZTAKI (Hungary), NAVUS GmbH and D-3-Group GmbH (both of Germany) as participants. GeneSyS started in March 2002 with planned completion in October 2004 [10]. The project is aimed at developing a new, open, generic and modular middleware for distributed systems supervision. Besides, the consortium intends to make GeneSyS an open standard in the distributed system supervision domain.

3.2 Contexts

This section presents three contexts that were chosen as validation scenarios for the project purposes. These quite different application coming from different industrial domains helped to identify a list of requirements that needed to be fulfiled by GeneSyS (see [11]).

3.2.1 Preliminary Design Review

This scenario was brought by EADS SPACE Transportation, the European aerospace industry leader. It concerns the spacecraft production process and, in particular, Automated Transfer Vehicle (ATV) design. The Preliminary Design Review (PDR) is a design process stage, involving hundreds of engineers from different European countries, that meet regularly to discuss ATV technical documentation, to release comments and change proposals.

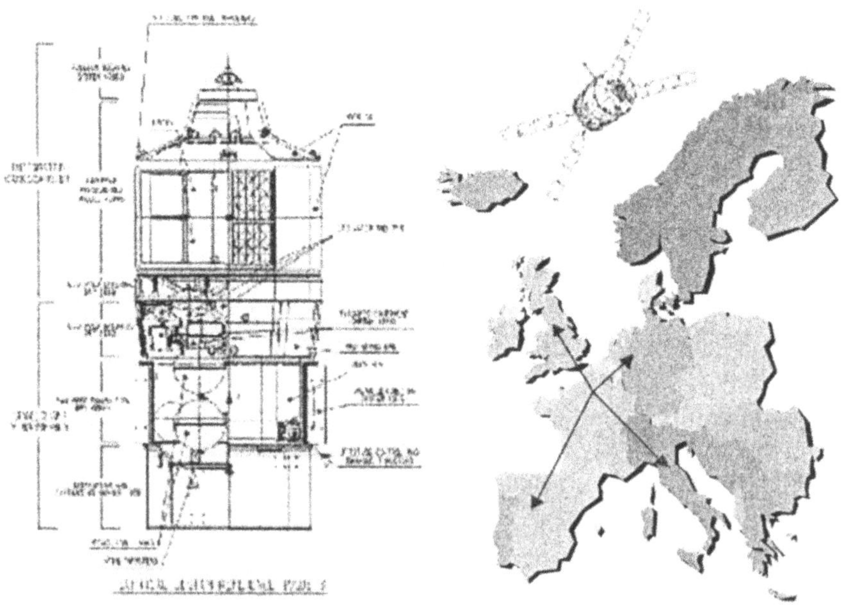

Figure 3. Preliminary Design Review, an ATV design phase.

To reduce the travel costs, a groupware application is used, which allows collaborative work on the documentation and visio conference meetings to discuss comments and change proposals.

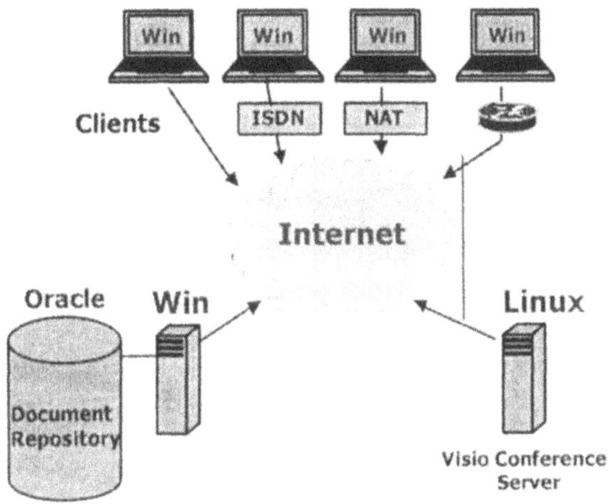

Figure 4. PDR Application, Groupware Application for Collaborative Engineering

The groupware application comprises mainly a Document Repository and a Visio Conference Server supporting multiple simultaneous client access. The application is physically highly distributed, different operating systems and access means are used. In addition, a database management system with a web front-end and the visio conference server require specific supervision on the application level.

Thus the system maintenance and the client technical support seems to be extremely difficult without common generic supervision framework.

3.2.2 Distributed Training

The following scenario is also from the space domain and concerns HLA-based simulations. HLA (see [12]) is a DoD standard for real-time interactive simulations. This standard is widely used in military, aerospace and automotive industries. The Distributed Training Scenario involves 4 real-time simulators playing different roles in joint training sessions of astronauts and ground controllers in order to prepare them in advance for contingency situation during the ATV to International Space Station (ISS) approach manoeuvre.

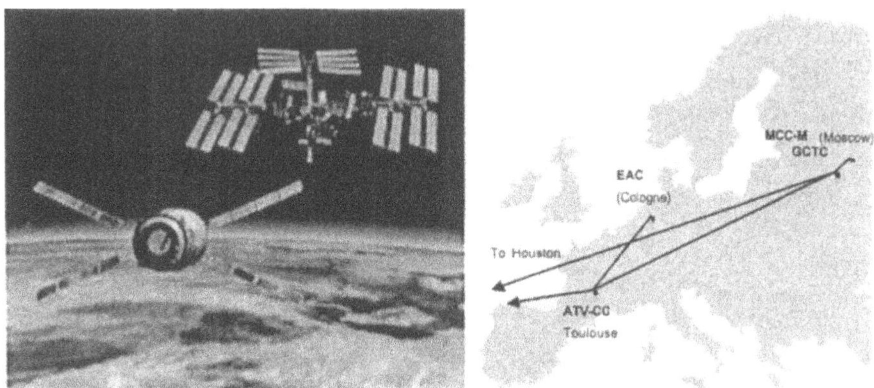

Figure 5. Distributed Training - HLA-based Interactive Simulation

The trainee teams are located in different places all over the world (Toulouse, Houston, Moscow), which imposes performance constraints on a supervision solution.

The supervision is needed at all levels starting from operating system, up to HLA middleware and Training application.

3.2.3 Web-Servers Monitoring

Today's web servers implement a distributed, multi layered architecture hosting complex applications. The situation is even complex if such web applications are connected to each other requiring continuous synchronisation with each other. In the Web Servers monitoring scenario, the supervision of such complex web based applications are contemplated. One such application is the so-called "node server" of the StreamOnTheFly (SOTF) application. SOTF provides a peer-to-peer network for community radios to share their shows (see figure 6).

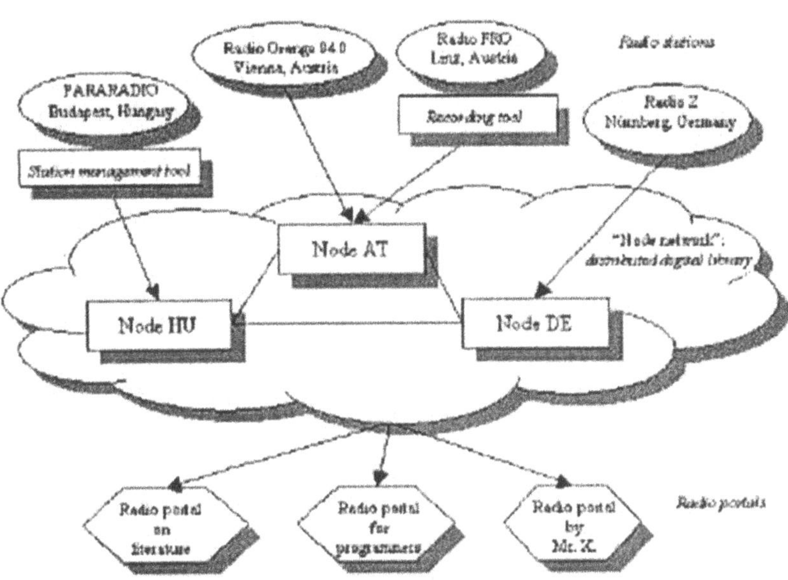

Figure 6. Web Servers Monitoring Scenario - Stream on the Fly Application

Nodes are the repositories of the shows, collecting the audio files and their associated metadata. The metadata is periodically exchanged by the highly distributed nodes of the SOTF network. Each node itself is typically a distributed system as the HTTP server and database servers are typically located on different machines or in different domain, therefore not only the collaboration of these nodes but the operation of a single node requires a complex supervision solution.

3.3 Requirements

Analysing the need of supervision for the mentioned distributed applications, the following common requirements were identified:

Comprehensiveness - the supervision should be provided for all levels of a computer infrastructure.

Flexibility - all kinds of data types and complex data structures should be supported.

Portability - the supervision system should by compatible with distributed applications, that are often multi-platform, involving different access means.

Integration capability - a global supervision system should be capable to benefit from existing solutions for local supervision and from available application extension mechanisms.

Security - authorisation, authentication, data integrity and privacy are extremely important for the distributed systems with control functionality.

4. GENESYS FRAMEWORK

4.1 Constraints of Existing Solutions

The commercial supervision systems like Tivoli, OpenView, Unicenter TNG, mentioned earlier, are aimed at different aspects of system monitoring starting from operating systems to network and up to some commercial standard applications.

However most of them have several common constraints, which should be overcome:

- proprietary interfaces;
- proprietary protocols;
- operating system dependent implementation;
- non-flexible architecture;
- dedication to particular commercial application (Oracle, SAP, etc.).

Although these supervision systems use open standards (SNMP, JMX, Corba), the mentioned constraints complicate integration with third-party monitoring tools to achieve system control at all levels. At the same time, proprietary solutions slow down pace of development of the whole domain.

With the advancement of Web technologies, more and more works appeared to introduce these technologies in the world of supervision (DMTF WBEM, OASIS WSDM, etc.). GeneSyS was one of the first to bring the Web Services to this domain. Besides, the GeneSyS consortium intends to make the GeneSyS achievements a new open standard.

4.2 Design Objectives

Thus, the main GeneSyS objective is to design a system supervision middleware that can be used in a wide range of applications (examples are listed in the applicability section). The planned outcome of the specification phase was a communication and messaging API for the middleware components as well as the functional design of these components.

While designing the GeneSyS framework, the consortium continuously aligned the design to meet the following aspects of a new solution in order to fit the requirements:

- the framework must clearly separate supervision (collection and processing of data) from visualisation (display and analysis of data)
- the framework must support both passive monitoring (collection of runtime data) and active control (start, stop, reconfiguration) of monitored entities
- the framework must provide all functionality related to the communication between middleware components
- the communication protocol must provide secure message exchange between middleware components
- the framework must be based on open standards and protocols to assure its openness and easy adaptation by anyone in need of a supervision facility; dependency on third party or proprietary software is not permissible
- the specified API must be language and implementation neutral
- authors of new monitoring components should only bother with the details of how to get the monitoring data from a monitored entity and how to control it - the rest (transferring the data to other components, storing the data, querying historical data, visualising monitoring data, etc.) should all be handled by GeneSyS.

4.3 Web Technologies as a Platform for a Supervision Framework

As the result of our research matched with the requirements outlined for GeneSyS, an agent based approach was implemented which separates the monitoring/controlling and visualisation of monitoring data. Web Services technologies were chosen as the base for GeneSyS messaging protocol.

Basing the supervision infrastructure on agents seems logical, because the monitoring of IT entities requires properties that are available with software agents. A software agent is a program that is authorised to act for another program or human (see [13]). Agents possess the characteristics of delegacy, competency and amenability that are the exact properties needed for a monitoring software component.

Delegacy for software agents centres on persistence. Delegacy provides the base for an agent to be an autonomous software component, which can act without the intervention of other programs or human operators. "Fire-and-forget" software agents stay resident, or persistent, as background processes after being launched. By making decisions and acting on their environment independently, software agents reduce human workload by generally only interacting with their end-clients when it is time to deliver results. In case of GeneSyS, the agents reside either on the computer hosting the monitored entity or on a computer that is able to communicate with the monitored entity.

Competency within a software environment requires knowledge of the specific communication protocols of the domain (SQL, HTTP, API calls). A monitoring agent competency is to have knowledge about the monitored entity to be able to collect runtime information from it or to control it with commands.

Amenability for non-intelligent software agents is generally limited to providing control options and the generation of status reports that require human review. Such agents often tend to be brittle in the face of a changing environment, necessitating a modification of their programming to restore performance.

Amenability in intelligent software agents can include self-monitoring of achievement toward client goals combined with continuous, online learning to improve performance. GeneSyS makes no restriction on its agents or on their intelligence or autonomous operations, but provides the ability to include it as found necessary by agent writers and also provides some middleware components (like monitoring data repository) that can be used to implement amenability.

Openness and standards based solution was one of the key requirements of GeneSyS especially in the light of the Consortium's intention to turn GeneSyS itself into an industry standard. After a number of iterations, we had two candidates for the realisation of the communication protocol:

- InterAgent Communication Model (ICM - FIPA based) (cf. [14])
- Web Services technologies (see [15])

The ICM framework has not been designed for monitoring or supervision needs but is a general communication framework for inter-agent communication. The Web Services framework standardised by the W3C is a generic framework for the interaction of Services over the Internet and is designed to exploit as much as possible existing protocol frameworks such as SOAP and HTTP. The Web Services framework is in contrast to ICM more a hierarchical or client-sever communication model.

ICM is a very efficient system for the transmission of messages between agents. However for supervision in general and especially in the area of standardisation and flexibility, major disadvantages have been identified. The most important issue against ICM was that the GeneSyS Message format would be tight to the ICM communication protocol and would bring GeneSyS in a complete dependency to ICM. This is a serious risk as ICM is not used at all by important software companies and no activity in the development has been identified since autumn 2001.

Web Services has a major problem with respect to performance. The use of an XML based protocol cannot be as efficient as a binary protocol due to the consuming text processing. Additionally, the most common transport protocol used for SOAP messages, the Hypertext Transfer Protocol (HTTP), is not very efficient as it lacks stateful connections. However we are convinced that these problems can be solved as Web Services potentially can use different protocols. The feature of alternative protocol bindings is already used for example in the .NET framework using Remoting, which uses different (proprietary) protocols. As this problem is not solely part of GeneSyS but the whole community including the major software vendors that are committed to Web Services will face this problem, the assumption that this limitation will disappear seems reasonable.

After a detailed comparison of these two technologies, we selected Web Services, including the SOAP XML based communication protocol as a base for GeneSyS. Going on the Web Services path, we have a strong industry backing with tools available for many languages. With this decision, we also defined the first instance of a Web Services based supervision system that has recently been followed by other companies and standards organisations (OASIS WSDM, DataPower Technology [16])

On top of SOAP and Web Services, a new layer of the GeneSyS protocol has been established called the GeneSyS Messaging Protocol (GMP). GeneSyS Messaging Protocol is a lightweight messaging protocol for exchanging structured supervision information in a decentralised, distributed environment. It is an XML protocol based on XML 1.0, XML Schema and XML Namespaces. GMP is intended to be used in the Web Services Architecture, thus, SOAP is considered as a default underlying protocol. However, other protocol bindings can be equally applied. Using XML to represent monitoring data was a natural choice. XML is a widely accepted industry standard that supports structured representation of complex data types, structures (enumerations, arrays, lists, hash maps, choices, sequences) and it can be easily processed by both humans and computers. With the wide acceptance of XML, an integration with supervised application and 3d party monitoring solutions can be smoothly achieved, since XML toolkits are available for every platform.

4.4 Basic Components and Communication Model

This section provides implementation details, illustrating a common supervision framework architecture.

Fig.7 depicts the basic GeneSyS functionality.

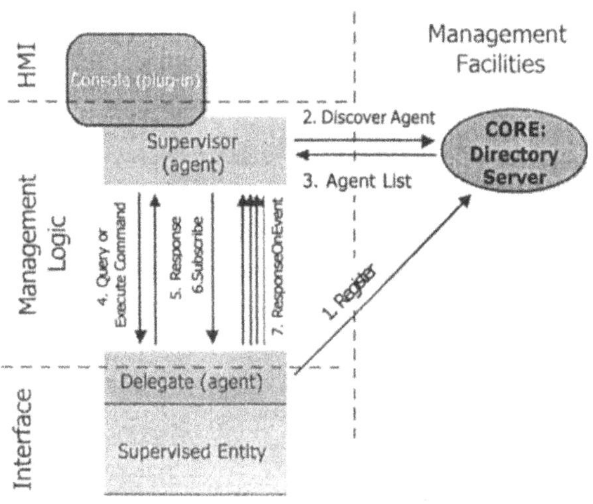

Figure 7. GeneSyS Communication Model

As showed above, supervision process involves several generic components. The Delegate implements an interface to the Supervised Entity (Operating System, Network, Applications, etc.), retrieves and evaluates monitoring information and generates monitoring events. The Supervisor is a remote controller entity that communicates with one or more Delegates. It may encapsulate management automation functionality (intelligence), recognising state patterns and making recovery actions. The Console is connected to one or many Supervisors to visualise the monitoring information in a synthetic way, and to allow for efficient controlling of Supervised Entity. The Core implements Directory Server, a location storage being updated dynamically.

The agents register to the Core to make them discoverable by other agents. Hereafter, the "agent" is a generic term comprising the Supervisor and the Delegate.

Both "pull" and "push" interaction models are available. The pull model is realised by the Query/Response mechanism, while the Event Subscribe mechanism secures the push model. All interactions between agents are provided for by the SOAP-RPC. The flexibility of XML standard is used to encode communication messages (GeneSyS Messaging Protocol) supporting complex data structures and custom data types.

4.5 Intelligence

An inherent property of software agents is autonomy, that is, the ability to work without the intervention of other programs or humans. Autonomous work requires some level of intelligence so that the agent can react on changes in its environment or can make decision based on its internal logic driven by rules or other means. Intelligence in agents is also required because in a complex environment with some 10 or 100 monitored entities, an administrator could be easily flooded with low level warnings like "memory is running low" or "maximum number of users almost reached". Instead, the administrator first needs a general, summarised view about the health of the systems and then can look at the details as necessary.

GeneSyS agents can work autonomously in a hosting environment connected to a monitored entity from which it collects data or controls its operation. The GeneSyS framework provides API hooks for adding intelligence to agents as well as components for supporting the implementation of intelligence. Intelligence can be accomplished in several ways, that are only outlined here, as the actual implementation of this feature is not a main goal of GeneSyS:

- Specific Implementation: the „intelligence" to react on the system status can be done as part of the program code of the agent.
- Parameter based Generic Solution. The rules can be configured through parameters. A basic example is a „Threshold Miss Agent" where the parameters would be min and max values.
- Rule Based Systems. In complex settings, the usage of rule based systems could be an option where the rules can be expressed in an external file e.g. based on JESS.
- Workflow based systems. Another option could be to use workflow languages such as BPEL4WS to define workflows that act depending on events receive.

GeneSyS provides a data Repository that is connected to the middleware bus via the same API as any other agents, which means its functionality is available to all other agents connected to a given CORE. The Repository provides a generic XML data storage facility. Agents can store monitoring or control messages in the Repository, which can later be queried. With the use of the Repository, an agent can base its decisions on archived data, for example, by analysing past messages for detecting trends in the operation of the monitored entity. More over, the Repository is also capable for storing control messages – or a list of control messages – which can be "replayed" any number of times at any time it is necessary.

The Agent Dependency Framework (ADF) is another aid for adding intelligence to monitoring. ADF allows defining dependencies of monitored entities. To be more precise, not directly the dependencies of monitored entities but the dependencies of the agents monitoring the entity can be described. Each delegate agent can describe in its component description (which is stored in the CORE) what agents it depends on. The dependency forms a directed graph that should never cause a circular reference. Once the dependency of each delegate is described, the dependency graph can be queried from the CORE. Based on the dependency graph, a special supervisor console view can be created that draws a tree view of the dependent entities and gives a quick overview of the health of the system with green, yellow and red light depicting a healthy, questionable or erroneous state of the dependant systems. This way of visualising the monitored system with all its dependent components provides a way for tracking root cause of problems. For example, an administrator seeing a red light in the top of the dependency hierarchy can expand the tree until he finds the subsystem that generates the red light and which has been "propagated" up in the dependency tree. In the same way, an autonomous intelligent agent can walk this tree and find the root cause of the problem and can work only with that subsystem that was the source of the problem.

5. APPLICABILITY RESULTS

This section presents the applicability results in accordance with the industrial contexts in order to give real examples of the GeneSyS framework in use.

5.1 Preliminary Design Review Scenario

This scenario was intended to prove a viability of the GeneSyS concept. Common system and network agents were developed to reflect system administrator needs. Custom application agents were used to monitor the system functional status (application load, resources used by applications, etc), user activities (documentation in use, on-line meetings, access violation, etc). The figure 8 depicts the deployment of GeneSyS components involved in the scenario.

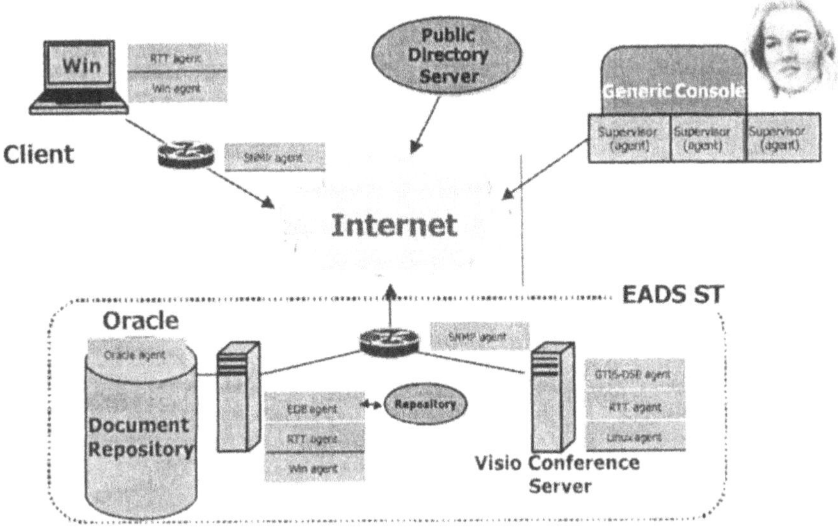

Figure 8. The PDR Application Supervision

The main goals for this scenario was to prove a capability of Web Services based distributed system to work in an heterogeneous environment. It includes support of different operating systems (Windows, Linux), programming languages and toolkits(C/C++/gSOAP, Java/Axis, .Net). Besides, developing custom application agents (Oracle, EDB, GTI6-DSE, Mbone, Tomcat), the integration capability was ensured.

The validation showed that, besides some ergonomy and performance issues, the solution is ready for the large community of the internet users. That is why, generic components for system and network monitoring, as well as, visualisation tools, service components and development toolkits were released under open source policy and can be found at the GeneSyS SourceForge repository (see [17]).

5.2 Distributed Training Scenario

The Distributed Training scenario was implemented in order to improve the GeneSyS V1 functionality and usability as well as to introduce an intelligence basis.

The flexible GeneSyS information allowed customising of System and

Figure 9 depicts the deployment schema and gives intelligence implementation hints.

The "synthetic view" and "agent dependencies framework" approaches were used to provide administrators with a run-time system operation status summary and to allow a fast problem location.

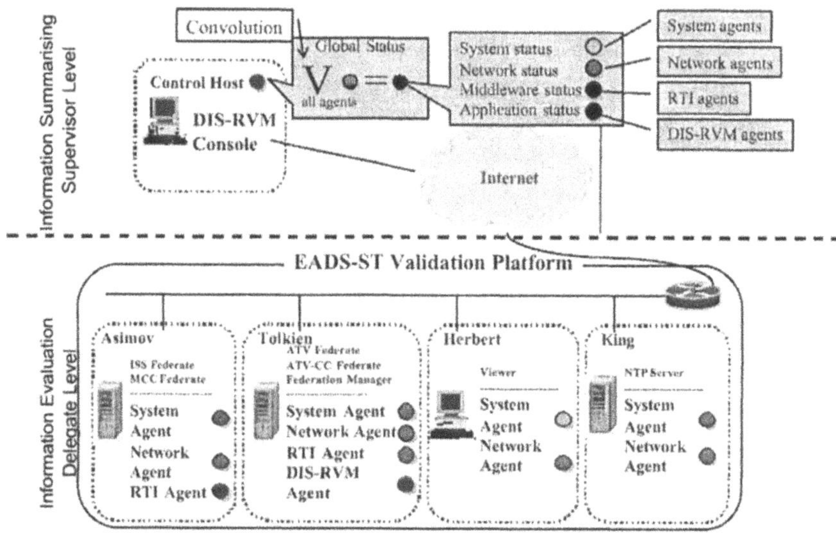

Figure 9. Intelligence in Distributed Training Supervision

Thus an administrator could browse down the agents to find a problem origin and then maintain the system.

5.3 Web Servers Scenario

The Web Servers Monitoring validation scenario aims at using GeneSyS for monitoring and controlling web servers and web based on-line services.

A Web Server is typically more than just an HTTP daemon: it may invoke external programs and those programs may use other programs for their execution, and so on. A typical Web Server can include, for example, an Apache server with a PHP interpreter and a MySQL database used by a number of PHP application. The Web Server is considered "healthy" only if all of these components are in good condition. Because these components may be dependent of each other it is not enough to have separate agents for all entities but these agents must be connected in a way to reflect the dependencies of the monitored entities.

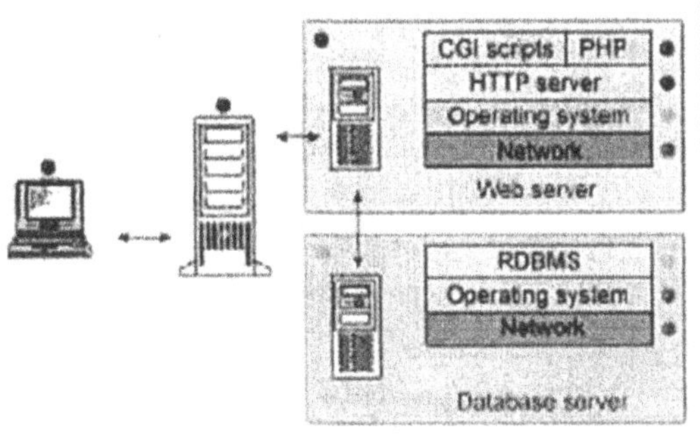

Figure 10. Web Application - A Common Deployment

Going on with the previous example: a Web Server could be considered healthy if the Apache daemon is up and running, the PHP applications it hosts respond in an acceptable time interval and the MySQL server has enough space for new records. If any of these conditions are not met the system should notify the administrator. More over, the unresponsiveness of Apache may be the result of a number of other dependent subsystems, like the operating or network system. So the "monitoring entity" could be divided into some more elements, namely the Apache server itself, the underlying operating system and the network connecting the server machine to the outer world. In this case even if Apache is found to be alive the operating system agent may report that the CPU load is too high and this could cause in a short time the Apache server being unable to respond to requests.

The Web Servers Monitoring scenario extensively uses the Agent Dependency Framework of GeneSyS, which provides the ability to describe the dependencies of system components and use this dependency graph to detect and find root cause of an erroneous system state.

6. CONCLUSION

Today, the distributed systems supervision is a very complex and important issue. The main purpose of this chapter was to give some useful information :

- To understand the problematic of this specific supervision,
- To know the existing technologies, tools in this domain,
- To see what are the main innovative features needed,
- To illustrate, through a case study - the GeneSyS project, the real-life needs, the architecture and design of a generic supervision solution.

In comparison with other solutions, among other advantages, the authors would like to emphasise that the GeneSyS architecture is open to be extended with custom agents for all kind of applications. Besides the proposed framework is published on SourceForge repository under an open source policy and already available for deploying (see [17]).

REFERENCIES

[1] JSR-000048 WBEM Services Specification, Sun Microsystems, Inc. October, 2002

[2] Hatonen, K. ; Klemettinen, M. ; H., Mannila: Knowledge discovery from telecommunication network alarm databases. In: International Conference on Data Engineering (ICDE'96), 1996, S. 115–122

[3] LEWIS, L.: A case-based reasoning approach to the resolution of faults in communication networks. In: Integrated Network Management III, 1993, S. 671–682

[4] RODOSEK, G. D. A Framework for Supporting Fault Diagnosis in Integrated Network and Systems Management: Methodologies for the Correlation of Trouble Tickets and Access to Problem-Solving Expertise. 1995

[5] R. Gardner and D. Harle. Pattern discovery and specification translation for alarm correlation. In Proceedings of Network Operations and Management Symposium (NOMS'98), New Orleans, USA, February 1998, pages 713–722.

[6] D. Ohsie, A. Mayer, S. Kliger, et al. Event modeling with the model language. In A. Lazar, R. Saracco, and R. Stadler, editors. Integrated Network Management V (IM'97), San Diego, USA, May 1997. Chapman & Hall, pages 625–637.

[7] GRUSCHKE, Boris: Integrated Event Management: Event Correlation using Dependency Graphs. In: Proceedings of DSOM'98, 1998

[8] Rich Wolski et.al., The Network Weather Service

[9] A. DeWitt, T. Gross, B. Lowekamp, N. Miller, P. Steenkiste, J. Subhlok, D. Sutherland, *"ReMoS: A Resource Monitoring System for Network-Aware Applications"* Carnegie Mellon School of Computer Science, CMU-CS-97-194.

[10] GeneSyS project official web-site : http://genesys.sztaki.hu

[11] GeneSyS V2 User Requirements Document - D1.2.1

[12] Institute of Electrical and Electronic Engineers - IEEE 1516.1, IEEE 1516.2, IEEE 1516.3

[13] Wallace Croft, David, "Intelligent Software Agents: Definitions and Applications", 1997, http://www.alumni.caltech.edu/~croft/research/agent/definition

[14] The Inter-Agent Communication Model (ICM), Fujitsu Laboratories of America, Inc., http://www.nar.fujitsulabs.com/icm/about.html

[15] Web Service Activity of W3C, http://www.w3.org/2002/ws/

[16] DataPower Offering Web Services-Based Network Device Management, http://www.ebizq.net/news/2534.html

[17] GeneSyS project SourceForge file repository, http://www.sourceforge.net/projects/genesys-mw

SOFTWARE REJUVENATION - MODELING AND ANALYSIS

Kishor S. Trivedi
Dept. of Electrical & Computer Engineering
Duke University, Durham, NC 27708, USA
kst@ee.duke.edu

Kalyanaraman Vaidyanathan
Sun Microsystems, Inc.
San Diego, CA 92121, USA
kalyan.vaidyanathan@sun.com

Abstract Several recent studies have established that most system outages are due to software faults. Given the ever increasing complexity of software and the well-developed techniques and analysis for hardware reliability, this trend is not likely to change in the near future. In this paper, we first classify software faults and discuss various techniques to deal with them in the testing/debugging phase and the operational phase of the software. We discuss the phenomenon of software aging and a preventive maintenance technique to deal with this problem called software rejuvenation. Stochastic models to evaluate the effectiveness of preventive maintenance in operational software systems and to determine optimal times to perform rejuvenation for different scenarios are described. We also present measurement-based methodologies to detect software aging and estimate its effect on various system resources. These models are intended to help develop software rejuvenation policies. An automated online measurement-based approach has been used in the software rejuvenation agent implemented in a major commercial server.

Keywords: Availability, Measurement-based dependability evaluation, Software reliability, Software aging, Software rejuvenation

1. Introduction

Several studies have now shown that outages in computer systems are more due to software faults than due to hardware faults [24, 42]. Recent studies have also reported the phenomenon of "software aging" [20, 29] in which the state of the software degrades with time. The primary causes of this degradation are the exhaustion of operating system resources, data corruption and numerical error accumulation. Eventually, this may lead to performance degradation of the software or crash/hang failure or both. Some common examples of "software aging" are memory bloating and leaking, unreleased file-locks, data corruption, storage space fragmentation and accumulation of round-off errors [20]. Aging has not only been observed in software used on a mass scale but also in specialized software used in high-availability and safety-critical applications [29]. Since aging leads to transient failures in software systems, environment diversity, a software fault tolerance technique, can be employed proactively to prevent degradation or crashes. This involves occasionally stopping the running software, "cleaning" its internal state or its environment and restarting it. Such a technique known as "software rejuvenation" was proposed by Huang et al. [29].[1] This counteracts the aging phenomenon in a proactive manner by removing the accumulated error conditions and freeing up operating system resources. Garbage collection, flushing operating system kernel tables and reinitializing internal data structures are some examples by which the internal state or the environment of the software can be cleaned.

Software rejuvenation has been implemented in the AT&T billing applications [29]. An extreme example of a system level rejuvenation, proactive hardware reboot, has been implemented in the real-time system collecting billing data for most telephone exchanges in the United States [7]. Occasional reboot is also performed in the AT&T telecommunications switching software [3]. On reboot, called *software capacity restoration*, the service rate is restored to its peak value. On-board preventive maintenance in spacecraft has been proposed and analyzed by Tai et al. [43]. This maximizes the probability of successful mission completion by the spacecraft. These operations, called *operational redundancy*, are invoked whether or not faults exist. Proactive fault management was also recommended for the Patriot missiles' software system [36]. A warning was issued saying that a very long running time could affect the targeting accuracy. This decrease in accuracy was evidently due to error accumulation caused by software aging. The warning however failed to inform the troops how many hours "very long" was and that it would help if the computer system was switched off and on every eight hours. This exemplifies the necessity and the use of proactive fault management even in safety critical systems. More recently, rejuvenation has been implemented in cluster systems to improve performance and availability [11, 30, 47]. Two kinds of policies have been implemented taking advantage of the cluster failover feature. In the periodic policy, rejuvenation of the cluster nodes is done in a rolling fashion after every deterministic interval. In the prediction-based policy, the time to rejuvenate is estimated based on the collection and statistical analysis of system data. The implementation and analysis are described in detail in [11, 47]. A software rejuvenation feature known as process recycling has been implemented in the Microsoft IIS 5.0 web server software [48]. The popular web server software Apache implements a form of rejuvenation by killing and recreating processes after a certain numbers of requests have been served [34, 49]. Software rejuvenation is also implemented in specialized transaction processing servers [10]. Rejuvenation has also been proposed for cable and DSL modem gateways [15], in Motorola's Cable Modem Termination System [35] and in middleware applications [9] for failure detection and prevention. Automated rejuvenation strategies have been proposed in the context of self-healing and autonomic computing systems [27]. Software rejuvenation (preventive maintenance) incurs an overhead (in terms of performance, cost and downtime) which should be balanced against the loss incurred due to unexpected outage caused by a failure. Thus, an important research issue is to determine the optimal times to perform rejuvenation.

In this paper, we present two approaches for analyzing software aging and studying aging-related failures. The rest of this paper is organized as follows. In Section 2, we show how to include faults attributed to software aging into the framework of traditional classification of software faults - deterministic and transient. We also study the treatment and recovery strategies for each of the fault classes, discussing the relative advantages and disadvantages. This will help us choose the best possible recovery strategy when a fault is triggered and the system experiences a crash or a performance degradation. Section 3 describes various analytical models for software aging and to determine optimal times to perform rejuvenation. Measurement-based models are dealt with in Section 4. The implementation of a software rejuvenation agent in a major commercial server is discussed in Section 5. Section 6 describes various approaches and methods of rejuvenation and Section 7 concludes the paper with pointers to future work.

2. Classification and Treatment of Software Faults

In this section, we describe how we can include software faults attributed to software aging into Jim Gray's fault classification [22] and discuss the various fault tolerance techniques to deal with these faults in the operational phase of the software. Particular attention is given to environment diversity, explaining its need, various approaches and methods in practice.

Classification of software faults

Faults, in both hardware and software, can be classified according to their phase of creation or occurrence, system boundaries (internal or external), domain (hardware or software), phenomenological cause, intent and persistence [5]. In this section, we restrict ourselves to the classification software faults based on their phase of creation.

Some studies have suggested that since software is not a physical entity and hence not subject to transient physical phenomena (as opposed to hardware), software faults are permanent in nature [28]. Some other studies classify software faults as both permanent and transient. Gray [22] classifies software faults into *Bohrbugs* and *Heisenbugs*. Bohrbugs are essentially permanent design faults and hence almost deterministic in nature. They can be identified easily and weeded out during the testing and debugging phase (or early deployment phase) of the software life cycle. A software system with Bohrbugs is analogous to a faulty deterministic finite state machine. Heisenbugs, on the other hand, are design faults that behave in a way similar to hardware transient or intermittent faults. Their conditions of activation occur rarely or are not easily reproducible. These faults are extremely dependent on the operating environment (other programs, OS and hardware resources). Hence these faults result in transient failures, i.e., failures which may not recur if the software is restarted. Some typical situations in which Heisenbugs might surface are boundaries between various software components, improper or insufficient exception handling and interdependent timing of various events. It is for this reason that Heisenbugs are extremely difficult to identify through testing. In fact, any attempt to detect such a bug may alter the operating environment enough to change the symptoms. A software system with Heisenbugs is analogous to a faulty non-deterministic finite state machine. A mature piece of software in the operational phase, released after its development and testing stage, is more likely to experience failures caused by Heisenbugs than due to Bohrbugs. Most recent studies on failure data have reported that a large proportion of software failures are transient in nature [22, 23], caused by phenomena such as overloads or timing and exception errors [12, 42]. The study of failure data from Tandem's fault tolerant computer system indicated that 70% of the failures were transient failures, caused by race conditions and timing problems [33].

We now describe how to explicitly account for the phenomenon of software aging in Gray's classification of software faults. We designate faults attributed to software aging as *aging-related* faults. Aging-related faults can fall under Bohrbugs or Heisenbugs depending on whether the failure is deterministic (repeatable) or transient.

Figure 1 illustrates this classification of software faults. Following are examples of software faults in each of these categories. A software fault which is environment independent and hence deterministic, falls under the category of non-aging related Bohrbug (for example, a set of inputs resulting in the same failure every time). If the software bug, for example, is related to the arrival order of messages to a process, it is classified as a non-aging related Heisenbug. Reorder of messages and replay might result in the system working correctly. A bug causing a gradual resource exhaustion deterministically every time is classified as an aging-related Bohrbug. A bug causing an unknown resource leak during rare instances which are difficult to reproduce could be classified as an aging-related Heisenbug.

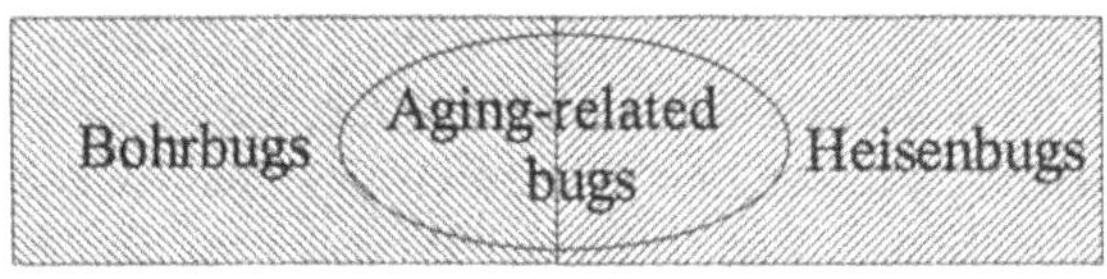

Figure 1. Venn diagram of software fault types

Software fault tolerance techniques

Design diversity [4] has been advocated as a technique for software fault tolerance. The design diversity approach was developed mainly to deal with Bohrbugs. It relies on the assumption of independence between multiple variants of software. However, as some studies have shown, this assumption may not always be valid [32]. Design diversity can also be used to treat Heisenbugs. Since there are multiple versions of software operating, it not likely that all of them will experience the same transient failure. One of the disadvantages of design diversity is the high cost involved in developing multiple variants of software.

Data diversity [2] can work well with Bohrbugs and is less expensive to implement than design diversity. To some extent, data diversity can also deal with Heisenbugs since different input data is presented and by definition, these bugs are non-deterministic and non-repeatable.

Environment diversity is the simplest technique for software fault tolerance and it effectively deals with Heisenbugs and aging-related bugs. Although this technique has been used for long in an *ad hoc* manner, only recently has it gained recognition and importance. Having its basis on the observation that most software failures are transient in nature, environment diversity utilizes reexecuting the software in a different environment [31].

Adams [1] has proposed restarting the system as the best approach to masking software faults. Environment diversity, a generalization of restart, has been proposed in [28, 31] as a cheap but effective technique for fault tolerance in software. Transient faults typically occur in computer systems due to design faults in software which result in unacceptable and erroneous states in the OS environment. Therefore, environment diversity attempts to provide a new or modified operating environment for the running software. Usually, this is done at the instance of a failure in the software. When the software fails, it is restarted in a different, error-free OS environment state which is achieved by some clean up operations. Examples of environment diversity techniques include retry operation, restart application and rebooting the node. The retry and restart operations can be done on the same node or on another spare (cold/warm/hot) node.

Tandem's fault tolerant computer system [33] is based on the *process pair* approach. It was noted that many application failures did not recur once the application was restarted on the second processor. This was due to the fact that the second processor provided a different environment which did not trigger the same error conditions which led to the failure of the application on the first processor. Hence, in this case (as well as in Avaya's SwiFT [21]), hardware redundancy coupled with software replication[2] was used to tolerate most of the software faults.

The basic observation in all these transient failures is that the same error condition is unlikely to occur if the software is reexecuted in a different environment. For aging-related bugs, environment diversity can be particularly effective if utilized proactively in the form of software rejuvenation.

3. Analytic Models for Software Rejuvenation

The aim of the analytic modeling is to determine optimal times to perform rejuvenation which maximize *availability* and minimize the *probability of loss* or the *response time of a transaction* (in the case of a transaction processing system). This is particularly important for business-critical applications for which adequate response time can be as important as system uptime. The analysis is done for different kinds of software systems exhibiting varied failure/aging characteristics.

The accuracy of a modeling based approach is determined by the assumptions made in capturing aging. In [16–18, 29, 43] only the failures causing unavailability of the software are considered, while in [38] only a gradually decreasing service rate of a software which serves transactions is assumed. Garg et al. [19], however, consider both these effects of aging together in a single model. Models proposed in [16, 17, 29] are restricted to hypo-exponentially distributed time to failure. Those proposed in [18, 38, 43] can accommodate general distributions but only for the specific aging effect they capture. Generally distributed time to failure, as well as the service rate being an arbitrary function of time are allowed in [19]. It has been noted [42] that transient failures are partly caused by overload conditions. Only the model presented by Garg et al. [19] captures the effect of load on aging. Existing models also differ in the measures being evaluated. In [18, 43] software with a finite mission time is considered. In the [16, 17, 19, 29] measures of interest in a transaction based software intended to run forever are evaluated.

Bobbio et al.[8] present fine grained software degradation models, where one can identify the current degradation level based on the observation of a system parameter, are considered. Optimal rejuvenation policies based on a risk criterion and an alert threshold are then presented. Dohi et al. [13, 14] present software rejuvenation models based on semi-Markov processes. The models are analyzed for optimal rejuvenation strategies based on cost as well as steady-state availability. Given a sample data of failure times, statistical non-parametric algorithms based on the total time on test transform are presented to obtain the optimal rejuvenation interval.

Basic model for rejuvenation

Figure 2 shows the basic software rejuvenation model proposed by Huang et al. [29]. The software system is initially in a "robust" working state, 0. As time progresses, it eventually transits to a "failure-probable" state 1. The system is still operational in this state but can fail (move to state 2) with a non-zero probability. The system can be repaired and brought back to the initial state 0. The software system is also rejuvenated at regular intervals from the failure probable state 1 and brought back to the robust state 0.

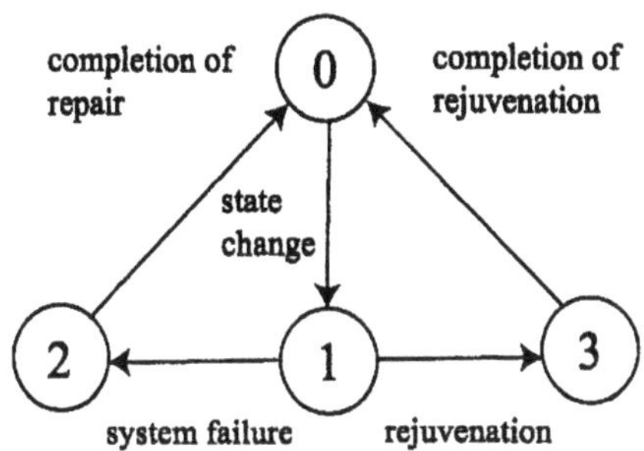

Figure 2. State transition diagram for rejuvenation

Huang et al. [29] assume that the stochastic behavior of the system can be described by a simple continuous-time Markov chain (CTMC) [45]. Let Z be the random time interval when the highly robust state changes to the failure probable state, having the exponential distribution $\Pr\{Z \leq t\} = F_0(t) = 1 - \exp(-t/\mu_0)$ $(\mu_0 > 0)$. Just after the state becomes the failure probable state, a system failure may occur with a positive probability. Without loss of generality, we assume that the random variable Z is observable during the system operation. Define the failure time X (from state 1) and the repair time Y, having the exponential distributions $\Pr\{X \leq t\} = F_f(t) = 1 - \exp(-t/\lambda_f)$ and $\Pr\{Y \leq t\} = F_a(t) = 1 - \exp(-t/\mu_a)$ $(\lambda_f > 0,\ \mu_a > 0)$. If the system failure occurs before triggering a software rejuvenation, then the repair is started immediately at that time and is completed after the random time Y elapses. Otherwise, the software rejuvenation is started. Note that the software rejuvenation cycle is measured from the time instant just after the system enters state 1. Define the distribution functions of the time to invoke the software rejuvenation and of the time to complete software rejuvenation by $F_r(t) = 1 - \exp(-t/\mu_r)$ and $F_c(t) = 1 - \exp(-t/\mu_c)$ ($\mu_c > 0$, $\mu_r > 0$), respectively. The CTMC is then analyzed and the expected system down time and the expected cost per unit time in the steady state is computed. An optimal rejuvenation interval which minimizes expected downtime (or expected cost) is obtained.

It is not difficult to introduce the periodic rejuvenation schedule and to extend the CTMC model to the general one. Dohi et al. [13, 14] developed semi-Markov models with the periodic rejuvenation and general transition distribution functions. More specifically, let Z be the random variable having the common distribution function $\Pr\{Z \leq t\} = F_0(t)$ with finite mean μ_0 (> 0). Also, let X and Y be the random variables having the common distribution functions $\Pr\{X \leq t\} = F_f(t)$ and $\Pr\{Y \leq t\} = F_a(t)$ with finite means λ_f (> 0) and μ_a (> 0), respectively. Denote the distribution function of the time to invoke the software rejuvenation and the distribution of the time to complete software rejuvenation by $F_r(t)$ and $F_c(t)$ (with mean μ_c (> 0)), respectively. After completing the repair or the rejuvenation, the software system becomes as good as new, and the software age is initiated at the beginning of the next highly robust state. Consequently, we define the time interval from the beginning of the system operation to the next one as one cycle, and the same cycle is repeated again and again. The time to software rejuvenation (the rejuvenation interval) is a constant, t_0, i.e., $F_r(t) = U(t - t_0)$, where $U(\cdot)$ is the unit step function.

The underlying stochastic process is a semi-Markov process with four regeneration states. If the sojourn times in all states are exponentially distributed, this model is the CTMC in Huang et al. [29]. Using the renewal theory [39], the steady-state system availability is computed as

$$
\begin{aligned}
A(t_0) &= \Pr\Big\{\text{software system is operative in the steady state}\Big\} \\
&= \frac{\mu_0 + \int_0^{t_0} \overline{F}_f(t)dt}{\mu_0 + \mu_a F_f(t_0) + \mu_c \overline{F}_f(t_0) + \int_0^{t_0} \overline{F}_f(t)dt} \\
&= S(t_0)/T(t_0), \qquad (1)
\end{aligned}
$$

where in general $\overline{\phi}(\cdot) = 1 - \phi(\cdot)$ The problem is to derive the optimal software rejuvenation interval t_0^* which maximizes the system availability in the steady state $A(t_0)$. We make the following assumption that the mean time to repair is strictly larger than the mean time to complete the software rejuvenation (i.e., $\mu_a > \mu_c$). This assumption is quite reasonable and intuitive. The following result gives the optimal software rejuvenation schedule for the semi-Markov model.

Assume that the failure time distribution is strictly IFR (increasing failure rate) [45]. Define the following non-linear function:

$$q(t_0) = T(t_0) - \Big\{(\mu_a - \mu_c)r_f(t_0) + 1\Big\}S(t_0), \tag{2}$$

where $r_f(t) = (dF_f(t)/dt)/\overline{F}_f(t)$ is the failure rate.

(i) If $q(0) > 0$ and $q(\infty) < 0$, then there exists a finite and unique optimal software rejuvenation schedule t_0^* $(0 < t_0^* < \infty)$ satisfying $q(t_0^*) = 0$, and the maximum system availability is

$$A(t_0^*) = \frac{1}{(\mu_a - \mu_c)r_f(t_0^*) + 1}. \tag{3}$$

(ii) If $q(0) \leq 0$, then the optimal software rejuvenation schedule is $t_0^* = 0$, *i.e.* it is optimal to start the rejuvenation just after entering the failure probable state, and the maximum system availability is $A(0) = \mu_0/(\mu_0 + \mu_c)$.

(iii) If $q(\infty) \geq 0$, then the optimal rejuvenation schedule is $t_0^* \to \infty$, *i.e.* it is optimal not to carry out the rejuvenation, and the maximum system availability is $A(\infty) = (\mu_0 + \lambda_f)/(\mu_0 + \mu_a + \lambda_f)$.

If the failure time distribution is DFR (decreasing failure rate), then the system availability $A(t_0)$ is a convex function of t_0, and the optimal rejuvenation schedule is $t_0^* = 0$ or $t_0^* \to \infty$ [13, 14].

Garg et al. [16] have developed a Markov Regenerative Stochastic Petri Net (MRSPN) model where rejuvenation is performed at deterministic intervals assuming that the failure probable state 1 is not observable.

Preventive maintenance in transactions based software systems

In [19], Garg et al. consider a transaction-based software system whose macro-states representation is presented in Figure 3. The state in which the software is available for service (albeit with decreasing service rate) is denoted as state A. After failure a recovery procedure is started. In state B the software is recovering from failure and is unavailable for service. Lastly, the software occasionally undergoes preventive maintenance (PM), denoted by state C. PM is allowed only from state A. Once recovery from failure or PM is complete, the software is reset to state A and is as good as new. From this moment, which constitutes a renewal, the whole process stochastically repeats itself.

The system consists of a server type software to which transactions arrive at a constant rate λ. Each transaction receives service for a random period. The service rate of the software is an arbitrary function measured from the

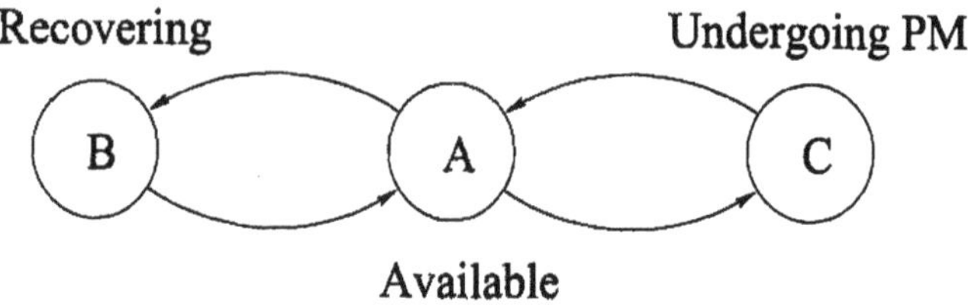

Figure 3. Macro-states representation of the software behavior

last renewal of the software (because of aging) denoted by $\mu(\cdot)$. Therefore, a transaction which starts service at time t_1, occupies the server for a time whose distribution is given by $1 - e^{-\int_{t_1}^{t} \mu(\cdot)\,dt}$. If the software is busy processing a transaction, arriving customers are queued. Total number of transactions that the software can accommodate is K (including the one being processed) and any more arriving when the queue is full are lost. The service discipline is FCFS. The software fails with a rate $\rho(\cdot)$, that is, the *CDF* of the time to failure X is given by $F_X(t) = 1 - e^{-\int_0^t \rho(\cdot)\,dt}$. Times to recover from failure Y_f and to perform PM Y_r are random variables with associated general *CDFs* F_{Y_f} and F_{Y_r} respectively. The model does not require any assumptions on the nature of F_{Y_f} and F_{Y_r}. Only the respective expectations $\gamma_f = E[Y_f]$ and $\gamma_r = E[Y_r]$ are assumed to be finite. Any transactions in the queue at the time of failure or at the time of initiation of PM are assumed to be lost. Moreover, any transactions which arrive while the software is recovering or undergoing PM are also lost.

The effect of aging in the model may be captured by using decreasing service rate and increasing failure rate, where the decrease or the increase respectively can be a function of time, instantaneous load, mean accumulated load or a combination of the above.

Two policies which can be used to determine the time to perform PM are considered. Under policy I which is purely time-based, PM is initiated after a constant time δ has elapsed since it was started (or restarted). Under policy II, which is based on instantaneous load and time, a constant waiting period δ must elapse before PM is attempted. After this time PM is initiated if and only if there are no transactions in the system. Otherwise, the software waits until the queue is empty upon which PM is initiated. The actual PM interval under Policy II is determined by the sum of PM wait δ and the time it takes for the queue to get empty from that point onwards B. Since the latter quantity is dependent on system parameters and can not be controlled, the actual PM interval has a range $[\delta, \infty)$.

Given the above behavioral model the following measures are derived for each policy: steady state availability of the software A_{SS}, long run probability of loss of a transaction P_{loss}, and expected response time of a transaction given that it is successfully served T_{res}. The goal is to determine optimal values of δ (PM interval under policy I and PM wait under policy II) based on the constraints on one or more of these measures.

According to the model described above at any time t the software can be in any one of three states: up and available for service (state A), recovering from a failure (state B) or undergoing PM (state C). Let $\{Z(t), t \geq 0\}$ be a stochastic process which represents the state of the software at time t. Further, let the sequence of random variables $S_i, i > 0$ represent the times at which transitions among different states take place. Since the entrance times S_i constitute renewal points $\{Z(S_i), i > 0\}$ is an embedded discrete time Markov chain (DTMC) with a transition probability matrix P given by:

$$\mathbf{P} = \begin{bmatrix} 0 & P_{AB} & P_{AC} \\ 1 & 0 & 0 \\ 1 & 0 & 0 \end{bmatrix}. \tag{4}$$

The steady state probability π_i of the DTMC being in state $i, i \in \{A, B, C\}$ is:

$$\pi = [\pi_A, \pi_B, \pi_C] = \left[\frac{1}{2}, \frac{1}{2}P_{AB}, \frac{1}{2}P_{AC}\right]. \tag{5}$$

The software behavior is modeled via the stochastic process $\{(Z(t), N(t)), t \geq 0\}$. If $Z(t) = A$, then $N(t) \in \{0, 1, \ldots, K\}$ as the queue can accommodate up to K transactions. If $Z(t) \in \{B, C\}$, then $N(t) = 0$, since by assumption all transactions arriving while the software is either recovering or undergoing PM are lost. Further, the transactions already in the queue at the transition instant are also discarded. It can be shown that the process $\{(Z(t), N(t)), t \geq 0\}$ is a Markov regenerative process (MRGP). Transition to state A from either B or C constitutes a regeneration instant.

Let U be a random variable denoting the sojourn time in state A, and denote its expectation by $E[U]$. Expected sojourn times of the MRGP in states B and C are already defined to be γ_f and γ_r. The steady state availability is obtained using the standard formulae from MRGP theory:

$$A_{SS} = Pr\{\textit{software is in state } A\}$$

$$= \frac{\pi_A E[U]}{\pi_B \gamma_f + \pi_C \gamma_r + \pi_A E[U]}. \tag{6}$$

The probability that a transaction is lost is defined as the ratio of expected number of transactions which are lost in an interval to the expected total number of transactions which arrive during that interval. Since the evolution of

$\{Z(t), N(t)), t > 0\}$ in the intervals comprising of successive visits to state A is stochastically identical it suffices to consider just one such interval. The number of transactions lost is given by the summation of three quantities: (1) transactions in the queue when the system is exiting state A because of the failure or initiation of PM (2) transactions that arrive while failure recovery or PM is in progress and (3) transactions that are disregarded due to the buffer being full. The last quantity is of special significance since the probability of buffer being full will increase due to the degrading service rate. It follows that the probability of loss is given by

$$P_{loss} = \frac{\pi_A E[N_l] + \lambda \left(\pi_B \gamma_f + \pi_C \gamma_r + \pi_A \int_0^\infty p_K(t)dt \right)}{\lambda \left(\pi_B \gamma_f + \pi_C \gamma_r + \pi_A E[U] \right)} \tag{7}$$

where $E[N_l]$ is the expected number of transactions in the buffer when the system is exiting state A. Equation 7 is valid only for policy II. Under policy I sojourn time in state A is limited by δ, so the upper limit in the integral $\int_0^\infty p_K(t)dt$ is δ instead of ∞.

Next an upper bound on the mean response time of a transaction given that it is successfully served, T_{res}, is derived. The mean number of transactions, denoted by E, which are accepted for service while the software is in state A is given by the mean number of transactions which are not accepted due to the buffer being full, subtracted from the mean total number of transactions which arrive while the software is in state A, that is, $E = \lambda \left[E[U] - \int_{t=0}^\infty p_K(t)dt \right]$. Out of these transactions, on the average, $E[N_l]$ are discarded later because of failure or initiation of PM. Therefore, the mean number of transactions which actually receive service given that they were accepted is given by $E - E[N_l]$. The mean total amount of time the transactions spent in the system while the software is in state A is $W = \int_{t=0}^\infty \sum_i i p_i(t)\ dt$. This time is composed of the mean time spent by the transactions which were served as well as those which were discarded, denoted as W_S and W_D, respectively. Therefore, $W = W_S + W_D$. The response time we are interested in is given by $T_{res} = W_S/(E - E[N_l])$, which is upper bounded by $T_{res} < \frac{W}{E - E[N_l]}$.

$p_i(t)$ is the probability that there are i transactions queued for service, which is also the probability of being in state i of the subordinated process at time t. $p_{i'}(t)$ is the probability that the system failed when there were i transactions queued for service. These transient probabilities for both policies can be obtained by solving the systems of forward differential-difference equations given in [19]. In general they do not have a closed-form analytical solution and must be evaluated numerically. Once these probabilities are obtained, the rest of the quantities P_{AB}, P_{AC}, $E[U]$ and $E[N_l]$ can be easily computed [19] and then used to obtain the steady state availability A_{SS}, the probability of transaction lost P_{loss} and the upper bound on the response time of a transaction T_{res}.

Examples are presented to illustrate the usefulness of the presented model in determining the optimum value of δ (PM interval in the case of policy I and PM wait in the case of policy II). First, the service rate and failure rate are assumed to be functions of real time, where $\rho(t)$ is defined to be the hazard function of Weibull distribution, while $\mu(t)$ is defined to be a monotone non-increasing function that approximates the service degradation. Figure 4 shows A_{ss} and P_{loss} for both policies plotted against δ for different values of the mean time to perform PM γ_r. Under both policies, it can be seen that for any

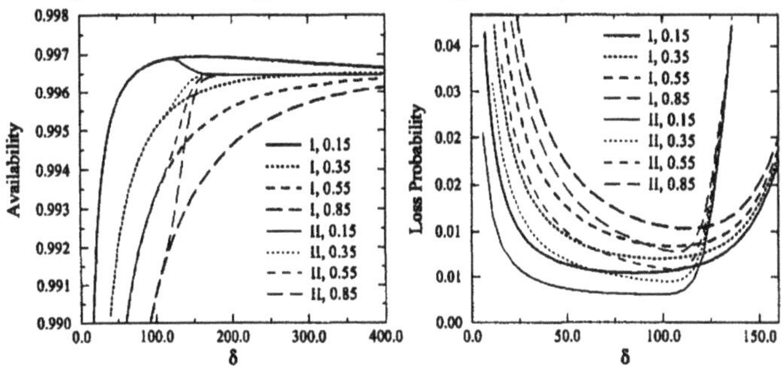

Figure 4. Results for experiment 1

particular value of δ, higher the value of γ_r, lower is the availability and higher is the corresponding loss probability. It can also be observed that the value of δ which minimizes probability of loss is much lower than the one which maximizes availability. In fact, the probability of loss becomes very high at values of δ which maximize availability. For any specific value of γ_r, policy II results in a lower minima in loss probability than that achieved under policy I. Therefore, if the objective is to minimize long run probability of loss, such as in the case of telecommunication switching software, policy II always fares better than policy I.

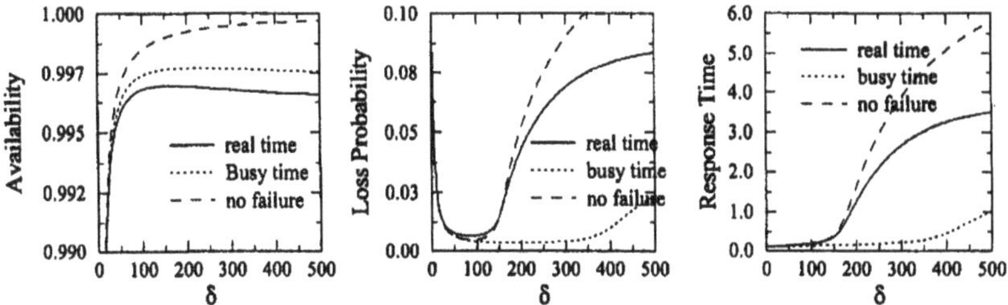

Figure 5. Results of experiment 2

Figure 5 shows A_{SS}, P_{loss} and upper bound on T_{res} plotted against δ under policy I. Each of the figures contains three curves. $\mu(\cdot)$ and $\rho(\cdot)$ in the solid curve are functions of real time $\mu(t)$ and $\rho(t)$, whereas in the dotted curve they are functions (with the same parameters) of the mean total processing time $\mu(L(t))$ and $\rho(L(t))$. The dashed curve represents a third system in which no crash/hang failures occur $\rho(\cdot) = 0$, but service degradation is present with $\mu(\cdot) = \mu(t)$. This experiment illustrates the importance of making the right assumptions in capturing aging because as seen from the figure, depending on the forms chosen for $\mu(\cdot)$ and $\rho(\cdot)$, the measures vary in a wide range.

Software rejuvenation in a cluster system

Software rejuvenation has been applied to cluster systems [11, 47]. This is a novel application, which significantly improves cluster system availability and productivity. The Stochastic Reward Net (SRN) model of a cluster system employing simple time-based rejuvenation is shown in Figure 6. The cluster consists of n nodes which are initially in a "robust" working state, P_{up}. The aging process is modeled as a 2-stage hypo-exponential distribution (increasing failure rate) [45] with transitions T_{fprob} and $T_{noderepair}$. Place P_{fprob} represents a "failure-probable" state in which the nodes are still operational. The nodes then can eventually transit to the fail state, $P_{nodefail1}$. A node can be repaired through the transition $T_{noderepair}$, with a coverage c. In addition to individual node failures, there is also a common-mode failure (transition T_{cmode}). The system is also considered down when there are a ($a \leq n$) individual node failures. The system is repaired through the transition $T_{sysrepair}$.

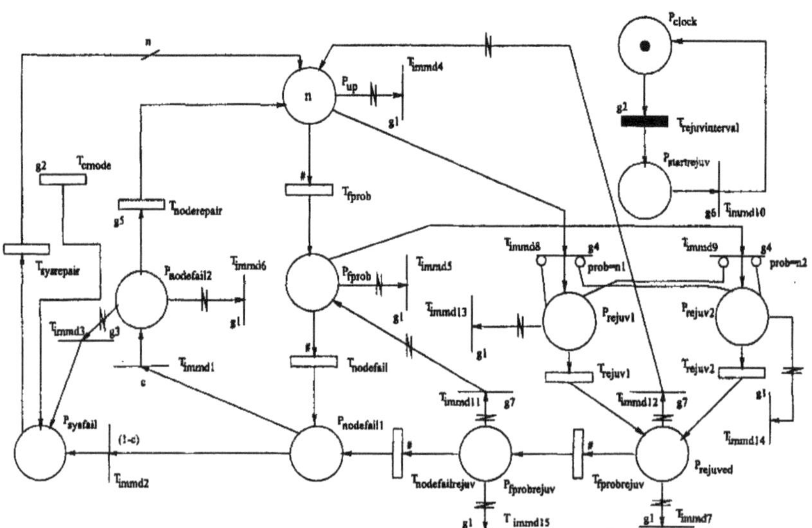

Figure 6. SRN model of a cluster system employing simple time-based rejuvenation

classified as an aging-related Bohrbug. A bug causing an unknown resource leak during rare instances which are difficult to reproduce could be classified as an aging-related Heisenbug.

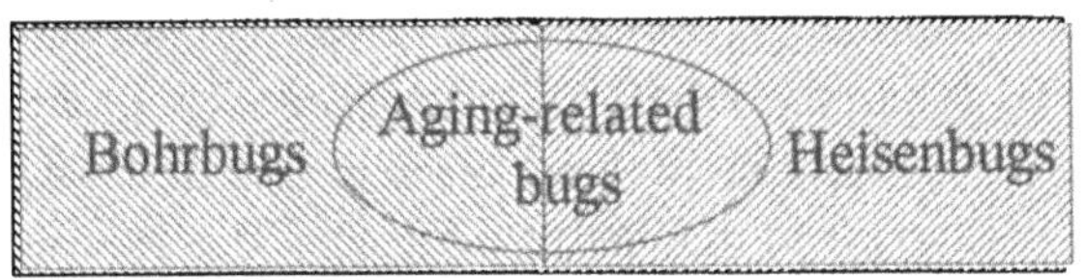

Figure 1. Venn diagram of software fault types

Software fault tolerance techniques

Design diversity [4] has been advocated as a technique for software fault tolerance. The design diversity approach was developed mainly to deal with Bohrbugs. It relies on the assumption of independence between multiple variants of software. However, as some studies have shown, this assumption may not always be valid [32]. Design diversity can also be used to treat Heisenbugs. Since there are multiple versions of software operating, it not likely that all of them will experience the same transient failure. One of the disadvantages of design diversity is the high cost involved in developing multiple variants of software.

Data diversity [2] can work well with Bohrbugs and is less expensive to implement than design diversity. To some extent, data diversity can also deal with Heisenbugs since different input data is presented and by definition, these bugs are non-deterministic and non-repeatable.

Environment diversity is the simplest technique for software fault tolerance and it effectively deals with Heisenbugs and aging-related bugs. Although this technique has been used for long in an *ad hoc* manner, only recently has it gained recognition and importance. Having its basis on the observation that most software failures are transient in nature, environment diversity utilizes reexecuting the software in a different environment [31].

Adams [1] has proposed restarting the system as the best approach to masking software faults. Environment diversity, a generalization of restart, has been proposed in [28, 31] as a cheap but effective technique for fault tolerance in software. Transient faults typically occur in computer systems due to design faults in software which result in unacceptable and erroneous states in the OS environment. Therefore, environment diversity attempts to provide a new or modified operating environment for the running software. Usually, this is done at the instance of a failure in the software. When the software fails, it is restarted in a different, error-free OS environment state which is achieved by some clean up operations. Examples of environment diversity

For the analyses, the following values are assumed. The mean times spent in places P_{up} and P_{fprob} are 240 hrs and 720 hrs respectively. The mean times to repair a node, to rejuvenate a node and to repair the system are 30 min, 10 min and 4 hrs respectively. In this analysis, the common-mode failure is disabled and node failure coverage is assumed to be perfect. All the models were solved using the SPNP (Stochastic Petri Net Package) tool [26]. The measures computed were expected unavailability and the expected cost incurred over a fixed time interval. It is assumed that the cost incurred due to node rejuvenation is much less than the cost of a node or system failure since rejuvenation can be done at predetermined or scheduled times. In our analysis, we fix the value for $cost_{nodefail}$ at \$5,000/hr, the $cost_{rejuv}$ at \$250/hr. The value of $cost_{sysfail}$ is computed as the number of nodes, n, times $cost_{nodefail}$.

Figure 8 shows the plots for an 8/1 configuration (8 nodes including 1 spare) system employing simple time-based rejuvenation. The upper plot and lower plots show the expected cost incurred and the expected downtime (in hours) respectively in a given time interval, versus rejuvenation interval (time between successive rejuvenation) in hours. If the rejuvenation interval is close to zero, the system is always rejuvenating and thus incurs high cost and downtime. As the rejuvenation interval increases, both expected unavailability and cost incurred decrease and reach an optimum value. If the rejuvenation interval goes beyond the optimal value, the system failure has more influence on these measures than rejuvenation. The analysis was repeated for 2/1, 8/2, 16/1 and 16/2 configurations. For time-based rejuvenation, the optimal rejuvenation interval was 100 hours for the 1-spare clusters, and approximately 1 hour for the 2-spare clusters. In our analysis of condition-based rejuvenation, we assumed 90% prediction coverage. For systems that have one spare, time-based rejuvenation can reduce downtime by 26% relative to no rejuvenation. Condition-based rejuvenation does somewhat better, reducing downtime by 62% relative to no rejuvenation. However, when the system can tolerate more than one failure at a time, downtime is reduced by 98% to 95% via time-based rejuvenation, compared to a mere 85% for condition-based rejuvenation.

4. Measurement Based Models for Software Rejuvenation

While all the analytical models are based on the assumption that the rate of software aging is known, in the measurement based approach, the basic idea is to monitor and collect data on the attributes responsible for determining the health of the executing software. The data is then analyzed to obtain predictions about possible impending failures due to resource exhaustion.

In this section we describe the measurement-based approach for detection and validation of the existence of software aging. The basic idea is to periodically monitor and collect data on the attributes responsible for determining the

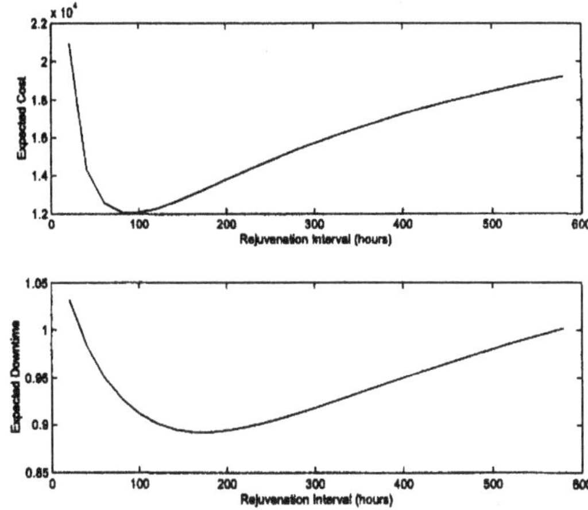

Figure 8. Results for an 8/1 cluster system employing time-based rejuvenation

health of the executing software, in this case the UNIX operating system. Garg et al. [20] propose a methodology for detection and estimation of aging in the UNIX operating system. An SNMP-based distributed resource monitoring tool was used to collect operating system resource usage and system activity data from nine heterogeneous UNIX workstations connected by an Ethernet LAN at the Department of Electrical and Computer Engineering at Duke University. A central monitoring station runs the manager program which sends *get* requests periodically to each of the agent programs running on the monitored workstations. The agent programs in turn obtain data for the manager from their respective machines by executing various standard UNIX utility programs like *pstat, iostat* and *vmstat.* For quantifying the effect of aging in operating system resources, the metric *Estimated time to exhaustion* is proposed. The earlier work [20] uses a purely time-based approach to estimate resource exhaustion times, whereas the the work presented in [46] takes into account the current system workload as well.

A methodology based on time-series analysis to detect and estimate resource exhaustion times due to software aging in a web server while subjecting it to an artificial workload, is proposed in [34]. Avritzer and Weyuker [3] monitor production traffic data of a large telecommunication system and describe a rejuvenation strategy which increases system availability and minimizes packet loss. Cassidy et al. [10] have developed an approach to rejuvenation for large online transaction processing servers. They monitor various system parameters over a period of time. Using pattern recognition methods, they come to the conclusion that 13 of those parameters deviate from normal behavior just prior to a crash, providing sufficient warning to initiate rejuvenation.

Time-based estimation

In the time-based estimation method presented by Garg et al. [20], data was collected from the UNIX machines at intervals of 15 minutes for about 53 days. Time-ordered values for each monitored object are obtained, constituting a time series for that object. The objective is to detect aging or a long term trend (increasing or decreasing) in the values. Only results for the data collected from the machine *Rossby* are discussed here.

First, the trends in operating system resource usage and system activity are detected using *smoothing* of observed data by *robust locally weighted regression*, proposed by Cleveland [20]. This technique is used to get the global trend between outages by removing the local variations. Then, the slope of the trend is estimated in order to do prediction. Figure 9 shows the smoothed data superimposed on the original data points from the time series of objects for Rossby. Amount of *real memory free* (plot 1) shows an overall decrease, whereas *file table size* (plot 2) shows an increase. Plots of some other resources not discussed here also showed an increase or decrease. This corroborates the hypothesis of aging with respect to various objects.

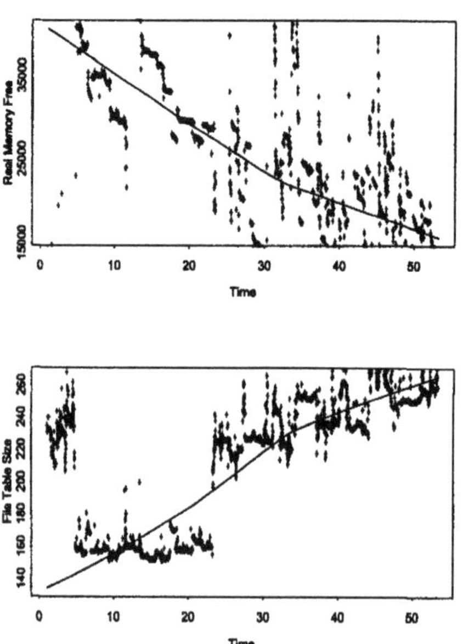

Figure 9. Non-parametric regression smoothing for Rossby objects

The seasonal Kendall test [20] was applied to each of these time series to detect the presence of any global trends at a significance level, α, of 0.05. With Z_α=1.96, all values are such that the null hypothesis (H_0) that no trend

Table 1. Estimated slope and time to exhaustion for Rossby, Velum and Jefferson objects

Resource Name	*Initial Value*	*Max Value*	*Sen's Slope Estimation*	*95% Confidence Interval*	*Estimated Time to Exh. (days)*
Rossby					
Real Memory Free	40814.17	84980	-252.00	-287.75 : -219.34	161.96
File Table Size	220	7110	1.33	1.30 : 1.39	5167.50
Process Table Size	57	2058	0.43	0.41 : 0.45	4602.30
Used Swap Space	39372	312724	267.08	220.09 : 295.50	1023.50
Jefferson					
Real Memory Free	67638.54	114608	-972.00	-1006.81 : -939.08	69.59
File Table Size	268.83	7110	1.33	1.30 : 1.38	5144.36
Process Table Size	67.18	2058	0.30	0.29 : 0.31	6696.41
Used Swap Space	47148.02	524156	577.44	545.69 : 603.14	826.07

exists is rejected for the variables considered. Given that a global trend is present and that its slope is calculated for a particular resource, the time at which the resource will be exhausted because of aging only, is estimated. Table 1 refers to several objects on Rossby and lists an estimate of the slope (change per day) of the trend obtained by applying Sen's slope estimate for data with seasons [20]. The values for real memory and swap space are in Kilobytes. A negative slope, as in the case of *real memory*, indicates a decreasing trend, whereas a positive slope, as in the case of *file table size*, is indicative of an increasing trend. Given the slope estimate, the table lists the estimated time to failure of the machine due to aging only with respect to this particular resource. The calculation of the time to exhaustion is done by using the standard linear approximation $y = mx + c$.

A comparative effect of aging on different system resources can be obtained from the above estimates. Overall, it was found that *file table size* and *process table size* are not as important as *used swap space* and *real memory free* since they have a very small slope and high estimated times to failure due to exhaustion. Based on such comparisons, we can identify important resources to monitor and manage in order to deal with aging related software failures. For example, the resource *used swap space* has the highest slope and *real memory free* has the second highest slope. However, *real memory free* has a lower time to exhaustion than *used swap space*.

Time and workload-based estimation

The method discussed in the previous subsection assumes that accumulated use of a resource over a time period depends only on the elapsed time. However, it is intuitive that the rate at which a resource is consumed is dependent on the current workload. In this subsection, we discuss a measurement-based model to estimate the rate of exhaustion of operating system resources as a function of both time and the system workload [46]. The SNMP-based distributed resource monitoring tool described previously was used for collecting operating system resource usage and system activity parameters (at 10 min intervals) for over 3 months. Only results for the data collected from the machine Rossby are discussed here. The *longest* stretch of sample points in which no reboots or failures occurred were used for building the model. A semi-Markov reward model [44] is constructed using the data. First different workload states are identified using statistical cluster analysis and a state-space model is constructed. Corresponding to each resource, a reward function based on the rate of resource exhaustion in the different states is then defined. Finally the model is solved to obtain trends and the estimated exhaustion rates and time to exhaustion for the resources.

The following variables were chosen to characterize the system workload - *cpuContextSwitch, sysCall, pageIn,* and *pageOut*. *Hartigan's k-means clustering algorithm* [25] was used for partitioning the data points into clusters based on workload. The statistics for the eleven workload clusters obtained are shown in Table 2. Clusters whose centroids were relatively close to each other and those with a small percentage of data points in them, were merged to simplify computations. The resulting clusters are $W_1 = \{1,2,3\}$, $W_2 = \{4,5\}$, $W_3 = \{6\}$, $W_4 = \{7\}$, $W_5 = \{8\}$, $W_6 = \{9\}$, $W_7 = \{10\}$ and $W_8 = \{11\}$.

Table 2. Statistics for the workload clusters

No.	Cluster Center				% of
	cpuConSw	sysCall	pgOut	pgIn	pts.
1	48405.16	94194.66	5.16	677.83	0.98
2	54184.56	122229.68	5.39	81.41	0.76
3	34059.61	193927.00	0.02	136.73	0.93
4	20479.21	45811.71	0.53	243.40	1.89
5	21361.38	37027.41	0.26	12.64	7.17
6	15734.65	54056.27	0.27	14.45	6.55
7	37825.76	40912.18	0.91	12.21	11.77
8	11013.22	38682.46	0.03	10.43	42.87
9	67290.83	37246.76	7.58	19.88	4.93
10	10003.94	32067.20	0.01	9.61	21.23
11	197934.42	67822.48	415.71	184.38	0.93

Transition probabilities from one state to another were computed from data, resulting in transition probability matrix P of the embedded discrete time

Markov chain The sojourn time distribution for each of the workload states was fitted to either 2-stage hyper-exponential or 2-stage hypo-exponential distribution functions. The fitted distributions were tested using the Kolmogorov-Smirnov test at a significance level of 0.01.

Two resources, *usedSwapSpace* and *realMemoryFree*, are considered for the analysis, since the previous time-based analysis suggested that they are critical resources. For each resource, the reward function is defined as the rate of corresponding resource exhaustion in different states. The true slope (rate of increase/decrease) of a resource at every workload state is estimated by using Sen's non-parametric method [46]. Table 3 shows the slopes with 95% confidence intervals.

It was observed that slopes in a given workload state for a particular resource during different visits to that state are almost the same. Further, the slopes across different workload states are different and generally higher the system activity, higher is the resource utilization. This validates the assumption that resource usage *does* depend on the system workload and the rates of exhaustion vary with workload changes. It can also be observed from Table 3 that the slopes for *usedSwapSpace* in all the workload states are non-negative, and the slopes for *realMemoryFree* are non-positive in all the workload states except in one. It follows that *usedSwapSpace* increases whereas *realMemoryFree* decreases over time which validates the software aging phenomenon.

Table 3. Slope estimates (in KB/10 min)

State	usedSwapSpace		realMemoryFree	
	Slope Est.	95 % Conf. Interval	Slope Est.	95 % Conf. Interval
W_1	119.3	5.5 - 222.4	-133.7	-137.7 - -133.3
W_2	0.57	0.40 - 0.71	-1.47	-1.78 - -1.09
W_3	0.76	0.73 - 0.80	-1.43	-2.50 - -0.62
W_4	0.57	0.00 - 0.69	-1.23	-1.67 - -0.80
W_5	0.78	0.75 - 0.80	0.00	-5.65 - 6.00
W_6	0.81	0.64 - 1.00	-1.14	-1.40 - -0.88
W_7	0.00	0.00 - 0.00	0.00	0.00 - 0.00
W_8	91.8	72.4 - 111.0	91.7	-369.9 - 475.2

The semi-Markov reward model was solved using the SHARPE tool [40] developed by researchers at Duke University. The slope for the workload-based estimation is computed as the expected reward rate in steady state from the model. The times to resource exhaustion is computed as the job completion time (mean time to accumulate x amount of reward) of the Markov reward model. Table 4 gives the estimates for the slope and time to exhaustion for

Table 4. Estimates for slope (in KB/10 min) and time to exhaustion (in days) for *usedSwapSpace* and *realMemoryFree*

Method of Estimation	usedSwapSpace			realMemoryFree		
	Slope Estimate	95 % Conf. Interval	Est. Time to Exh.	Slope Estimate	95 % Conf. Interval	Est. Time to Exh.
Time based	0.787	0.786 - 0.788	2276.46	-2.806	-3.026 - -2.630	60.81
Workload based	4.647	1.191 - 7.746	490.50	-4.1435	-9.968 - 2.592	41.38

usedSwapSpace and *realMemoryFree.* It can be seen that workload based estimations gave a lower time to resource exhaustion than those computed using time based estimations. Since the machine failures due to resource exhaustion were observed much before the times to resource exhaustion estimated by the time based method, it follows that the workload based approach results in better estimations.

Time Series and ARMA Models

In this section, a measurement-based approach based on time-series analysis to detect software aging and to estimate resource exhaustion times due to aging in a web server is described [34]. The experiments are conducted on an Apache web server running on the Linux platform. Before carrying out other experiments, the capacity of the web server is determined so that the appropriate workload to use in the experiments can be decided. The capacity of the web server was found to be around 390 requests/sec. In the next part of the experiment, the web server was run without rejuvenation for a long time until the performance degraded or until the server crashed. The requests were generated by *httperf* [37] to get one of five specified files from the server of sizes 500 bytes, 5KB, 50KB, 500KB and 5MB. The corresponding probabilities that a given file is requested are: 0.35, 0.5, 0.14, 0.009 and 0.001, respectively. During the period of running, the performance measured by the workload generator and system parameters collected by the Linux system monitoring tool, *procmon*, were recorded.

The first data set was collected in a 7-day period with a connection rate of 350 requests/sec. The second set was collected in a 25-day period with connection rate of 400 request/sec. During the experiment, we recorded more than 100 parameters, but for our modeling purposes, six representative parameters pertaining to system resources were selected (Table 5). In addition to the six system status parameters, the response time of the web server, recorded by

Table 5. Analyzed parameters and their physical meaning

Parameter	Physical meaning
PhysicalMemoryFree	Free physical memory
SwapSpaceUsed	Used swap space
LoadAvg5Min	Average CPU load in the last five minutes
NumberDiskRequests	Number of disk requests in the last five minutes
PageOutCounter	Number of pages paged out in the last five minutes
NewProcesses	Number of newly spawned processes in the last five minutes
ResponseTime	The interval from the time *httperf* sends out the first byte of request until it receives the first byte of reply

Table 6. Estimated slope of parameters

Data Set	Parameter	Slope	95% confidence interval
I	response time	0.027 ms/hour	(0.019, 0.036) ms/hour
	free physical memory	-88.472 KB/hour	(-93.337, -83.607) KB/hour
	used swap space	29.976 KB/hour	(29.290, 30.662) KB/hour
II	response time	0.063 ms/hour	(0.057, 0.068) ms/hour
	free physical memory	15.183 KB/hour	(14.094, 16.271) KB/hour
	used swap space	7.841 KB/hour	(7.658, 8.025) KB/hour

httperf on the client machine, is also included in the model as a measure of performance of the web server.

After collecting the data, it needs to be analyzed to determine if software aging exists, which is indicated by degradation in performance of the web server and/or exhaustion of system resources. The performance of the web server is measured by response time which is the interval from the time a client sends out the first byte of request until it receives the first byte of reply. Figure 10(a) shows the plot of the response time in data set I. To identify the trend, the range of y-axis is magnified (Figure 10(b)). The response time becomes longer with the running time of the experiment. To determine whether the trend is just a fluctuation due to noise or an essential characteristic of the data, a linear regression model is used to fit the time series of the response time. The least squares solution is $r = 15.5655 + 0.027t$, where r is response time in milliseconds, t is the time from the beginning of the experiment. The 95% confidence interval for the slope is $(0.019, 0.036)$ ms/hour. Since the slope is positive, it can be concluded that the performance of the web server is degrading.

Performing the same analysis to the parameters related to system resources, it was found that the available resources are decreasing. Estimated slopes of some of the parameters using linear regression model are listed in Table 6.

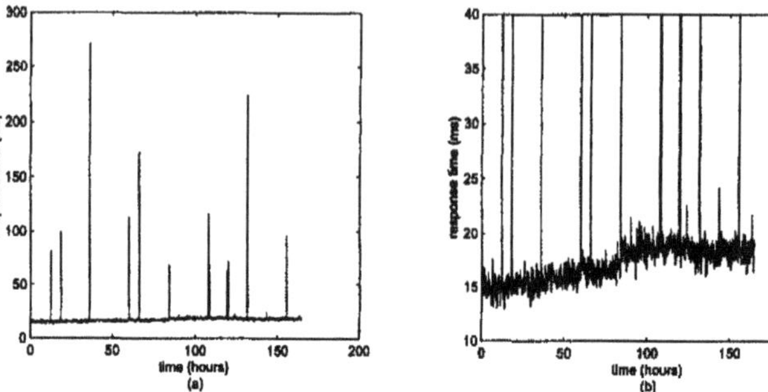

Figure 10. Response time of the web server

The parameters in data set II are used as the modeling objects since the duration of data set II is longer than that of data set I. In this case, there are seven parameters to be analyzed. The analysis can be done using two different approaches: (1) building a univariate model for each of the outputs or, 2) building only one multivariate model with seven outputs. In this case, seven univariate models are built and then combined into a single multivariate model. First, the parameters are determined to determine their characteristics and build an appropriate model with one output and four inputs for each parameter - connection rate, linear trend, periodic series with a period of one week, and periodic series with a period of one day. The autocorrelation function (ACF) and the partial autocorrelation function (PACF) for the output are computed. The ACF and the PACF help us decide the appropriate model for the data [41]. For example, from the ACF and PACF of *used swap space* it can be determined that an autoregressive model of order 1 [AR(1)] is suitable for this data series. Adding the inputs to the AR(1) model, we get the ARX(1) model for used swap space:

$$Y_t = aY_{t-1} + b_1X_t + b_2L_t + b_3W_t + b_4D_t, \tag{8}$$

where Y_t is the used swap space, X_t is the connection rate, L_t is the time step which represents the linear trend, W_t is the weekly periodic series and D_t is the daily periodic series. After observing the ACF and PACF of all the parameters, we find that all of the PACFs cut off at certain lags. So all the multiple input single output (MISO) models are of the ARX type, only with different orders. This gives great convenience in combining them into a multiple input multiple output (MIMO) ARX model which is described later.

In order to combine the MISO ARX models into a MIMO ARX model, we need to choose the order between different outputs. This is done by inspecting the CCF (cross-correlation function) between each pair of the outputs to find out the leading relationship between them. If the CCF between parameter A and B gets its peak value at a positive lag k, we say that A leads B by k steps and it might be possible to use A to predict B. In our analysis, there are 21

CCFs that need to be computed. And in order to reduce the complexity, we only use the CCFs that exhibit obvious leading relationship with lags less than 10 steps. The next step after determination of the orders is to estimate the coefficients of the model by the least squares method. The first half of the data is used to estimate the parameters and the rest of the data is then used to verify the model. Figure 11 shows the two-hour-ahead (24-step) predicted used swap

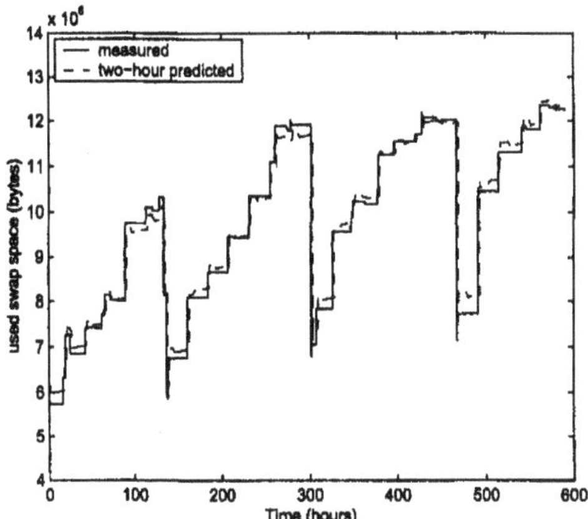

Figure 11. Measured and two-hour ahead predicted used swap space

space which is computed using the established model and the data measured up to two hours before the predicted time point. From the plots, we can see that the predicted values are very close to the measured values.

Explicit link between resource leaks and software aging

In [6] a model is developed to account for the gradual loss of system resources, especially, the memory resource. In a client-server system, for example, every client process issues memory requests at varying points in time. An amount of memory is granted to each new request (when there is enough memory available), held by the requesting process for a period of time, and presumably released back to the system resource reservoir when it is no longer in use. A memory leak occurs when the amount of allocated memory is not fully released. The available memory space is gradually reduced as such resource leaks accumulate over time. As a consequence, a resource request that would have been granted in the leak-less situation may not be granted when the system suffers from memory resource leaks. This model accommodates both the leak-free case and the leak-present case. The model relates system degradation to resource requests, releases or resource holding intervals and memory leaks. These quantities can be monitored and modeled directly from obtainable data measurements [34].

An operating software system is modeled as a continuous time Markov chain (CTMC). The ideal, leak-free case is shown in Figure 12.

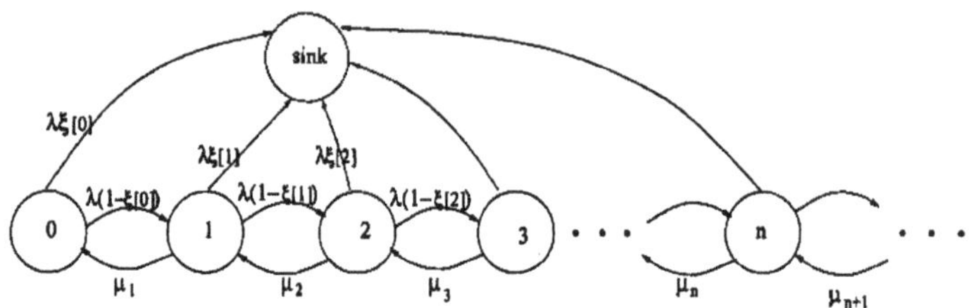

Figure 12. Leak-free model of a system

Denote by M the initial total amount of available memory. The memory unit is application-specific. The system is in workload state k, $k \geq 0$, when there are k independent processes holding a portion of the resource. The total number of states is practically finite. It is assumed that the memory requests are independent of each other and arrive from a Poisson process with rate λ. A request is granted when sufficient memory is available, else the system is considered to have failed. In other words, each incoming request may cause the system to transit to the sink state when it asks for more memory than the available amount. Denote by $\xi[k]$ the conditional probability that the system fails in state k upon the arrival of a new request. The amount of each memory request is modeled as a continuous random variable with the density function $g(x)$. The allocated resource is held for a random period of time, which is dependent upon the processing or service rate and determines the resource release rate. When the holding time per request is exponentially distributed with rate μ, the release rate μ_k at state is equal to $k\,\mu$. Here, the time unit is also application-specific.

Provided with the specification of the leak-free model, one can derive system failure rate $h(t)$ and the system reliability $R(t) = 1 - \pi_{\text{sink}}(t) = \sum_k \pi_k(t)$. Conversely, given a specified requirement on system reliability, the model can be used to derive a lower bound on the total amount M of system resource to meet this requirement.

In a system with a leak present, the conditional probability that the system transits to the sink state from state k upon a new request becomes leak dependent and hence time dependent. The memory leak function $\ell(t)$ is related to the system failure via the variable of available resource amount. The variable is bounded from above by the total amount M of the system resource. The failure rate of a leak-present system with the initial amount M of available memory, is denoted by $h(t, M)$.

5. Implementation of a Software Rejuvenation Agent

The first commercial version of a software rejuvenation agent (SRA) for the IBM xSeries line of cluster servers has been implemented with our collaboration [11, 30, 47]. The SRA was designed to monitor consumable resources, estimate the time to exhaustion of those resources, and generate alerts to the management infrastructure when the time to exhaustion is less than a user-defined notification horizon. For Windows operating systems, the SRA acquires data on exhaustible resources by reading the registry performance counters and collecting parameters such as available bytes, committed bytes, non-paged pool, paged pool, handles, threads, semaphores, mutexes, and logical disk utilization. For Linux, the agent accesses the /proc directory structure and collects equivalent parameters such as memory utilization, swap space, file descriptors and inodes. All collected parameters are logged on to disk. They are also stored in memory preparatory to time-to-exhaustion analysis.

In the current version of the SRA, rejuvenation can be based on elapsed time since the last rejuvenation, or on prediction of impending exhaustion. When using Timed Rejuvenation, a user interface is used to schedule and perform rejuvenation at a period specified by the user. It allows the user to select when to rejuvenate different nodes of the cluster, and to select "blackout" times during which no rejuvenation is to be allowed. Predictive Rejuvenation relies on curve-fitting analysis and projection of the utilization of key resources, using recently observed data. The projected data is compared to prespecified upper and lower exhaustion thresholds, within a notification time horizon. The user specifies the notification horizon and the parameters to be monitored (some parameters believed to be highly indicative are always monitored by default), and the agent periodically samples the data and performs the analysis. The prediction algorithm fits several types of curves to the data in the fitting window. These different curve types have been selected for their ability to capture different types of temporal trends. A model-selection criterion is applied to choose the "best" prediction curve, which is then extrapolated to the user-specified horizon. The several parameters that are indicative of resource exhaustion are monitored and extrapolated independently. If any monitored parameter exceeds the specified minimum or maximum value within the horizon, a request to rejuvenate is sent to the management infrastructure. In most cases, it is also possible to identify which process is consuming the preponderance of the resource being exhausted, in order to support selective rejuvenation of just the offending process or a group of processes.

6. Approaches and Methods of Software Rejuvenation

Software rejuvenation can be divided broadly into two approaches as follows:

- **Open-loop approach:** In this approach, rejuvenation is performed without any feedback from the system. Rejuvenation in this case, can be based just on elapsed time (periodic rejuvenation) [29, 16] and/or instantaneous/cumulative number of jobs on the system [19].

- **Closed-loop approach:** In the closed-loop approach, rejuvenation is performed based on information on the system "health". The system is monitored continuously (in practice, at small deterministic intervals) and data is collected on the operating system resource usage and system activity. This data is then analyzed to estimate time to exhaustion of a resource which may lead to a component or an entire system degradation/crash. This estimation can be based purely on time, and workload-independent [20, 11] or can be based on both time and system workload [46].

  The closed-loop approach can be further classified based on whether the data analysis is done off-line or on-line. Off-line data analysis is done based on system data collected over a period of time (usually weeks or months). The analysis is done to estimate time to rejuvenation. This off-line analysis approach is best suited for systems whose behavior is fairly deterministic. The on-line closed-loop approach, on the other hand, performs on-line analysis of system data collected at deterministic intervals. Another approach to estimate the optimal time to rejuvenation could be based on system failure data [14]. This approach is more suited for off-line data analysis.

This classification of approaches to rejuvenation is shown in Figure 13.

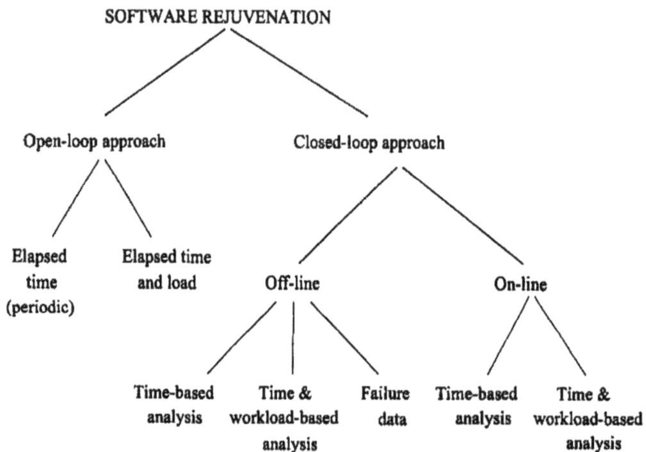

Figure 13. Approaches to software rejuvenation

Rejuvenation is a very general proactive fault management approach and can be performed at different levels - the system level or the application level. An example of a system level rejuvenation is a hardware-reboot. At the application level, rejuvenation is performed by stopping and restarting a particular offending application, process or a group of processes. This is also known as a *partial rejuvenation*. The above rejuvenation approaches when performed on a single node can lead to undesired and often costly downtime. Rejuvenation has been recently extended for cluster systems, in which two or more nodes work together as a single system [11, 47]. In this case, rejuvenation can be performed by causing no or minimal downtime by failing over applications to another spare node.

7. Conclusions

In this paper, we classified software faults based on an extension of Gray's classification and discussed the various techniques to deal with them. Attention was devoted to software rejuvenation, a proactive technique to counteract the phenomenon of software aging. Various analytical models for software aging and to determine optimal times to perform rejuvenation were described. Measurement-based models based on data collected from operating systems were also discussed. The implementation of a software rejuvenation agent in a major commercial server was then briefly described. Finally, various approaches to rejuvenation and rejuvenation granularity were discussed.

In the measurement-based models presented in this paper, only aging due to each individual resource has been captured. In the future, one could improve the algorithm used for aging detection to involve multiple parameters simultaneously, for better prediction capability and reduced false alarms. Dependences between the various system parameters could be studied. The best statistical data analysis method for a given system is also yet to be determined.

Notes

1. Although we use the by-now-established phrase "software aging", it should be clear that no deterioration of the software system per se is implied but rather, the software appears to age due to the gradual depletion of resources [6]. Likewise, "software rejuvenation" actually refers to rejuvenation of the environment in which the software is executing.
2. identical copies

References

[1] E. Adams. Optimizing Preventive Service of the Software Products. *IBM Journal of R&D*, 28(1):2-14, January 1984.

[2] P. E. Amman and J. C. Knight. Data Diversity: An Approach to Software Fault Tolerance. In *Proc. of 17th Int'l. Symposium on Fault Tolerant Computing*, pages 122-126, June 1987.

[3] A. Avritzer and E. J. Weyuker. Monitoring Smoothly Degrading Systems for Increased Dependability. *Empirical Software Eng. Journal*, Vol.2, No.1, pages 59-77, 1997.

[4] A. Avizienis and L. Chen. On the Implementation of N-version Programming for Software Fault Tolerance During Execution. In *Proc. IEEE COMPSAC 77*, pages 149-155, November 1977.

[5] A. Avizienis, J-C. Laprie and B. Randell. Fundamental Concepts of Dependability LAAS Technical Report No. 01-145, LAAS, France, April 2001.

[6] Y. Bao, X. Sun and K. Trivedi. Adaptive Software Rejuvenation: Degradation Models and Rejuvenation Schemes. In *Proc. of The Int'l. Conference on Dependable Systems and Networks, DSN-2003* June 2003.

[7] L. Bernstein. Text of Seminar Delivered by Mr. Bernstein. *University Learning Center*, George Mason University, January 29, 1996.

[8] A. Bobbio, A. Sereno and C. Anglano. Fine grained software degradation models for optimal rejuvenation policies. *Performance Evaluation*, Vol. 46, pp 45-62, 2001.

[9] T. Boyd and P. Dasgupta Premptive Module Replacement Using the Virtualizing Operating System In *Proc. of the Workshop on self-healing, adaptive and self-managed systems, SHAMAN 2002*, New York, NY, June 2002.

[10] K. Cassidy, K. Gross and A. Malekpour. Advanced Pattern Recognition for Detection of Complex Software Aging in Online Transaction Processing Servers. In *Proc. of DSN 2002*, Washington D.C., June 2002.

[11] V. Castelli, R. E. Harper, P. Heidelberger, S. W. Hunter, K. S. Trivedi, K. Vaidyanathan and W. Zeggert. Proactive Management of Software Aging. *IBM Journal of Research & Development*, Vol. 45, No.2, March 2001.

[12] R. Chillarege, S. Biyani, and J. Rosenthal. Measurement of Failure Rate in Widely Distributed Software. In *Proc. of 25th IEEE Int'l. Symposium on Fault Tolerant Computing*, pages 424–433, Pasadena, CA, July 1995.

[13] T. Dohi, K. Goseva–Popstojanova and K. S. Trivedi. Analysis of Software Cost Models with Rejuvenation. In *Proc. of the 5th IEEE International Symposium on High Assurance Systems Engineering, HASE 2000*, Albuquerque, NM, Nov. 2000.

[14] T. Dohi, K. Goseva–Popstojanova and K. S. Trivedi. Statistical Non-Parametric Algorithms to Estimate the Optimal Software Rejuvenation Schedule. *Proc. of the 2000 Pacific Rim International Symposium on Dependable Computing, PRDC 2000*, Los Angeles, CA, Dec. 2000.

[15] C. Fetzer and K. Hostedt Rejuvenation and Failure Detection in Partitionable Systems In *Proc. of the Pacific Rim Int'l. Symposium on Dependable Computing, PRDC 2001*, Seoul, South Korea, December 2001.

[16] S. Garg, A. Puliafito and K. S. Trivedi. Analysis of Software Rejuvenation Using Markov Regenerative Stochastic Petri Net. In *Proc. of the Sixth Int'l. Symposium on Software Reliability Engineering*, pages 180-187, Toulouse, France, October 1995.

[17] S. Garg, Y. Huang, C. Kintala and K. S. Trivedi. Time and Load Based Software Rejuvenation: Policy, Evaluation and Optimality. In *Proc. of the First Fault-Tolerant Symposium*, Madras, India, December 1995.

[18] S. Garg, Y. Huang and C. Kintala, K.S. Trivedi, Minimizing Completion Time of a Program by Checkpointing and Rejuvenation. *Proc. 1996 ACM SIGMETRICS Conference*, Philadelphia, PA, pp. 252-261, May 1996.

[19] S. Garg, A. Puliafito, M. Telek and K. S. Trivedi. Analysis of Preventive Maintenance in Transactions Based Software Systems. *IEEE Trans. on Computers*, pages 96-107, Vol. 47, No. 1, January 1998.

[20] S. Garg, A. van Moorsel, K. Vaidyanathan, K. Trivedi. A Methodology for Detection and Estimation of Software Aging. In *Proc. of 9th Int'l. Symposium on Software Reliability Engineering*, pages 282-292, Paderborn, Germany, November 1998.

[21] S. Garg, Y. Huang, C. M. R. Kintala, K. S. Trivedi and S. Yagnik. Performance and Reliability Evaluation of Passive Replication Scheme s in Application Level Fault Tolerance. In *Proc. of the Fault Tolerant Computing Symp., FTCS 1999*, Madison, WI, pp. 322-329, June 1999.

[22] J. Gray. Why do Computers Stop and What Can be Done About it? In *Proc. of 5th Symposium on Reliability in Distributed Software and Database Systems*, pages 3-12, January 1986.

[23] J. Gray. A Census of Tandem System Availability Between 1985 and 1990. *IEEE Trans. on Reliability*, 39:409-418, October 1990.

[24] J. Gray and D. P. Siewiorek. High-availability Computer Systems. *IEEE Computer*, pages 39–48, September 1991.

[25] J. A. Hartigan. *Clustering Algorithms*. New York:Wiley, 1975.

[26] C. Hirel, B. Tuffin and K. S. Trivedi. SPNP: Stochastic Petri Net Package. Version 6.0. B. R. Haverkort et al. (eds.): TOOLS 2000, Lecture Notes in Computer Science 1786, pp 354-357, Springer-Verlag Heidelberg, 2000.

[27] Y. Hong, D. Chen, L. Li and K.S. Trivedi. Closed Loop Design for Software Rejuvenation In *Proc. of the Workshop on self-healing, adaptive and self-managed systems, SHAMAN 2002*, New York, NY, June 2002.

[28] Y. Huang, P. Jalote, and C. Kintala. *Lecture Notes in Computer Science, Vol. 774*, Two techniques for transient software error recovery, pages 159–170. Springer Verlag, Berlin, 1994.

[29] Y. Huang, C. Kintala, N. Kolettis, and N. D. Fulton. Software Rejuvenation: Analysis, Module and Applications. In *Proc. of 25th Symposium on Fault Tolerant Computing, FTCS-25*, pages 381–390, Pasadena, California, June 1995.

[30] IBM Netfinity Director Software Rejuvenation - White Paper. IBM Corp., Research Triangle Park, NC, Jan 2001.

[31] P. Jalote, Y. Huang, and C. Kintala. A Framework for Understanding and Handling Transient Software Failures. In *Proc. 2nd ISSAT Int'l. Conf. on Reliability and Quality in Design*, Orlando, FL, 1995.

[32] J. C. Knight and N. G. Leveson. An Experimental Evaluation of the Assumption of Independence in Multiversion Programming *Software Engineering Journal*, pages 96-109, Vol. 12, No. 1, 1986.

[33] I. Lee and R. K. Iyer. Software Dependability in the Tandem GUARDIAN System. *IEEE Trans. on Software Engineering*, pages 455-467, Vol. 21, No. 5, May 1995.

[34] L. Li, K. Vaidyanathan and K. S. Trivedi. An Approach to Estimation of Software Aging in a Web Server. In *Proc. of the Int'l. Symp. on Empirical Software Engineering, ISESE 2002*, Nara, Japan, October 2002.

[35] Y. Liu, Y. Ma, J.J. Han, H. Levendel and K.S. Trivedi. Modeling and Analysis of Software Rejuvenation in Cable Modem Termination System. In *Proc. of the Int'l. Symp. on Software Reliability Engineering, ISSRE 2002*, Annapolis, MD, November 2002.

[36] E. Marshall. Fatal Error: How Patriot Overlooked a Scud. *Science*, page 1347, March 13, 1992.

[37] D. Mosberger and T. Jin. Httperf - A Tool for Measuring Web Server Performance *In First Workshop on Internet Server Performance, WISP*, Madison, WI, pp.59-67, June 1998.

[38] A. Pfening, S. Garg, A. Puliafito, M. Telek and K. S. Trivedi. Optimal Rejuvenation for Tolerating Soft Failures. *Performance Evaluation*, 27 & 28, pages 491-506, October 1996.

[39] S. M. Ross. *Stochastic Processes*. John Wiley & Sons, New York, 1983.

[40] R. A. Sahner, K. S. Trivedi, A. Puliafito. *Performance and Reliability Analysis of Computer Systems - An Example-Based Approach Using the SHARPE Software Package*. Kluwer Academic Publishers, Norwell, MA, 1996.

[41] R. H. Shumway and D. S. Stoffer. *Time Series Analysis and Its Applications*, Springer-Verlag, New York, 2000.

[42] M. Sullivan and R. Chillarege. Software Defects and Their Impact on System Availability - A Study of Field Failures in Operating Systems. In *Proc. 21st IEEE Int'l. Symposium on Fault-Tolerant Computing*, pages 2–9, 1991.

[43] A. T. Tai, S. N. Chau, L. Alkalaj and H. Hecht. On-Board Preventive Maintenance: Analysis of Effectiveness and Optimal Duty Period. In *3rd Int'l. Workshop on Object Oriented Real-time Dependable Systems*, Newport Beach, CA, February 1997.

[44] K. S. Trivedi, J. Muppala, S. Woolet and B. R. Haverkort. Composite Performance and Dependability Analysis. *Performance Evaluation*, Vol. 14, nos. 3-4, pp. 197-216, February 1992.

[45] K. S. Trivedi. *Probability and Statistics, with Reliability, Queuing and Computer Science Applications*, 2nd edition. John Wiley, 2001.

[46] K. Vaidyanathan and K. S. Trivedi. A Measurement-Based Model for Estimation of Resource Exhaustion in Operational Software Systems. In *Proc. of the Tenth IEEE Int'l. Symposium on Software Reliability Engineering*, pages 84-93, Boca Raton, Florida, November 1999.

[47] K. Vaidyanathan, R. E. Harper, S. W. Hunter, K. S. Trivedi. Analysis and Implementation of Software Rejuvenation in Cluster Systems. In *Proc. of the Joint Int'l. Conference on Measurement and Modeling of Computer Systems, ACM SIGMETRICS 2001/Performance 2001*, Cambridge, MA, June 2001.

[48] http://www.microsoft.com/technet/prodtechnol/windows2000serv/technologies/iis/default.mspx

[49] http://www.apache.org

TEST AND DESIGN-FOR-TEST OF MIXED-SIGNAL INTEGRATED CIRCUITS

Marcelo Lubaszewski[1] and Jose Luis Huertas[2]
[1]*Electrical Engineering Department, Universidade Federal do Rio Grande do Sul (UFRGS), Av. Osvaldo Aranha esquina Sarmento Leite 103, 90035-190 Porto Alegre RS, Brazil;*
[2]*Instituto de Microelectrónica de Sevilla, Centro Nacional de Microelectrónica (IMSE-CNM), Universidad de Sevilla, Av. Reina Mercedes s/n, Edificio CICA, 41012 Sevilla, Spain*

Abstract: Although most electronic circuits are almost entirely digital, many include at least a small part that is essentially analog. This is due to the need to interface with the real physical world, that is analog in nature. As demanding market segments require ever more complex mixed-signal solutions, high quality tests become essential to meet circuit design specifications in terms of reliability, time-to-market, costs, etc. In order to lower costs associated to traditional specification-driven tests and, additionally, achieve acceptable fault coverages for analog and mixed-signal circuits, it is reasonable to expect that no other solution than a move towards defect-oriented design-for-test methods will be applicable in the near future. Therefore, testing tends to be dominated by embedded mechanisms to allow for accessibility to internal test points, to achieve on-chip test generation, on-chip test response evaluation, or even to make it possible the detection of errors concurrently to the circuit application. Within this context, an overview of existing test methods is given in this chapter, focusing on design-for-testability, built-in self-test and self-checking techniques suitable for the detection of realistic defects in analog and mixed-signal integrated circuits.

Keywords: Analog and mixed-signal test, fault modelling, fault simulation, test generation, defect-oriented test, design-for-test, design-for-testability, built-in self-test, self-checking circuits.

1. INTRODUCTION

Today's telecommunications, consumer electronics and other demanding market segments, require that more complex, faster and denser circuits are designed in shorter times and at lower costs. Obviously, the ultimate goal is to maximise profits.

Although most electronic circuits are almost entirely digital, many include at least a small part that is essentially analog. This is due to the need to interface with the real physical world, that is analog in nature. Therefore, transducers, signal conditioning and data converter components add to the final circuit architecture, leading to ever more complex mixed-signal chips with an increasing analog-digital interaction.

Nevertheless, the development of reliable products cannot be achieved without high quality methods and efficient mechanisms for testing Integrated Circuits (ICs). If, on one hand, test methods have already reached an important level of maturity in the domain of digital logic, unfortunately, on the other hand, practical analog solutions are still lagging behind their digital counterparts. Analog and mixed-signal testing has traditionally been achieved by functional test techniques, based on the measurement of circuit specification parameters. However, measuring such parameters is a time consuming task, requires costly test equipment and does not ensure that a device passing the test is actually defect-free. Then, to ensure the quality required for product competitiveness, one can no more rely on conventional functional tests: a move is needed towards methods that search for manufacturing defects and faults occurring during a circuit's lifetime. Moreover, to achieve acceptable fault coverages has become a very hard and costly task for external testing: test mechanisms need to be built into integrated circuits early in the design process. Ideally, these mechanisms should be reused to test for internal defects and environmental conditions that may affect the operation of the systems into which the circuits will be embedded. This would provide for amplified payback. To give an estimate about the price to pay for faults escaping the testing process, fault detection costs can increase by a factor of ten, when moving from the circuit to the board level, then from the board to the system level, and lastly, from the final test of the system to its application in the field.

Therefore, design-for-test seems to be the only reasonable answer to the testing challenges posed by state-of-the-art integrated circuits. Mechanisms that allow for accessibility to internal test points, that achieve on-chip test generation, on-chip test response evaluation, and that make it possible the detection of errors concurrently to the application, are examples of structures that may be embedded into circuits to ensure system testability. They obviously incur penalties in terms of silicon overhead and performance degradation. These penalties must definitely account for finding the best trade off between quality and cost. However, the industrial participation to recent test standardisation initiatives confirms that, in many commercial applications, design-for-test can prove economical.

Within this context, the aim of this chapter is to give a glimpse into the area of design-for-test of analog and mixed-signal integrated circuits. First of all, the test methods of interest to existing design-for-test techniques are revisited. Finally, design-for-testability, built-in self-test and self-checking techniques are discussed and illustrated in the realm of integrated circuits.

2. TEST METHODS

2.1 General background

From the very first design, any circuit undergoes *prototype debugging*, *production* and periodic *maintenance tests* to simply identify and isolate, or even replace faulty parts. Those are called *off-line tests,* since they are independent of the circuit application and need, in the field, that the application is stopped before the related testing procedures can be run.

In high safety systems, such as automotive, avionics, high speed train and nuclear plants, poor functioning cannot be tolerated and detecting faults concurrently to the application becomes also essential. The *on-line detection* capability, used for checking the validity of undertaken operations, can be ensured by special mechanisms, such as self-checking hardware.

In general, tests must check whether, according to the specifications, the circuit has a correct functional behaviour (*functional testing*), or whether the physical implementation of the circuit matches its schematics (*structural testing*). The former, also called specification-driven test, is based on measuring parameters that are part of the functional specification of the circuit under test. The latter, also called defect-oriented test, is based on catching physical defects that are modelled as *faults* representing, at the level of design description (algorithmic, logic, electrical, etc), the impact of mismatches between the actually implemented and the expected implementation of the device. The structural, opposed to the functional testing, can more easily provide a quantitative measure of test effectiveness (*fault coverage*), due to its fault-based nature. If, for any reason, structural tests cannot reach the required fault coverage, they must be followed by functional tests, although this leads to a longer test time because of redundant testing.

On one hand, test methods have already reached an important level of maturity in the domain of digital systems: *digital testing* has been dominated by structured fault-based techniques and by successfully developed and automated standardised test configurations. On the other hand, practical analog solutions are still lagging behind their digital counterparts: *analog and mixed-signal testing* has traditionally been achieved by functional test techniques, based on the measurement of circuit specification parameters, such as gain, bandwidth, distortion, impedance, noise, etc. Analysing aspects such as size, accuracy, sensitivity, tolerances and modelling, helps understanding why this digital vs. analog testing contrast exists:

Compared to digital logic, analog circuits are usually made up of much fewer elementary devices that interface with the external world through a much smaller number of inputs and outputs. Thus, the difficulties of testing analog circuits do not reside in sizing, but in the precision and accuracy that the measures require. Additionally, analog circuits are much more sensitive to loading effects than digital circuits. The simple flow of an analog signal to an output pin may have an important impact on the final circuit topology and behaviour.

Digital signals have discrete values. Analog signals, however, have an infinite range, and good signal values are referred to certain tolerance margins that depend on process variations and measurement inaccuracies. Absolute tolerances in analog components can be very large (around 20%), but relative matching is usually very good (0.1% in some cases). Although multiple component deviations may occur, in general, analog design methods promote that deviations cancel each other's effect, placing design robustness on the opposite direction of fault detection. Additionally, simulation time very quickly gets prohibitive for multiple component deviations.

For the reasons above, modelling the circuit behaviour is far more difficult in analog than in digital circuits. Furthermore, the function of analog circuits cannot be described by closed-form expressions as in Boolean algebra, that allows for the use of very simple fault models such as the widely accepted digital stuck-at. Instead, the behaviour of an analog circuit depends on the exact behaviour of a transistor, whose model requires a set of complex equations containing lots of parameters. As a consequence, it turns difficult to map defects to suitable fault models and thus, to accurate simulate the circuit behaviour in presence of faults.

Independently of the digital or analog nature of the circuit under test, the application of input stimuli followed by the observation of output voltages has been a widely used test technique. However, it has been shown that such a *voltage testing* cannot detect many physical defects that lead to unusual circuit consumptions. This is the reason why the practice of *current testing*, based on the measurement of the current consumption between the power supplies, has been increasing in importance in the last years. Current testing has been mostly faced as a complementary technique to the voltage testing approach.

2.2 Defects and fault models

Efficient tests can only be produced if realistic fault models, based on physical failure mechanisms and actual layouts, are considered.

Many defects may be inherent to the silicon substrate on which the integrated structures will be fabricated. Those may result from impurities found in the material used to produce the wafers, for example. Others may be due to problems occurring during the various *manufacturing* steps: the resistivity of contacts, for instance, will depend on the doping quality; the presence of dust particles in the clean room or in the materials may lead to the occurrence of spot defects; the misalignment of masks may result in deviations of transistor sizes, etc. All these defects lead, in general, to faults that simultaneously affect several devices, i.e. *multiple faults*.

Other defects occur during a circuit's *lifetime*. They are usually due to failure mechanisms associated to transport and electromechanical phenomena, thermal weakness, etc. In general, those defects produce *single faults*.

Permanent faults, like interconnect opens and shorts, floating gates, etc, can be produced by defects resulting from manufacturing and circuit usage. *Transient faults*, on the contrary, will appear due to intermittent phenomena, such as electromagnetic interference or space radiations.

Although defects are absolutely the same for digital and analog circuits, fault modelling is a much harder task in the analog case. This is mainly due to a larger number of possible misbehaviours resulting from defects that may affect a circuit dealing with analog signals.

The most intuitive fault model is the one that simply translates the various facets of the expected behaviour of a circuit to a number of parameters that shall conform for the circuit to be considered fault-free. These parameters are obviously extracted from the circuit design specification and measuring all of them equals to checking the whole circuit functionality, at a cost that may approach the one of full device characterisation. In the case of operational amplifiers, such functional fault model may consider accepted intervals for input offset voltage, common-mode rejection ratio, slew-rate, open-loop gain, output resistance and other parameters (Calvano, 2001). In respect to analog filters, functional faults may comprise parameters such as cut-off frequency, pole factor quality, DC-gain, maximum ripple in the pass and reject band, dynamic range, total harmonic distortion, noise, etc (Calvano, 2000). Fault models for Analog-to-Digital (A/D) and Digital-to-Analog (D/A) converters bring up static performance parameters, such as gain, offset, differential and integral non-linearity, as well as dynamic parameters, such as signal-to-noise and distortion ratio, effective number of bits, total harmonic distortion and spurious free dynamic range (Bernard, 2003).

In terms of structural testing, three categories of faults have been guiding most works on analog testing: *hard faults* (Milor, 1989), *soft* and *large deviations* (Slamani, 1995). Hard faults are serious changes in component values or in circuit topology, usually resulting from catastrophic opens or short circuits. In continuous-time analog integrated circuits, this involves transistors, resistors, capacitors and wires opens and shorts. In discrete-time implementations, switches stuck-on and stuck-open add to the fault model. Figure 1 shows an example of hard faults at the transistor level. Soft faults are small deviations around component nominal values, such as small changes in transistor gains, in capacitor and resistor values, etc. They may cause circuit malfunctions by slightly displacing the cut-off frequency of filters or the output gain of amplifiers, for example. Large deviations are also deviations in the nominal value of components, but of a greater magnitude. They still cause circuit malfunctions, but their effects are quite harder than those observed for soft faults. Some few works also consider interaction faults in analog and mixed-signal circuits (Caunegre, 1996; Cota, 1997). These faults are shorts between nodes of the circuit that are not terminals of the same digital or analog component.

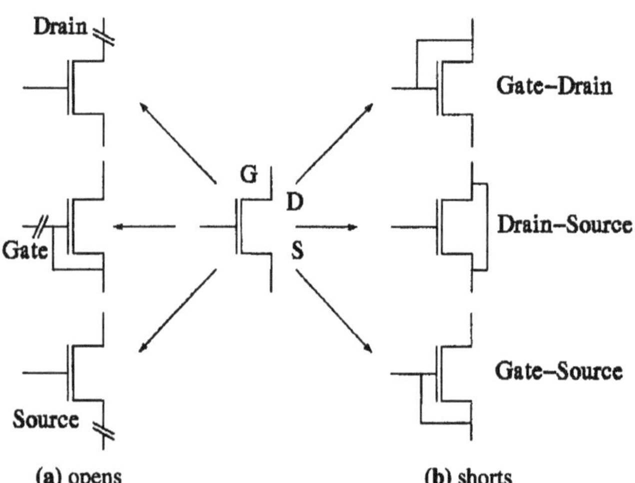

Figure 1. Fault model for hard faults in a MOS transistor.

Finally, from the knowledge about defect sizes and defect occurrences in a process, layouts can be analysed and the probabilities of occurrence of opens, shorts, etc, in different layout portions and layers, can be derived by *inductive fault analysis - IFA* (Meixner, 1991). The IFA technique has the advantage of considerably reducing the list of faults, by taking into account only those with reasonable chances of occurrence (*realistic faults*).

2.3 Functional Test

In IC industry, most practices for mixed-signal testing are functional and thus, build upon specification-driven procedures. The approaches in use are based on time- or frequency-domain analysis. Many of them make use of Digital Signal Processing (DSP) techniques.

Time-domain analysis is used to check circuit time responses from transient, DC static or AC dynamic measurements. They apply to both filters and data converters.

An example of test procedure based on transient response analysis is given in (Calvano, 2000). That work considers that deviations in the cut-off frequency and in the pole quality factor are the faults to detect in 2nd order sections of analog filters. A pulse, a step or a ramp is applied to a low-pass, band-pass or high-pass filter, respectively, and the peak-time and/or overshoot of the 2nd order dynamic system response is observed. Those parameters prove to be good indirect measures of the filter cut-off frequency and pole quality factor.

For more complex linear (Carro, 1998) and even for non-linear analog circuits (Nácul, 2002), duplication-like testing can be performed by training a digital filter such as it can mimic the expected behaviour of the circuit under test. Once the adaptive filter has all its coefficients determined, then a test stimulus is simultaneously applied to the trained filter and the circuit under test, and the outputs of both circuits are compared to check whether the circuit is faulty or fault free. A broadband test stimulus, such as white noise, is the preferable choice for both the training and the testing phases of the method.

Another example of time-domain analysis is the histogram testing of A/D converters. In this technique, code transition levels are not measured directly, but determined through statistical analysis of converter activity. For a known periodic input stimulus, the histogram of code occurrences (code counts) is computed over an integer number of input waveform periods. Figure 2 shows a *ramp histogram*, also called linear histogram, computed for a linear - typically triangular – waveform. The computation is illustrated for an ideal 3-bit converter. Generally, histograms support analysis of the converter's static performance parameters. A missing code m is easily identified as the corresponding code count $H[m]$ is equal to zero. Also offset is easily identified as a shift in the code counts and gain directly relates to average code count. Finally, the converter linearity can be assessed via the detailed determination of code transition levels.

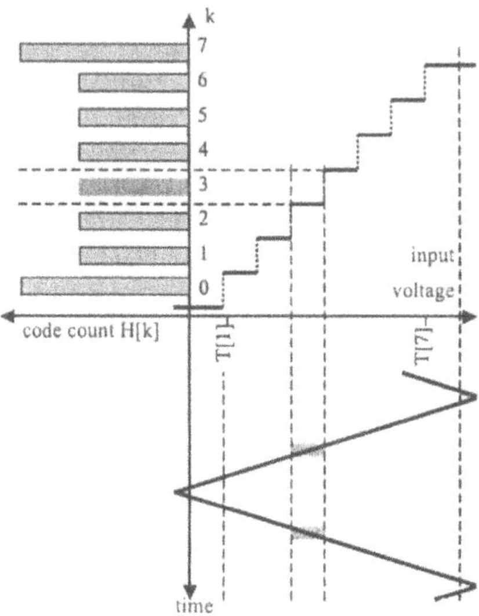

Figure 2. Linear histogram for an ideal 3-bit A/D converter.

A frequency-domain based test typically builds upon a conversion of a signal from the time-domain to a spectral representation.

A Bode plot is the most intuitive and the most frequent representation for the behaviour of a filter in frequency-domain. From a Bode plot, parameters such as gain in the pass and reject band, cut-off frequency and pole quality factor of a filter, can be easily extracted. In practice, a complete frequency sweep is needed to experimentally obtain such a plot, which requires long test application and measurement times.

Another type of frequency-domain test samples signals in the time-domain and then convert to the frequency-domain by applying a Fast Fourier Transform (FFT) or a Discrete Fourier Transform (DFT) to the samples. The resulting spectrum is a plot of frequency component magnitudes over a range of frequency bins. Further details on fundamentals of DSP testing can be found in (Mahoney, 1987; Burns, 2001). Figure 3 illustrates an A/D converter output spectrum obtained from the application of a DFT to the response of the converter to a spectrally pure sine-wave input of frequency f_i. The second to k^{th} harmonic distortion components, A_{H2} to A_{Hk}, occur at frequencies that are integer multiples of f_i. Additionally, spurious components, such as A_{Si} in figure 3, can be seen at other than the input signal or harmonics frequencies. The main dynamic and some static performance parameters can be extracted from the output spectrum in the form of ratios of RMS amplitudes of particular spectral components (Bernard, 2003). Similarly, such a spectrum can be obtained for a filter, for which f_i is usually its cut-off frequency.

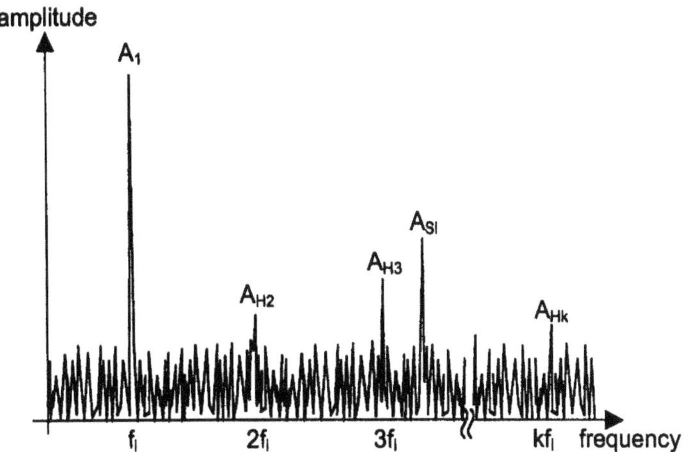

Figure 3. A/D converter output spectrum

2.4 Structural Test

Existing structural fault models give the opportunity of precisely determining input test stimuli that provoke that the faulty circuit behaves differently from the expected fault-free outputs. In next sections, available tools for fault simulation and automatic test generation are described. Those tools make it possible to build structural test sequences for fault detection and fault diagnosis in analog and mixed-signal integrated circuits.

2.4.1 Fault simulation

Fault simulation consists, basically, of simulating the circuit in the presence of the faults of the model, and of comparing the individual results with the fault-free simulations. The goal is to check whether or not these faults are detected by the applied input stimuli. The steps involved in the fault simulation process are:

- fault-free simulation;
- reduction of the fault list (*fault collapsing*), by deleting faults that present the same structure as expected for a particular circuit topology;
- insertion of the fault model into the fault-free circuit description (*fault injection*);
- simulation of the faulty circuit;
- comparison of the faulty and fault-free simulation results and, in case of mismatch, deletion of the fault from the initial fault list (*fault dropping*).

A typical fault simulation environment is given in figure 4.

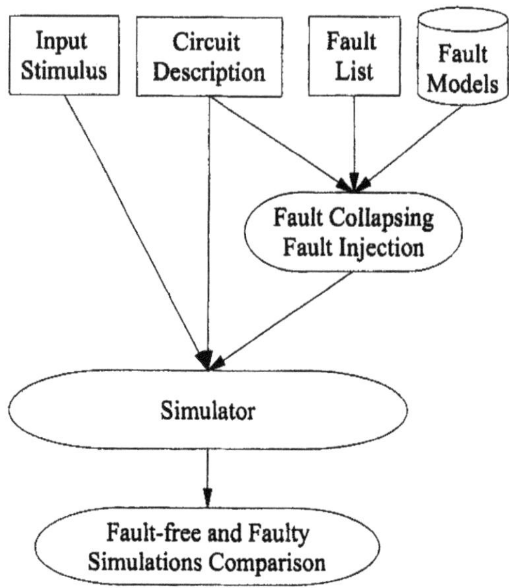

Figure 4. A generic fault simulation procedure.

Fault simulation is widely used for:

- test evaluation, by checking the fault coverage, i.e. the percentage of faults detected by a set of input stimuli;
- fault dropping in test generation, by verifying which faults of the model a computed test stimulus detects; and,
- diagnosis, by making it possible the construction of *fault dictionaries* that identify which faults are detected by every test stimulus.

Contrarily to the digital case, where some degree of parallelism is possible in fault simulation (Abramovici, 1990), in analog and mixed-signal circuits faults are injected and simulated sequentially, making fault simulation a very time consuming task. For analog circuits, fault simulation is traditionally performed at the transistor-level using circuit simulators. For the fault simulation of continuous-time analog circuits, (Sebeke, 1995) proposes a computer-aided testing tool based on a transistor-level hard fault model. This fault model is made up of local shorts, local opens, global shorts and split nodes. The tool injects into the fault-free circuit realistic faults obtained from layouts by an IFA-based fault extractor. For switched-capacitor analog circuits, (Mir, 1997) presents a switch-level fault simulator that models shorts, opens and deviations in capacitors, stuck-on, stuck-open and shorts between analog terminals of switches. An automatic tool is introduced that performs time- and frequency-domain switch-level fault simulations, keeping simulation times orders of magnitude lower than for transistor-level simulations. A behavioural-level fault simulation approach is proposed in (Nagi, 1993a). It has practical use only for continuos-time linear analog circuits. First of all, the circuit under test, originally expressed as a system of linear state variables, suffers a bilinear transformation from the s-domain equations to the z-domain. Next, the equations are solved to give a discretized solution. In this approach, soft faults in passive components are directly mapped onto the state equations, while hard faults require, in general, that the transfer function is recomputed for the affected blocks. Finally, operational amplifier faults are modelled in the s-domain, before mapping them to the z-domain.

2.4.2 Test generation

Following the choice of a suitable fault model and fault simulator, test generation is the natural step to define an efficient test procedure to apply to the circuit under test.

The problem of generating tests consists, basically, of finding a set of input test stimuli and a set of output measures, which guarantee a maximum fault coverage. If the fault detection goal is extended to include fault diagnosis, the computed test stimuli must, additionally, be capable of distinguishing between faults. A typical test generation environment is given in figure 5.

Over the last decade, some test generation procedures for analog circuits have been proposed in the literature. The technique reported in (Tsai, 1991), one of the earliest contributions to test generation of linear circuits, formulates the analog test generation task as a quadratic programming problem, and it derives pulsed waveforms as input test stimuli. DC test generation is dealt with in (Devarayanadurg, 1994) as a min-max optimisation problem that considers process variations for the detection of hard faults in analog macros. This min-max formulation of the static test problem is extended to the dynamic case (AC) in (Devarayanadurg, 1995). The automatic generation of AC tests has also been addressed in other works (Nagi, 1993b; Slamani, 1995; Mir, 1996a; Cota, 1997). (Nagi, 1993b) uses a heuristic based on sensitivity calculations to choose the circuit frequencies to consider. After each choice, fault simulation is performed as the means to drop from the fault list all detected faults. From a multifrequency analysis, the approach in (Slamani, 1995) selects the test frequencies that maximise the sensitivity of the output parameters measured for each individual faulty component. (Mir, 1996a) also proposes a multifrequency test generation procedure, but computes a minimal set of test measures and a minimal set of test frequencies which guarantee maximum fault coverage and maximal diagnosis. Finally, (Cota, 1997) enlarges the set of faults including interaction shorts, and merges the sensitivity analysis (Slamani, 1995) and the search of minimal sets (Mir, 1996a), with test generation based on fault simulation (Nagi, 1993b). Additionally, it applies the new automatic test generation procedure to linear and non-linear analog and mixed-signal circuits.

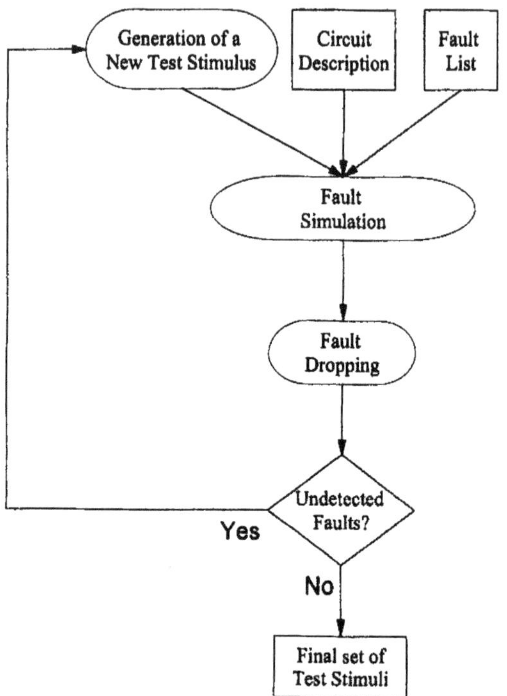

Figure 5. A generic test generation procedure.

3. DESIGN-FOR-TEST

Even though a test generation tool is available for testing, hard-to-detect faults can prevent that a good trade off between fault coverage and testing time is achieved. In these cases, the redesign of parts of the circuit can represent a possible solution to improve the accessibility to hard-to-test elements (*design-for-testability*).

Considering the increasing complexity of integrated circuits, another design-for-test possibility is to build self-test capabilities into circuits (*built-in self-test*). In general, the use of on-chip structures for test generation and test evaluation allows for significant savings in test equipment, reducing the final chip cost.

In case the application requires that faults are detected on-line, the circuit can be made *self-checking* by encoding the outputs of functional blocks and verifying them through embedded checkers. Unlike built-in self-test approaches, concurrent checking is performed using functional signals, rather than signals specifically generated for testing the circuit.

In the following sections, these three design-for-test approaches, i.e. design-for-testability, built-in self-test and self-checking technique, are further discussed and illustrated. The discussion ends up by the proposal of an unified approach for off-line and on-line testing of analog and mixed-signal integrated circuits.

3.1 Design-for-testability

Design-for-testability approaches aim at improving the capability of observing, at the circuit outputs, the behaviour of internal nodes (*observability*), and at improving the capability of getting test signals from the circuit inputs to internal nodes (*controllability*).

Ad-hoc techniques, that are in general based on partitioning, on the use of multiplexers to give access to hard-to-test nodes, on disabling feedback paths, etc, can be used to enhance the testability of circuits. Nevertheless, structured approaches are far more suitable to face testing problems in highly complex integrated circuits.

In the digital domain, the most successful structured approach is undoubtedly the *scan path* technique (Eichelberger, 1978). In test mode, a set of circuit flip-flops is connected into a shift register configuration, so that scan-in of test vectors and scan-out of test responses are made possible. Similarly, the testability of internal nodes of printed circuit boards can be improved by extending the internal scan path to the interface of integrated circuits. This technique is referred to as *boundary scan* (LeBlanc, 1984) and is the basis of a very successful test standard (IEEE, 1990), implemented in many products available in the market (Maunder, 1994).

In the analog case, the first attempt to apply the idea of the scan path to test filters was made by (Soma, 1990). The basis of this design-for-testability methodology consists of dynamically broadening the bandwidth of each stage of a filter, in order to improve the controllability and observability of circuit internal nodes. This bandwidth expansion is performed by disconnecting the capacitors of the filter stages by using MOS switches. The main drawback of this approach is that the additional switches impact the filter performance. Although in the extension of this technique to switched-capacitor implementations (Soma, 1994) no extra switches are needed in the main signal path, additional control signals and associated circuitry and routing are required. In order to reduce the impact on performance of the additional scan circuitry, operational amplifiers with duplicated input stages have been used in (Bratt, 1995). This technique is illustrated in figure 6: in scan mode, a filter stage can be reprogrammed to work as a voltage follower, and propagate to the next stage the output of the previous stage.

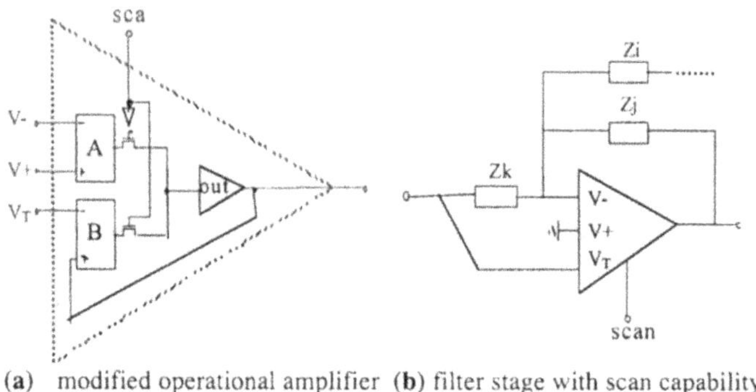

(a) modified operational amplifier (b) filter stage with scan capability

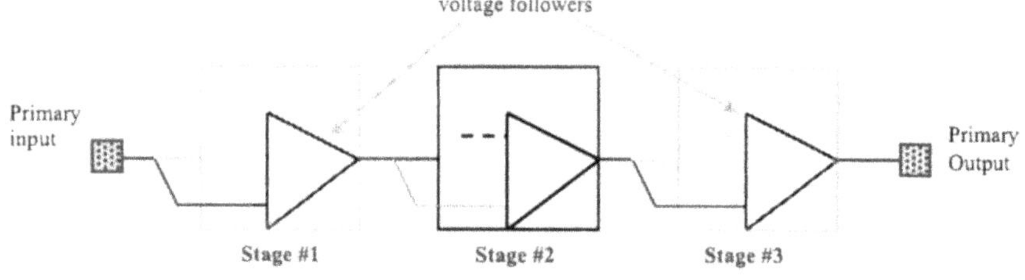

(c) using modified amplifier to test filter stage#2

Figure 6. Analog scan based on operational amplifier with duplicated input stage.

At the board level, the main problem to face in testing mixed-signal circuits is the detection and diagnosis of interconnect faults. While shorts and opens in digital wiring can be easily checked by means of boundary scan, analog interconnects (made up of discrete components in addition to wires) require specific mechanisms to measure impedance values. The principle of the most usual impedance measurement technique is shown in figure 7 (Osseiran, 1995). Zx is the impedance to measure. Z1 and Z2 are two other impedances connected to Zx. Zs is the probe impedance of the test stimuli source (including the source output impedance), Zi is the impedance of the probe to the virtual ground of the operational amplifier (including the input impedance of the measuring circuitry) and Zg is the impedance of circuit internal probes connecting Z1 and Z2 to ground. If Zs, Zi and Zg are very low, Zx will be given by the formula in figure 7.

Assuming that the terminals of Zx, Z1 and Z2 are connected to chips (IC1 and IC2 in figure 7), electronic access to these points can be achieved by building into I/O interfaces the *analog boundary modules* (ABM) given in figure 8. While applying the measurement procedure described above, those cells to which Zx is connected will switch on bus AB1 for stimulus application, and switch on bus AB2 for response measurement. The cells connected to the ends of Z1 and Z2 that are opposed to Zx will be pulled down by switching on VL. All analog boundary scan modules will provide for isolation of integrated circuit cores. The measurement technique in figure 7 and the analog module in figure 8 are part of the IEEE 1149.4 standard for mixed-signal test (IEEE, 1999).

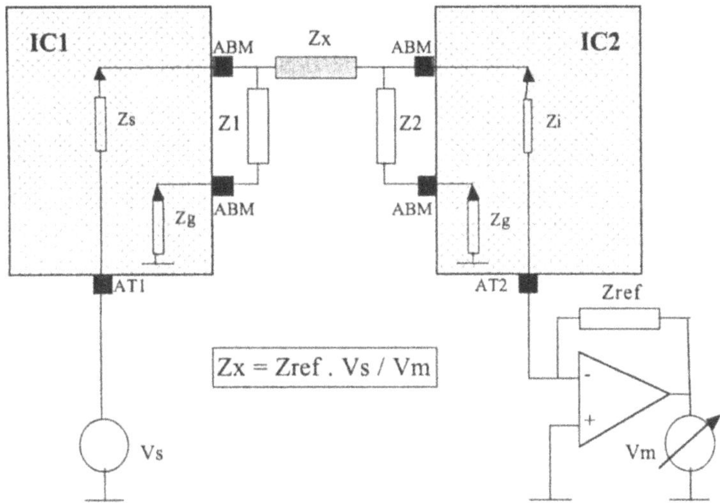

Figure 7. Analog in-circuit test.

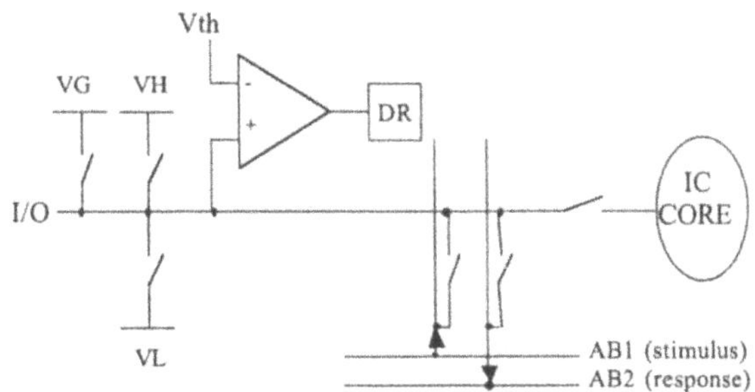

Figure 8. Analog boundary module (ABM).

As it can be seen from figure 9, this test standard extends the IEEE Std. 1149.1 to cope with the test of analog circuitry. The general architecture of the IEEE Std. 1149.4 infrastructure is given in the figure. To comply with the IEEE 1149.1 standard, it comprises a dedicated Test Access Port (TAP) composed of four required pins *TDI*, *TDO*, *TMS* and *TCK*, a collection of Digital Boundary Modules (DBM) associated with every digital function pin, and a test control circuitry composed of a TAP controller, an instruction register and an instruction decoder. These features permit loading and unloading of both instructions and test data and provide access to the core circuitry for application and monitoring of digital test signals. The IEEE 1149.4 standard adds an Analog Test Access Port (ATAP), a Test Bus Interface Circuit (TBIC), Analog Boundary Modules (ABM) associated to every analog function pin and a two-wire internal analog test bus (*AB1/2*).

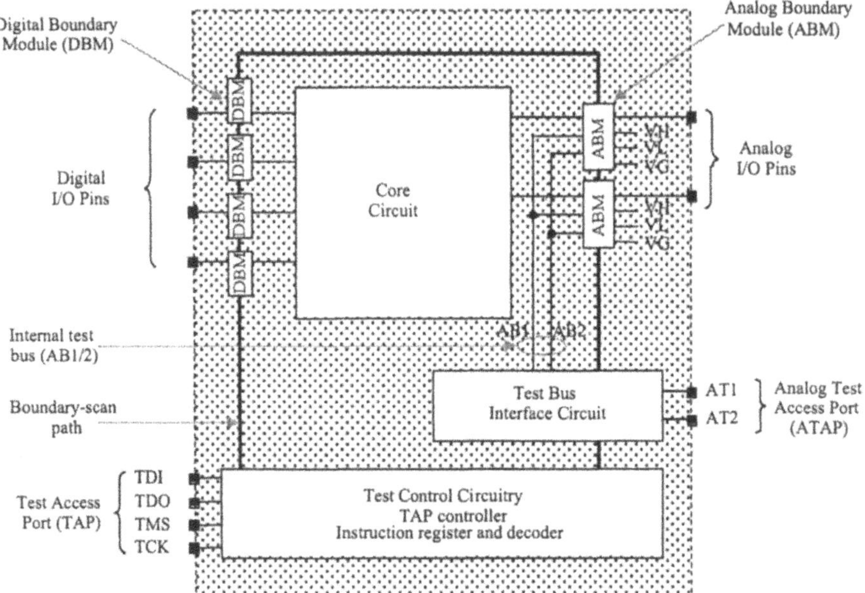

Figure 9. On-chip test architecture of an 1149.4-compliant integrated circuit.

More recently, the problem of ensuring good test accessibility to internal nodes has been considered at a much earlier stage of the IC design process, at the moment of choosing the method for the synthesis of the desired function. (Calvano, 2002), for example, presents a design for testability method that relies on the synthesis of filter transfer functions using partial fraction extraction. The transfer functions are built from 1st order building blocks for which very simple stimuli are disclosed for testing. The resulting filter is partitioned by construction and each individual fraction is made externally accessible through the available infrastructure provided by the IEEE Std.1149.4.

3.2 Built-in self-test

With the advances on integrated circuits, faster and more complex test equipments are needed to meet ever more demanding test specifications. Testers with demanding requirements of speed, precision, memory and noise are in general very expensive. An attractive alternative is to move some or all of the tester functions onto the chip itself. The use of built-in self-test (BIST) for high volume production of integrated circuits is desirable to reduce the cost per chip during production-time testing.

An ideal BIST scheme should provide means of on-chip test stimulus generation, on-chip test response evaluation, on-chip test control and I/O isolation. The interest in a particular approach depends on its suitability to address the circuit faulty behaviours, and the cost and applicability of the technique.

All BIST methods have some associated cost in terms of area overhead and additional test pins. The additional BIST area required in the chip results in a decrease in yield. This penalty must be compensated by reducing test and maintenance costs. Moreover, by adding circuitry to the signal path, the BIST scheme in use can degrade the circuit performance.

Ideally, a BIST structure would be applicable for any kind of functional circuit. The diversity in design topologies and functional and parametric specifications prevents reaching this aim. However, some structured approaches are applicable to wide classes of circuits. The interest in a BIST technique is also related to the ability to perform diagnosis in the field and the possibility of reusing circuitry already available in the functional design.

3.2.1 Test generation and test compaction

Several BIST approaches were proposed in the past that are now common practice among digital designers. For instance, the merger of at-speed built-in test generation and output response analysis, with the scan path technique, culminated with the proposal of a multifunctional digital BIST structure named BILBO: Built-In Logic Block Observer (Koenemann, 1979).

In the realm of analog circuits, in last years some works have proposed on-chip structures for test generation and response evaluation.

In general, the stimulus generation for analog BIST depends on the type of test measurement to apply (Mir, 1995): DC static, AC dynamic or transient response measurements. DC faults are usually detected by a single set of steady state inputs; AC testing is typically performed using sine-wave forms with variable frequency; finally, pulse signals, ramps or triangular waveforms are the input stimuli for transient response measurements. Relaxation and sine-wave oscillators (Gregorian, 1986) are used for the generation of test signals. Dedicated sine-wave oscillators have already been proposed for multifrequency testing (Khaled, 1995). To minimise the test effort, individual test signals can be combined to form a multi-tone test signal (Lu, 1994; Nagi, 1995). To save hardware, a method to reconvert a sigma-delta D/A converter into a precision analog sine-wave oscillator has been proposed in (Toner, 1993). A practical approach to generate on-chip precise and slow analog ramps, intended for analog testing, has been prototyped and validated in (Provost, 2003). (Azaïs, 2001) uses a similar on-chip ramp generator to perform histogram based tests of A/D converters. A different way of generating analog test stimuli consists on feeding pseudo-random digital test patterns into a D/A converter. In this method, called hybrid test stimulus generator (Ohletz, 1991), the digital patterns are generated as in a digital BILBO.

An alternative to existing on-chip test stimuli generators is the vectorless technique called Oscillation Test Method, OTM (Arabi, 1997a). In this approach, the Circuit Under Test (CUT) is converted into an oscillator by adding circuitry in a feedback loop, as shown in figure 10. The resulting circuit generates an oscillation frequency that can be expressed as a function of either the CUT components or its important parameters. In order to increase the fault coverage or to make the fault detection easier, the amplitude of the generated signal must be taken as a test measurement complementary to the oscillation frequency (Huertas, 2002a).

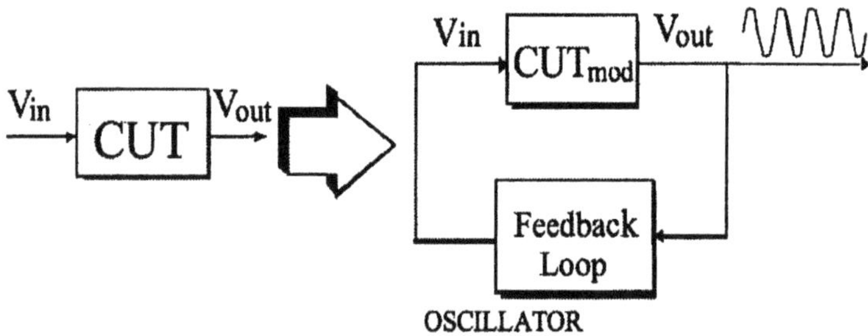

Figure 10. Basic idea of the oscillation test method.

The OTM was successfully applied to filters (Huertas, 2002b) and also to A/D converters (Arabi, 1997b; Huertas, 2003). Figure 11 illustrates the application of this test method to the built-in self-test of a converter (Arabi, 1997b). The oscillating input signal is generated through the charging or discharging of a capacitor with a positive or a negative reference current I, generated on-chip. The reference current is toggled depending on a comparison result between the A/D converter output code, C, and a desired output code, D, after each conversion. If $C < D$, the positive reference current is connected to the capacitor to set a positive slope in the test stimulus. If $C > D$, the negative reference current is chosen to obtain a negative slope in the test stimulus. Testing for the non-linearities of the converter is based on the measurement of the frequency of the signal on the switch control line (*ctrl*), that oscillates around a desired code transition level set by the BIST logic.

For analog circuits, the analysis of the output response is complicated by the fact that analog signals are inherently imprecise. The analysis of the output response can be done by matching the outputs of two identical circuits. This is possible if the function designed leads to replicated sub-functions or because the circuit is duplicated for concurrent checking (Lubaszewski, 1995). When identical outputs are not available, three main approaches can be considered for analysing the test response (Mir, 1995): In the first approach, the analog BIST includes analog checkers which verify the parameters associated with the analog behaviour (according to the specification) for known input test signals (Slamani, 1993). The second approach consists on the generation of a signature that describes the waveform of the output response. A compaction scheme that uses a digital integrator has been reported in (Nagi, 1994). The third approach is based on the conversion of the analog test responses into digital vectors. This conversion can be performed by available blocks as they appear in the circuit under test or by means of some CUT reconfiguration. Similarly to a digital BILBO, whenever an A/D converter is available, the analog test responses can be fed into an output response analysis register to generate a signature (Ohletz, 1991). A bit-stream can also be obtained as test response output, if there exists in the CUT a block that can be configured as a sigma-delta modulator, for example. This is shown in (Cassol, 2003) for the case of analog filters built from a cascade of second order blocks. In that work, every filter stage is tested using a neighbour block that is reconfigured to work as a sigma-delta converter.

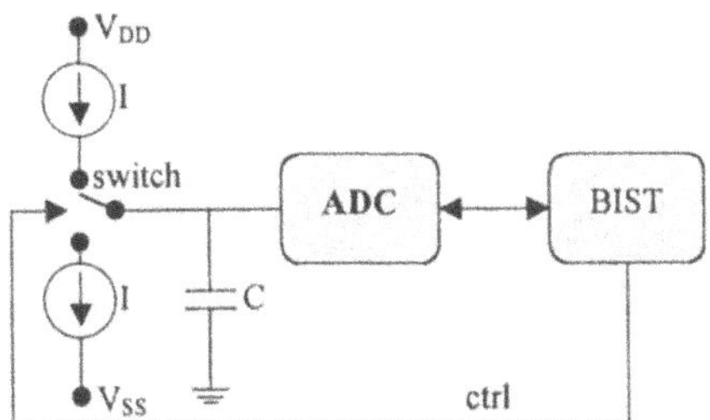

Figure 11. Oscillation BIST applied to A/D converter.

The ability of scanning signals and generating/compacting analog AC-tests using the same hardware has recently led to the proposal of a novel multifunctional BIST structure. This structure, called analog built-in block observer (ABILBO), recreates the digital BILBO versatility in the analog domain (Lubaszewski, 1996). Basically, the ABILBO structure is made up of two analog integrators and one comparator. A switched-capacitor implementation is given in figure 12. Since integrators have duplicated input stages as in figure 6, the operational amplifiers can work as voltage followers and then perform analog scan (mode1). With the operational amplifiers in the normal mode, switches can be properly programmed, such that either a sine-wave oscillator (mode2) or a double-integration signature analyser (mode3) results. The frequency of the quadrature oscillator obtained in mode2 depends linearly on the frequency of the switching clock (Φ1,Φ2). The signature resulting from the selection of mode3 in the ABILBO structure corresponds to the time for the output of the second integrator to reach a predefined reference voltage (V_{REF}). If a counter is used for computing digital signatures, counting must be enabled from the integration start up to the time when the comparator output goes high. In (Renovell, 1997), the ABILBO mode for signature analysis is extended to cope with transient tests. Finally, both integrators can be reset by shorting their integration capacitors (mode4).

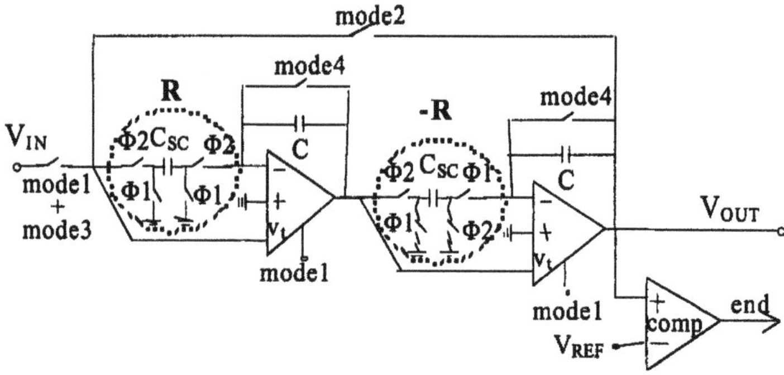

Figure 12. A switched-capacitor analog BILBO.

3.2.2 Current testing

Many faults, such as stuck-on transistors and bridging faults, result in higher than normal currents flowing through the power supplies of the circuit under test (Maly, 1988).

In the case of digital CMOS circuits, for example, these faults create a path between VDD and GND that should not exist in the fault-free circuit. Since the quiescent current becomes orders of magnitude higher than the expected leakage currents, these faults can be detected by using off-chip current sensors. This test method simplifies the test generation process, since the propagation of faults to the circuit primary outputs is no more required. In order to lower the evaluation time of the off-chip approach, intrinsically faster *built-in current sensors* can be used.

In the analog world, the same test method may apply to those circuits that present medium to low quiescent currents. For circuits with high quiescent currents, a possibility is to measure transients using specific *built-in dynamic current sensors*. The sensor proposed in (Argüelles, 1994) is shown in figure 13. It can be used to measure the dynamic current across the most sensitive branches of the circuit under test. To avoid performance degradation, this sensor is coupled to the circuit by means of an additional stage to existing current mirrors. As it can be seen from figure 13, in test mode (Enable=1), the transient current is firstly copied, next converted to a voltage and amplified, and finally digitised. The sensor outputs a signature characterised by the number and width of pulses fitting a predefined time window.

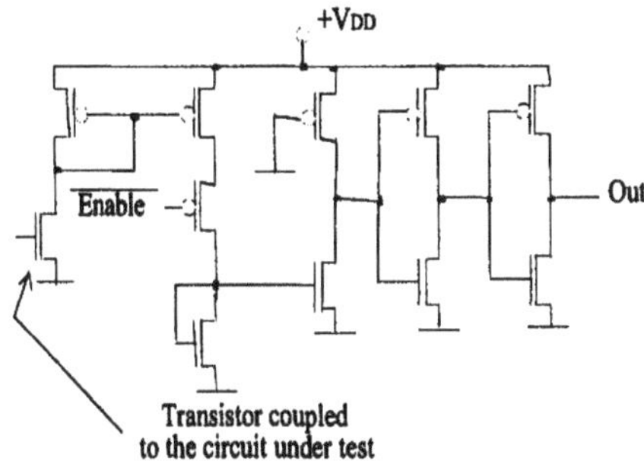

Figure 13. Built-in dynamic current sensor.

Potentially, methods based on current measurements can lead to unified solutions for testing digital and analog parts of mixed-signal integrated circuits (Bracho, 1995).

3.3 Self-checking circuits

In digital self-checking circuits, the concurrent error detection capability is achieved by means of functional circuits, which deliver encoded outputs, and checkers, which verify whether these outputs belong to error detecting codes. The most usual codes are the parity, the Berger and the double-rail code. The general structure of a self-checking circuit is shown in figure 14.

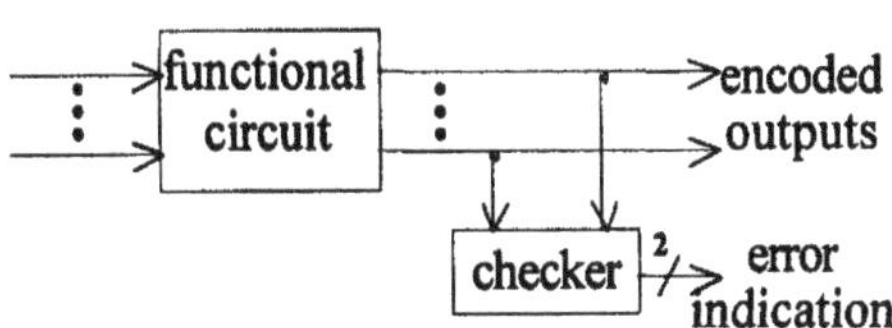

Figure 14. Self-checking circuit.

Most often, self-checking circuits are aimed at reaching the *totally self-checking goal*: the first erroneous output of the functional circuit results in an error indication in the checker outputs.

Similarly to digital self-checking circuits, the aim of designing *analog self-checking circuits* is to meet the totally self-checking goal. This is possible since analog codes can also be defined, for example the differential and duplication codes (Kolarík, 1995). A tolerance is required for checking the validity of an analog functional circuit and this is taken into account within the analog code.

The nodes to be monitored by an analog checker are not necessarily those associated with the circuit outputs, due to commonly used feedback circuitry. In addition, the most important difference is that the input and output code spaces of an analog circuit have an infinite number of elements. Therefore, the hypothesis considered for digital circuits becomes unrealistic, since an infinite number of input signals might be applied within a finite lapse of time. In order to cope with this problem, the self-checking properties are redefined for the analog world in (Nicolaidis, 1993).

In the last years, the self-checking principle has been applied to on-line testing analog and mixed-signal circuits, including filters and A/D converters (Lubaszewski, 1995). The major techniques employed for concurrent error detection are: *partial replication* of modular architectures, e.g. filters based on a cascade of biquads (Huertas, 1992) and pipelined A/D converters (Peralías, 1995); *continuous checksums* in state variable filters (Chatterjee, 1991); *time replication* in current mode A/D converters (Krishnan, 1992); and *balance checking* of fully differential circuits (Mir, 1996b).

The partial replication approach is illustrated in figure 15 for the case of a multistage pipelined A/D converter. Since the converter is built from a *cascade of identical functional modules*, the on-line testing capability can be ensured by an additional *checking module* identical to the converter stages and a multiplexing system. The *multiplexing system* must be such that the outputs of every stage can be compared against the outputs of the checking module, when the latter receives the same input as the former. The *control* gives the sequence of testing that evolves sequentially from the first (1) to the last (L) stage, and then restarts.

Figure 16 illustrates the principle of balance checking applied to fully differential integrated filters. In a correctly balanced fully differential circuit, the operational amplifier inputs are at virtual ground. But, in general, transient faults, deviations in passive components and hard faults in operational amplifier transistors corrupt this balance. In (Mir, 1996b), an analog checker is proposed which is capable of signalling balance deviations, i.e. the occurrence of a common-mode signal at the inputs of fully differential operational amplifiers. This same technique was used for on-line testing A/D converters in (Lubaszewski, 1995) and in (Francesconi, 1996). To improve accuracy of concurrent error detection in fully differential circuits, (Stratigopoulos, 2003a) presented a novel analog checker that dynamically adjusts the error threshold to the magnitude of the input signals. This analog checker was used in (Stratigopoulos, 2003b) to validate a new analog on-line testing approach based on circuit state estimation.

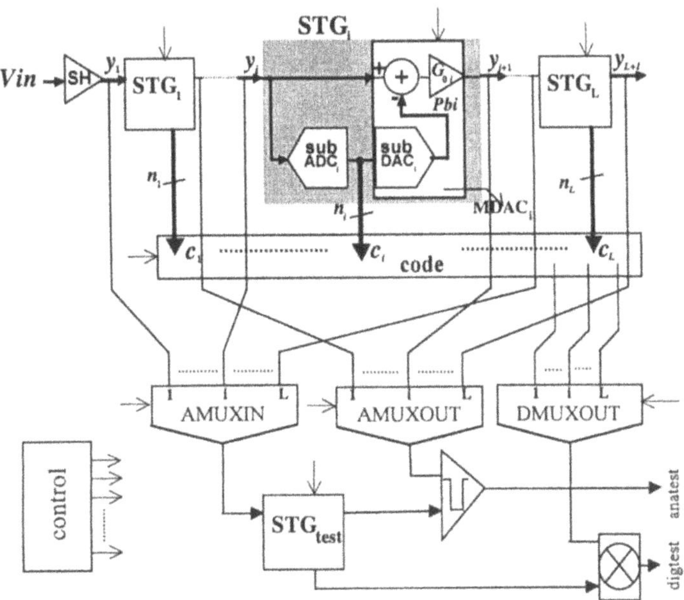

Figure 15. Pipelined A/D converter with on-line test capability.

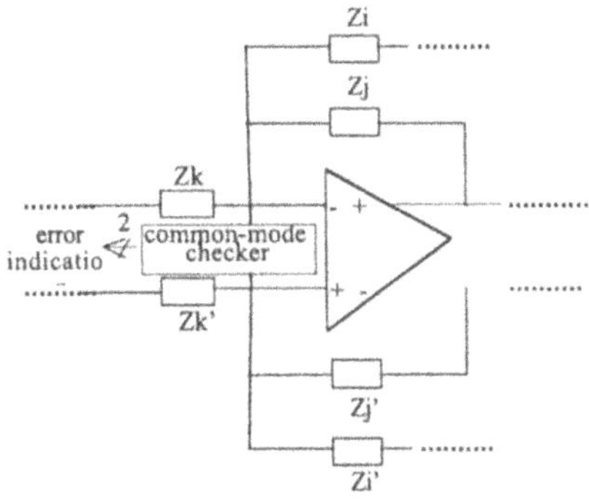

Figure 16. Generic stage of a self-checking fully differential filter.

3.4 Unified built-in self-test

Faults originating from an integrated circuit's manufacture typically manifest as multiple faults. However, conventional self-checking architectures only cover single faults. Besides that, fault latency may lead to the accumulation of faults and can invalidate the self-checking properties. In addition, when the checkers generate an error indication in these circuits, no mechanism exists to recognise if the detected fault is a transient or a permanent one. But this information is important to allow for diagnosis and repair in the field.

A solution to these problems has been given in (Nicolaidis, 1988). Nicolaidis proposes that built-in self-test capabilities similar to those used for production testing are embedded into self-checking circuits. These capabilities must be repeatedly activated, at periods of time no longer than the mean-time between failures. This technique, referred to as *unified built-in self-test (UBIST),* unifies *on-line and off-line tests,* covering all tests necessary during a system's lifetime: manufacturing, field testing and concurrent error detection. Moreover, it simplifies the design of checkers and increases the fault coverage of self-checking circuits.

In the analog domain, the first attempt to couple built-in self-test and self-checking capabilities was made by (Mir, 1996c). Mir proposes the design of a *test master* compliant with the IEEE Std. 1149.1 that efficiently shares hardware between the *off-line and on-line tests of fully differential circuits.* This test master relies on a programmable sine-wave oscillator for test generation and on common-mode analog checkers for test response evaluation. The frequencies to apply to the circuit under test are computed by the test generation tool described in (Mir, 1996a). For concurrent error detection, the checkers monitor the balance of the inputs of fully differential operational amplifiers. To allow for off-line fault detection and fault diagnosis, they additionally observe the balance of operational amplifier outputs (Mir, 1996b).

Another possibility of unifying tests is based on the partial replication scheme presented in the previous section. Assuming the analog filter based on a cascade of biquads shown in figure 17, the multiplexing scheme, the checking module and the comparison mechanism can ensure that *on-line tests* test 1, test 2 and test 3 are applied, in a time-shared manner, to individual filter stages. Since, in this case, the functional modules are not identical but similar, the checking module must be a programmable biquad capable of mimicking the behaviour of every individual filter stage.

The individual biquads can be designed such that they can accommodate, in *off-line test* mode, the *ABILBO structure* of figure 12. Then, off-line tests can be applied in three different phases: In phase test 1, biquad 1 will be tested with biquad 3 working as an oscillator (ABILBO 3) and biquad 2 working as a signature analyser (ABILBO 2). In phase test 2, biquad 2 will be tested with biquad 1 working as an oscillator (ABILBO 1) and biquad 3 working as a signature analyser (ABILBO 3). In phase test 3, biquad 3 will be tested with biquad 2 working as an oscillator (ABILBO 2) and biquad 1 working as a signature analyser (ABILBO 1). A feedback path from the output to the filter input is required to apply the phases test 1 and test 3. In summary, the biquads, while working as test generators, test individual filter stages off-line, and check the ability of the programmable biquad to mimic the filter stages on-line. While working as signature analysers, the biquads check that the test generators work properly, at the same time as they improve the fault diagnosis capability. This occurs because they make it possible to recognise if a fault affects the stage under test or the programmable biquad. As illustrated by this example, the unification of off-line and on-line tests in modular analog circuits is, in general, expected to result in low performance degradation and low overhead penalty.

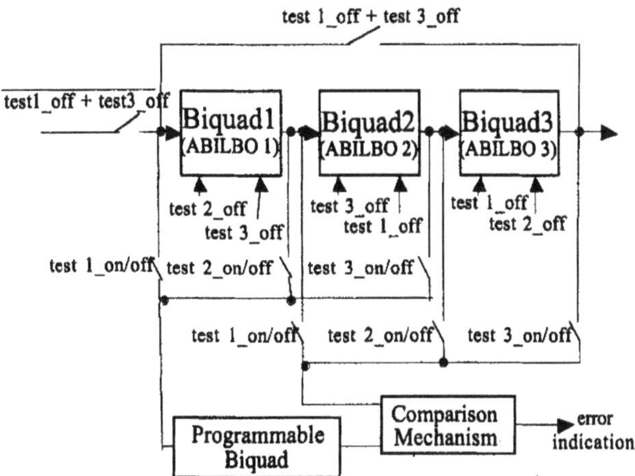

Figure 17. On-line/off-line test merger in a modular analog filter.

The unification of on and off-line tests was also proposed in the realm of data converters built from a cascade of identical functional modules. (Peralías, 1998) addressed the practical implementation of a test technique applicable to digitally-corrected pipelined A/D converters. Because of the self-correction capability, such a kind of converters has some inherent insensitivity to the effect of faults, which represents a disadvantage for testing and diagnosis. Authors show that potentially malfunctioning units can be concurrently identified with low extra circuitry and that the proposed test scheme can also be useful to reduce the time in production-level testing.

4. CONCLUSIONS

Existing design-for-test schemes and related test methods were extensively discussed in this chapter. The analog and mixed-signal cases were addressed, and testing issues were covered at the integrated circuit level. Some of these schemes are natural extensions of digital testing techniques that suffered some adaptations to cope with analog design constraints. Others are based on very specific functional and/or structural properties of particular classes of analog and mixed-signal circuits and signals.

Although structural design-for-test approaches offer, in general, more efficient implementations than specification-driven schemes, they cannot always ensure that the functional performances of the circuit are all met. Then, functional tests are still required, although they are much more time and resource consuming than fault-based approaches. A combination of functional and structural approaches may provide, in many situations, the best quality and cost trade off for analog and mixed-signal testing.

The major advantages of design-for-test over traditional external test methods can be summarised as follows:

- the enhanced accessibility to internal test points makes it possible to develop short test sequences that achieve high fault coverages. This leads to high quality tests, requiring short application times. As a consequence, reliability is improved and time-to-market is shortened;
- cheaper testers can be used, as performance, interfacing and functional requirements are relaxed. Design-for-testability, built-in self-test and self-checking alleviate the probing requirements for the test equipment. Built-in self-test and self-checking alleviate functionality, since test generation and/or response evaluation are performed on-chip.

The main drawbacks that come along with design-for-test are the following:

- an additional time is needed to design the test mechanisms to embed into integrated circuits and systems. However, the test development times for conventional testing methods are often longer. An alternative is to reuse pre-designed test cores;
- extra silicon is required to integrate test capabilities. However, embedded test structures have evolved over the years, and can now achieve very low area overheads. Additionally, the cost of transistors continues to drop.
- the performance of the circuit under test may be degraded by the additional test structures. Again, embedded test structures are expected to evolve, offering more efficient solutions. However, this is still a challenge for analog testing.

Reuse has been the keyword in the domain of integrated systems design. As new synthesis-for-test tools and test standards are developed, reuse tends also to dominate the testing of integrated circuits and systems. In fact, in the test domain this paradigm may not be limited to reuse pre-developed test cores in new designs. It can be further extended to reuse the same embedded test cores to perform different types of tests in different phases of a circuit's lifetime. These tests would allow for prototype debugging, manufacture testing, maintenance checking, and concurrent error detection in the field.

Only mechanisms based on unified off-line and on-line tests can add this dimension to the test reuse.

5. REFERENCES

Abramovici, M., Breuer, M.A. and Friedmann, A.D., 1990, *Digital Systems Testing and Testable Design*, Computer Science Press, New York.

Arabi, K. and Kaminska, B., 1997a, Testing analog and mixed-signal integrated circuits using oscillation-test method, *IEEE Trans. on CAD of Integrated Circuits and Systems* **16**(7).

Arabi, K. and Kaminska, B., 1997b, Oscillation built-in self test (OBIST) scheme for functional and structural testing of analog and mixed-signal circuits, in: *International Test Conference*, Proceedings, pp. 786-795

Argüelles, J., Martínez, M. and Bracho, S., 1994, Dynamic Idd test circuitry for mixed-signal ICs, *Electronics Letters* **30**(6).

Azaïs, F., Bernard, S., Bertrand, Y. and Renovell, M., 2001, Implementation of a linear histrogram BIST for ADCs, in: *Design Automation and Test in Europe*, Proceedings.

Bernard, S., Comte, M., Azaïs, F., Bertrand, Y. and Renovell, M., 2003, A new methodology for ADC test flow optimization, in: *International Test Conference*, Proceedings, pp. 201-209.

Bracho, S., Martínez, M. and Argüelles, J., 1995, Current test methods in mixed-signal circuits, in: *Midwest Symposium on Circuits and Systems*, Proceedings, pp. 1162-1167.

Bratt, A.H., Richardson, A.M.D., Harvey, R.J.A. and Dorey, A.P., 1995, A design-for-test structure for optimising analogue and mixed signal IC test, in: *European Design and Test Conference*, Proceedings, pp. 24-33.

Burns, M. and Roberts, G.W., 2001, *An Introduction to Mixed-Signal IC Test and Measurement*, Oxford University Press.

Calvano, J.V., Castro Alves, V., and Lubaszewski, M., 2000, Fault detection methodology and BIST method for 2nd order Butterworth, Chebyshev and Bessel Filter Approximations, in: *IEEE VLSI Test Symposium*, Proceedings.

Calvano, J.V., Mesquita Filho, A.C., Castro Alves, V. and Lubaszewski, M., 2001, Fault models and test generation for OpAmp circuits – the FFM, *KAP Journal of Electronic Testing: Theory and Applications* **17**:121-138.

Calvano, J.V., Castro Alves, V., Mesquita Filho, A.C. and Lubaszewski, M., 2002, Filters designed for testability wrapped on the mixed-signal test bus, in: *IEEE VLSI Test Symposium*, Proceedings, pp.201-206.

Carro, L. and Negreiros, M., 1998, Efficient analog test methodology based on adaptive algorithms, in: *Design Automation Conference*, pp. 32-37.

Cassol, L., Betat, O., Carro, L. and Lubaszewski, M., 2003, The ΣΔ-BIST method applied to analog filters, *KAP Journal of Electronic Testing: Theory and Applications* **19**:13-20.

Caunegre, P. and Abraham, C., 1996, Fault simulation for mixed-signal systems, *KAP Journal of Electronic Testing: Theory and Applications* **8**:143-152.

Chatterjee, A., 1991, Concurrent error detection in linear analog and switched-capacitor state variable systems using continuous checksums, in: *International Test Conference*, Proceedings, pp. 582-591.

Cota, E.F., Lubaszewski, M. and Di Domênico, E.J., 1997, A new frequency-domain analog test generation tool, in: *International Conference on Very Large Scale Integration*, Proceedings, pp. 503-514.

Devarayanadurg, G. and Soma, M., 1994, Analytical fault modelling and static test generation for analog ICs, in: *International Conference on Computer-Aided Design*, Proceedings, pp. 44-47.

Devarayanadurg, G. and Soma, M., 1995, Dynamic test signal design for analog ICs, in: *International Conference on Computer-Aided Design*, Proceedings, pp. 627-629.

Eichelberger, E.B. and Williams, T.W., 1978, A logic design structure for LSI testability, *Journal of Design Automation and Fault-Tolerant Computing* **2**(2): 165-178.

Francesconi, F., Liberali, V., Lubaszewski, M. and Mir, S., 1996, Design of high-performance band-pass sigma-delta modulator with concurrent error detection, in: *International Conference on Electronics, Circuits and Systems*, Proceedings, pp. 1202-1205.

Gregorian, R. and Temes, G.C., 1986, *Analog MOS Integrated Circuits for Signal Processing*, John Wiley and Sons, New York.

Huertas, G., Vázquez, D., Peralías, E.J., Rueda, A. and Huertas, J.L., 2002a, Testing mixed-signal cores: a practical oscillation-based test in an analog macrocell, *IEEE Design and Test of Computers* **19**(6):73-82.

Huertas, G., Vázquez, D., Rueda, A. and Huertas, J.L., 2002b, Practical oscillation-based test of integrated filters, *IEEE Design and Test of Computers* **19**(6):64-72.

Huertas, G., Vázquez, D., Rueda, A. and Huertas, J.L., 2003, Oscillation-based test in oversampling A/D converters, *Elsevier Microelectronics Journal* **34**(10):927-936.

Huertas, J.L., Vázquez, D. and Rueda, A., 1992, On-line testing of switched-capacitor filters, in: *IEEE VLSI Test Symposium*, Proceedings, pp. 102-106.

IEEE Standard 1149.1, 1990, *IEEE Standard Test Access Port and Boundary Scan Architecture*, IEEE Standards Board, New York.

IEEE Standard 1149-4, 1999, *IEEE Standard for a Mixed Signal Test Bus*, IEEE Standards Board, New York.

Khaled, S., Kaminska, B., Courtois, B. and Lubaszewski, M., 1995, Frequency-based BIST for analog circuit testing, in: *IEEE VLSI Test Symposium*, Proceedings, pp. 54-59.

Kolarík, V., Mir, S., Lubaszewski, M. and Courtois, B., 1995, Analogue checkers with absolute and relative tolerances, *IEEE Transactions on Computer-Aided Design of Integrated Circuits and Systems* **14**(5): 607-612.

Koenemann, B., Mucha, J. and Zwiehoff, G., 1979, Built-in logic block observation techniques, in: *Test Conference*, Proceedings, pp. 37-41.

Krishnan, S., Sahli, S. and Wey, C.-L., 1992, Test generation and concurrent error detection in current-mode A/D converter, in: *International Test Conference*, Proceedings, pp. 312-320.

LeBlanc, J.J., 1984, LOCST: A built-in self-test technique, *IEEE Design and Test of Computers*, November, pp. 45-52.

Lu, A.K. and Roberts, G.W., 1994, An analog multi-tone signal generator for built-in self-test applications, in: *International Test Conference*, Proceedings, pp. 650-659.

Lubaszewski, M., Mir, S., Rueda, A. and Huertas, J.L., 1995, Concurrent error detection in analog and mixed-signal integrated circuits, in: *Midwest Symposium on Circuits and Systems*, Proceedings, pp. 1151-1156.

Lubaszewski, M., Mir, S. and Pulz, L., 1996, ABILBO: Analog BuILt-in Block Observer, in: *International Conference on Computer-Aided Design*, Proceedings, pp. 600-603.

Mahoney, M., 1987, *DSP-based Testing of Analog and Mixed-Signal Circuits*, IEEE Computer Society Press, 1987.

Maly, W. and Nigh, P., 1988, Built-in current testing - feasibility study, in: *International Conference on Computer-Aided Design*, Proceedings, pp. 340-343.

Maunder, C.M., 1994, The test access port and boundary scan architecture: an introduction to ANSI/IEEE Std. 1149.1 and its applications, in: *Forum on Boundary Scan for Digital and Mixed-Signal Boards*, CERN, Geneva.

Meixner, A. and Maly, W., 1991, Fault modelling for the testing of mixed integrated circuits, in: *International Test Conference*, Proceedings, pp. 564-572.

Milor, L. and Visvanathan, V., 1989, Detection of catastrophic faults in analog integrated circuits, *IEEE Transactions on Computer-Aided Design* **8**(2): 114-130.

Mir, S., Lubaszewski, M., Liberali, V. and Courtois, B., 1995, Built-in self-test approaches for analogue and mixed-signal integrated circuits, in: *Midwest Symposium on Circuits and Systems*, Proceedings, pp. 1145-1150.

Mir, S., Lubaszewski, M. and Courtois, B., 1996a, Fault-based ATPG for linear analog circuits with minimal size multifrequency test sets, *KAP Journal of Electronic Testing: Theory and Applications* **9**:43-57.

Mir, S., Lubaszewski, M., Kolarík, V. and Courtois, B., 1996b, Fault-based testing and diagnosis of balanced filters, *KAP Journal on Analog Integrated Circuits and Signal Processing* **11**:5-19.

Mir, S., Lubaszewski, M. and Courtois, B., 1996c, Unified built-in self-test for fully differential analog circuits, *KAP Journal of Electronic Testing: Theory and Applications* **9**:135-151.

Mir, S., Rueda, A., Olbrich, T., Peralías, E. and Huertas, J.L., 1997, SWITTEST: Automatic switch-level fault simulation and test evaluation of switched-capacitor systems, in: *Design Automation Conference*, Proceedings.

Nácul, A.C., Carro, L., Janner, D. and Lubaszewski, M., 2002, Testing of RF mixers with adaptive filters, *Elsevier Microelectronics Journal* **(33)**10:847-853.

Nagi, N., Chatterjee, A. and Abraham, J.A., 1993a, DRAFTS: Discretized analog circuit fault simulator, in: *Design Automation Conference*, Proceedings, pp. 509-514.

Nagi, N., Chatterjee, A., Balivada, A. and Abraham, J.A., 1993b, Fault-based automatic test generator for linear analog circuits, in: *International Conference on Computer-Aided Design*, Proceedings, pp. 88-91.

Nagi, N., Chatterjee, A. and Abraham, J.A., 1994, A signature analyzer for analog and mixed-signal circuits, in: *International Conference on Computer Design*, Proceedings, pp. 284-287.

Nagi, N., Chatterjee, A., Balivada, A. and Abraham, J.A., 1995, Efficient multisine testing of analog circuits, in: *International Conference on VLSI Design*, Proceedings, pp. 234-238.

Nicolaidis, M., 1988, A Unified Built-In Self-Test Scheme: UBIST, in: *International Symposium on Fault Tolerant Computing*, Proceedings, pp. 157-163.

Nicolaidis, M., 1993, Finitely self-checking circuits and their application on current sensors, in: *IEEE VLSI Test Symposium*, Proceedings, pp. 66-69.

Ohletz, M., 1991, Hybrid Built-In Self-Test (HBIST) for mixed analog/digital integrated circuits, in: *European Test Conference*, Proceedings, pp. 307-316.

Osseiran, A., 1995, Getting to a test standard for mixed-signal boards, in: *Midwest Symposium on Circuits and Systems*, Proceedings, pp. 1157-1161.

Peralías, E., Rueda, A. and Huertas, J.L., 1995, An on-line testing approach for pipelined A/D converters, in: *IEEE International Mixed-Signal Testing Workshop*, Proceedings, pp.44-49.

Peralías, E., Rueda, A., Prieto, J.A. and Huertas, J.L., 1998, DFT & on-line test of high-performance data converters: a practical case, in: *International Test Conference*, Proceedings, pp.534-540.

Provost, B. and Sánchez-Sinencio E., 2003, On-chip ramp generators for mixed-signal BIST and ADC self-test, *IEEE Journal of Solid-State Circuits* **38**(2):263-273.

Renovell, M., Lubaszewski, M., Mir, S., Azais, F. and Bertrand, Y., 1997, A multi-mode signature analyzer for analog and mixed circuits, in: *International Conference on Very Large Scale Integration*, Proceedings, pp. 65-76.

Sebeke, C., Teixeira, J.P. and Ohletz, M.J., 1995, Automatic fault extraction and simulation of layout realistic faults for integrated analogue circuits, in: *European Design and Test Conference*, Proceedings, pp. 464-468.

Slamani, M. and Kaminska, B., 1993, T-BIST: A Built-In Self-Test for analog circuits based on parameter Translation, in: *Asian Test Symposium*, Proceedings, pp. 172-177.

Slamani, M. and Kaminska, B., 1995, Multifrequency analysis of faults in analog circuits, *IEEE Design and Test of Computers* **12**(2):70-80.

Soma, M., 1990, A design-for-test methodology for active analog filters, in: *International Test Conference*, Proceedings, pp. 183-192.

Soma, M. and Kolarík, V., 1994, A design-for-test technique for switched-capacitor filters, in: *VLSI Test Symposium*, Proceedings, pp. 42-47.

Stratigopoulos, H.-G.D. and Makris, Y., 2003a, An analog checker with dynamically adjustable error threshold for fully differential circuits, in: *IEEE VLSI Test Symposium*, Proceedings, pp. 209-214.

Stratigopoulos, H.-G.D. and Makris, Y., 2003b, Concurrent error detection in linear analog circuits using state estimation, in: *International Test Conference*, Proceedings, pp. 1164-1173.

Tsai, S.J., 1991, Test vector generation for linear analog devices, in: *International Test Conference*, Proceedings, pp. 592-597.

Toner, M.F. and Roberts, G.W., 1993, A BIST scheme for an SNR test of a sigma-delta ADC, in: *International Test Conference*, Proceedings, pp. 805-814.

WEB SERVICES

Mohand-Said Hacid
University Claude Bernard Lyon 1 - France

Abstract: In the emerging world of Web services, services will be combined in innovative ways to form elaborate services out of building blocks of other services. This is predicated on having a common ground of vocabulary and communication protocols operating in a secured environment. Currently, massive standardization efforts are aiming at achieving this common ground. We discuss aspects related to services, such as possible architectures, modeling, discovery, composition and security.

Key words: Web services architecture, Web services modeling, Web services discovery.

1. INTRODUCTION

A Web service is programmable application logic accessible using standard Internet protocols. Web services combine the best aspects of component-based development and the Web. Like components, Web services represent functionality that can be easily reused without knowing how the service is implemented. Unlike current component technologies which are accessed via proprietary protocols, Web services are accessed via ubiquitous Web protocols (ex: HTTP) using universally accepted data formats (ex: XML).

In practical business terms, Web services have emerged as a powerful mechanism for integrating disparate IT systems and assets. They work using widely accepted, ubiquitous technologies and are governed by commonly adopted standards. Web Services can be adopted incrementally at low cost. Today, enterprises use Web services for point-to-point application integration, to reuse existing IT assets, and to securely connecting to business partners or customers. Independent Software Vendors embed Web services functionality in their software products so they are easier to deploy.

From a historical perspective, Web services represent the convergence between the service-oriented architecture (SOA) and the Web. SOAs has evolved over the last years to support high performance, scalability, reliability, and availability. To achieve the best performance, applications are designed as services that run on a cluster of centralized application servers. A service is an application that can be accessed through a programmable interface. In the past, clients accessed these services using a tightly coupled, distributed computing protocol, such as DCOM, CORBA, or RMI. While these protocols are very effective for building a specific application, they limit the flexibility of the system. The tight coupling used in this architecture limits the reusability of individual services. Each of the protocols is constrained by dependencies on vendor implementations, platforms, languages, or data encoding schemes that severely limit interoperability. Additionally, none of these protocols operates effectively over the Web.

The Web services architecture takes all the best features of the service-oriented architecture and combines it with the Web. The Web supports universal communication using loosely coupled connections. Web protocols are completely vendor-,platform-, and language-independent. The resulting effect is an architecture that eliminates the usual constraints of distributed computing protocols. Web services support Web-based access, easy integration, and service reusability.

A Web service is an application or information resource that can be accessed using standard Web protocols. Any type of application can be offered as a Web service. Web services are applicable to any type of Web environment: Internet, intranet, or extranet. Web services can support business-to-consumer, business-to-business, department-to-department, or peer-to-peer interactions. A Web service consumer can be a human user accessing the service through a desktop or wireless browser, it can be an application program, or it can be another Web service. Web Services support existing security frameworks.

1.1 Characteristics of Web Services

A Web service exhibits the following characteristics:

- A Web service is accessible over the Web. Web services communicate using platform-independent and language-neutral Web

protocols. These Web protocols ensure easy integration of heterogeneous environments.
- A Web service provides an interface that can be called from another program. This application-to-application programming interface can be invoked from any type of application client or service. The Web service interface acts as a liaison between the Web and the actual application logic that implements the service.
- A Web service is registered and can be located through a Web service Registry. The registry enables service consumers to find services that match their needs.
- Web services support loosely coupled connections between systems. They communicate by passing messages to each other. The Web service interface adds a layer of abstraction to the environment that makes the connections flexible and adaptable.

1.2 Web Services Technologies

Web services can be developed using any programming language and can be deployed on any platform. Web services can communicate because they all speak the same language: the Extensible Markup Language (XML). Web services use XML to describe their interfaces and to encode their messages. XML-based Web services communicate over standard Web protocols using XML interfaces and XML messages, which any application can interpret.

However, XML by itself does not ensure effortless communication. The applications need standard formats and protocols that allow them to properly interpret the XML. Hence, three XML-based technologies are emerging as the standards for Web services:

- Simple Object Access Protocol (**SOAP**) [1] defines a standard communications protocol for Web services.
- Web Services Description Language (**WSDL**) [3] defines a standard mechanism to describe a Web service.
- Universal Description, Discovery and Integration (**UDDI**) [2] provides a standard mechanism to register and discover Web services.

The rest of the chapter is organized as follows: Section 2 gives an overview of the classical approach to Web services (architecture and components). Section 3 introduces semantic Web services. We conclude in section 4.

2. WEB SERVICES ARCHITECTURE

Distributed computing has always been difficult. Now the business world has lined up behind the term "Web services" to try and build services that are highly reliable and scalable.

Many Web services architectures today are based on three components (figure 1): the service requestor, the service provider, and the service registry, thereby closely following a client/server model with an explicit name and directory service (the service registry). Although simple, such an architecture illustrates quite well the basic infrastructure necessary to implement Web services: a way to communicate (SOAP), a way to describe services (WSDL), and a name and directory server (UDDI). SOAP, WSDL and UDDI are nowadays the core of Web services. Specifications covering other aspects are typically designed based on SOAP, WSDL and UDDI. This is similar to the way conventional middleware platforms are built, where the basic components are interaction protocols, IDLs, and name and directory services.

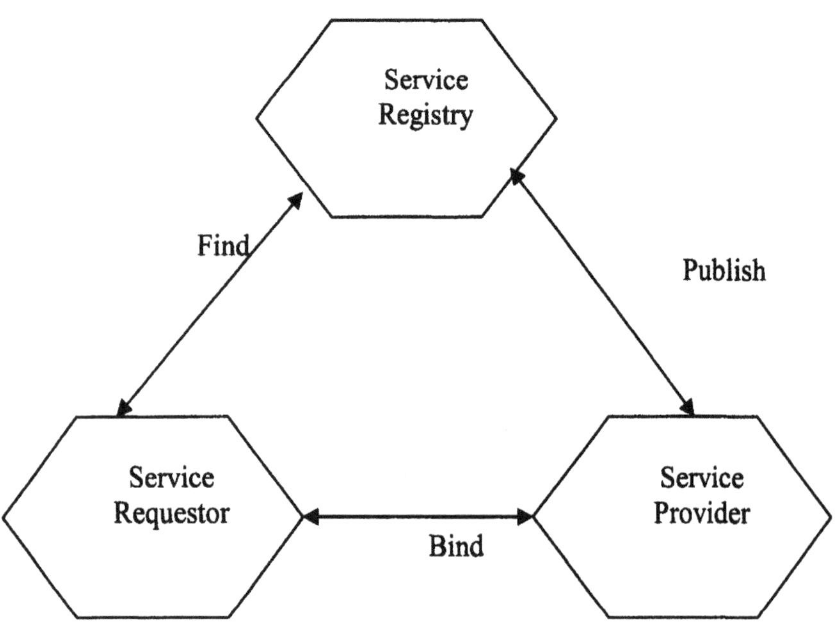

Figure 1. Web Services Architecture

Figure 2 shows how the main components of a Web service architecture relate to one another. When a service provider wants to make the service available to service consumers, he describes the service using WSDL and registers the service in a UDDI registry. The UDDI registry will then maintain pointers to the WSDL description and to the service. When a service consumer wants to use a service, he queries the UDDI registry to find a service that matches his needs and obtains the WSDL description of the service, as well as the access point of the service. The service consumer uses the WSDL description to construct a SOAP message with which to communicate with the service.

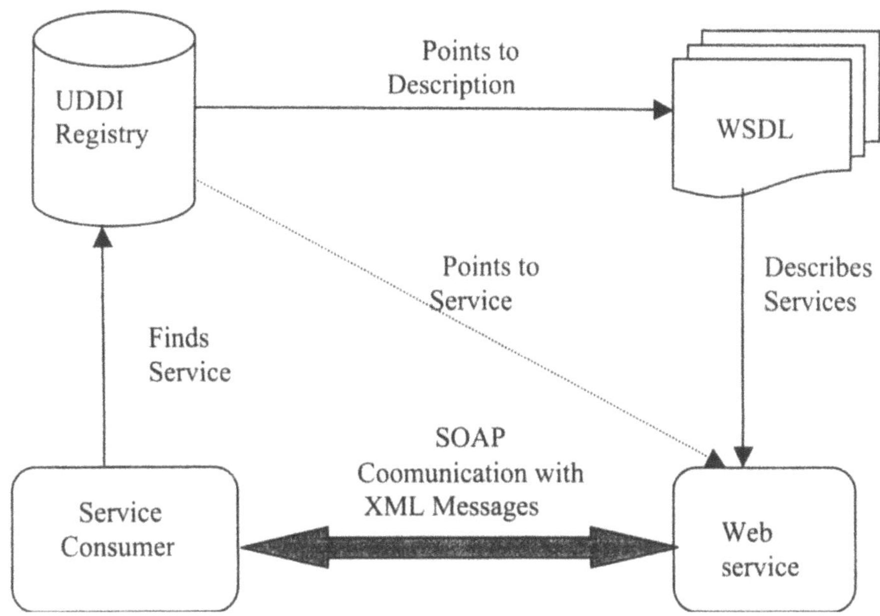

Figure 2. Web services Components – current technologies

2.1 SOAP

SOAP is an extensible XML messaging protocol that forms the foundation for Web Services. SOAP provides a simple and consistent mechanism that allows one application to send an XML message to another application. Fundamentally, SOAP supports peer-to-peer communications (figure 3). A SOAP message is a one-way transmission from a SOAP sender to a SOAP receiver, and any application can participate in an exchange as either a SOAP sender or a SOAP receiver. SOAP messages may be combined to support many communication behaviors, including request/ response, solicit response, and notification.

SOAP was first developed in late 1999 by DevelopMentor, Microsoft, and UserLand as a Windows-specific XML-based remote procedure call (RPC) protocol. In early 2000 Lotus and IBM joined the effort and helped produce an open, extensible version of the specification that is both platform-and language-neutral. This version of the specification, called SOAP 1.1 (see http://www.w3.org/TR/SOAP/), was submitted to the World Wide Web Consortium (W3C). W3C subsequently initiated a standardization effort.

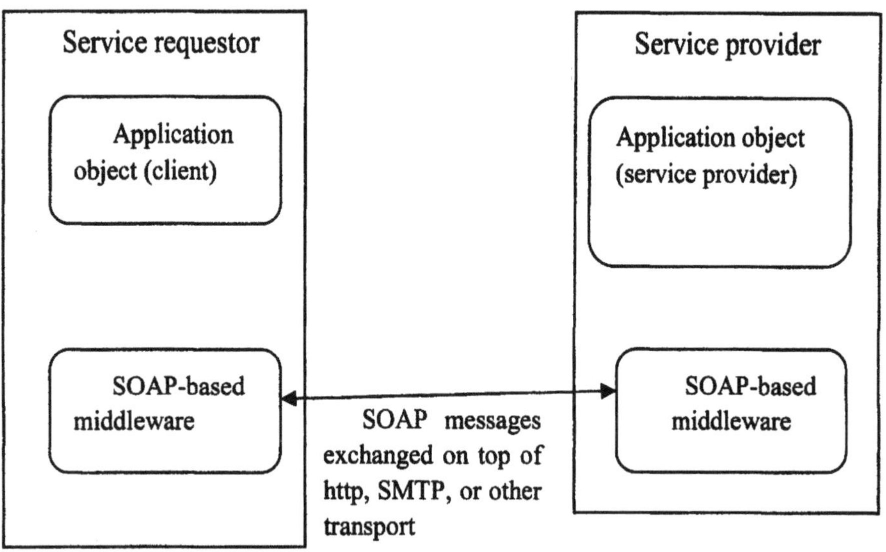

Figure 3. Clients can invoke Web services by exchanging SOAP messages

A pictorial representation of the SOAP message is given in figure 4. Clients can invoke Web services by exchanging SOAP messages.

- **SOAP Envelope.** The SOAP envelope provides a mechanism to identify the contents of a message and to explain how the message should be processed. A SOAP envelope includes a SOAP header and a SOAP body. The SOAP header provides an extensible mechanism to supply directive or control information about the message. For example, a SOAP header could be used to implement transactions, security, reliability, or payment mechanisms. The SOAP body contains the payload that is being sent in the SOAP message.

- **SOAP Transport Binding Framework.** It defines bindings for HTTP and the HTTP Extension Framework.
- **SOAP Serialization Framework.** All data passed through SOAP messages are encoded using XML, but there is no default serialization mechanism to map application-defined datatypes to XML elements. Data can be passed as literals or as encoded values. Users can define their own serialization mechanism, or they can use the serialization mechanism defined by the SOAP encoding rules. The SOAP encoding style is based on a simple type system derived from the W3C XML Schema Part 2:Datatypes Recommendation (see http://www.w3.org/TR/xmlschema-2/). It supports common features found in the type systems of most programming languages and databases. It supports simple scalar types, such as "string ", "integer ", and "enumeration ", and it supports complex types, such as "struct " and "array ".
- **SOAP RPC Representation.** SOAP messaging supports very loosely coupled communications between two applications. The SOAP sender sends a message and the SOAP receiver determines what to do with it. The SOAP sender does not really need to know anything about the implementation of the service other than the format of the message and the access point URI. It is entirely up to the SOAP receiver to determine, based on the contents of the message, what the sender is requesting and how to process it. SOAP also supports a more tightly coupled communication scheme based on the SOAP RPC representation. The SOAP RPC representation defines a programming convention that represents RPC requests and responses. Using SOAP RPC, the developer formulates the SOAP request as a method call with zero or more parameters. The SOAP response returns a return value and zero or more parameters. SOAP RPC requests and responses are marshaled into a "struct" datatype and passed in the SOAP body.

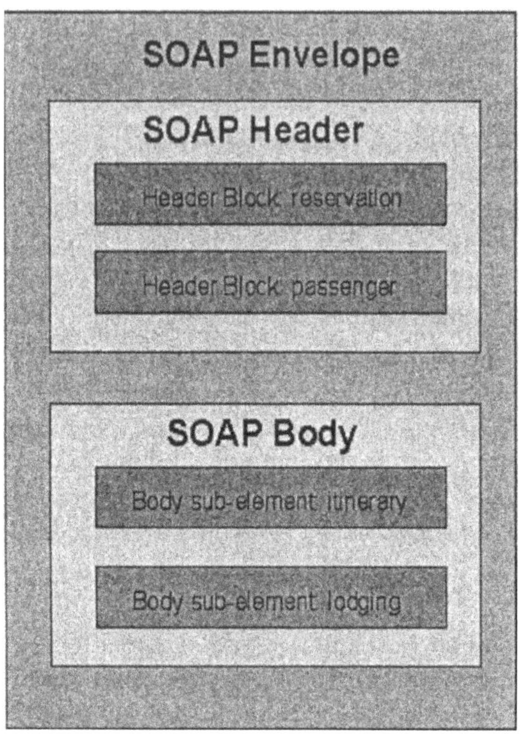

Figure 4. Structure of SOAP messages

2.1.1 SOAP Message Exchange

SOAP is a simple messaging framework for transferring information specified in the form of an XML infoset between an initial SOAP sender and an ultimate SOAP receiver. The more interesting scenarios typically involve multiple message exchanges between these two nodes. The simplest such exchange is a request-response pattern. Some early uses of SOAP emphasized the use of this pattern as means for conveying remote procedure calls (RPC), but it is important to note that not all SOAP request-response exchanges can or need to be modeled as RPCs. The latter is used when there is a need to model a certain programmatic behavior, with the exchanged messages conforming to a pre-defined description of the remote call and its return. A much larger set of usage scenarios than that covered by the request-response pattern can be modeled simply as XML-based content exchanged in SOAP messages to form a back-and-forth "conversation", where the semantics are at the level of the sending and receiving applications.

2.2 WSDL

WSDL is an XML format for describing network services as a set of endpoints operating on messages containing either document-oriented or procedure-oriented information. The operations and messages are described abstractly, and then bound to a concrete network protocol and message format to define an endpoint. Related concrete endpoints are combined into abstract endpoints (services). WSDL is extensible to allow description of endpoints and their messages regardless of what message formats or network protocols are used to communicate. WebMethods' Web Interface Definition Language (WIDL), one of the pioneering specifications for description of remote Web services, was an XML format that took familiar approach (which was accessing functionality on a remote machine as if it were on a local machine) to users of remote procedural technologies, such as RPC and CORBA. There was some fit between WIDL and the XML-RPC system by UserLand. The former has since faded away, as message-based XML technologies have proven more popular than their procedural equivalents. The latter seems to be giving way to SOAP, which has support for message-oriented as well as procedural approaches.

The Web services Description Language (WSDL) is an XML-based language used to describe the services a business offers and to provide a way for individuals and other businesses to access those services electronically. WSDL is the cornerstone of the Universal Description, Discovery, and Integration (UDDI) initiative spearheaded by Microsoft, IBM, and Ariba. UDDI is an XML-based registry for businesses worldwide, which enables businesses to list themselves and their services on the Internet. WSDL is the language used to do this.

WSDL is derived from Microsoft's Simple Object Access Protocol (SOAP) and IBM's Network Accessible Service Specification Language (NASSL). WSDL replaces both NASSL and SOAP as the means of expressing business services in the UDDI registry.

2.2.1 WSDL Document Types

To assist with publishing and finding WSDL service descriptions in a UDDI Registry, WSDL documents are divided into two types: *service interfaces* and *service implementations* (see figure 5).

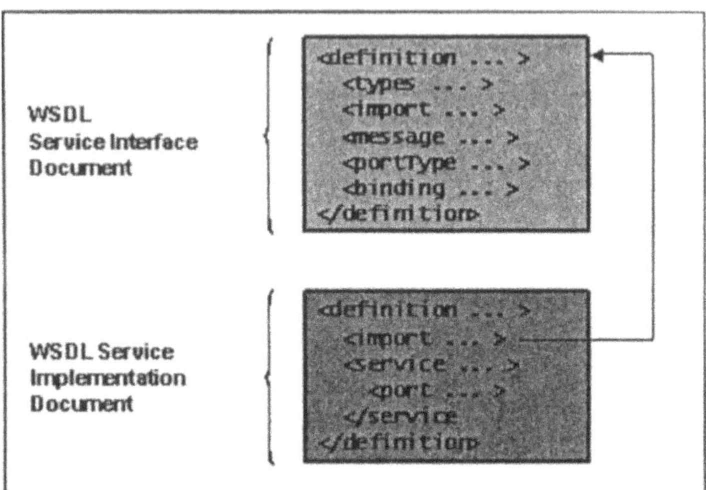

Figure 5. WSDL document types

A service interface is described by a WSDL document that contains the *types*, *import*, *message*, *portType*, and *binding* elements. A service interface contains the WSDL service definition that will be used to implement one or more services. It is an abstract definition of a Web service, and is used to describe a specific type of service.

A service interface document can reference another service interface document using an import element. For example, a service interface that contains only the message and portType elements can be referenced by another service interface that contains only bindings for the portType.

The WSDL service implementation document will contain the *import* and *service* elements. A service implementation document contains a description of a service that implements a service interface. At least one of the import elements will contain a reference to the WSDL service interface document. A service implementation document can contain references to more than one service interface document.

The import element in a WSDL service implementation document contains two attributes. The *namespace* attribute value is a URL that matches the *targetNamespace* in the service interface document. The *location* attribute is a URL that is used to reference the WSDL document that contains the complete service interface definition. The *binding* attribute on the port element contains a reference to a specific binding in the service interface document.

The service interface document is developed and published by the *service interface provider*. The service implementation document is created and published by the *service provider*. The roles of the service interface provider and service provider are logically separate, but they can be the same business entity.

A complete WSDL service description is a combination of a service interface and a service implementation document. Since the service interface represents a reusable definition of a service, it is published in a UDDI registry as a tModel. The service implementation describes instances of a service. Each instance is defined using a WSDL service element. Each service element in a service implementation document is used to publish a UDDI businessService.

When publishing a WSDL service description, a service interface must be published as a tModel before a service implementation is published as a businessService.

2.3 UDDI

Just before WSDL emerged, a consortium of 36 companies, including IBM, Ariba, and Microsoft, launched the Universal Description, Discovery and Integration (UDDI) system, an initiative to provide a standard directory of on-line business services with an elaborate API for querying the directories and service providers.

The key item of consideration in the UDDI specifications is the "Web service." A Web service describes specific business functionality exposed by a company, usually through an Internet connection, for the purpose of providing a way for another company or software program to use the service. The UDDI specifications define a way to publish and discover information about Web services. UDDI aims to automate the process of publishing your preferred way of doing business, finding trading partners and have them find you, and interoperate with these trading partners over the Internet.

Prior to the UDDI project, no industry-wide approach was available for businesses to reach their customers and partners with information about their products and Web services. Nor was there a uniform method that detailed how to integrate the systems and processes that are already in place at and between business partners. Nothing attempted to cover both the business and development aspects of publishing and locating information associated with a piece of software on a global scale.

Conceptually, a business can register three types of information into a UDDI registry. The specification does not call out these types specifically, but they provide a good summary of what UDDI can store for a business:

- **White pages**. Basic contact information and identifiers about a company, including business name, address, contact information, and unique identifiers such as tax IDs. This information allows others to discover your Web service based upon your business identification.
- **Yellow pages**. Information that describes a Web service using different categorizations (taxonomies). This information allows others to discover your Web service based upon its categorization (such as being in the manufacturing or car sales business).
- **Green pages**. Technical information that describes the behaviors and supported functions of a Web service hosted by your business. This information includes pointers to the grouping information of Web services and where the Web services are located.

2.3.1 Why UDDI?

Most eCommerce-enabling applications and Web services currently in place take divergent paths to connecting buyers, suppliers, marketplaces and service providers. Without large investments in technology infrastructure, businesses of all sizes and types can only transact Internet-based business with global trading partners they have discovered and who have the same applications and Web services.

UDDI aims to address this impediment by specifying a framework which will enable businesses to:

- Discover each other.
- Define how they interact over the Internet.
- Share information in a global registry that will more rapidly accelerate the global adoption of B2B eCommerce.

2.3.2 UDDI Business Registry

UDDI relies upon a distributed registry of businesses and their service descriptions implemented in a common XML format.

The UDDI Business Registry provides an implementation of the UDDI specification. Any company can access the registry on the Internet, enter the description of its business, reach a UDDI site and search through all the business services listed in the UDDI registry. There is no cost to access information in the registry. Though based on XML, the registry can also describe services implemented in HTML, CORBA, or any other type of programming model or language.

3. TOWARDS SEMANTIC WEB SERVICES

3.1 Introduction

Semantic Web services are emerging as a promising technology for the effective automation of services discovery, combination, and management [25, 21, 20]. They aim at leveraging two major trends in Web technologies, namely Web services and Semantic Web :

- Web services built upon XML as vehicle for exchanging messages across applications. The basic technological infrastructure for Web services is structured around three major standards: SOAP, WSDL, and UDDI [33, 16]. These standards provide the building blocks for service description, discovery, and communication. While Web services technologies have clearly influenced positively the potential of the Web infrastructure by providing programmatic access to information and services, they are hindered by lack of rich and machine-processable abstractions to describe service properties, capabilities, and behavior. As a result of these limitations, very little automation support can be provided to facilitate effective discovery, combination, and management of services. Automation support is considered as the cornerstone to provide effective and efficient access to services in large, heterogeneous, and dynamic environments [10, 33, 20]. Indeed, until recently the basic Web services infrastructure was mainly used to build simple Web services such as those providing information search capabilities to an open audience (e.g. stock quotes, search engine queries, auction monitoring).
- Semantic Web aims at improving the technology to organize, search, integrate, and evolve Web-accessible resources (e.g., Web documents, data) by using rich and machine-understandable abstractions for the representation of resources semantics. Ontologies are proposed as means to address semantic heterogeneity among Web-accessible information sources and services. They are used to provide meta-data for the effective manipulation of available information including discovering information sources and reasoning about their capabilities. Efforts in this area include the

development of ontology languages such as RDF, DAML, and DAML+OIL [18]. In the context of Web services, ontologies promise to take interoperability a step further by providing rich description and modeling of services properties, capabilities, and behavior.

By leveraging efforts in both Web services and semantic Web, semantic Web services paradigm promises to take Web technologies a step further by providing foundations to enable automated discovery, access, combination, and management of Web services. Efforts in this area focus on providing rich and machine understandable representation of services properties, capabilities, and behavior as well as reasoning mechanisms to support automation activities [25, 11, 21, 20, 13, 8]. Examples of such efforts include DAML-S, WSMF (Web services Modeling Framework) [21], and METEOR-S (http://lsdis.cs.uga.edu/proj/meteor/SWP.tm).Work in this area is still in its infancy. Many of the objectives of the semantic Web services paradigm, such as capability description of service, dynamic service discovery, and goal-driven composition of Web services remain to be reached.

3.2 Web Services and their Complexity

Many Web service description languages distinguish between elementary and complex Web services. Elementary Web services are simple input/output boxes, whereas complex Web services break down the overall process into sub-tasks that may call other web services. Strictly speaking, such a distinction is wrong and may lead to mis-conceptualizations in a Web service modeling framework. It is not the complexity of the Web service that makes an important distinction. It is rather the complexity of its *description* or its interface (in terms of static and dynamic) that makes a difference. A complex Web service such as a logical inference engine with a web interface can be *described* as rather elementary. It receives some input formulas and derives--after a while--a set of conclusions. A much simpler software product such as a simple traveling information system may be broken down into several Web services around hotel information, flight information, and general information about a certain location. Therefore, it is not the inherent complexity of a Web service, it is the complexity of its external visible description that makes the relevant difference in our context. This insight may look rather trivial, however, it has some important consequences:

- Many Web service description approaches do not make an explicit distinction between an internal description of a Web service and its external visible description. They provide description means such as data flow diagrams and control flow descriptions without making clear whether they should be understood as interface descriptions for accessing a Web service, or whether they should be understood as internal descriptions of the realization of a Web service. Often, the internal complexity of a Web service reflects the business intelligence of a Web service provider. Therefore, it is essential for him not to make it publicly accessible. This is the major conceptual distinction between an internal description of the workflow of a Web service and its interface description.

- The dichotomy of elementary and complex Web services is too simplistic. As we talk about the complexity of the *description* of a Web service it is necessary to provide a scale of complexity. That is, one starts with some description elements and gradually upscale the complexity of available description elements by adding additional means to describe various aspects of a Web service.

3.3 Functionalities Required for Successful Web Services

UDDI, WSDL, and SOAP are important steps in the direction of a web populated by services. However, they only address part of the overall stack that needs to be available in order to eventually achieve the semantic Web services vision. [9] identifies the following elements as being necessary to achieve scalable Web service discovery, selection, mediation and composition:

- **Document types**. Document types describe the content of business documents like purchase orders or invoices. The content is defined in terms of elements like an order number or a line item price. Document types are instantiated with actual business data when a service requester and a service provider exchange data. The payload of the messages sent back and forth is structured according to the document types defined.
- **Semantics**. The elements of document types must be populated with correct values so that they are semantically correct and are interpreted correctly by the service requesters and providers. This requires that vocabulary is defined that enumerates or describes valid element values. For example, a list of product names or products that can be ordered from a manufacturer. Further examples are units of measure as well as country codes. Ontologies provide a means for defining the concepts of the data exchanged. If ontologies are available document types refer to the ontology concepts. This

ensures consistency of the textual representation of the concepts exchanged and allows the same interpretation of the concepts by all trading partners involved. Finally, the intent of an exchanged document must be defined. For example, if a purchase order is sent, it is not clear if this means that a purchase order needs to be created, deleted or updated. The intent needs to make semantically clear how to interpret the sent document.

- **Transport binding**. Several transport mechanisms are available like HTTP/S, S/MIME, FTP or EDIINT. A service requester as well as a service provider has to agree on the transport mechanism to be used when service requests are executed. For each available transport mechanism the layout of the message must be agreed upon and how the document sent shall be represented in the message sent. SOAP for example defines the message layout and the position within the message layout where the document is to be found. In addition, header data are defined, a requirement for SOAP message processing.
- **Exchange sequence definition**. Communication over networks is currently inherently unreliable. It is therefore required that service requester and service provider make sure themselves through protocols that messages are transmitted exactly once. The exchange sequence definition achieves this by defining a sequence of acknowledgment messages in addition to time-outs, retry logic and upper retry limits.
- **Process definition**. Based on the assumption that messages can be exchanged exactly once between service requester and service provider, the business logic has to be defined in terms of the business message exchange sequence. For example, a purchase order might have to be confirmed with a purchase order acknowledgment. Or, a request for quotation can be responded to by one or more quotes. These processes define the required business message logic in order to derive to a consistent business state. For example, when goods are ordered by a purchase order and confirmed by a purchase order acknowledgment they have to be shipped and paid for, too.
- **Security**. Fundamentally, each message exchange should be private and unmodified between the service requester and service provider as well as non-reputable. Encryption, as well as signing, ensures the unmodified privacy whereby non-repudiation services ensure that neither service requester nor service provider can claim not to have sent a message or to have sent a different one.

- **Syntax**. Documents can be represented in different syntaxes available. XML is a popular syntax, although non-XML syntax is used, too (e.g. EDI).
- **Trading partner specific configuration**. Service requesters or service providers implement their business logic differently from each other. The reason is that they establish their business logic before any cooperation takes place. This might require adjustments once trading partners are found and the interaction should be formalized using Web services. In case modifications are necessary, trading partner specific changes have to be represented. Current Web service technology scares rather low compared to these requirements. Actually, SOAP provides support on information binding. Neither UDDI nor WSDL add any support in the terms enumerated above. Many organizations had the insight that message definition and exchange are not sufficient to build an expressive Web services infrastructure. In addition to UDDI, WSDL and SOAP standards for process definitions as well as exchange sequence definitions are proposed such as WSFL [23], XLANG [32], ebXML BPSS [35], BPML [5] and WSDL [12]. Still, there are important features missing in all of the mentioned frameworks. Very important is to reflect the *loose coupling* and *scalable mediation* of Web services in an appropriate modeling framework. This requires mediators that map between different document structures and different business logics as well as the ability to express the difference between publicly visible workflows (public processes) and internal business logics of a complex Web service (private processes). Therefore, a fully-fledged Web service Modeling Framework (WSMF) [4] was proposed.

3.4 Semantic Markup for Web Services

To make use of Web service, a software agent needs a computer-interpretable description of the service, and the means by which it is accessed. An important goal for Semantic Web markup languages, then, is to establish a framework within which these descriptions are made and shared. Web sites should be able to employ a set of basic classes and properties for declaring and describing services, and the ontology structuring mechanisms of DAML+OIL provide the appropriate framework within which to do this.

Services can be simple or primitive in the sense that they invoke only a single Web-accessible computer program, sensor, or device that does not rely upon another Web service, and there is no ongoing interaction between the user and the service, beyond a simple response. Alternatively, services can be complex, composed of multiple primitive services, often requiring an interaction or conversation between the user and the services, so that the user can make choices and provide information conditionally. DAML-S is meant to support both categories of services, but complex services have provided the primary motivations for the features of the language. The following tasks are expected from DAML-S [14, 27, 14, 15]:

- **Automatic Web service Discovery**. Automatic Web service discovery involves the automatic location of Web services that provide a particular service and that adhere to requested constraints. For example, the user may want to find a service that makes hotel reservations in a given city and accepts a particular credit card. Currently, this task must be performed by a human who might use a search engine to find a service, read the Web page, and execute the service manually, to determine if it satisfies the constraints. With DAML-S markup of services, the information necessary for Web service discovery could be specified as computer-interpretable semantic markup at the service Web sites, and a service registry or ontology-enhanced search engine could be used to locate the service automatically. Alternatively, a server could proactively advertise itself in DAML-S with a service registry, also called middle agent [17, 37, 24], so that the requesters can find it when they query the registry.

- **Automatic Web service Invocation**. Automatic Web service invocation involves the automatic execution of an identified Web service by a computer program or agent. For example, the user could request the purchase of an airline ticket from a particular site on a particular flight. Currently a user must go to the Web site offering that service, fill out a form, and click on a button to execute the service. Alternatively, the user might send an HTTP request directly to the service with the appropriate parameters in HTML. In either case, a human is necessary in the loop. Execution of a Web service can be thought of as a collection of function calls. DAML-S markup of Web services provides a declarative, computer-interpretable API for executing these function calls.

- **Automatic Web service Composition and Interoperation**. This task involves the automatic selection, composition, and interoperation of Web services to perform some task, given a high-level description of an objective. For example, the user may want to make all the travel arrangements for a trip to a conference. Currently, the user must select the Web services, specify the composition manually, and make sure that any software needed for the interoperation is custom-created. With DAML-S markup of Web services, the information necessary to select and compose services will be encoded at the service Web sites.

- **Automatic Web service Execution Monitoring**. Individual services and, even more, compositions of services, will often require some time to execute completely. A user may want to know during this period what the status of his or her request is, or plans may have changed, thus requiring alterations in the actions the software agent takes.

3.5 Services Composition

Composition of Web services that have been previously annotated with semantics and discovered by a mediation platform is another benefit proposed by Semantic Web for Web services. Composition of services can be quite simple sequence of service calls passing outputs of one service to the next and much more complex, where *execution path* (service workflow) is not a sequence but more sophisticated structure, or intermediate data transformation is required to join outputs of one service with inputs of another. Within traditional approach such service composition can be created but with limitations: since semantics of inputs/outputs is not introduced explicitly, the only way to find matching service is to follow data types of its inputs and/or know exactly what service is required. This approach works for simple composition problem but fails for problems required for the future Web services for e-commerce. As an example of composition, suppose there are two Web services, an on-line language translator and a dictionary service, where the first one translates text between several language pairs and the second returns the meaning of English words.

If a user needs a *FinnishDictionary* service, neither of these can satisfy the requirement. However, together they can (the input can be translated from Finnish to English, fed through the English Dictionary, and then translated back to Finnish). The dynamic composition of such services is difficult using just the WSDL descriptions, since each description would designate strings as input and output, rather than the necessary concept for combining them (that is, some of these input strings must be the name of languages, others must be the strings representing user inputs and the translator's outputs). To provide the semantic concepts, we can use the ontologies provided by the Semantic Web.

Service composition can also be used in linking Web (and Semantic Web) concepts to services provided in other network-based environments [31]. One example is the sensor network environment, which includes two types of services; basic sensor services and sensor processing services. Each sensor is related to one Web service, which returns the sensor data as the output. Sensor processing services combine the data coming from different sensors in some way and produce a new output. These sensors have properties that describe their capabilities, such as sensitivity, range, etc., as well as some non-functional attributes, such as name, location, etc. These attributes, taken together tell whether the sensor's service is relevant for some specific task. An example task in this environment would involve retrieving data from several sensors and using relevant fusion services to process them via SOAP calls. As an example, the data from several acoustic and infrared sensors can be combined together and after applying filters and special functions, this data may be used to identify the objects in the environment. In this setting, we need to describe the services that are available for combining sensors and the attributes of the sensors that are relevant to those services. More importantly, the user needs a flexible mechanism for filtering sensor services and combining only those that can realistically be fused.

In DAML-S *ServiceGrounding* part of service description provides knowledge required to access service (where, what data, in what sequence communication goes) and *ServiceProfile* part provides references to the *meaning* what service is used for. Both these pieces of information are enough (as it supposed by Semantic Web vision) to be used by intelligent mediator (intelligent agent, mediation platform, transaction manager etc.) for using this service directly or as a part of compound service. The implementation of service composer [31] have shown how to use semantic descriptions to aid in the composition of Web services-- it directly combines the DAML-S semantic service descriptions with actual invocations of the WSDL descriptions allowing us to execute the composed services on the Web. The prototype system can compose the actual Web services deployed on the Internet as well as providing filtering capabilities where a large number of similar services may be available.

3.6 Web Services and Security

The Industry view on Web services security [30, 34] is mostly focused on concerns such as data integrity and confidentiality, authentication, and non repudiation of messages. The way they are ensured is by adapting general information security technologies (such as cryptography or digital signature) to XML data. The advantages is that these technologies have been extensively tested and improved for many years and that they are still a lively topic in the research community. Some of the most significant specifications in XML services security are [29]:

- *XML Encryption* (XML Enc): It describes how to en-code an XML document or some parts of it, so that its confidentiality can be preserved. The document's en-coding procedure is usually included in the file, so that a peer possessing the required secrets can find the way to decrypt it.
- *XML Digital Signature* (XML DSig): Describes how to attach a digital signature to some XML Data. This will ensure data integrity and non repudiation. The goal is to ensure that the data has been issued by a precise peer.
- *Web services Security* (WSS): This standard is based on SOAP, XML Enc and XML DSig and describes a procedure to exchange XML data between Web services in a secure way.
- *Security Assertion Markup Language* (SAML): Specifies how to exchange (using XML) authentication and authorization information about users or entities. Two services can use SAML to share authentication data in order not to ask a client to log again when it switches from one service to the another (Single Sign On procedure).

Considering that Active XML is a language that is certified pure XML, all these recommendations (or specifications) can be used to ensure its security during the transfer and the storage of information.

3.6.1 Typing and Pattern Matching

We need to control the services calls in order to avoid the ones that could execute malicious actions (for example, buy a house, propose to sell my car on ebay at a tiny price, and so on). Active XML [38] relies on a typing and function pattern matching algorithm that will compare the structure of the answer returned by the service with a "allowed structure" provided by the client. If the structures can match (using rewriting), then answer's call can be invoked. Details on the algorithm are given in [28], but this algorithm is k-depth limited, and its decidability is not proved when ignoring the k-depth limit. CDuce [7] is an example of language with powerful pattern matching features. It can easily compare structures and corresponding data, and its strong capability to handle types (and subtyping) makes it a good candidate for defining structures precisely. However, CDuce is mostly oriented towards XML transformation, so Active XML is definitely more simple and adapted for Web services.

3.6.2 Trust in Web Services

There are many ways to consider the notion of "trust" in services. The most adopted vision of trust in services is based upon progressive requests and disclosures of credentials between the peers (according to a policy), that will gradually establish the trust relationship [6, 36]. The privacy of the peers can be preserved, and credentials do not have to be shown without a need for it, thus preventing the user to display some information that (s)he could want to keep from a non authorized peer [22]. In [19], the analysis of trust is based upon the basic beliefs that will lead to the decision of granting trust or not. This approach is much more sociological and context dependent from the previous one, but it is closer from the way a human being behaves when trusting or not another person. The conditions required for the final decision of trust granting are divided into two major parts :

- *internal attribution*, representing the conditions that depend on the trusting agent's personality and skills,
- *external attribution*, that represents conditions that are completely independent from the agent (opportunity, interferences, ...).

Depending on these factors, a value representing the "trustfulness" is computed using a fuzzy algorithm. This value will allow the agent to take the decision on trusting the peer or not.

4. CONCLUSION

One of Semantic Web promises is to provide intelligent access to the distributed and heterogeneous information and enable mediation via software products between user needs and the available information sources. Web Services technology resides on the edge of limitation of the current web and desperately needs advanced semantic provision oriented approach. At present, the Web is mainly a collection of information and does provide efficient support in its processing. Also the promising Web services idea to allow services to be automatically accessed and executed has no yet facilities to efficiently discover web services by those who need them. All service descriptions are based on semi-formal natural language descriptions and put limits to find them easily. Bringing Web services to their full potential requires their combination with approach proposed by Semantic Web technology. It will provide automation in service discovery, configuration, matching client's needs and composition. Today there are much less doubts both in research and development world, than few months ago, whether Semantic Web approach is feasible. The importance of Web services has been recognized and widely accepted by industry and academic research. However, the two worlds have proposed solutions that progress along different dimensions. Academic research has been mostly concerned with expressiveness of service descriptions, while industry has focused on modularization of service layers for usability in the short term.

References

1. http://www.w3.org/2002/ws/
2. http://www.uddi.org/
3. http://www.w3.org/2002/ws/desc/
4. http://devresource.hp.com/drc/specifications/wsmf/index.jsp
5. A. Arkin: Business Process Modeling Language (BPML), Working Draft 0.4, 2001. http://www.bpmi.org/.
6. K. E. S. T. Barlow, A. Hess. Trust negotiation in electronic markets. In *Proceedings of the Eighth Research Symposium on Emerging Electronic Markets (RSEEM 01)*, 2001.
7. V. Benzaken, G. Castagna, and A. Frisch. Cduce: An xml-centric general-purpose language. In *Proceedings of the ACM International Conference on Functional Programming*, Uppsala, SWEDEN, 2003.
8. A. Bernstein and M. Klein. Discovering Services: Towards High Precision Service Retrieval. In CaiSE workshop on Web services, e-Business, and the Semantic Web: Foundations, Models, Architecture, Engineering and Applications. Toronto, Canada ,May 2002.
9. C. Bussler: B2B Protocol Standards and their Role in Semantic B2B Integration Engines, *IEEE Data Engineering*, 24(1), 2001.
10. Fabio Casati and Ming-Chien Shan. Dynamic and adaptive composition of e-services. Information Systems ,26(3):143 –163,May 2001.
11. D. Chakraborty, F. Perich, S. Avancha, and A. Joshi. DReggie: Semantic Service Discovery for M-Commerce Applications. In Workshop on Reliable and Secure Applications in Mobile Environment,20th Symposium on Reliable Distributed System, pages 28 –31,Oct.2001.
12. E. Christensen, F. Curbera, G. Meredith, S. Weerawarana: Web Services Description Language (WSDL) 1.1,15 March 2001. http://www.w3.org/TR/wsdl.
13. The DAML Services Coalition. DAML-S: Web service Description for the Semantic Web. In The First International Semantic Web Conference (ISWC),pages 348 –363,Jun.2002.

14. The DAML Services Coalition (alphabetically Anupriya Ankolenkar, Mark Burstein, Jerry R. Hobbs, Ora Lassila, David L. Martin, Drew McDermott, Sheila A. McIlraith, Srini Narayanan, Massimo Paolucci, Terry R. Payne and Katia Sycara), "DAML-S: Web service Description for the Semantic Web", *The First International Semantic Web Conference (ISWC)*, Sardinia (Italy), June, 2002.
15. DAML Services Coalition (alphabetically A. Ankolekar, M. Burstein, J. Hobbs, O. Lassila, D. Martin, S. McIlraith, S. Narayanan, M. Paolucci, T. Payne, K. Sycara, H. Zeng), "DAML-S: Semantic Markup for Web services", in *Proceedings of the International Semantic Web Working Symposium (SWWS)*, July 30-August 1, 2001.
16. Data Engineering Bulletin: Special Issue on Infrastructure for Advanced E-Services.24(1), IEEE Computer Society, 2001.
17. K. Decker, K. Sycara, and M. Williamson. Middle-agents for the Internet. In IJCAI'97, 1997.
18. Y.Ding, D. Fensel and B. Omelayenko M.C.A. Klein. The semantic web: yet another hip? DKE ,6(2-3):205 –227,2002.
19. Rino Falcone, Giovanni Pezzulo, Cristiano Castelfranchi. A fuzzy approach to a belief-based trust computation. In Trust, Reputation, and Security: Theories and Practice, AAMAS 2002 International Workshop. LNCS 2631 Springer 2003. Pages 73-86.
20. D. Fensel and C. Bussler. The Web service Modeling Framework WSMF. http://www.cs.vu.nl/diete /wese/publications.html.
21. D. Fensel, C. Bussler, and A. Maedche. Semantic Web Enabled Web services. In International Semantic Web Conference,Sardinia,Italy ,pages 1 –2,Jun.2002.
22. K. E. S. J. Holt, R. Bradshaw and H. Orman. Hidden credentials. In *2nd ACM Workshop on Privacy in the Electronic Society (WPES'03)*, Washington DC, USA, October 2003.
23. F. Leymann: Web Service Flow Language (WSFL 1.0), May 2001. http://www-4.ibm.com/software/solutions/webservices/pdf/WSFL.pdf.
24. D. Martin, A. Cheyer, and D. Moran. The Open Agent Architecture: A Framework for Building Distributed Software Systems. Applied Artificial Intelligence, 13(1-2):92-128, 1999.
25. S. McIlraith,T.C. Son,and H. Zeng.Semantic Web services. IEEE Intelligent Systems. Special Issue on the Semantic Web ,16(2):46 – 53,March/April 2001.
26. S. McIlraith, T. C. Son, and H. Zeng. Mobilizing the Web with DAML-Enabled Web service. In Proceedings of the Second International Workshop Semantic Web (SemWeb'2001), 2001.
27. S. McIlraith, T. C. Son, and H. Zeng. Semantic Web service. IEEE Intelligent Systems, 16(2):46-53, 2001.

28. T. Milo, S. Abiteboul, B. Amann, O. Benjelloun, and F. D. Ngoc. Exchanging intensional xml data. In *Proc. of ACM SIGMOD 2003*, June 2003.
29. M. Naedele. Standards for xml and Web services security. *IEEE Computer*, pages 96–98, April 2003.
30. O. for the Advancement of Structured Information Standards (OASIS). http://www.oasis-open.org/
31. E. Sirin, J. Hendler, B. Parsia, Semi-Automatic Composition of Web services Using Semantic Descriptions, In proceedings of "Web services: Modeling, Architecture and Infrastructure" workshop in conjunction with *ICEIS2003*, 2003.
32. S. Thatte: XLANG: Web Services for Business Process Design, Microsoft Corporation, 2001. http://www.gotdotnet.com/team/xml_wsspecs/xlang-c/default.htm.
33. The VLDB Journal: Special Issue on E-Services.10(1),Springer-Verlag Berlin Heidelberg, 2001.
34. W. W. W. C. (W3C). http://www.w3.org/
35. D. Waldt and R. Drummond: EBXML: The Global Standard for Electronic Business, http://www.ebxml.org/presentations/global_standard.htm.
36. M. Winslett, T. Yu, K. E. Seamons, A. Hess, J. Jacobson, R. Jarvis, B. Smith, and L. Yu. Negotiating trust on the web. *IEEE Internet Computing*, 6(6):30–37, November/December 2002.
37. H.-C. Wong and K. Sycara. A Taxonomy of Middle-agents for the Internet. In ICMAS'2000, 2000.
38. http://www-rocq.inria.fr/gemo/Gemo/Projects/axml/

APPLICATIONS OF MULTI-AGENT SYSTEMS

Mihaela Oprea
University of Ploiesti, Department of Informatics, Bd. Bucuresti Nr. 39, Ploiesti, Romania

Abstract: Agent-based computing has the potential to improve the theory and practice of modelling, designing, and implementing complex systems. The paper presents that basic notions of intelligent agents and multi-agent systems and focus on some applications of multi-agent systems in different domains.

Key words: intelligent agents; multi-agent systems; coordination; negotiation; learning; agent-oriented methodologies; applications.

1. INTRODUCTION

In the last decade, Intelligent Agents and more recently, Multi-Agent Systems appeared as new software technologies that integrate a variety of Artificial Intelligence techniques from different subfields (reasoning, knowledge representation, machine learning, planning, coordination, communication and so on), and which offer an efficient and more natural alternative to build intelligent systems, thus giving a solution to the current complex real world problems that need to be solved. For example, a complex system could be decomposed in components and again the components in sub-components and so on, till some primitive entities are obtained. Some of these primitive entities could be viewed as being agents that solve their local problems and interact between them in order to solve the goal of the initial complex system. However, most of the real world complex systems are only nearly decomposable, and a solution would be to endow the components with the ability of making decisions about the nature and the scope of their interactions at run time. Still, from this simplistic view, we could figure out a new type of computing, based on agents. In [1], Jennings argued that agent-of the Fishmarket system is that it is left to the buyers and sellers to encode their own bidding strategies. Also, the auctions could be monitored by the FM Monitoring Agent that keeps track of every single event taking place during a tournament. In Fishmarket each agent in a MAS is dynamically attached to a controller module, and it's in charge of controlling its external actions (i.e. protocol execution).

3.11 SARDINE

In [62] it is described an alternative airline flight bidding prototype system, called SARDINE (System for Airline Reservations Demonstrating the Integration of Negotiation and Evaluation), which offers better choices in comparison to the Priceline system. The SARDINE system uses software agents to coordinate the preferences and interests of each party involved. The buyer agent takes the buyer's preferences and correlates these parameters with the available flights from a reservation database. The user then tells the buyer agent how much to bid and the airline agents accept the ticket bids from the buyer agent. Finally, the airline agents consider individual bids based on flight yield management techniques and specific buyer information. The SARDINE system uses the OR combinatorial auction. A combinatorial auction is one in which the user submits simultaneous multiple bids. The bids are mutually exclusive of one another, thus an OR combinatorial auction is used.

3.12 eMediator

The eMediator [63], [64] is a next generation electronic commerce server that has three components: an auction house (*eAuctionHouse*), a leveled commitment contract optimizer (*eCommitter*), and a safe exchange planner (*eExchangeHouse*). The eAuction House allows users from Internet to buy and sell goods as well as to set up auctions. It is a third party site, and therefore both sellers and buyers can trust that it executes the auction protocols as stated. It is implemented in Java and uses some of the computationally intensive matching algorithms in C++. In order to increase reliability the information about the auctions is stored in a relational database. The server is the first Internet auction that supports combinatorial auctions, bidding via graphically drawn price-quantity graphs, and by mobile agents.

oriented approaches can significantly enhance our ability to model, design and build complex (distributed) software systems.

A natural way to modularise a complex system is in terms of multiple, interacting autonomous components that have particular goals to achieve, i.e. of a multi-agent system (MAS). A multi-agent approach is an attempt to solve problems that are inherently (physically or geographically) distributed where independent processes can be clearly distinguished. Such problems include, for example, decision support systems, networked or distributed control systems, air traffic control. Therefore, multi-agent systems approach is appropriate for distributed intelligence applications: network based, human involved, physically distributed, decentralized controlled, etc.

The basic notion of agent-computing is the agent with its derivation, the software agent. Several definitions has been given to the notion of agent. According to Michael Wooldridge, an *agent* is a computer system that is situated in some environment, and is capable of flexible, autonomous action in that environment in order to meet its design objectives [2]. The flexibility characteristic means that the agent is reactive, pro-active and social. Therefore, the key characteristics of agents are autonomy, proactivity, situatedness, and interactivity. More characteristics could be added, such as mobility, locality, openness, believability, learning, adaptation capabilities, comprehensibility, etc. A *software agent* is an independently executing program able to handle autonomously the selections of actions when expected or limited unexpected events occur.

Summarizing, an agent need to have computational abilities (reasoning, searching, etc) and can use its knowledge and rationality models to map inputs to outputs that would maximize its utility (its performance measure according to the rationality). According to the interaction strategy that is used, an agent could be *cooperative*, *self-interested*, and *hostile*. Cooperative agents could work together with other agents and humans with the intention of solving a joint problem. Self-interested agents try to maximize their own goods without any concern for the global good, and will perform services for other agents only for compensation (e.g. in terms of money). Hostile agents have a utility that increases with their own gains, and increases also with the competitor's losses.

The agents can be viewed as living in a society where they have to respect the rules of that society. They also live in an organization, which can be effectively executed only in respect with organizational patterns of interactions. In general, multi-agent systems represent institutions where agents must fulfill a set of expected behaviours in their interactions.

2. MULTI-AGENT SYSTEMS

Multi-agent systems are a particular type of distributed intelligent systems in which autonomous agents inhabit a world with no global control or globally consistent knowledge. Figure 1 presents the so called multi-agent system equation, which states that in a multi-agent system a task is solved by agents that communicate among them.

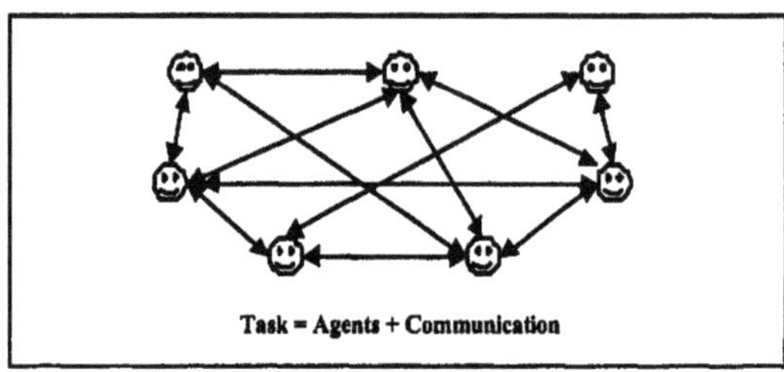

Figure 1. The multi-agent system equation.

We could view a multi-agent system as a society of individuals (agents) that interact by exchanging knowledge and by negotiating with each other in order to achieve either their own interest or some global goal. One of the characteristics of some MASs is the openness, which means that new agents can be created or can enter a MAS (i.e. mobile agents can arrive), and some unknown entities (e.g. legacy and elsewhere implemented entities) may enter a MAS. This characteristic has some technological implications: the need for standards (such as FIPA [3]) and the existence of a proper infrastructure that support interoperations.

In a MAS, agents are embedded in a certain environment which could be dynamic, unpredictable and open. This environment is the world of resources the agents perceive. The interactions between agents are the core of a multi-agent system functioning. Starting from [4], Nick Jennings has introduced the definition of a new computer level, the Social Level (SL) [5] in order to solve the problems related to flexible social interactions. With a SL incorporated, above the Knowledge Level (KL), the prediction of the behaviour of the social agents and of the whole MAS could be easily made. Following the Newell's notation, a preliminary version of the SL is given by: the system (an agent organization), the components (primitive elements from which the agent organization is built), composition laws (e.g. roles of agents in the organization), behaviour laws, and the medium (the elements the system processes in order to obtain the desired behaviour). The social level allows to create organizational models of multi-agent systems.

In a multi-agent system, agents are connected through different schemes, usually following mesh and hierachical structures.

The main characteristics of a multi-agent system are: *autonomy* (agents may be active and are responsible for their own activities), *complexity* (induced by the mechanisms of decision-making, learning, reasoning, etc), *adaptability* (adjust the agents activities to the dynamic environmental changes), *concurrency* (in case of tasks parallel processing), *communication* (inter-agent, intra-agent), *distribution* (MASs often operate on different hosts and are distributed over a network), *mobility* (agents need to migrate between platforms and environments), *security and privacy* (possible intrusion of the agents' data, state, or activities), and *openness* (MASs can dynamically decide upon their participants).

A multi-agent system has functional and non-functional properties. The functional properties are coordination, rationality, knowledge modelling. The non-functional properties are performance (response time, number of concurrent agents/task, computational time, communication overhead, etc), scalability (increased loading on an agent which is caused by its need to interact with more agents because the size of the society has increased), stability (a property of an equilibrium). The non-functional properties are discussed in [6]. Scalability is a property that becomes important when developing practical MASs. Most agent systems that have beein built so far involve a relatively small number of agents. When multi-agent systems are employed in larger applications this property need a very careful analysis. The scalability of a MAS is the average measure of the degree of performance degradation of individual agents in the society as their environmental loading increases, due to an expansion in the size of the society [6].

In a multi-agent system, agents have only local views, goals and knowledge that may conflict with others, and they can interact and work with other agents for the desired overall system's behavior. In order to achieve the common goals, a multi-agent system need to be coordinated. Coordination has to solve several problems such as the distributed expertise, resources or information, dependencies between agents' actions, efficiency. Two main dependencies can be encountered in a MAS, inter-agent dependencies and intra-agent dependencies. Several approaches that tackle the coordination problem were developed in Distributed Artificial Intelligence and Social Sciences, starting with diferent interaction protocol, partial global planning, and ending with the social laws. Depending on the domain of application specific coordination techniques are more appropriate. Also, the type of coordination protocol that is employed will influence the performance of the MAS.

A multi-agent infrastructure has to enable and rule interactions. It is the "middleware" layer that supports communication and coordination activities. The communication infrastructures (e.g. FIPA defined communication infrastructures) are dedicated to the control of the global interaction in a MAS. It includes routing messages and facilitators. The coordination infrastructures (e.g. MARS and Tucson coordination infrastructures [7]) are dedicated to laws that establish which agents can execute which protocols and where. It includes synchronization and constraints on interactions.

The main benefits of multi-agent systems approaches are the following: address problems that are too large for a centralized single agent (e.g. because of resource limitations or for robustness concerns), allow the interconnection and interoperation of multiple existing legacy systems (e.g. expert systems, decision support systems, legacy network protocols), improve scalability, provide solutions to inherently distributed problems (e.g. telecommunication control, workflow management), and provide solutions where the expertise is distributed. Some of the problems that could appear in a MAS are related to the emergent behaviour, system robustness, and system reliability.

A major characteristic in agent research and applications is the high heterogeneity of the field. The heterogeneity means agent model heterogeneity (different models and formalisms for agents), language heterogeneity (different communication and interaction schemes used by agents), and application heterogeneity (various goals of a MAS for many application domains). The heterogeneity has to be manageable with appropriate models and software toolkits. In the next sections we briefly discuss some models for agent architectures, communication, coordination, negotiation, learning in a multi-agent system, and, finally, we made a short presentation of the most known and used MAS development methodologies, and MAS development software.

2.1 Agent architectures

Two main complementary approaches are currently used to characterize intelligent (i.e. rational) agents and multi-agent systems: operational (agents and MASs are systems with particular features, i.e. a particular structure and a particular behaviour), and based on system levels (agents and MASs are new system levels). The first approach define rational agents in terms of *beliefs* (information about the current world state), *desires* (preferences over future world states) and *intentions* (set of goals the agent is committed to achieve) - BDI, thus being independent from the internal agent architecture. The advantage is that uses the well founded logics (e.g. modal logics). One of the problems is related to the ground of rationality on axioms of a logic.

The second approach hides details in hardware design. System levels are levels of abstraction. The agent is modelled as being composed of a body (i.e. means for the agent to interact with its environment), a set of actions the agent can perform on its environment, and a set of goals.

Figure 2 presents the general architecture of an agent.

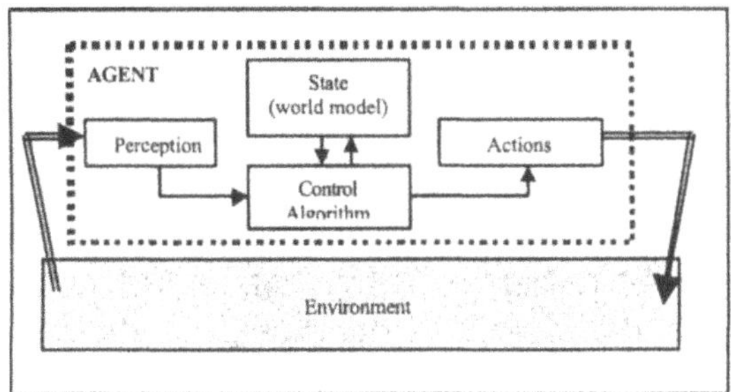

Figure 2. The general architecture of an agent.

The main agent architectures reported in the literature (see e.g. [8]) are the deliberative architecture, the reactive architecture, and the hybrid architecture. Most agent architectures are dedicated to the fulfillment of precise tasks or to problem solving, typically requiring reasoning and planning. Other approaches simulate emotions, which direct the agent in a more reactive way.

An agent that uses *the deliberative architecture* contains a symbolic world model, develops plans and makes decisions in the way proposed by symbolic artificial intelligence. Two important problems need to be solved in this case: the transduction problem and the representation/reasoning problem. The solution of the first problem led to work on vision, speech understanding, learning, etc. The solution for the second problem led to work on knowledge representation, automated reasoning/planning etc. The answer to the question "*how should an agent decide what to do*?" is that it should deduce its best action in light of its current goals and world model, so, it should plan. The world model can be constructed through *learning*.

An agent that uses *the reactive architecture* does not include any kind of central symbolic world model, and does not use complex symbolic reasoning. Rodney Brooks [9] had introduced two ideas: situatedness and embodiment. In his view "intelligent" behaviour arises as a result of an agent's interaction with its environment, and the agent is specified in terms of perceptions and actions. It is not a central dogma of the embodied approach that no internal representations exist. The being of the agent is dependent on the context in which it is encountered, and it is derived from purposeful interaction with the world. A possible answer to the question "*how should an agent decide what to do*?" is to do planning in advance and compile the result into a set of rapid reactions, or situation-action rules, which are then used for real-time decision making, or to learn a good set of reactions by trial and error.

An agent that uses a *hybrid architecture* has a layered architecture with both components: deliberative and reactive, usually, the reactive one having some kind of precedence over the deliberative one. Two important problems need to be solved: the management of the interactions between different layers and the development of the internal structure of an internally unknown system characterized by its I/O behavior. A possible answer to the question "*how should an agent decide what to do*?" is by integrating planning system, reactive system and learning system into a hybrid architecture, even included into a single algorithm, where each appears as a different facet or different use of that algorithm. This answer was given by the Dyna architecture [10].

How to choose the agent architecture is not an easy problem and is mainly application domain dependent. In [11] it is claimed that evolution has solved this problem in natural systems with a hybrid architecture involving closely integrated concurrently active deliberative and reactive sub-architectures.

2.2 Communication

Interaction is a fundamental characteristic of a multi-agent system. The agent communication capability is needed in most cases for the coordination of activities. A conversation is a pattern of message exchange that two or more agents agree to follow in communicating with one another. Actually, it is a pre-established coordination protocol. Several methods could be used for the representation of conversations: state transition diagrams, finite-state machines, Petri nets, etc. An Agent Communication Language (ACL) is a collection of speech-act-like message types, with agreed-upon semantics, which facilitates the knowledge and information exchange between software agents. The standardization efforts made so far generated a standard framework for agent communication (a standard agent communication language – KQML [12], FIPA ACL – both based on the notion of speech act). Current used ACLs are not accepted by all researchers due to some problems they have: the formal semantics for such languages (define semantics based on mental states, or equate the meaning of a speech act with the set of allowable responses), the relationships between speech acts and various related entities such as conversations, agent mental state. A possible alternative model of agent communication is *Albatross* (Agent language based on a treatment of social semantics, [13]) that has a commitment-based semantics for speech acts.

KQML (Knowledge Query and Manipulation Language) is a high level message-oriented communication language and protocol for information exchange independent of content syntax and applicable ontology. It is independent of the transport mechanism (TCP/IP, SMTP, etc), independent of the content language (KIF, SQL, Prolog, etc), and independent of the ontology assumed by the content. A KQML message has three layers: content, communication, and message. The syntax of KQML is based on the s-expression used in Lisp (*performative arguments*). The semantics of KQML is provided in terms of pre-conditions, post-conditions, and completion conditions for each performative. FIPA ACL is similar to KQML. The communication primitives are called *communicative acts* (CA). SL is the formal language used to define the semantics of FIPA ACL. It is a multi-modal logic with modal BDI operators, and can represent propositions, objects, and actions. In FIPA ACL, the semantics of each CA are specified as sets of SL formulae that describes the act's feasability pre-conditions and its rational effect.

A message has three aspects: *locution* (how is the message phrased), *illocution* (how is the message meant by the sender or understood by the receiver), and *perlocution* (how does the message influence the receiver's behavior). Figure 3 shows an example of ACL message.

```
(inform
: sender agent1
: receiver tim-auction-server
: content
        (price (bid computer_11) 1700)
: in-reply-to round-3
: language sl
: ontology tim-auction
)
```

Figure 3. Example of an ACL message.

One important issue in agent communication is the understanding of messages meaning. The message ontology gives the meaning of a message. The ontology provides interpretation of the message, giving a meaning for each word included in the content of the message. More generally, ontology is a description of the concepts and relationships that can exist for an agent. Usually, an ontology is designed for a specific multi-agent system, thus being aplication domain dependent. Therefore, one of the problems that may occur is the communication among agents that use different ontologies.

Agent communication languages such as KQML and FIPA ACL have provided a tool and framework to tackle the interoperability problems of inter-agent communication.

2.3 Coordination

In a multi-agent system agents have their own plans, intentions and knowledge, and are willing to solve their local goals, while for the global goal of the system it is needed a coordination mechanism to solve the conflicts that may arise due to limited resources or to the opposite intentions the agents might have. Coordination is a process in which the agents engage in order to ensure that the multi-agent system acts in a coherent manner. For this purpose, the agents must share information about their activities. One way the agents may achieve coordination is by communication. Another way, without communication, assume that the agents have models of each others' behaviors. Coordination avoids unnecessary activity and allows a reduce resource contention, avoids deadlock, and livelock and maintains safety conditions (minimizing the conflicts). Deadlock refers to a state of affairs in which further action between two or more agents is impossible. Livelock refers to a scenario where agents continuously act (exchange tasks, for example), but no progress is made.

According to [14], any comprehensive coordination technique must have four major components: (1) a set of structures that enable the agents' interaction in predictable ways; (2) flexibility in order to allow the agents to operate in dynamic environment and to cope with their inherently partial and imprecise viewpoint of the community; (3) a set of social structures which describe how agents should behave towards one another when they are engaged in the coordination process; (4) sufficient knowledge and reasoning capabilities must be incorporated in order to exploit both the available structure (individual and social) and the flexibility. In [15], a coordination model is described by three elements: *the coordinables*, i.e. the objects of the coordination (e.g. the software agents), *the coordination media*, i.e. what enables the interaction between the coordinables (e.g. the agent communication language), and *the coordination laws* that govern the interaction between the coordination media and the coordinables, and the rules that the coordination media employs (e.g. the finite state machine that describes the interaction protocol).

Coordination may require cooperation between agents, but sometimes, coordination may occur without cooperation. The design of a specific coordination mechanism will take into account appart from the domain of the application, the type of architecture that is adopted for the MAS design. There are mediated interaction coordination models (e.g. blackboard based interaction), and non mediated interaction ones. When a mediated interaction coordination protocol is applied, the state of the interaction could be inspected in order to check the coordination trace.

In the literature there have been reported different coordination techniques. In [14] it is made a classification of the existing coordination techniques applied to software agent systems. Four broad categories were identified: organizational structuring, contracting, multi-agent planning, and negotiation. The first category includes coordination techniques like the classical client-server or master-slave techniques. A high level coordination strategy from the second category is given by the Contract Net Protocol (CNP). A multi-agent planning technique, from the third category, involves the construction of a multi-agent plan that details all the agents' future actions and interactions required to achieve their goals, and interleave execution with more planning and re-planning. The fourth category of coordination techniques uses negotiation to solve the conflicts that may arise in a MAS. Usually, negotiation compromises speed for quality because there is an overhead during negotiation before compromise is made.

In [15] it is made a comparison between three types of coordination models: hybrid coordination models based on tuple centers [16], interaction protocols as a coordination mechanism, and implicit coordination through the semantic of classic ACLs. All these models were proposed by different research communities. The coordination community proposed the first one, while the second one was proposed by the agent community, and the last one by the more formally inclined part of the agent community.

In [17] it is presented a framework that enables agents to dynamically select the mechanism they employ in order to coordinate their inter-related activities. The classification made in [17] reveals two extreme classes, the social laws (long-term rules that prescribe how to behave in a given society), and the interaction protocols (e.g. CNP, that coordinates the short-term activities of agents in order to accomplish a specific task). Between these classes it is situated partial global planning. In [18] another approach is described, the use of coordination evaluation signals to guide an agent's behavior. In [19] it is presented a precise conceptual model of coordination as structured "conversations" involving communicative actions amongst agents. The model was extended with the COOL (COOrdination Language) language and it was applied in several industrial MAS. A social based coordination mechanism is described in [20]. Coordination gradually emerges among agents and their social context. The agents are embedded in a social context in which a set of norms is in force. These norms influence the agents' decision-making and goal generation processes by modifying their context.

In cases where the communication costs are prohibitive, a solution is to coordinate a set of individually motivated agents by choosing an equilibrium point. Such an evolutionary approach is used in [21], where by learning from observations the coordination point (viewed as an equilibrium point) is reached.

Another coordination model is given by stigmergy [22], [23], which means that agents put signs, called sigma in Greek, in their environment to mutually influence each other's behaviour. Such indirect coordination mechanism is suitable for small-grained interactions compared to coordination methods that usually require an explicit interaction between the agents. With stigmergy, agents observe signs in their environment and act upon them without needing any synchronization with other agents. The signs are typically multi-dimensional and reflect relevant aspects of the coordination task. For example, the display of apples provides the agents with information through look, smell, and packaging of the apples. A multi-agent coordination and control system design, inspired by the behaviour of social insects such as food foraging ants is discussed in [24].

2.4 Negotiation

Negotiation is a discussion in which interested parties exchange information and, eventually, come to an agreement [25]. In a multi-agent system, negotiation has been viewed as a solution for problems such as network coherency, the problem decomposition and allocation, and more generally for the coordination problems. Negotiation can be viewed as a process whereby agents communicate to reach a common decision. Thus, the negotiation process involves the identification of interactions (through communication) and the modification of requirements through proposals and counter-proposals. The main steps of negotiation are (1) exchange of information; (2) each party evaluates information from its own perspective; (3) final agreement is reached by mutual selection. Two main types of negotiation were reported in the literature [26], [27], [28]: distributive negotiation and integrative negotiation.

2.4.1 Distributive negotiation

The distributive negotiation (win-lose type of negotiation, such as auctions) involves a decision-making process of solving a conflict between two or more parties over a single mutually exclusive goal. In the game theory this is a zero-sum game. Auctions are methods for allocating tasks, goods, resources, etc. The participants are auctioneer and bidders. Example of applications includes delivery tasks among carriers, electricity, stocks, bandwidth allocation, heating, contracts among construction companies, fine art, selling perishable goods, and so on.

Different types of distributive negotiation are available: the Contract Net Protocol, and auction mechanisms such as first-price sealed-bid, second-price sealed-bid, English auction, Dutch auction, etc.

One of the problems encountered when adopting an auction mechanism is how to incorporate a fair bidding mechanism, i.e. keeping important information secure or isolated from competing agents. Another problem is that the auction protocol may not always converges in finite time. Still, the main advantage of auctions is that in certain domains, because the goods are of uncertain value, dynamic price adjustment often maximize revenue for a seller.

2.4.2 Integrative negotiation

The integrative negotiation (win-win type of negotiation, such as desired retail merchant-customer relationships and interactions) involves a decision-making process of solving a conflict between two or more parties over a multiple interdependent, but non-mutually exclusive goals. In game theory this is a non-zero-sum game. Usually, integrative negotiation deals with multi-attribute utility theory. Negotiation involves determining a contract under certain terms and conditions. An integrative negotiation model is characterized by three key information: the negotiation protocol, the list of issues over which negotiation takes place, and the reasoning model used by the agents (i.e. the negotiation strategy).

Several negotiation models were proposed, service-oriented negotiation models, persuasive argumentation, strategic negotiation, etc.

A service-oriented negotiation model that was used with success in MAS applications is presented in [29]. Suppose that one agent (the client) requires a service to be performed on its behalf by some other agent (the server). The negotiation between the client and the server may be iterative with several rounds of offers and counter-offers that may occur before an agreement is reached or the negotiation process is terminated. The negotiation can ranged over a set of issues (quantitative and qualitative). The sequence of offers and counter-offers in a two-party negotiation is called the negotiation thread. Offers and counter-offers are generated by linear combination of simple functions called tactics. Different weights in the linear combination allow the varying importance of the criteria to be modeled. Tactics generate an offer or a counter-offer, for a single component of the negotiation issue using a single criterion (time, resource, behavior of the other agent, etc). The way in which an agent changes the weights of the different tactics over time is given by the agent negotiation strategy. Different types of tactics were used by the service-oriented negotiation model, time dependent tactics (including Boulware, and Conceder tactics), resource dependent tactics (dynamic deadline tactics and resource estimation tactics), and behaviour dependent tactics (relative Tit-For-Tat, random absolute Tit-For-Tat, average Tit-For-Tat). In this model, the agent has a representation of its mental state containing information about its beliefs, its knowledge of the environment and any other attitudes like desires, goals, intentions and so on, which are important to the agent.

Let's consider the case of two agents, a seller and a buyer, that are negotiating the price of a specific product. Each agent knows its own reservation price, RP, which is how much the agent is willing to pay or to receive in the deal. A possible deal can be made only if there exists an overlapping zone between the reservation prices of the two agents. The agents don't even know if there is an agreement zone. The ideal rule to find if there is an agreement zone is given in figure 4.

if $RP^{seller} \leq RP^{buyer}$ **then**
  * Possible deal - the zone of agreement exists;
else
  * No deal - the zone of agreement doesn't exist;

where RP^{buyer} is the maximum price the buyer is willing to pay for the product, and RP^{seller} is the minimum price the seller will accept to receive.

Figure 4 Rule for agreement zone search.

The way in which each agent is making a proposal for the price of the product is given by its pricing strategy. Usually, it cannot be forecast if an agreement will be made between two agents that negotiate. The convergence in negotiation is achieved when the scoring value of the received offer is greater than the scoring value of the counter-offer the agent intend to respond with.

The PERSUADER system [30] was developed to model adversial conflict resolution in the domain of labour relations which can be multi-agent, multi-issue, single or repeated negotiation encounters. The system uses both case-based reasoning and multi-attribute utility theory. The negotiation is modeled as an incremental modification of solution parts through proposals and counter-proposals. In this model the agents try to influence the goals and intentions of their opponents through persuasive argumentation. In [31] and [32] more details are given regarding the negotiation by arguing.

In the strategic negotiation model [33], a game-theory based technique, there are no rules which bind the agents to any specific strategy. The agents are not bound to any previous offers that have been made. After an offer is rejected, an agent whose turn it is to suggest a new offer can decide whether to make the same offer again, or to propose a new one. In this case, the negotiation protocol provides a framework for the negotiation process and specifies the termination condition, but without a limit on the number of the negotiation rounds. It is assumed that the agents can take actions only at certain times in the set T={0, 1, 2, ...}, that are determined in advance and are known to the agents. Strategic negotiation is appropriate for dynamic real-world domains such as resource allocation, task distribution, human high pressure crisis negotiation.

2.5 Learning

In a multi-agent system the agents are embedded in the environment where they live, and need to interact with other agents in order to achieve their goals. Usually, they try to adapt to the environment by learning or by an evolutionary process, thus doing an anticipation of the interaction with the other agents. Learning in a multi-agent environment is complicated by the fact that, as other agents learn, the environment effectively changes. When agents are acting and learning simultaneously, their decisions affect and limit what they subsequently learn.

Adaptability and embodiment are two important issues that need to be addressed when designing flexible multi-agent systems [28], [34]. Adaptability allows the generation of a model of the selection process within the system and thus results in internal representations that can indicate future successful interactions. Agents can be seen as having a "body" that is embedded in their work environment, and is adapted to this environment by learning or by an evolutionary process. In the context of a multi-agent system, the two properties, adaptability and embodiment, are tightly related to each other.

The most used learning algorithms that were experimented in the case of multi-agent systems are reinforcement learning (e.g. Q-learning [35]), Bayesian learning, and model-based learning.

2.5.1 Reinforcement learning

The reinforcement learning is a common technique used by adaptive agents in MASs and its basic idea is to revise beliefs and strategies based on the success or failure of observed performance. Q-learning is a particular reinforcement learning algorithm (an incremental reinforcement learning) that works by estimating the values of all state-action pairs. An agent that uses a Q-learning algorithm selects an action based on the action-value function, called the Q-function. $Q_j(s, a) = Q_j(s, a) + \lambda(r_j - Q_j(s, a))$, where λ is a constant, r_j is the immediate reward received by agent j after performing action a in state s. The Q-function defines the expected sum of the discounted reward attained by executing an action a in state s and determining the subsequent actions by the current policy π. The Q-function is updated using the agent's experience.

The reinforcement learning techniques have to deal with the exploration-exploitation dilemma. Some experimental comparisons between several explore/exploit strategies are presented in [36] showing the risk of exploration in multi-agent systems. In [35] it is demonstrated that genetic algorithm based classifier systems can be used effectively to achieve near-optimal solutions more quickly than Q-learning, this result revealing the problem of slow convergence that is specific to reinforcement learning techniques.

2.5.2 Bayesian learning

Usually, Bayesian behaviour is considered as the only rational agent's behaviour, i.e. the behaviour that maximizes the utility. Bayesian learning is built on bayesian reasoning which provides a probabilistic approach to inference. The bayesian learning algorithms manipulates probabilities together with observed data. In [37] it is presented a sequential decision making model of negotiation called Bazaar, in which learning is modeled as a Bayesian belief update process. During negotiation, the agents use the Bayesian framework to update knowledge and belief that they have about the other agents and the environment. For example, an agent (buyer/seller) could update his belief about the reservation price of the other agent (seller/buyer) based on his interactions with the seller/buyer and on his domain knowledge. The agent's belief is represented as a set of hypotheses. Each agent tries to model the others in a recursive way during the negotiation process, and any change in the environment, if relevant and perceived by an agent, will have an impact on the agent's subsequent decision making. The experiments showed that greater the zone of agreement, the better the learning agents seize the opportunity.

2.5.3 Model-based learning

In [38] it is described a model-based learning framework that model the interaction between agents by the game-theoretic concept of repeated games. The approach tries to reduce the number of interaction examples needed for adaptation, by investing more computational resources in deeper analysis of past interaction experience. The learning process has two stages: (1) the learning agent infers a model of the other agent based on past interaction and

(2) the learning agent uses the learned model for designing effective interaction strategy for the future. The experimental results presented in [38] showed that a model-based learning agent performed significantly better than a Q-learning agent.

2.5.4 Nested representations

An important aspect that should be taken into account when designing adaptive multi-agent systems is the utility of nested representations that are essential for agents that must cooperate with other agents [7]. In [39] it is introduced a method of learning nested models, in order to decide when an agent should behave strategically and when it should act as a simple price-taker, in an information economy. In general, learning abilities consists in making a choice from among a set of fixed strategies and do not consider the fact that the agents are embedded in an environment (i.e. inhabit communities of learning agents).

2.6 Methodologies for multi-agent system development

The development of multi-agent systems applications has generated the development of an agent-specific software engineering, called Agent-Oriented Software Engineering (AOSE), which defines abstractions (of agents, environment, interaction protocols, context), specific methodologies and tools, and could be applicable to a very wide range of distributed computing applications. The adoption of object-oriented (OO) methodologies from object-oriented software engineering is an option, but some mismatches could appeared, as each methodology may introduce new abstractions (e.g. roles, organisation, responsibility, belief, desire, and intentions).

Usually, the whole life-cycle of system development (analysis, design, implementation, validation) is covered by a methodology. Let's consider the analysis and design steps. During the analysis step, agents are associated with the entities of the analyzed scenarios. Then, roles, responsibilities and capabilities are associated accordingly. Finally, interaction patterns between agents are identified. At the knowledge level, for each agent we need to identify its beliefs, goals, body (i.e. the way it interacts with the environment), and actions. The environment behaviour should be identified. At the social level, the analysis step focus on the analysis of an organization and it is needed to identify the roles in the organization, the organizational relations between roles, the dependency between roles, the interaction

There are two approaches for tackle the Agent-Oriented Methodologies (AOM), the Knowledge Engineering (KE) approach and the Software Engineering (SE) approach. The KE approach provides techniques for agent's knowledge modelling. Example of such tools are DESIRE and MAS-CommonKADS [40]. The SE approach used the OO approach, in which an agent is viewed as an active object. Examples of such tools are AUML, GAIA, ADEPT, MESSAGE/UML, OPM/MAS [41]. AUML [42] is an extension of the standard SE approach, UML (Unified Modeling Language). The FIPA Agent UML (AUML) standard is under development. MASs are sometimes characterized as extensions of object-oriented systems. This overlay simplified view has often troubled system designers as they try to capture the unique features of MASs using OO tools. Therefore, an agent-based unified modeling language (AUML) is being developed [43]. The ZEUS toolkit was developed in parallel with an agent development methodology [44], which is supported by the ZEUS Agent Generator tool. DESIRE provides formal specifications to automatically generate a prototype. It has a design approach more than an analysis approach. Agents are viewed as composed components, and MAS interaction as components interaction. OPM/MAS offers an approach that combines OO and process orientation. GAIA is a top-down design methodology that has a solid social foundation and is an extension of the SE approach.

2.7 Multi-agent system development software

Agent platforms support effective design and construction of agents and multi-agent systems. An agent platform has to provide the following functions: agent management, agent mobility, agent communication, directory services (yellow pages), and interface to plug-in additional services. Figure 5 presents the architecture of a FIPA Agent Platform [3]. Several agent platforms are available: JADE (CSELT&Univ. of Parma, [45]), ZEUS (British Telecom, [44], [46]), AgentBuilder (Reticular Systems Inc., [47]), MadKit (LIRMM Montpellier [48], [49]), Volcano (LEIBNIZ, [40]), etc.

JADE (Java Agent Development framework) [45] is a free software framework for the development of agent applications in compliance with the FIPA specifications for interoperable intelligent multi-agent systems. JADE is written in Java language and is made by various Java packages, giving application programmers both ready-made pieces of functionality and abstract interfaces for custom, application dependent tasks. The main tools provided by JADE are the Remote Management Agent (RMA), the Dummy Agent, the Sniffer agent, the Introspector Agent, the SocketProxyAgent, the

DF GUI (a complete graphical user interface that is used by the default Directory Facilitator). The latest available version is JADE 3.1 (Dec. 2003).

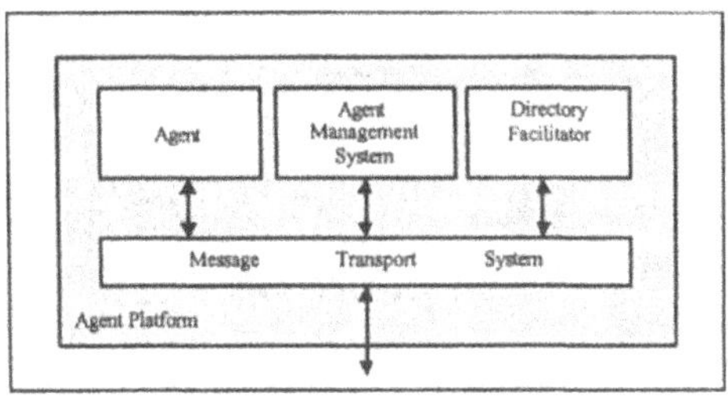

Figure 5. The architecture of a FIPA Agent Platform.

ZEUS is a generic, customisable, and scaleable industrial-strength collaborative agent toolkit. It consists in a package of classes implemented in Java, allowing it to run on a variety of hardware platforms [46]. The classes of the ZEUS toolkit are classified in three groups: an agent component library, an agent building tool, and an agent visualisation tool. ZEUS toolkit covers all stages of a MAS development, from analysis to deployment. It is limited to a single agent model.

AgentBuilder is an integrated software toolkit that allows software developers to quickly implement intelligent agents and agent-based applications [47]. The latest version is AgentBuilder 1.3 (based on Java 1.3), Windows XP compatible. Two versions are currently available: LITE, ideal for building single-agent, stand-alone applications and small agencies, and PRO, that has all the features of LITE plus an advanced suite of tools for testing and building multi-agent systems. AgentBuilder is grounded on Agent0/Placa BDI architecture. It is limited to a single agent model. Almost all stages of a MAS development are covered.

The MadKit toolkit provides a generic, highly customizable and scalable agent platform [48]. It is a generic multi-agent platform based on an organizational model called AGR (agent-group-role). MadKit is composed by a set of Java classes that implements the agent kernel, and various libraries of messages, probes and agents. Also, it includes a graphical development environment, system and demonstration agents. The MadKit micro-kernel is a small and optimized agent kernel which handles several tasks (control of local groups and roles, agent life-cycle management, and local message passing). The kernel is extensible through "kernel hooks". MadKit has a good versatility and light methodology (no BDI).

Volcano is a multi-agent platform that is under development [40], and whose aims are to fulfill the criteria of completeness (e.g. inclusion of MAS analysis and design phases), applicability (e.g. the versatility of the platform) and complexity (e.g. more friendly user interface, reuse of the platform). It is based on the Agents Environment Interactions Organisations (AEIO) MAS decomposition. In this framework, *agents* are internal architectures of the processing entities, the *environment* is composed by the domain-dependent elements for structuring external interactions between entities, the *interactions* are elements for structuring internal interactions between entities, and *organisations* are elements for structuring sets of entities within the MAS. Volcano has a full analysis-to-deployment chain, including an open library of models and intelligent deployment tools.

3. APPLICATIONS

As reported in [50], the main application domains of multi-agent systems are ambient intelligence, grid computing, electronic business, the semantic web, bioinformatics and computational biology, monitoring and control, resource management, education, space, military and manufacturing applications, and so on. Many researchers has applied agent technology to industrial applications such as manufacturing enterprise integration, supply chain management, manufacturing planning, scheduling and control, holonic manufacturing systems.

In order to support interoperability and to allow heterogeneus agents and MASs to work together, some infrastructures are needed. Most of the multi-agent system applications adopted ad-hoc designs for the MAS infrastructure. However, in the recent years some MAS infrastructures were proposed.

3.1 Multi-agent systems infrastructures

Each multi-agent system architecture has its specific features: agent registration, agent capability advertisements, strategy for finding agents, agent communication language, agent dialogue mediation, agent content language, default agent query preference, etc. As multi-agent systems are open, in complex applications, homogeneity cannot be achieved with respect to the MAS architecture specific features. Thus, interoperation mechanisms must be designed and implemented.

3.1.1 RETSINA

RETSINA (Reusable Task Structure-based Intelligent Network Agents) [51] multi-agent infrastructure has been developed at the Carnegie Mellon University in Pittsburgh, USA. It is composed by four different reusable agent types that can be adapted to different applications, the interface agents, task agents, information/resource agents, and middle agents. A collection of RETSINA agents forms an open society of reusable agents that self-organize and cooperate in response to task requirements. The RETSINA framework was implemented in Java. It is constructed on the principle that all agents should communicate directly with each other, if necessary. Agents find each other through a Matchmaker agent, who does not manage the transaction between the two agents, it just allow the direct communication between the two agents.

RETSINA is an open MAS infrastructure that supports communities of heterogeneus agents. It does not employ any centralized control on the MAS, rather implements distributed infrastructural services that facilitate the relations between the agents instead of managing them.

The RETSINA-OAA InterOperator acts as a connection between two MASs with two radically different agent architectures: the RETSINA capability-based MAS architecture and SRI' Open Agent Architecture (OAA). Agents in the OAA system "speak" Prolog-based OAA ICL, while agents in RETSINA system use KQML. The two languages has very different syntactic and semantic structures. OAA is organized around an agent called the Facilitator, which manages all the communications between agents in such a way that OAA agents cannot communicate directly.

3.1.2 SICS

SICS MarketSpace [52] is an agent-based market infrastructure implemented in Java. The goal of SICS is to enable automation of consumer goods markets distributed over the Internet. It consists in an information model for participant interests, and an interaction model that defines a basic vocabulary for advertising, searching, negotiating and settling deals. The interaction model is asynchronous message communication in a simple speech act based language, the *Market Interaction Format* (MIL).

3.2 Application areas

We have selected various MAS application areas (which are not disjunctive) and for each area a brief presentation of some MASs developments (the majority being simulations or prototypes) is made. The general application domains selected for this presentation are resource management (ADEPT business management, FACTS telecommunication service, TeleMACS, Challenger, MetaMorphII, MACIV); manufacturing planning, scheduling and control (TELE TRUCK); monitoring, diagnosis and control (ARCHON energy management); electronic commerce

(Fishmarket, SARDINE, eMediator, SMACE, COM_ELECTRON), and virtual enterprise (VIRT_CONSTRUCT).

3.3 ARCHON's electricity transportation management application

Energy management is the process of monitoring and controlling the cycle of generating, transporting and distributing electrical energy to industrial and domestic customers. A Spanish company, Iberdrola, that works in the energy domain decided to develop a set of decision support systems (DSS) in order to reduce the operators' cognitive load in critical situations, and to decrease the response time for making decisions. The DSS were interconnected and extended using the ARCHON technology. In [53] it is discussed the problem of development and deployment of MASs in real world settings, and it is analysed under the ARCHON project and applied to electricity transport management. ARCHON provides a descentralised software platform which offers the necessary control and level of integration to help the subcomponents to work together. Each agent consists of an ARCHON Layer (AL) and an application program (Intelligent System - IS).

Seven agents are running on five different machines. The agents are: BAI (Black-out Area Identifier), CSI-D and CSI-R (pre-existing Control System Interface), BRS (Breaks and Relays Supervisor), AAA (Alarms Analysis Agent), SRA (Service Restoration Agent), and UIA (User Interface Agent). The BAI agent identifies which elements of the network are initially out of service. CSI is the application's front end to the control system computers and consists of two agents: CSI-D detects the occurrence of disturbances and preprocesses the chronological and non chronological alarm messages which are used by the agents AAA, BAI and BRS; and CSI-R detects and corrects inconsistencies in the snapshot data file of the network, computes the power flowing through it and makes it available to SRA and UIA. The BRS agent detects the occurrence of a disturbance, determine the type of fault, generates an ordered list of fault hypotheses, validates hypotheses and identifies malfunctioning equipment. The AAA agent has similar goals with BRS. The SRA agent devises a service restoration plan to return the network to a steady state after a blackout has occurred. The UIA agent implements the interface between the users and the MAS.

Due to parallel activation of tasks, efficiency is achieved. Reliability is increased because even if one of the agents break down, the rest of agents can produce a result (not the best one) that could be used by the operator.

The application is operational since 1994. The MAS gives better results because it takes multiple types of knowledge and data into account and integrates them in a consistent manner. Also, the system is robust because there are overlapping functionalities which means that partial results can be produced in the case of agent failure. The system is open, so new agents could be added in an incremental manner.

3.4 ADEPT business process management application

An agent-based system developed for managing a British Telecom (BT) business process is presented in [54]. The business process consists in providing customers with a quote for installing a network to deliver a particular type of telecommunications service. The process is dynamic and unpredictable, it has a high degree of natural concurrency, and there is a need to respect departmental and organisational boundaries. In this process, the following departments are involved: the customer service division (CSD), the design divison (DD), the surveyor department (SD), the legal department (LD), and the organisations that provide the out-sourced service of vetting customers (VCs). In the multi-agent system, each department is represented by an agent, and all the interactions between them take the form of negotiations (based on a service-oriented negotiation model). All negotiations are centered on a multi-attribute object, where attributes are, for instance, price, quality, duration of a service.

3.5 FACTS telecommunication service management

In the FACTS telecommunication service management [55], the problem scenario is based on the use of negotiation to coordinate the dynamic provisioning of resources for a Virtual Private Network (VPN) used for meeting scheduling by end users. A VPN refers to the use of a public network (as is the Internet) in a private manner. This service is provided to the users by service and network providers. The multi-agent system consists in a number of agents representing the users (Personal Communication Agents), and the service and network providers.

3.6 Challenger

In [56] it is described a MAS for distributed resource allocation, *Challenger*. The MAS consists of agents which individually manage local resources and which communicate with one another in order to share their resources (e.g. CPU time) in an attempt to efficiently use of them. *Challenger* is similar to other market-based control systems as the agents act as buyers and sellers in a marketplace, always trying to maximize their own utility. Experimental results of using the MAS to perform CPU load balancing in a network of computers (small sized networks, e.g. of maximum 10 machines) are presented in [56]. Challenger was designed to be robust and adaptive. It is completely descentralized and consist of a distributed set of agents that run locally on every machine in the network. The main agent behaviour is based on a market/bidding metaphor with the following four steps: job origination, making bids, evaluation of bids, and returning results. Several simulations were run, including learning behaviours of the agents in order to improve the performance of the whole system in some critical situations such as large message delays and inaccurate bids made by the agents.

3.7 Tele-MACS

Tele-MACS [57] applied a multi-agent control approach to the management of an ATM network. In telecommunications, Tele-MACS considers link bandwidth allocation and dynamic routing. A multi-layered control architecture has been implemented in Java. Tele-MACS consists of multiple layers of MASs, where each layer is defined to conduct the control of the network infrastructure to a certain level of competence.

3.8 TELE TRUCK

Real-life transport scheduling can be solved by a multi-agent system. Each resource could be represented as an agent and market algorithms are applied to find and optimize solutions. The TELE TRUCK system, presented in [58], can be applied to online dispatching in a logistics management node of a supply web, and uses telecommunication technologies (satellite, GPS, mobile phones). The truck drivers, trucks, (semi)-trailers are autonomous entities with their own objectives, and only an appropriate group of these entities can perform together the transportation task. Thus the whole problem can be modeled as a MAS. Each entity is an intelligent agent, and has its own plan, goal, and communication facilities in order to provide the resources for the transportation plans according to their role in the society. In the TELE TRUCK system different types of negotiation techniques are used for the allocation of transportation tasks in a network of shipping companies. In the case of vertical cooperation, i.e. the allocation of orders within one shipping company, the simulated trading algorithm is used for dynamic optimization, and also an extended contract net protocol is used for fast and efficient initial solution (e.g. one order can be split to multiple trucks). The simulated trading algorithm is a randomized algorithm that realizes a market mechanism where contractors attempt to optimize a task allocation by successively selling and buying tasks in several trading rounds. In the case of horizontal cooperation, i.e. the order allocation across shipping companies, a brokering mechanism is used for short-term cooperation. The matrix auction is another negotiation technique that is used. This type of auction is truth revealing and applicable for the simultaneous assignment of multiple items or tasks to bidders. For example, in the case of orders assignment to the vehicles, a bidding procedure is used. The dispatch officer in the shipping company interacts with a dispatch agent. The dispatch agent announces the newly incoming orders via an extended contract net protocol.

3.9 MetaMorphII

The MetaMorphII system [59] enables the development of a mediator-based multi-agent architecture to support enterprise integration and supply chain management. A federated-based approach is applied. A manufacturing system is seen as a set of subsystems that are connected through special interface agents called facilitators or mediators. Each enterprise has at least one mediator. In the supply chain network, partners, suppliers and customers are connected through their mediators. Other levels of mediators can exist inside an enterprise. The coordination mechanisms that are used include communication between agents through facilitators. Local agents use a restricted subset of an Agent Communication Language (ACL) to inform facilitators about their needs and services they offer. Facilitators use this information as well as their knowledge of the global MAS network to transform local agents' messages and route them to other facilitators. In this way, local agents give a part of their autonomy to facilitators and in turn, the facilitators satisfy their requirements.

3.10 Fishmarket

The Fishmarket project conducted at the Artificial Intelligence Research Institute (IIIA-CSIC), Barcelona, developed an agent-mediated electronic institution [60], [61]. FM100 is a Java-based version of the Fishmarket auction house, that allows to define auction-based trading scenarios where goods can be traded using the classical auction protocols (Dutch, English, Vickrey, and First-price Sealed Bid). It has a library of agent templates written in Java, Lisp, and C.

Fishmarket is one of the most popular simulations of an agent-mediated auction house, which offers a convinient mechanism for automated trading due to the simplicity of the conventions used for the interaction when multi-party negotiations are involved, and to the fact that on-line auctions may successfully reduce storage, delivery or clearing house costs in the fish market. FM was designed for the Spanish fish market. One main advantage

3.13 MACIV

MACIV is a multi-agent system for resource management on civil construction companies, developed in Java as an academic prototype used for demonstration of negotiation techniques [65]. In order to achieve an adequate solution and take into account the specific characteristics of the problem, it was decided to adopt a decentralized solution based on multi-agent systems techniques. The agents behaviours were improved through reinforcement learning. A multi-criteria negotiation protocol is used for a society of buyers and sellers, where buyer agents represent human operators requesting for tasks to be executed and seller agents represent resources competing for being used for those task execution.

3.14 SMACE

SMACE [66] is a MAS for e-commerce that supports and assists the creation of customised software agents to be used in agent-mediated e-commerce transactions. It has been used for testing automated negotiation protocols, including those based on the continuous double auction that support a multi-issue approach in the bargaining process. Learning is also included as a capability that enhance the MAS performance. The agents may have any negotiation strategy. SMACE was implemented in Java and JATLite was used to provide the communication infrastructure.

3.15 COM_ELECTRON

COM_ELECTRON is a multi-agent system developed at University of Ploiesti [67], which is dedicated to second hand electronic products selling. It has been implemented in JADE as a simulation. For the shopping agents architecture we have used the SmartAgent architecture [68]. The role of a SmartAgent is to assist users while doing electronic shopping in the Internet. The shopping agent may receive proposals from multiple seller agents. Each proposal defines a complete product offering including a product configuration, price, warranty, and the merchant's value-added services. The shopping agent evaluates and orders these proposals based on how they satisfy its owner's preferences (expressed as multi-attribute utilities). He negotiates over a set of issues that describe the characteristics of a good (such as: type of processor, memory capacity, price, hard disk capacity, in the case of a second hand laptop).

The main purpose of the agent-mediated electronic commerce system COM_ELECTRON is the maximization of the profit viewed as an increased number of transactions and deals agreed after some rounds of bilateral negotiation. In order to achieve this purpose, the negotiation model that was adopted by an agent (buyer/seller) is the service-oriented negotiation model described in [29] extended with an adaptability component capability implemented by a feed-forward artificial neural network [69], that allows him to model the other agent's negotiation strategy, thus doing an adaptive negotiation in order to make a better deal. The adaptive negotiation model was included in the architecture of the SmartAgent [70]. Figure 6 describes the price negotiation context.

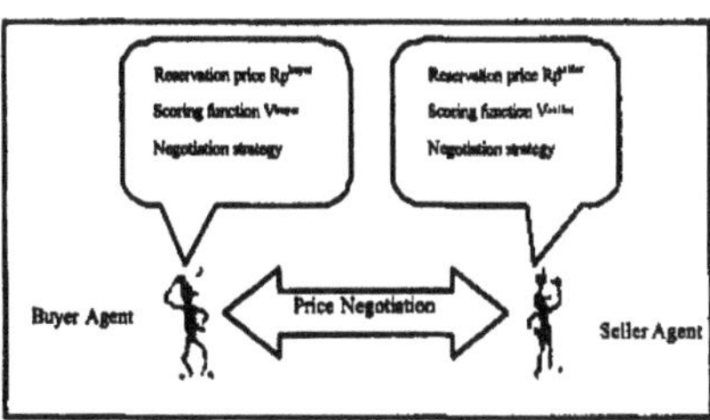

Figure 6. The price negotiation context.

This history of price proposals is a time series and the prediction of the next price proposal is made by using a feed forward artificial neural network. The learning capability is activated during the process of proposals and counterproposals exchanging and will influence the way in which the negotiation will evolve to an agreement. For example, the seller agent will reason about the buyer agent based solely on his observations of buyer's actions.

Currently, the COM_ELECTRON system uses a non-mediated interaction coordination model. If a coordination trace inspection it is needed, the architecture of the MAS can be modified by including some mediator agents which will capture the state of the interaction.

3.16 VIRT_CONSTRUCT

The agent-based virtual enterprise, VIRT_CONSTRUCT [71], [72], is under development at University of Ploiesti. The implementation of the system is made in JADE The goal of VIRT_CONSTRUCT is the

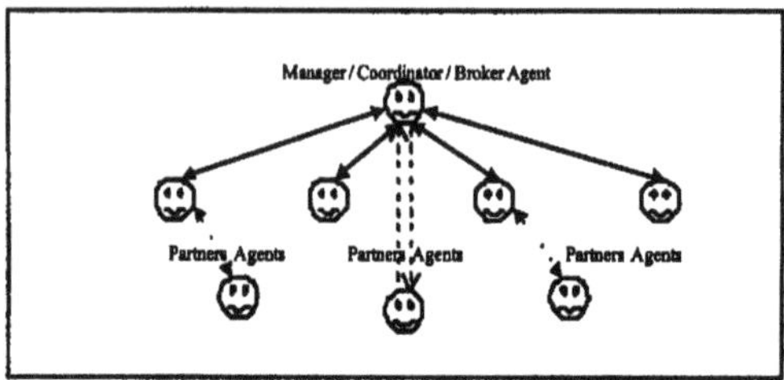

Figure 7. The MAS view of VIRT_CONSTRUCT.

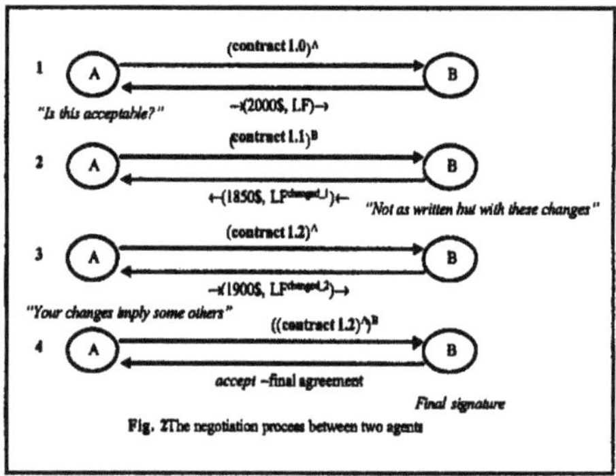

Figure 8. The negotiation process between two agents.

In the case of an agent-based VE, each partner is an agent that will act on behalf of the partner via delegation or in negotiation processes. In the context of an electronic marketplace, the creation of a VE involves the initiation of a competition between different agents that send bids in order to become the VE partners. Figure 8 describes an example of negotiation process between two agents, the Broker-Agent (A) and a potential partner's agent (B) that has the capability of specialized roof construction.

We have used two coordination mechanisms, the contract net protocol and a service-oriented negotiation model. Several simulations with different environment settings were run in JADE.

4. CONCLUSION

The multi-agent system approach has proved to be a proper solution for the design of complex, distributed computational systems. The main functionalities that a MAS has to provide are reasoning, communication, coordination, learning, planning, etc. Currently, the MAS developments have ad-hoc designs, predefined communication protocols and scalability only in simulations. Therefore, problems with external non-agent legacy systems could arise. A lot of problems need to be solved. One of these is the lack of mature software development methodologies for agent-based systems. Currently, research work is focused in this direction, and the basic principles of software and knowledge engineering need to be applied to the development and deployment of multi-agent systems. Another is the need for standard languages and interaction protocols especially for their use in open agents societies. Also, there is a demanding need for developing reasoning capabilities for agents in open environments.

Summarizing, the problems that might appear when using a multi-agent system approach are the coordination in an open environment, the distributed resource allocation, the distribution of tasks, the agents interoperability, the privacy concerns, and the overall system stability.

From a software engineering point of view it is important to have some coordination tools that help engineers harnessing the intrinsic complexity of agent interaction by providing them with the most effective views on the state and evolution over time of interaction within the multi-agent system. Depending on the application domain that is modeled by a multi-agent system and on the specific type of negotiation needed at a specific moment, a distributive or an integrative negotiation model could be chosen. Usually, the integrative negotiation is applied to task/resource allocation, while for more complex domains, with multiple goals, an integrative negotiation model would be proper. An important aspect that need to be addressed when designing a multi-agent system is learning, which has the ability to improve the whole behaviour of a MAS.

Agent-based computing has the potential to improve the theory and the practice of modelling, designing, and implementing of complex systems. The main benefit of applying a multi-agent approach is that the partial subsystems can be integrated into a coherent and consistent super-system in which they work together to better meet the needs of the entire application.

References

1. N. R. Jennings, Agent-Based Computing: Promises and Perils, *Proceedings of the 16th International Joint Conference on Artificial Intelligence IJCAI99*, Stockholm, Sweden, pp. 1429-1436 (1999).
2. M. Wooldridge, Agent-based software engineering, *IEE Proceedings on Software Engineering*, **144**(1), 26-37 (1997).
3. FIPA (Foundation for Intelligent Physical Agents): http://www.fipa.org
4. A. Newell, The Knowledge Level, *Artificial Intelligence*, **18**:87-127 (1982).
5. N. R. Jennings, and J. R. Campos, Towards a Social Level Characterisation of Socially Responsible Agents, *IEE Proceedings on Software Engineering*, **144**(1), 11-25 (1997).
6. L. C. Lee, H. S. Nwana, D. T. Ndumu, and P. de Wilde, The stability, scalability and performance of multi-agent systems, *British Telecom Journal*, **16**(3), 94-103 (1998).

7. M. Wooldridge, The theory of multi-agent systems, *lecture notes*, UPC-Barcelona (2000).
8. M. Wooldridge, and N. Jennings, Intelligent agent: theory and practice, *The Knowledge Engineering Review*, **10**(2), 115-152 (1995).
9. R. Brooks, Intelligence without representation, *Artificial Intelligence*, **47**(1-3), 139-159 (1991).
10. R. Sutton, Integrated Architectures for Learning, Planning, and Reacting Based on Approximating Dynamic Programming, *Proceedings of the 7th ICML*, Morgan Kaufmann (1990), 216-224.
11. A. Sloman, and B. Logan, Building Cognitively Rich Agents Using the SIM_AGENT Toolkit, *Communications of ACM* (1999).
12. KQML: http://www.cs.umbc.edu/kqml/.
13. M. Colombetti, A Commitment-Based Approach to Agent Speech Acts and Conversations, *Proceedings of Agent Languages and Conversation Policies workshop – Autonomous Agents 2000*, pp. 21-29 (2000).
14. H. Nwana, L. Lee, and N. Jennings, Coordination in Software Agent Systems, *BT Technology Journal*, **14**(4) (1996).
15. F. Bergenti, and A. Ricci, Three Approaches to the Coordination of Multiagent Systems, *Proceedings of the international ACM conference SAC2002*, Madrid, Spain (2002).
16. A. Omicini, and E. Denti, From tuple spaces to tuple centres, *Science of Computer Programming*, **42**(3):277-294 (2001).
17. R. Bourne, C. B. Excelente-Toledo, and N. R. Jennings, Run-Time Selection of Coordination Mechanisms in Multi-Agent Systems, *Proceedings of ECAI2000*, Berlin, Germany (2000).
18. E. de Jong, Multi-Agent Coordination by Communication of Evaluations, *technical report*, Artificial Intelligence Laboratory, Vrije Universiteit Brussel (1997).
19. M. Barbuceanu, and M. S. Fox, Integrating Communicative Action, Conversations and Decision Theory to Coordinate Agents, *ACM Proceedings of Autonomous Agents 97*, Marina Del Rey, California, USA, pp. 49-58 (1997).
20. S. Ossowski, A. Garcia-Serrano, and J. Cuena, Emergent Co-ordination of Flow Control Actions through Functional Co-operation of Social Agents, *Proceedings of the 12th European Conference on Artificial Intelligence-ECAI96*, Budapest, Hungary, pp. 539-543 (1996).
21. A. Bazzan, Evolution of Coordination as a Metaphor for Learning in Multi-Agent Systems, *Proceedings of the ECAI96 workshop W26*, Budapest, Hungary (1996).
22. P. P. Grassé, La theorie de la stigmergie: essai d'interpretation du comportament des termites constructeurs, Insectes Sociaux 6 (1959).
23. G. Theraulaz, G., A brief history of Stigmergy, *Artificial Life*, **5**, pp. 97-116 (1999).
24. P. Valckenaers, H. Van Brussel, M. Kollingbaum, and O. Bochmann, Multi-agent Coordination and Control Using Stigmergy Applied to Manufacturing Control, *Multi-Agent Systems and Applications*, Lecture Notes in Artificial Intelligence – LNAI 2086, Springer (2001).
25. D. G. Pruitt, *Negotiation Behavior*, Academic Press, New York (1981).
26. M. Fisher, Characterising Simple Negotiation as Distributed Agent-Based Theorem-Proving – A Preliminary Report, *Proceedings of the International Conference on Multi-Agent Systems* – ICMAS, pp. 127-134 (2000).
27. S. Kraus, Automated Negotiation and Decision Making in Multiagent Environments, M. Luck et al. (Editors), *Multi-Agent Systems and Applications*, LNAI 2086, (2001), 150-172.
28. M. Oprea, Adaptability in Agent-Based E-Commerce Negotiation, *tutorial notes* of the 20th IASTED International Conference Applied Informatics AI'02 – symposium Artificial Intelligence Applications–AIA'02, February, Innsbruck, Austria (2002).

29. P. Faratin, C. Sierra, and N. R. Jennings, Negotiation decision functions for autonomous agents, *Robotics and Autonomous Systems*, **24**:159-182 (1998).
30. K. P. Sycara, Persuasive argumentation in negotiation, *Theory and Decision*, **28**:203-242 (1990).
31. S. Kraus, K. Sycara, and A. Evenchik, Reaching agreements through argumentation: a logical model and implementation, *Artificial Intelligence*, **104**(1-2), 1-69 (1998).
32. S. Parsons, C. Sierra, and N. R. Jennings, Agents that reason and negotiate by arguing, *Journal of Logic and Computation*, **8**(3), 261-292 (1998).
33. S. Kraus, *Strategic Negotiation in Multiagent Environments*, MIT Press, Cambridge, USA (2001).
34. M. Oprea, Adaptability and Embodiment in Agent-Based E-Commerce Negotiation, *Proceedings of the Workshop Adaptability and Embodiment Using Multi-Agent Systems-* AEMAS01, Prague, (2001) 257-265.
35. S. Sen, and M. Sekaran, Individual Learning of coordination knowledge, *Journal of Experimental & Theoretical Artificial Intelligence*, **10**(3), 333-356 (1998).
36. A. Pérez-Uribe, and B. Hirsbrunner, The Risk of Exploration in Multi-Agent Learning Systems: A Case Study, *Proceedings of the Agents-00/ECML-00 workshop on Learning Agents*, Barcelona, (2000), 33-37.
37. D. Zeng, D., and K. Sycara, How Can an Agent Learn to Negotiate, *Intelligent Agents III. Agent Theories, Architectures and Languages*, LNAI 1193, Springer, 233-244, (1997).
38. D. Carmel, and S. Markovitch, Model-based learning of interaction strategies in multi-agent systems, *JETAI* **10**, 309-332 (1998).
39. J. Vidal, and E. Durfee, Learning nested agent models in an information economy, *Journal of Experimental & Theoretical Artificial Intelligence*, **10**(3), 291-308 (1998).
40. Y. Demazeau, Multi-Agent Methodology and Programming, *tutorial notes*, ACAI'2001 & EASSS'2001, Prague (2001).
41. F. Bergenti, O. Shehory, and F. Zambonelli, Agent-Oriented Software Engineering, *tutorial notes*, EASSS2002, Bologna (2002).
42. AUML: http://auml.org
43. B. Bauer, J. P. Müller, and J. Odell, Agent UML: A Formalism for Specifying Multiagent Interaction, *Agent-Oriented Software Engineering*, P. Ciancarini and M. Wooldridge (Eds.), Springer, Berlin, pp. 91-103 (2001).
44. H. S. Nwana, D. T. Ndumu, L. Lee, and J. C. Collis, A Toolkit for Building Distributed Multi-Agent Systems, *Applied Artificial Intelligence Journal*, **13**(1) (1999) - Available on line from http://www.labs.bt.com/projects/agents.
45. JADE (Java Agent Development Framework), http://jade.cselt.it/.
46. J. C. Collis, and L. C. Lee, Building Electronic Commerce Marketplaces with ZEUS Agent Tool-Kit, *Agent Mediated Electronic Commerce*, P. Noriega, C. Sierra (Eds.), LNAI 1571, Springer, (1999), pp. 1-24.
47. AgentBuilder: http://www.agentbuilder.com.
48. MadKit: http://www.madkit.org
49. O. Gutknecht, and J. Ferber, MadKit: A generic multi-agent platform, *Proceedings of the Fourth International Conference on Autonomous Agents – AA2000*, Barcelona, (2000), pp. 78-79.
50. M. Luck, P. McBurney, and C. Preist, Agent Technology: Enabling Next Generation Computing – A Roadmap for Agent Based Computing, AgentLink II (Jan. 2003).
51. K. Sycara, Multi-agent Infrastructure, Agent Discovery, Middle Agents for Web Services and Interoperation, *Multi-Agent Systems and Applications*, M. Luch et al. (Eds), LNAI 2086, Springer, (2001), pp.17-49.

52. J. Eriksson, N. Finne, and S. Janson, SICS MarketSpace – An Agent-Based Market Infrastructure, *Agent Mediated Electronic Commerce*, LNAI 1571, Springer, pp. 41-53 (1999).
53. N. R. Jennings, J. M. Corera, I. Laresgoiti, Developing Industrial Multi-Agent Systems, *Proceedings of ICMAS* (1995), pp. 423-430.
54. N. R. Jennings, P. Faratin, M. J. Johnson, T. J. Norman, P. O'Brien, and M. E. Wiegand, Agent-based business process management, *International Journal of Cooperative Information Systems*, **5**(2&3):105-130 (1996).
55. FACTS (1998) http://www.labs.bt.com/profsoc/facts.
56. A. Chavez, A. Moukas, and P. Maes, *Challenger*: A Multi-agent System for Distributed Resource Allocation, Proceedings of Autonomous Agents 97, Marina Del Rey, USA, (1997), pp. 323-331.
57. Tele-MACS: http://www.agentcom.org/agentcom/.
58. H. –J. Bürckert, K. Fisher, and G. Vierke, Transportation scheduling with holonic MAS – the teletruck approach, *Proceedings of the 3rd International Conference on Practical Applications of Intelligent Agents and Multiagents - PAAM'98*, UK (1998).
59. W. Shen, Agent-based cooperative manufacturing scheduling: an overview, *COVE Newsletter*, No. 2, (March 2001).
60. Fishmarket, http://www.iiia.csic.es/Projects/fishmarket/newindex.html.
61. P. Noriega, Agent-Mediated Auctions: The Fishmarket Metaphor, *PhD Thesis*, Artificial Intelligence Research Institute-IIIA-CSIC, Barcelona (1997).
62. J. Morris, P. Ree, and P. Maes, Sardine: Dynamic Seller Strategies in an Auction Marketplace, *Proceedings of the International Conference Electronic Commerce*, Minneapolis, Minnesota, USA, ACM Press, (2000).
63. eMediator, http://www.ecommerce.cs.wustl.edu/eMediator.
64. T. Sandholm, *eMediator*: A Next Generation Electronic Commerce Server, *Proceedings of the 4th International Conference Autonomous Agents*, Barcelona, ACM Press, (2000), pp. 341-348.
65. J. M. Fonseca, A. D. Mora, and E. Oliveira, MACIV: A Multi-Agent System for Resource Selection on Civil Construction Companies, *Technical Summaries of the Software Demonstration Session – in conjunction with Autonomous Agents '00* (2000).
66. H. L. Cardoso, and E. Oliveira, SMACE, *Technical Summaries of the Software Demonstration Session – in conjunction with Autonomous Agents '00* (2000).
67. M. Oprea, COM_ELECTRON a multi-agent system for second hand products selling – a preliminary report, *research report*, University of Ploiesti (2003).
68. M. Oprea, The Architecture of a Shopping Agent, *Economy Informatics*, **II**(1), 63-68 (2002).
69. M. Oprea, The Use of Adaptive Negotiation by a Shopping Agent in Agent-Mediated Electronic Commerce, *Multi-Agent Systems and Applications III*, LNAI 2691, Springer, 594-605 (2003).
70. M. Oprea, An Adaptive Negotiation Model for Agent-Based Electronic Commerce, *Studies in Informatics and Control*, **11**(3), 271-279 (2002).
71. M. Oprea, Coordination in an Agent-Based Virtual Enterprise, *Studies in Informatics and Control*, **12**(3), 215-225 (2003).
72. M. Oprea, The Agent-Based Virtual Enterprise, *Journal of Economy Informatics*, **3**(1), 21-25 (2003).

DISCRETE EVENT SIMULATION WITH APPLICATION TO COMPUTER COMMUNICATION SYSTEMS PERFORMANCE

Introduction to Simulation

Helena Szczerbicka[1], Kishor S. Trivedi[2] and Pawan K. Choudhary[2]
[1]*University of Hannover, Germany* ; [2]*Duke University, Durham, NC*

Abstract: As complexity of computer and communication systems increases, it becomes hard to analyze the system via analytic models. Measurement based system evaluation may be too expensive. In this tutorial, discrete event simulation as a model based technique is introduced. This is widely used for the performance/availability assessment of complex stochastic systems. Importance of applying a systematic methodology for building correct, problem dependent, and credible simulation models is discussed. These will be made evident by relevant experiments for different real-life problems and interpreting their results. The tutorial starts providing motivation for using simulation as a methodology for solving problems, different types of simulation (steady state vs. terminating simulation) and pros and cons of analytic versus simulative solution of a model. This also includes different classes of simulation tools existing today. Methods of random deviate generation to drive simulations are discussed. Output analysis, involving statistical concepts like point estimate, interval estimate, confidence interval and methods for generating it, is also covered. Variance reduction and speed-up techniques like importance sampling, importance splitting and regenerative simulation are also mentioned. The tutorial discusses some of the most widely used simulation packages like *OPNET MODELER* and *ns-2*. Finally the tutorial provides several networking examples covering TCP/IP, FTP and RED.

Key words: Simulation, Statistical Analysis, random variate, TCP/IP, OPNET MODELER and ns-2

In many fields of engineering and science, we can use a computer to simulate natural or man-made phenomena rather than to experiment with the real system. Examples of such computer experiments are simulation studies of congestion control in a network and competition for resources in a computer operating system. A simulation is an experiment to determine characteristics of a system empirically. It is a modeling method that mimics or emulates the behavior of a system over time. It involves generation and observation of artificial history of the system under study, which leads to drawing inferences concerning the dynamic behavior of the real system.

A *computer simulation* is a discipline of designing a model of an actual or theoretical system, executing the model (an experiment) on a digital computer, and statistically analyzing the execution output (see Fig. 1). The current state of the physical system is represented by state variables (program variables). Simulation program modifies state variables to reproduce the evolution of the physical system over time.

This tutorial provides an introductory treatment of various concepts related to simulation. In Section 1 we discuss the basic notion of going from the system description to its simulation model. In Section 2, we provide a broad classification of simulation models followed by a classification of simulation modeling tools/languages in Section 3. In Section 4 we discuss the role of probability and statistics in simulation while in Section 5 we develop several networking applications using the simulation tools OPNET MODELER and ns-2. Finally, we conclude in Section 6.

1. FROM SYSTEM TO MODEL

System can be viewed as a set of objects with their attributes and functions that are joined together in some regular interaction toward the accomplishment of some goal. Model is an abstract representation of a system under study. Some commonly used model types are:

1. Analytical Models. These employ mathematical formal descriptions like algebraic equations, differential equations or stochastic processes and associated solution procedures to solve the model. For example continuous time Markov chains, discrete time Markov chains, semi-Markov and Markov regenerative models have been used extensively for studying reliability/availability/performance and performability of computer and communication systems [1].
    1. Closed form Solutions: Underlying equations describing the dynamic behavior of such models can sometimes be solved in closed form if the model is small in size (either by hand or by such packages as Mathematica) or if the model is highly structured such as the Markov chain underlying a product-form queuing network [1].
    2. Numerical Methods: When the solution of an analytic model cannot be obtained in a closed form, then computational procedures are used to

numerically solve analytical models using packages such as SHARPE [2] or SPNP [3]

2. Simulation models: Employ methods to "run" the model so as to mimic the underlying system behavior; no attempt is made to solve the equations describing system behavior as such equations may be either too complex or not possible to formulate. An artificial history of the system under study is generated based on model assumptions. Observations are collected and analyzed to estimate the dynamic behavior of the system being simulated. Note that simulation provides a model-based evaluation method of system behavior but it shares its experimental nature with measurement-based evaluation and as such needs the statistical analysis of its outputs.

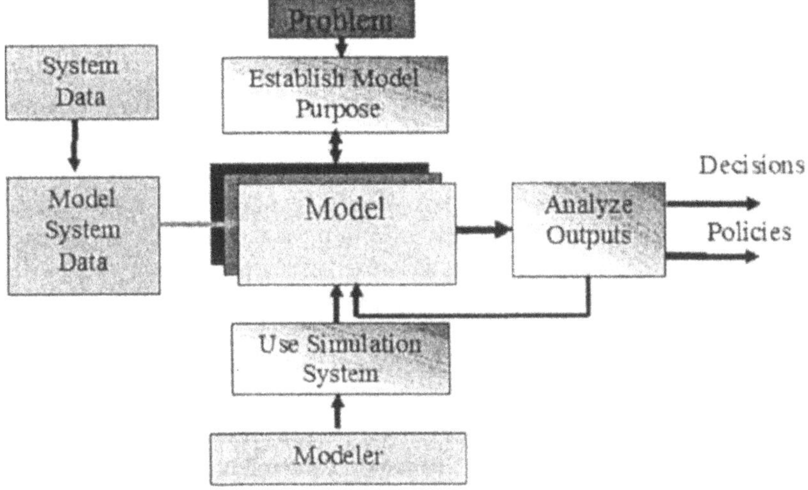

Figure 1. Simulation based problem solving

Simulation or analytic models are useful in many scenarios. As the real system becomes more complex and computing power becomes faster and cheaper, modeling is being used increasingly for the following reasons [4]:

1. If the system is unavailable for measurement the only option available for its evaluation is to use a model. This can be the case if system is being designed or it is too expensive to experiment with the real system
2. Evaluation of system under wide variety of workloads and network types (or protocols).

3. Suggesting improvement in the system under investigation based on knowledge gained during modeling.
4. Gaining insight into which variables are most important and how variables interact.
5. New polices, decision rules, information flows can be explored without disrupting ongoing operations of the real system.
6. New hardware architectures, scheduling algorithms, routing protocols, reconfiguration strategies can be tested without committing resources for their acquisition/implementation.

While modeling has proved to be a viable and reliable alternative to measurements on the real system, the choice between analytical and simulation is still a matter of importance For large and complex systems, analytic model formulation and/or solution may require making unrealistic assumptions and approximations. For such systems simulation models can be easily created and solved to study the whole system more accurately. Nevertheless, many users often employ simulation where a faster analytic model would have served the purpose.

Some of difficulties in application of simulation are:

1. Model building requires special training. Frequently, simulation languages like Simula [5], Simscript [6], Automod [7], Csim [8], etc are used. Users need some programming expertise before using these languages.
2. Simulation results are difficult to interpret, since most simulation outputs are samples of random variables. However most of the recent simulation packages have inbuilt output analysis capabilities to statistically analyze the outputs of simulation experiments.
3. Though the proper use of these tools requires a deep understanding statistical methods and necessary assumptions to assert the credibility of obtained results. Due to a lack of understanding of statistical techniques frequently simulation results can be wrongly interpreted [9].
4. Simulation modeling and analysis are time consuming and expensive. With availability of faster machines, development in parallel and distributed simulation [10, 11] and in variance reduction techniques such as importance sampling [12, 13, 14], importance splitting [15, 16, 17] and regenerative simulation [18], this difficulty is being alleviated.

In spite of some of the difficulties, simulation is widely used in practice and the use of simulation will surely increase manifold as experimenting with real systems gets increasingly difficult due to cost and other reasons. Hence it is important for every computer engineer (in fact, any engineer) to be familiar with the basics of simulation.

2. CLASSIFICATION OF SIMULATION MODELS

Simulation models can be classified according to several criteria [19]:

1. *Continuous vs. Discrete:* Depending upon the way in which state variables of the modeled system change over time. For example concentration of a substance in a chemical reactor changes in a smooth, continuous fashion like in a fluid flow whereas changes in the length of a queue in a packet switching network can be tracked at discrete points in time. In a *discrete event simulation* changes in the modeled state variable are triggered by scheduled events [20].
2. *Deterministic vs. stochastic*
This classification refers to type of variables used in the model being simulated. The choice of stochastic simulation makes it experimental in nature and hence necessitates statistical analysis of results.
3. *Terminating vs. Steady state:* A terminating simulation is used to study the behavior of a system over a well-defined period of time, for example for the reliability analysis of a flight control system over a designated mission time. This corresponds to transient analysis put in the context of analytic models. Whereas steady state simulation corresponds to the steady state analysis in the context of analytic models. As such, we have to wait for the simulation system output variables to reach steady state values. For example, the performance evaluation of a computer or networking system is normally (but not always) is done using steady state simulation. Likewise, the availability analysis is typically carried out for steady state behavior.
4. *Synthetic or distribution driven vs. Trace driven:* A time-stamped sequence of input events is required to drive a simulation model. Such an event trace may already be available to drive the simulation hence making it a trace driven simulation. Examples are cache simulations for which many traces are available. Similarly, traces of packet arrival events (packet size, etc.) are first captured by using a performance measurement tool such as tcpdump. Then these traces are used as input traffic to the simulation. Lots of traces are freely available on Web. One of Internet traces archive is http://ita.ee.lbl.gov. Alternatively, event traces can be synthetically generated. For the synthetic generation, distributions of all inter-event times are assumed to be known or given and then random deviates of the corresponding distributions are used as the time to next event of that type. We will show how to generate random deviates of important distributions such as the exponential, the Weibull and the Pareto distribution. The distribution needed to drive such distribution

driven simulations may have been obtained by statistical inference based on real measurement data.

5. *Sequential vs. Distributed simulation:* Sequential simulation processes events in a non-decreasing time order. In distributed simulation a primary model is distributed over heterogeneous computers, which independently perform simulations locally. The challenge is to produce such a final overall order of events, which is identical with the order that would be generated when simulating the primary model on a single computer, sequentially. There is extensive research in parallel and distributed simulation [10, 11].

The rest of this tutorial is concerned with sequential, distribution driven discrete event simulation.

3. CLASSIFICATION OF SIMULATION TOOLS

Simulation tools can be broadly divided into three basic categories:

1. *General Purpose Programming Language (GPPL):* - C, C++, Java are some of the languages which have the advantage of being readily available. These also provide a total control over software development process. But the disadvantage is that model construction takes considerable time. Also it doesn't have support for any control of a simulation process. Furthermore, generation of random deviates for various needed distributions and the statistical analysis of output will have to be learned and programmed.
2. *Plain Simulation Language (PSL)* - SIMULA, SIMSCRIPT II.5 [6], SIMAN, GPSS, JSIM, SILK are some of the examples. Almost all of them have basic support for discrete event simulation. One drawback is that they are not readily available. There is also the need for programming expertise in a new language.
3. *Simulation Packages (SPs)*- like OPNET MODELER [21], ns-2 [22], CSIM [8], COMMNET III, Arena [23], Automod [7], SPNP [3] etc. They have a big advantage of being user-friendly, with some of them having graphical user interface. They provide basic support for discrete event simulation (DES) and statistical analysis as well as several application domains like TCP/IP networks. This ensures that model construction time is shorter. Some simulation tools like OPNET MODELER also provide user an option of doing analytical modeling of the network. The negative side is that they are generally expensive, although most of them have free academic version for research. Like PSL, SPs require some expertise in new language/environment, and they tend to be less flexible than the PSLs.

Information about a variety of available simulation tools can be found at: http://www.idsia.ch/~andrea/simtools.html

4. THE ROLE OF STATISTICS IN SIMULATION

There are two different uses of statistical methods and one use of probabilistic methods in distribution driven simulations. First, the distributions of input random variables such as inter-arrival times, times to failure, service times, times to repair, etc. need to be estimated from real measurement data. Statistical inference techniques for parameter estimation and fitting distributions are covered in [1] and will be reviewed in the tutorial. Using random number generators, probabilistic methods of generating random deviates are then used to obtain inter-event times and drive the simulation. Once again this topic is covered in [1] and will be reviewed. Simulation runs are performed as computer experiments in order to determine the characteristics of its output random variables. A single simulation run produces sample of values of an output variable over time. Statistical techniques are employed here to examine the data and to get meaningful output from the experiment. Also they are used to define the necessary length of simulation (the size of the sample), characteristics of output variables like mean value and some assessments regarding an accuracy of results. Two principal methods, independent replication and the method of batch means, will be discussed.

In the following subsections we discuss random variate generation methods and the statistical analysis of simulation output.

4.1 Random Variate generation

In this section we describe methods of generating random deviates of any arbitrary distribution, assuming a routine to generate uniformly distributed random numbers is available. The distribution can be either continuous or discrete. Most of the simulation packages like OPNET MODELER, ns-2 and CSIM have built-in routines for generating random variates. But still knowledge of random variate generation is necessary to more accurately model the real world problem especially when available built-in generators in simulation packages do not support the needed distribution. Some of the popular methods for generating variates are [1, 4]:

1. *Inverse Transform:* In this method the following property is used: if X is a continuous random variable with the CDF F, than the new random variable $Y=F(X)$ is uniformly distributed over the interval (0, 1). Thus to

generate a random deviate x of X first a random number u from a uniform distribution over (0, 1) is generated and then the F is inverted. $F^{-1}(u)$ gives the required value of x. This can be used to sample from exponential, uniform, Weibull, triangular, as well as empirical and discrete distributions. It is most useful when the inverse of the CDF, $F(.)$ can be easily computed. Taking the example of exponential distribution (see Eq.1) given u drawn from $U(0,1)$, generate x drawn from *exponential distribution* (see Eq. 2).

$$F(x) = 1 - e^{-\lambda x}, \quad x \geq 0 \tag{1}$$

$$x = -\frac{\ln(1-u)}{\lambda} \tag{2}$$

Some distribution which can be easily inverted are exponential, Weibull, Pareto and log-logistic.

For Weibull distribution whose distribution is given by Eq. (3).

$$F_X(x) = 1 - e^{-\lambda x^{\alpha}} \tag{3}$$

The random variate is generated using Eq. (4)

$$x = \left(\frac{-\ln(1-u)}{\lambda} \right)^{\frac{1}{\alpha}} \tag{4}$$

Similarly Pareto distribution is given by Eq. (5)

$$\begin{aligned} F_X(x) &= 1 - \left(\frac{k}{x} \right)^{\alpha} \quad & x \geq k \\ &= 0 & x \leq k \end{aligned} \tag{5}$$

The random variate is generated using Eq. (6)

$$x = \frac{k}{(1-u)^{\frac{1}{\alpha}}} \tag{6}$$

For Rayleigh distribution given by

$$F_X(x) = 1 - e^{-x^2/2\sigma^2} \quad x \geq 0$$
$$= 0 \qquad otherwise \tag{7}$$

The random variate can be generated using:

$$x = \sqrt{-2\sigma^2 \ln(1-u)} \tag{8}$$

Similarly for Log-Logistic Distribution given by

$$F_X(x) = 1 - \frac{1}{1+(\lambda t)^{\kappa}} \tag{9}$$

The random deviate is generated using

$$x = \frac{1}{\lambda}\left(\frac{u}{1-u}\right)^{\kappa} \tag{10}$$

Random variate of (discrete) Bernoulli distribution with parameter (1-q) can also be generated by the inverse transform technique. The CDF is given by

$$\begin{aligned} F_X(x) &= 0 \quad x < 0 \\ &= q \quad 0 \leq x < 1 \\ &= 1 \quad x \geq 1 \end{aligned} \tag{11}$$

The inverse function for Bernoulli distribution becomes

$$\begin{aligned} F^{-1}(u) &= 0 \quad 0 < u \leq q \\ &= 1 \quad q < u \leq 1 \end{aligned} \tag{12}$$

Now by generating u between (0, 1) we can obtain a random deviate of the Bernoulli distribution by Eq. (12).

For *Hyperexponential distribution* given by

$$F(t) = \sum_i \alpha_i (1 - e^{-\lambda_i t}) \quad t \geq 0 \tag{13}$$

Random variate for Hyperexponential can be generated in two steps. Consider for example a three stage Hyperexponential distribution with parameters α_1, α_2, α_3 and λ_1, λ_2 λ_3. First a uniform random number u is generated and like Eq. (12) the following inverse function is generated:

$$\begin{aligned} F^{-1}(u) &= 1 \quad 0 < u \leq \alpha_1 \\ &= 2 \quad \alpha_1 < u \leq \alpha_1 + \alpha_2 \\ &= 3 \quad \alpha_1 + \alpha_2 < u \leq 1 \end{aligned} \tag{14}$$

Now if $u < \alpha_1$, $F^{-1}(u) = 1$, and the variate is then generated from exponential distribution which occur with probability α_1.

$$x = -\frac{\ln(1-u)}{\lambda_1} \tag{15}$$

Similarly if $F^{-1}(u)=2$, Hyperexponential variate is given as

$$x = -\frac{\ln(1-u)}{\lambda_2} \tag{16}$$

Similarly depending upon the output of Bernoulli variate, Hyperexponential variate can be generated. Note that this example was for $k=3$, but it can be easily extended to $k=n$ stages.

2. *Convolution Method:* This is very helpful in such cases when the random variable Y can be expressed as a sum of other random variables that are independent and easier to generate than Y. Let

$$Y = X_1 + X_2 + \ldots + X_k \tag{17}$$

Taking an example of Hypoexponential case, random variable X with parameters $(\mu_1, \ldots \mu_k)$ is sum of k independent exponential RV's Y_i with mean $1/\mu_i$. For example, a 2-stage hypoexponential distribution is given by

$$F(t) = 1 - \frac{\lambda_2}{\lambda_2 - \lambda_1} e^{-\lambda_1 t} + \frac{\lambda_1}{\lambda_2 - \lambda_1} e^{-\lambda_2 t} \tag{18}$$

From the inverse transform technique, each Y_i is generated using Eq. (2) and their sum is the required result. Note that Erlang is a special case of the

Hypoexponential distribution when all the k sequential phases have identical distribution. Random variate for hypoexponential distribution is given as Eq. (19).

$$x = \sum_{i=1}^{k} -\frac{1}{\mu_i} \ln(1-u_i) \tag{19}$$

Binomial random variable is known to be the sum of n independent and identically distributed Bernoulli random variables hence generating n Bernoulli random variates and adding, this sum will result in a random variate of the Binomial. If $(x_1, x_2, .. x_n)$ are the Bernoulli random variates given by Eq.(12) and let y be Binomial random variate then,

$$y = \sum_{i=1}^{n} x_i \tag{20}$$

3. Direct Transform of Normal Distribution: Since inverse of a normal distribution cannot be expressed in closed form we cannot apply inverse transform method. The CDF is given by:

$$\Phi(x) = \int_{-\infty}^{x} \frac{1}{\sqrt{2\pi}} e^{-\frac{t^2}{2}} dt \tag{21}$$

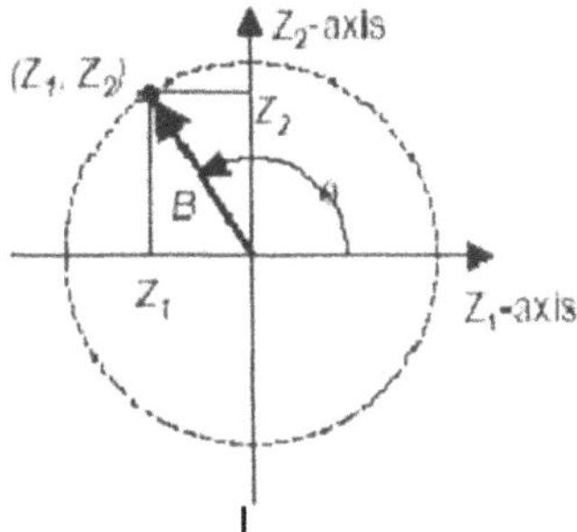

Figure 2. Polar representation

In order to derive a method of generating a random deviate of this distribution, we use a property of the normal distribution that relates it to the Rayleigh distribution. Assume that Z_1 and Z_2 are independent standard normal random variables. Then the square root of their sum $Z_1^2 + Z_2^2$ is known to have the Rayleigh distribution [1] for which we know how to generate its random deviate.

Now in polar coordinates, the original normal random variable can be written as:

$$Z_1 = B\cos\theta \qquad B^2 = Z_1^2 + Z_2^2$$
$$Z_2 = B\sin\theta \tag{22}$$

Using the inverse transform technique (see Eq. 8) we have:

$$b = \sqrt{-2\ln(1-u)} \tag{23}$$

Next we generate a random value of θ to finally get two random deviates of the standard normal:

$$z_1 = \sqrt{-2\ln(1-u_1)}\cos(2\pi u_2)$$
$$z_2 = \sqrt{-2\ln(1-u_1)}\sin(2\pi u_2) \tag{24}$$

4.2 Output Analysis

Discrete-event simulation takes random numbers as inputs that result in each set of study to produce different set of outputs. Output analysis is done to examine data generated by a simulation. It can be used to predict the performance/reliability/availability of a system or compare attributes of different systems. While estimating some measure of the system, sayθ, simulation will generate an estimator$\hat{\Theta}$ ofθ due to presence of random variability. The precision of the estimator $\hat{\Theta}$ will depend upon its variance. Output analysis will help in estimating this variance and also in determining number of observations needed to achieve a desired accuracy. Phenomenon like *sampling error* and *systematic error* influence how well an estimate $\hat{\theta}$ will approximateθ. Sampling error is introduced due to random inputs and dependence or correlation among observations. Systematic errors occur due to dependence of the observations on initially chosen state and initial condition of the system.

4.2.1 Point and Interval Estimates

Estimation of parameter by a single number from the output of a simulation is called point estimate. Let random variables $\{Y_1, Y_2 .. Y_n\}$ are set of observations obtained after simulation. Then a common point estimator for parameter θ is given by Eq. (25).

$$\hat{\Theta} = \frac{1}{n}\sum_{i=1}^{n} Y_i \tag{25}$$

The point estimator $\hat{\Theta}$ is also a random variable and called unbiased if its expected value is θ i.e.

$$E[\hat{\Theta}] = \theta \tag{26}$$

If $E[\hat{\Theta}] = \theta + b$, then b is called bias of the point estimator.

The confidence interval provides an interval or range of values around the point estimate [1]. Confidence interval is defined as

$$P(A < \hat{\Theta} < B) = 1 - \alpha \text{ where } A \text{ and } B \text{ are functions of parameter } \theta \tag{27}$$

For a single parameter, such as the mean, the standard deviation, or probability level, the most common intervals are two sided (i.e., the statistic is between the lower and upper limit) and one sided (i.e., the statistic is smaller or larger than the end point). For the simultaneous estimation of two or more parameters, a confidence region, the generalization of a confidence interval, can take on arbitrary shapes [24, 25].

4.2.2 Terminating vs. Steady State simulation

Output analysis is discussed here for two classes of simulations: terminating simulation and steady state simulation.

Terminating simulation: This applies to the situation wherein we are interested in the transient value of some measure, e.g., channel utilization after 10 minutes of system operation or the transient availability of the system after 10 hours of operation. In these cases each simulation run is conducted until the required simulated time and from each run a single sample value of the measure is collected. By making m independent simulation runs, point and interval estimates of the required measure are obtained using standard statistical techniques. In both the cited examples, each simulation run will provide a binary value of the measure and hence we use the inference procedure based on sampling from the Bernoulli random variable [1]. Yet another situation for terminating simulation arises when the system being modeled has some absorbing states. For instance we are interested in estimating the mean time to failure of a system then form each simulation run a single value is obtained and multiple independent runs are used to get the required estimate. In this case, we could use inference procedure assuming sampling from the exponential or the Weibull distribution [1].

Steady-State Simulation: In this case, we can in principle make independent runs but since the transient phase needs to be thrown away and since it can be long, this approach is wasteful. Attempt is therefore made to get the required statistics from a long single run. The first problem encountered then is to estimate the length of the transient phase. The second problem is the dependence in the resulting sequence. [1] talks about how to estimate the correlation in the sequence first using independent runs. Instead of using independent runs, we can divide a single sequence into first the transient phase and then a batch of steady state runs. Then there are dependencies not only within a batch but also across batches.

The estimator random variable of the mean measure, θ to be estimated is given by Eq. (28) where n is number of observations.

$$\Theta = \lim_{n\to\infty} \frac{1}{n}\sum_{i=1}^{n} Y_i \tag{28}$$

This value should be independent of the initial conditions. But in real system, simulation is stopped after some number of observations n have been collected. The simulation run length is decided on the basis of how large the bias in the point estimator is, the precision desired or resource constraint for computing.

4.2.3 Initialization Bias

Initial conditions may be artificial or unrealistic. There are methods that reduce the point-estimator bias in steady state simulation. One method is called *intelligent initialization* that involves initialization of simulation in a state that is more representative of long-run conditions. But if the system doesn't exist or it is very difficult to obtain data directly from the system, any data on similar systems or simplified model is collected.

The second method involves dividing the simulation into two phases. One of them is called the *initialization phase* from time *0* to T_0 and the other is called the *data-collection phase* from T_0 to $T_0 + T_E$.

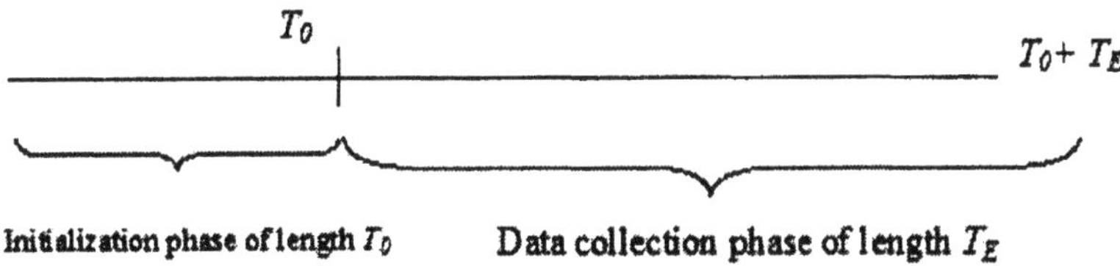

Figure 3. Initialization and Data Collection phase

The choice of T_0 [26, 27, 28] is important as system state at time T_0 will be more representative of steady state behavior than at the time of original initial conditions (i.e., at time $t=0$). Generally T_0 is taken to be more than five times T_E [29].

4.2.4 Dealing with Dependency [1]

Successive values of variables monitored from a simulation run exhibit dependencies, such as high correlation between the response times of consecutive requests to a file server. Assume that the observed quantities are dependent random variables, $(Y_1, Y_2 \ldots Y_m)$ having index invariant mean μ and variance σ^2. The sample mean is given by

$$\bar{Y} = \sum_{i=1}^{m} \frac{Y_i}{m} \tag{29}$$

Sample mean is unbiased point estimator of population mean but variance of sample mean is not equal to σ^2/n. Taking sequence to be wide sense stationary the variance is given by Eq.(30)

$$Var[\overline{Y}] = \frac{\sigma^2}{m} + \frac{2}{m}\sum_{i=1}^{m-1}\left(1 - \frac{i}{m}\right)K_i \tag{30}$$

$$So\ m Var[\bar{Y}] = \sigma^2 a \quad where\ a = 1 + 2\sum_{i=1}^{\infty}\frac{K_i}{\sigma^2} \tag{31}$$

The statistic $\dfrac{\bar{Y} - \mu}{\sigma\sqrt{a/m}}$ approaches standard normal distribution as m approaches infinity. Therefore an approximate $100(1\text{-}\alpha)\%$ confidence interval becomes

$$\overline{Y} \pm \sigma z_{\alpha/2}\sqrt{\frac{a}{m}} \tag{32}$$

The need to estimate $\sigma^2 a$ can be avoided using *Replication method.* It is used to estimate point-estimator variability. In this method, simulation experiment is replicated m times with n observations each. If initial state is chosen randomly for all m observations, the result will be independent of each other. But the n observations within each experiment will be dependent. Let the sample mean and sample variance of the jth experiment be given by $\overline{Y}(j)\ and\ S^2(j)$ respectively. From individual sample means, point estimator of population mean is given by

$$\overline{Y} = \frac{1}{m}\sum_{j=1}^{m}\overline{Y}(j) = \frac{1}{mn}\sum_{j=1}^{m}\sum_{i=1}^{n}Y_i(j) \tag{33}$$

All $\overline{Y}(1), \overline{Y}(2)..\overline{Y}(m)$, are independent and identically distributed (*i.i.d*) random variables. Assume that the common variance of $\overline{Y}(j)$, is denoted by v^2. The estimator of the variance v^2 is given by

$$\overline{V^2} = \frac{1}{m-1}\sum_{j=1}^{m}[\overline{Y}(j)-\bar{Y}]^2 \quad (34)$$

And $100(1\text{-}\alpha)\%$ confidence interval for θ, is approximately given by

$$\bar{y} - t_{\alpha/2,m-1}\frac{v}{\sqrt{m}} \leq \theta \leq \bar{y} + t_{\alpha/2,m-1}\frac{v}{\sqrt{m}} \quad (35)$$

where '*t*' represents *t-student* distribution with *(m-1)* degree of freedom.

4.2.5 Method of Batch Means

One major disadvantage of the replication method is that initialization phase data from each replication is wasted. To address the issue, we use a design based on a single, long simulation run divided into contiguous segments (or batches), each having length *n*. The sample mean Y_r of rth segment is then treated as an individual observation. This method called the *method of batch means,* reduces the unproductive portion of simulation time to just one initial stabilization period. But the disadvantage is the set of sample means are not statistically independent and usually the estimator is biased. Estimation of the confidence interval for a single run method can be done following the same procedure as done for replication method. We just replace r^{th} replication in independent replication by the rth batch. *Method of batch means* is also called *single run method.*

4.2.6 Variance Reduction Techniques

Variance reduction techniques help in obtaining greater precision of simulation results (smaller confidence interval) for the same number of simulation runs, or in reducing the number of runs required for the desired precision. They are used to improve the efficiency and accuracy of the simulation process.

One of frequently used technique is importance sampling [12, 13, 14]. In this approach the stochastic behavior of the system is modified in such a way that some events occur more often. This helps in dealing with rare events scenarios. But this modification causes model to be biased, which can be removed using the likelihood ratio function. If carefully done, the variance of the estimator of the simulated variable is smaller than the original implying reduction in the size of the confidence interval. Other techniques include importance splitting [15, 16, 17] and regenerative simulation [18].

Some of the other methods that are used to speed up of simulations are parallel and distributed simulation [10, 11].

To summarize, before generating any sound conclusions on the basis of the simulation-generated output data, a proper statistical analysis is required. The simulation experiment helps in estimating different measures of the system. The statistical analysis helps in acquiring some assurance that these estimates are sufficiently precise for the proposed use of the model. Depending on the initial conditions and choice of run length terminating simulations or steady-state simulations can be performed. Standard error or a confidence interval can be used to measure the precision of point estimators.

5. SOME APPLICATIONS

In this section we discuss some of the simulation packages like OPNET MODELER [21] and ns-2 [22]. We also discuss Network Animator (NAM) [30] which generates graphs and animation in ns-2. OPNET MODELER and ns-2 are application oriented simulation packages. While OPNET MODELER uses GUI extensively for configuring network, ns-2 is OTcl Interpreter and uses code in OTCL and C++ to connect network.

5.1 OPNET MODELER

This simulation package uses an object oriented approach in formulating the simulation model. One of the powers of OPNET MODELER comes from its simplicity that is due to its menu-driven graphical user interface. Some of the application areas where OPNET can be used are:

1. For network (LAN/WAN) planning. It has built-in libraries for all the standard TCP/IP protocol and applications including IP Quality of Service (QoS), Resource Reservation Protocol (RSVP) etc.
2. It supports wireless and satellite communication schemes and protocols.
3. It can be used for microwave and fiber-optic based network management.

4. Can be used for evaluating new routing algorithms for routers, switches and other connecting devices, before plugging them physically in the network.

Features of OPNET MODELER that make it a comprehensive tool for simulation are:

1. It uses hierarchical model structure. The model can be nested within layers.
2. Multiple scenarios can be simulated simultaneously and results can be compared. This is very useful when deciding the amount of resource needed for a network configuration. This also helps in pinpointing which system parameter is affecting the system output most.
3. OPNET MODELER gives an option of importing traffic patterns from an external source.
4. It has many of built-in graphing tools that make the output analysis easier.
5. It has the capability of automatically generating models with live network information (topobgy, device configurations, traffic flows, network management data repositories, etc.).
6. OPNET MODELER has animation capabilities that can help in understanding and debugging the network.

5.1.1 Construction of Model in OPNET MODELER [19]

OPNET MODELER allows to model network topologies using three hierarchical levels:

1. *Network Level:* It is the highest level of modeling in OPNET MODELER. Topologies are modeled using network level components like routers, hosts and links. These network models can be dragged and dropped from object palette, can be chosen from OPNET MODELER menu which contain numerous topologies like star, bus, ring, mesh etc. or can be imported from a real network by collecting network topology information. (See Fig. 4)
2. *Node level:* It is used to model internal structure of a network level component. It captures the architecture of a network device or system by depicting the interactions between functional elements called modules. Modules have the capability of generating, sending and receiving packets from other modules to perform their functions within the node. They typically represent applications, protocol layers and physical resources ports, buses and buffers. Modules are connected by "streams" that can be a packet stream, a statistic stream or an association stream. As the name suggests packet stream represents packet flows between modules, a

statistic stream is used to convey statistics of the between modules. An association stream is used for logically associating different modules and it does not carry any information. (See Fig. 5)

3. *Process Level:* It uses a Finite State Machine (FSM) description to support specification at any level of detail of protocols, resources, applications, algorithms and queuing policies. States and transitions graphically define the evolution of a process in response to events. Each state of the process model contains C/C++ code, supported by an extensive library for protocol programming. Actions taken in a state are divided into enter executives and exit executives which are described by Proto-C (See Fig. 6).

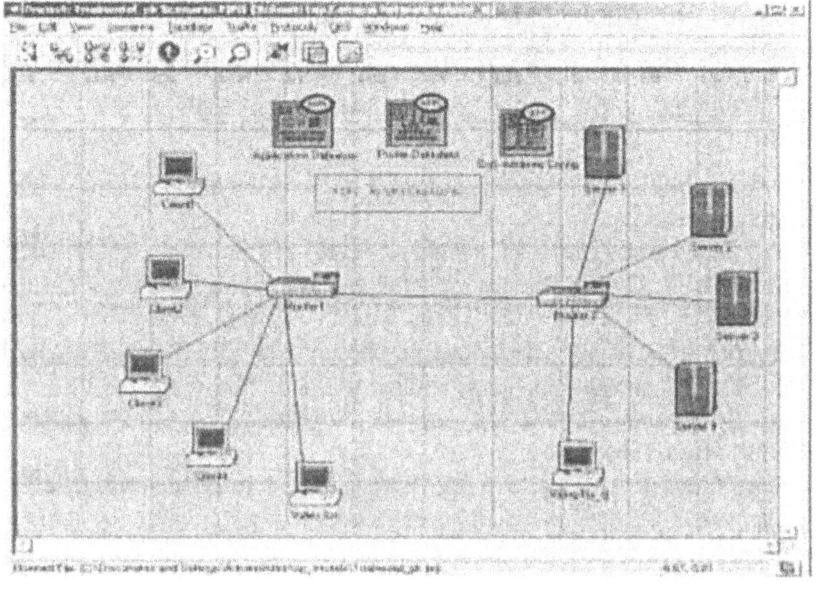

Figure 4. Screen Shot for Network level Modeling. Detail of an FIFO architecture.

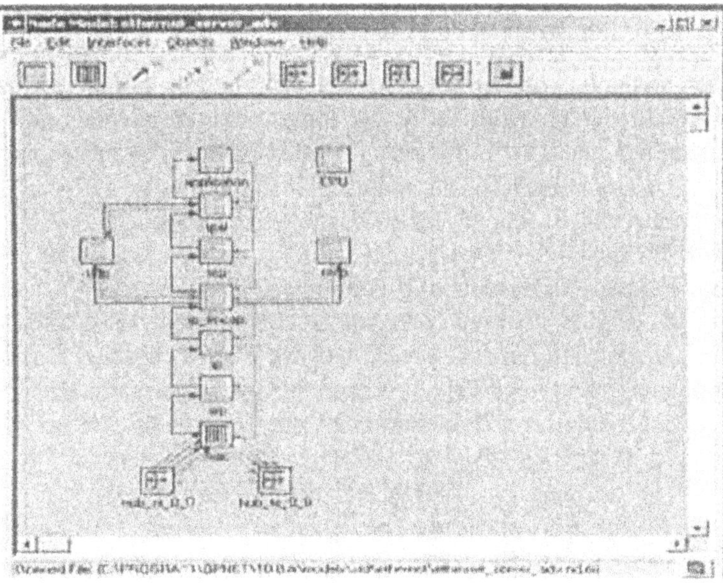

Figure 5. Screen Shot for Node level Modeling. Detail of server using Ethernet link.

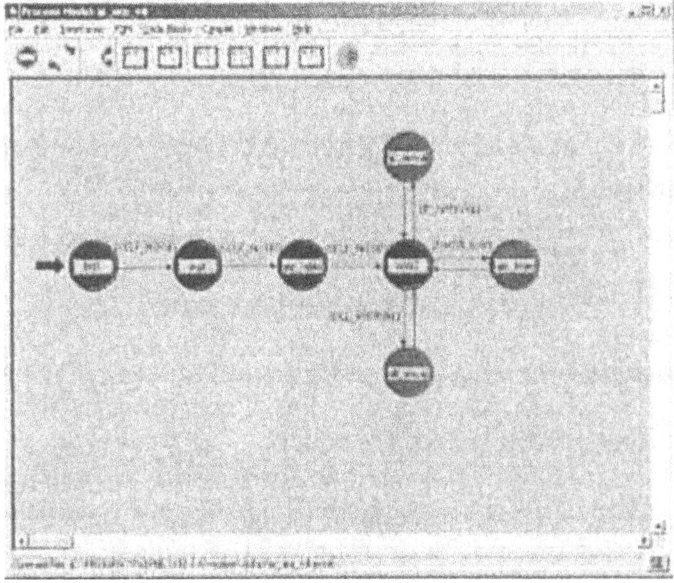

Figure 6. Screen Shot for Process Level Modeling. Details of an IP Node

5.1.2 Example- Comparison of RED vs. FIFO with Tail-drop

The normal behavior of router queues on the Internet is called tail-drop. Tail-drop works by queuing the incoming messages up to a certain queue length and then dropping all traffic that comes when the queue is full. This could be unfair, and may lead to many retransmissions. The sudden burst of drops from a router that has reached its buffer size will cause a delayed burst of retransmits, which will over fill the congested router again.

RED (Random Early Detection) [31] is an active queue management scheme proposed for IP routers. It is a router based congestion avoidance mechanism. RED is effective in preventing congestion collapse when TCP window size is configured to exceed network storage capacity. It reduces congestion and end-to-end delay by controlling the average queue size. It drops packets randomly with certain probability even before the queue gets full (see Fig. 7).

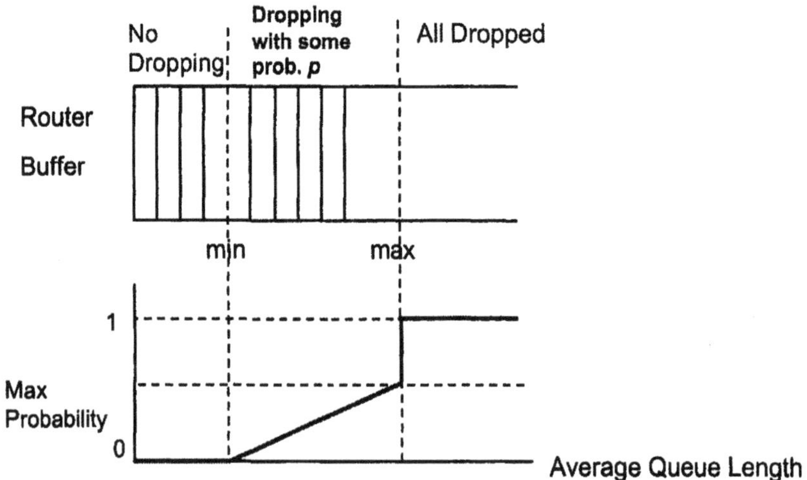

Figure 7. Active Queue Management by RED

In this example we compare the performance of RED and FIFO with Tail Drop. The network for the example consists of two routers and five clients with their corresponding servers. The capacity of link between two routers is taken to be 2.048Mbps. All other links have capacity of 100Mbps fast Ethernet. Clearly the link between Router 1 and Router 2 is the bottleneck. Our goal is the buffer occupancy at Router 1 for the two schemes.

Model is constructed using network level editor of OPNET MODELER. Hosts and servers are joined together with the help of routers and switches that are simply dragged and dropped from object palette. Attributes are assigned for various components. Configuration parameters are assigned with the help of utility objects. Some of the utility objects like Application configuration, Profile configuration and QoS configuration are shown in following screen shots. The application chosen is video conferencing with each of the clients having different parameters set- Heavy, Streaming Multimedia, Best Effort, Standard and with Background Traffic. Incoming and outgoing frame sizes are set to 1500 bytes.

All the screen shots from (Fig.8-11) were for the FIFO scheme. OPNET MODELER has a facility for generating duplicate scenario using which we generate the model for the RED scheme. The applications and profile configuration for RED remains the same as in the FIFO case. Only the QoS attributes configuration needs to be changed (See Fig. 12). RED parameters are set as in Table 1. After this, discrete event simulation is run and different statistics like buffer size for Router 1 are collected. All five clients are sending video packets having length 1500 bytes with interarrival time and service time derived from *constant* distribution.

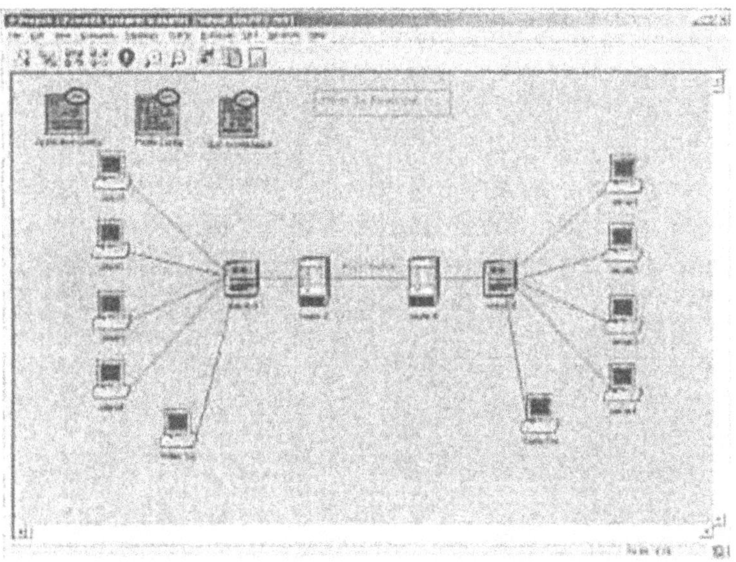

Figure 8. Network level modeling for FIFO arrangement. 5 clients are connected to 2 switches and 2 routers. They are connected with 5 servers.

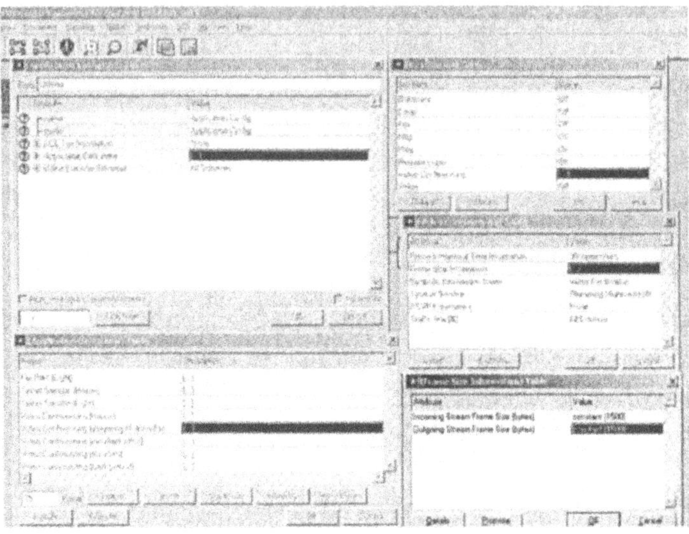

Figure 9. Application Configuration- Different window showing assignment of parameter to video conferencing (streaming Multimedia)

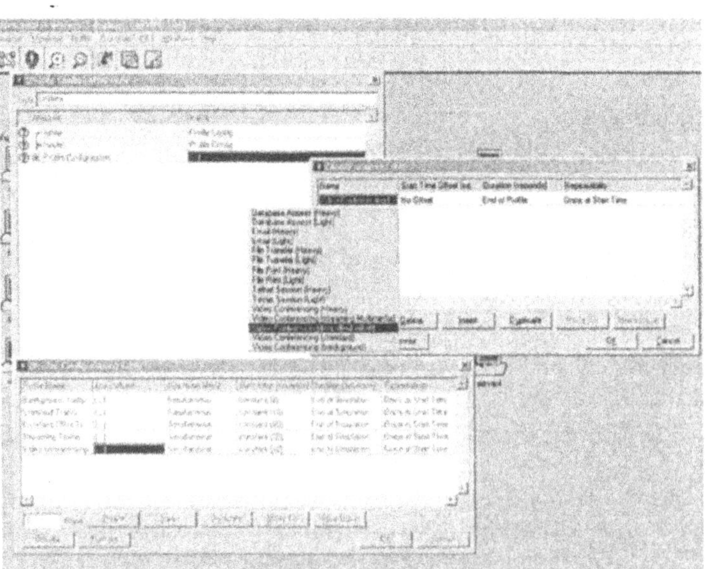

Figure 10. Profile Configuration -Different Screen shot for entering Video conferencing (various modes) to each of the client.

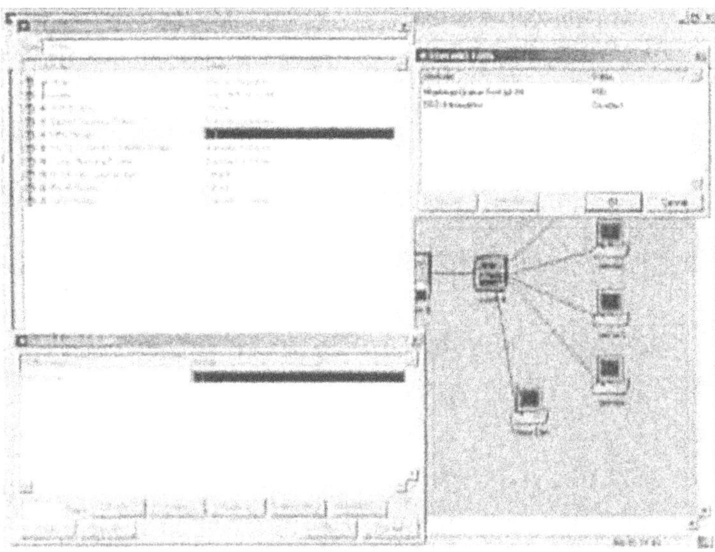

Figure 11 QoS Attribute Configuration- This shows that FIFO is selected with queue size of 100 and RED is disabled.

Figure 13 shows the result of simulation where the buffer sizes for the two cases are plotted as a function of time. Notice that both buffers using RED and FIFO taildrop behave similarly when link utilization is low. After 40 seconds, when utilization jumps to almost 100 %, congestion starts to build at router buffer that uses FIFO taildrop. In case of active queue management (RED case), the buffer occupancy remains low and it never saturates. In fact buffer occupancy is much smaller than that of FIFO during the conges tion period.

Table 1. RED parameters

Parameters	Values
min_{th}	25
max_{th}	90
max_p	0.15
w_q	0.01

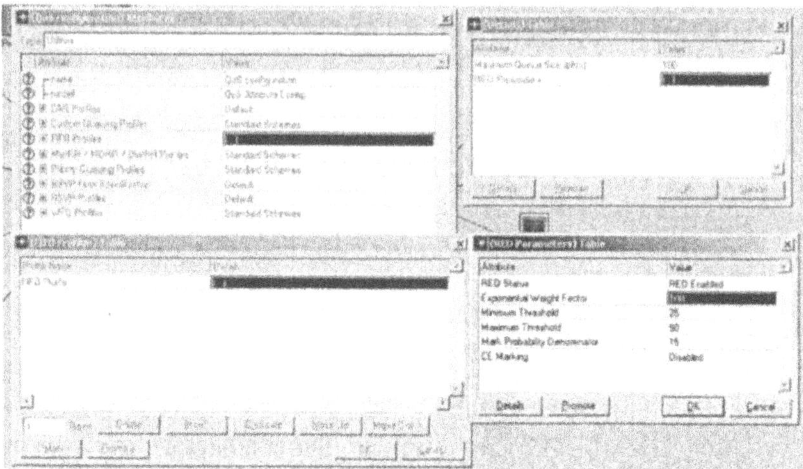

Figure 12. QoS Attribute configuration for RED case. Application and Profile configuration remains same as FIFO

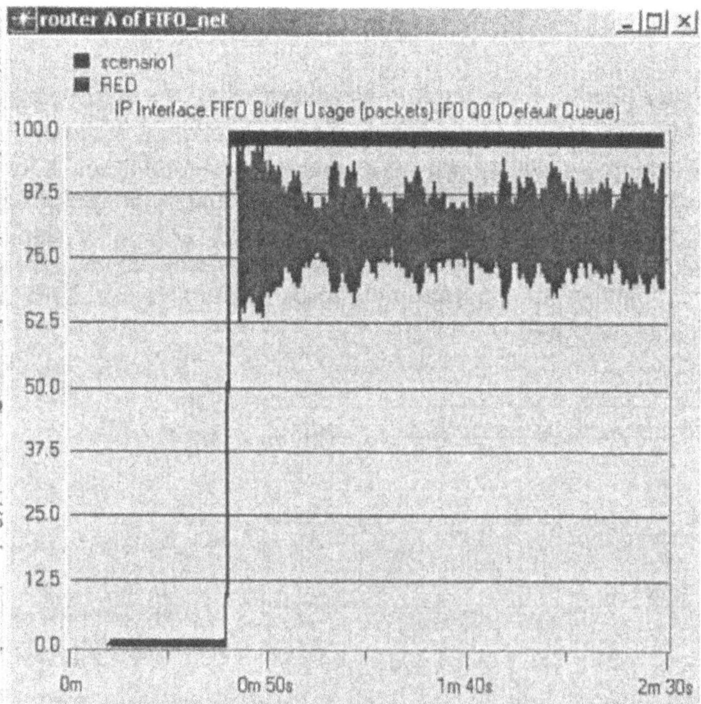

Figure 13. RED vs. FIFO for buffer occupancy

5.2 ns-2 and NAM

Network Simulator (ns) started as a variant of REAL network simulator [32] with the support of DARPA and several companies/universities. It has evolved and is now known as ns-2. It is a public domain simulation package in contrast to OPNET MODELER which is a commercial package. Like OPNET MODELER, it also uses an object oriented approach towards problem solving. It is written in C++ and object oriented TCL [33]. All network components and characteristics are represented by classes. ns-2 provides a substantial support for simulation of TCP, routing and multicast protocols over wired and wireless networks. Details about ns-2can be found from http://www.isi.edu/nsnam/ns/.

5.2.1 Overview and Model construction in ns-2

ns-2 provides canned sub-models for several network protocols like TCP and UDP, router queue management mechanism like Tail Drop, RED, routing algorithms like Dijkstra [34] and traffic source behavior like telnet, FTP, CBR etc. It contains simulation event scheduler and a large number of network objects, such as routers, links etc. which are interconnected to form a network. The user needs to write an OTcl script that initiates an event scheduler, sets up the network topology using network objects and tells traffic sources when to start and stop transmitting packets through the event scheduler.

5.2.2 Network Components (ns objects)

Objects are built from a hierarchical C++ class structure. As shown in Fig. 14, all objects are derived from class NsObject. It consists of two classes- connectors and classifiers. Connector is an NsObject from which links like queue and delay are derived. Classifiers examine packets and forward them to appropriate destinations. Some of the most frequently used objects are:

1. *Nodes*: This represents clients, hosts, router and switches. For example, a node n1 can be created by using command *set n1 [$ns node]*.
2. *Classifiers:* It determines the outgoing interface object based on source address and packet destination address. Some of the classifiers are Address classifier, Multicast classifier, Multipath classifier and Replicators.

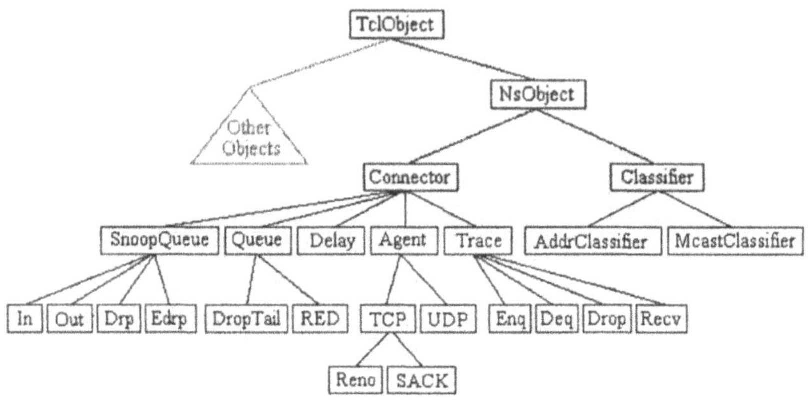

Figure 14. Class Hierarchy (Taken from "NS by example" [35])

3. *Links:* These are used for connection of nodes to form a network topology. A link is defined by its head which becomes its entry point, a reference to main queue element and a queue to process packets dropped at the link. Its format is *$ns <type>-link <node1> <node2> <bandwidth> <delay> <queue-type>*.
4. *Agents:* these are the transport end-points where packets originate or are destined. Two types of agents are TCP and UDP. ns-2 supports wide variants of TCP and it gives an option for setting ECN bit specification, congestion control mechanism and window settings. For more details about Agent specification see [14]
5. *Application:* The major types of applications that ns-2 supports are traffic generators and simulated applications. *Attach-agent* is used to attach application to transport end-points. Some of the TCP based applications supported by ns-2 are Telnet and FTP.
6. *Traffic generators:* In cases of a distribution driven simulation automated traffic generation with desired shape and pattern is required. Some of traffic generators which ns-2 provide are Poisson, On-OFF, Constant bit rate and Pareto On-OFF.

5.2.3 Event Schedulers

Event scheduler is used by network components that simulate packet-handling delay or components that need timers. The network object that issues an event will handle that event later at a scheduled time. Event scheduler is also used to schedule simulated events, such as when to start a Telnet application, when to finish a simulation, etc. ns-2 has real-time and non-real-time event schedulers. Non-real-time scheduler can be implemented either by a list, heap or a calendar.

5.2.4 Data collection and Execution

ns-2 uses tracing and monitoring for data collection. Events such as a packet arrival, packet departure or a packet drop from a link/queue are recorded by tracing. Since tracing module does not collect data for any specific performance metrics, it is only useful for debugging and verification purposes. The command in ns-2 for activating tracing is *$ns trace-all <tracefile>*.

Monitoring is a better alternative to tracing where we need to monitor a specific link or node. Several trace objects are created which are then inserted into a network topology at desired places. These trace objects collect different performance metrics. Monitoring objects can also be written in C++ (Tracing can written in OTcl only) and inserted into source or sink functions.

After constructing network model and setting different parameters, ns-2 model is executed by using *run* command. (*$ns run*).

5.2.5 Network Animator

NAM is an animation tool that is used extensively along with ns-2. It was developed in LBL. It is used for viewing network simulation packet traces and real world packet traces. It supports packet level animation that shows packets flowing through the link, packets being accumulated in the buffer and packets dropping when the buffer is full. It also supports topology layout that can be rearranged to suit user's needs. It has various data inspection tools that help in better understanding of the output. More information about NAM can be found at http://www.isi.edu/nsnam/ns/tutorial/index.html.

5.2.6 Example- RED Analysis

Objective: Studying the dynamics of current and average queue size in a RED queue.

In this example we have taken six nodes. All links are duplex in nature with their speed and delay shown in the Fig.16. In this example FTP application is chosen for both source nodes *n1* and *n3*. Node *n2* is the sink node. The window size for TCP application is taken to be 15. RED buffer can hold a maximum of 30 packets in this example. First FTP application starts from 0 till 12 seconds and second FTP application starts from 4 to 12 seconds. For output data collection, monitoring feature is used. NAM is used to display graph of buffer size vs. time

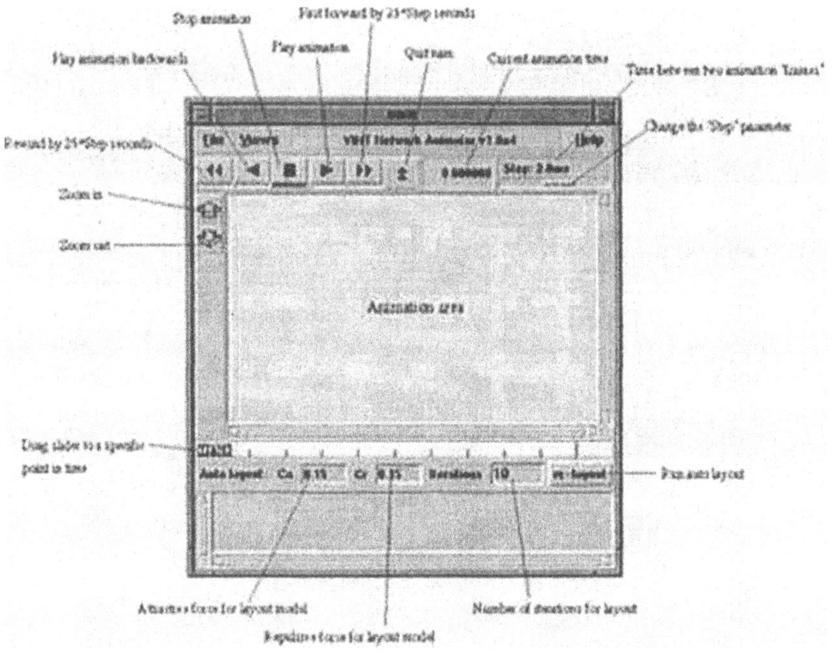

Figure 15. NAM Window (picture taken from "Marc Greis Tutorial" [36])

In this File Transfer Protocol has been simulated over TCP network. By default FTP is modeled by simulating the transfer of a large file between two endpoints. By large file we mean that FTP keeps on packetizing the file and sending it continuously between the specified start and stop times. The number of packets to be sent between start and stop time can also be specified using *produce* command. Traffic is controlled by TCP which performs the appropriate congestion control and transmits the data reliably. The buffer size is taken to be 14000 packets and router parameters are given in table 2. The output shows the buffer occupancy at router *r1*, for instantaneous and average value case. From the graph it becomes clear that during higher utilization also, RED helps in reducing congestion.

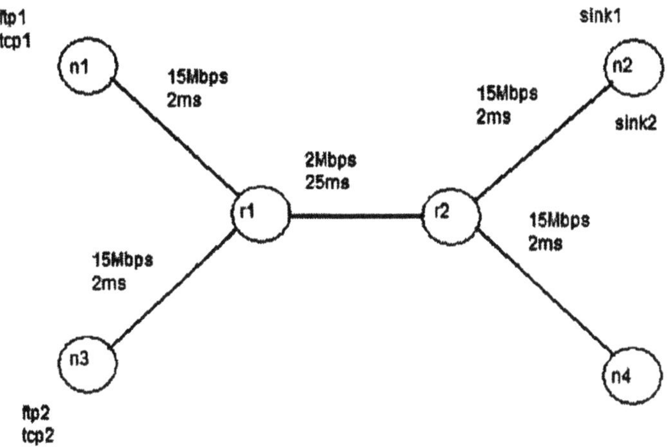

Figure 16. Network connection for an RED configuration

Table 2. RED parameters

Parameters	Values
minth	6000 packets
maxth	12000 packets
max_p	0.15
w_q	0.01

6. SUMMARY

This tutorial discussed simulation modeling basics and some of its applications. Role of statistics in different aspects of simulation was discussed. This includes random variate generation and the statistical analysis of simulation output.

Different classes of simulation were discussed. Simulation packages like OPNET MODELER and ns-2 along with some applications were discussed in the last section. These packages are extensively used in research and industry for real-life applications.

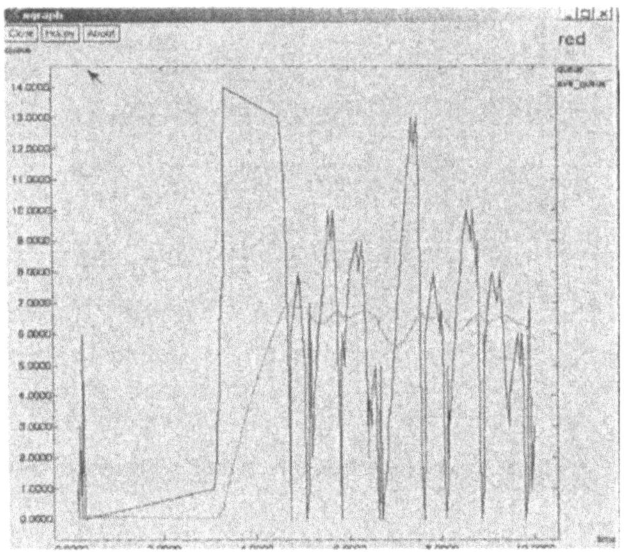

Figure 17. Plot of RED Queue Trace path

REFERENCES

1. Kishor S. Trivedi, *Probability and Statistics with Reliability, Queuing, and Computer Science Applications,* (John Wiley and Sons, New York, 2001).
2. Robin A. Sahner, Kishor S. Trivedi, and Antonio Puliafito, *Performance and Reliability Analysis of Computer Systems: An Example-Based Approach Using the SHARPE Software Package,* (Kluwer Academic Publishers, 1996).
3. Kishor S. Trivedi, G. Ciardo, and J. Muppala, SPNP: Stochastic Petri Net Package, *Proc. Third Int. Workshop on Petri Nets and Performance Models (PNPM89)*, Kyoto, pp. 142 - 151, 1989.
4. J. Banks, John S. Carson, Barry L. Nelson and David M. Nicol, *Discrete –Event System Simulation*, Third Edition, (Prentice Hall, NJ, 2001).
5. Simula Simulator; http://www.isima.fr/asu/ .
6. Simscript II.5 Simulator; http://www.caciasl.com/ .
7. AUTOMOD Simulator; http://www.autosim.com/.
8. CSIM 19 Simulator; http://www.mesquite.com/.

9. K, Pawlikowski, H. D. Jeong and J. S. Lee, On credibility of simulation studies of telecommunication networks, *IEEE Communication Magazine, 4(1)*, 132-139, Jan 2002.
10. H. M. Soliman, A.S. Elmaghraby, M.A. El-sharkawy, Parallel and Distributed Simulation System: an overview, *Proceedings of IEEE Symposium on Computer and Communications*, pp 270-276, 1995.
11. R.M. Fujimoto, Parallel and Distributed Simulation System, Simulation Conference, *Proceeding of winter, Vol. 1*, 9-12 Dec. 2001.
12. B. Tuffin, Kishor S. Trivedi, Importance Sampling for the Simulation of Stochastic Petri Nets and Fluid Stochastic Petri Nets, *Proceeding of High Performance Computing*, Seattle, WA, April 2001.
13. G. S. Fishman, *Concepts Algorithms and Applications*, (Springer-Verlag, 1997).
14. P.W. Glynn and D.L. Iglehart, Importance Sampling for stochastic Simulations, *Management Science, 35(11)*, 1367-1392, 1989.
15. P. Glasserman, P. Heidelberger, P. Shahabuddin, and T. Zajic, Splitting for rare event simulation: analysis of simple cases. In *Proceedings of the 1996 Winter Simulation Conference* edited by D.T. Brunner J.M. Charnes, D.J. Morice and J.J. Swain editors, pages 302-308, 1996.
16. P. Glasserman, P. Heidelberger, P. Shahabuddin, and T. Zajic, A look at multilevel splitting. In *Second International conference on Monte-Carlo and Quasi- Monte Carlo Methods in Scientific Computing* edited by G. Larcher, H. Niederreiter, P. Hellekalek and P. Zinterhof, Volume 127 of Lecture Series in Statistics, pages 98-108, (Springer-Verlag, 1997).
17. B. Tuffin, Kishor S. Trivedi, Implementation of Importance Splitting techniques in Stochastic Petri Net Package," in *Computer performance evaluation: Modeling tools and techniques; 11th International Conference; TOOLS 2000, Schaumburg, Il. USA*, edited by B. Haverkort, H. Bohnenkamp, C. Smith, Lecture Notes in Computer Science 1786, (Springer Verlag, 2000).
18. S. Nananukul, Wei-Bo-Gong, A quasi Monte-Carlo Simulation for regenerative simulation, *Proceeding of 34th IEEE conference on Decision and control*, Volume 2, Dec. 1995.
19. M. Hassan, and R. Jain, *High Performance TCP/IP Networking: Concepts, Issues, and Solutions*, (Prentice-Hall, 2003).
20. Bernard Zeigler, T. G. Kim, and Herbert Praehofer, *Theory of Modeling and Simulation*, Second Edition, (Academic Press, New York, 2000).
21. OPNET Technologies Inc. ; http://www.opnet.com/.
22. Network Simulator; http://www.isi.edu/nsnam/ns/.
23. Arena Simulator; http://www.arenasimulation.com/.

24. Liang Yin, Marcel A. J. Smith, and K.S. Trivedi, Uncertainty analysis in reliability modeling, In *Proc. of the Annual Reliability and Maintainability Symposium, (RAMS)*, Philadelphia, PA, January 2001.
25. Wayne Nelson. *Applied Life Data Analysis.* John Wiley and Sons, New York, 1982.
26. L.W. Schruben, Control of initialization Bias in multivariate simulation response, *Communications of the Association for Computing machinery*, 246-252, 1981.
27. A.M. Law and J.M. Carlson, A sequential Procedure for determining the length of steady state simulation, *Operations Research,* Vol. 27, pp-131-143, 1979.
28. Peter P. Welch, *Statistical analysis of simulation result, Computer performance Modeling Handbook,* edited by Stephen S. Lavenberg, Academic Press,1983
29. W.D. Kelton, Replication Splitting and Variance for simulating Discrete Parameter Stochastic Process, *Operations Research Letters*, Vol.4,pp-275-279, 1986.
30. Network Animator. ; http://www.isi.edu/nsnam/nam/.
31. S. Floyd, and V. Jacobson, Random early detection gateways for congestion avoidance, *IEEE/ACM Transactions on Networking*, Volume1, Issue 4 , Aug. 1993 Pages:397 – 413.
32. REAL network simulator. ; http://www.cs.cornell.edu/skeshav/real/overview.html
33. OTCL-Object TCL extensions. ; http://bmrc.berkeley.edu/research/cmt/cmtdoc/otcl/
34. E. W. Dijkstra, A Note on Two Problems in Connection with Graphs. *Numerische Math. 1*, 269-271, 1959.
35. Jay Cheung, Claypool, NS by example. ; http://nile.wpi.edu/NS/
36. Marc Greis, Tutorial on ns. ; http://www.isi.edu/nsnam/ns/tutorial/

HUMAN-CENTERED AUTOMATION: A MATTER OF AGENT DESIGN AND COGNITIVE FUNCTION ALLOCATION

Guy Boy
European Institute of Cognitive Sciences and Engineering (EURISCO International), 4 Avenue Edouard Belin, 31400 Toulouse, France.

Abstract: This chapter presents an analytical framework that brings answers to and overcomes the "classical" debate on direct manipulation versus interface agents. Direct manipulation is always appropriate when the system to be controlled is simple. However, when users need to interact with complex systems, direct manipulation is also complex and requires a sufficient level of expertise. Users need to be trained, and in some cases deeply trained. They also need to be assisted to fulfill overall criteria such as safety, comfort or high performance. Artificial agents are developed to assist users in the control of complex systems. They are usually developed to simplify work, in reality they tend to change the nature of work. They do not remove training. Artificial agents are evolving very rapidly, and incrementally create new practices. An artificial agent is associated to a cognitive function. Cognitive function analysis enables human-centered design of artificial agents by providing answers to questions such as: Artificial agents for what? Why are artificial agents not accepted or usable by users? An example is provided, analyzed and evaluated. Current critical issues are discussed.

Key words agents; cognitive functions; human-centered automation; safety; direct manipulation; expertise.

1. INTRODUCTION

The concept of artificial agent, and automaton in general, is very clumsy. The term clumsy automation was introduced by Earl Wiener who has studied aircraft cockpit automation for the past three decades (Wiener, 1989). Wiener criticizes the fact that the traditional answer of engineers to human-machine interaction problems was to automate. His research results suggest that particular attention should be paid to the way automation is done. In addition to these very well documented results, there are pessimistic views on the development of software agents:

"Agents are the work of lazy programmers. Writing a good user-interface for a complicated task, like finding and filtering a ton of information, is much harder to do than making an intelligent agent. From a user's point of view, an agent is something you give slack to by making your mind mushy, while a user interface is a tool that you use, and you can tell whether you are using a good tool or not." (Lanier, 1995, page 68).

This is a partial view of the problem. Agents cannot be thrown to the trash based only on this argument. There are at least three reasons to reconsider Lanier's view seriously:

- agents have been used for years in aeronautics, and there are lessons learned from this deep experience;
- since our occidental societies are moving from energy-based interaction (sensory-motoric activities) to information-based interaction (cognitive activities), the concept of agent has become extremely important for analyzing this evolution from a socio-cognitive viewpoint;
- the concept of agent needs to be taken in a broader sense than the description provided by Jaron Lanier.

More recently, Ben Shneiderman and Pattie Maes (1997) resumed a debate on direct manipulation versus interface agents that has been ongoing for long time in the intelligent interface community (Chin, 1991). Direct manipulation affords the user control and predictability in their interfaces. Software agents open the way to some kind of delegation. I take the view that software agents make new practices emerge. Software agents are no more than new tools that enable people to perform new tasks. The main flaw in current direct manipulation argumentations is that interaction is implicitly thought with an 'acceptable' level of current practice in mind. Current practice evolves as new tools emerge. When steam engines started to appear, the practice of riding horses or driving carriages needed to evolve towards driving cars. Instead of using current practice based on knowledge of horses' behavior, drivers needed to acquire new practice based on knowledge of cars' behavior. For example, when someone driving a carriage wanted to turn right, he or she needed to pull the rein to the right but according to a very specific knowledge of what the horse could accept, understand and follow. Driving a car, someone who want to turn right simply pull the steering wheel to the right according to a very specific knowledge of what the car could accept, 'understand' and follow. It will not shock anyone to say that today pulling the steering wheel to the right is direct manipulation. However, pulling the rein to the right will not necessarily always cause the expected result for all of us, especially for those who do not know horses very well. This kind of human-horse interaction is obviously agent-based. Conversely, horse riders who discovered car driving at the beginning of the twentieth century did not find this practice very natural compared to riding a horse. In this case, the artificial agent was the car engine that the driver needed to control. Today, new generation commercial aircraft include more artificial agents that constitute a *deeper interface* between the pilots and the mechanical devices of the aircraft. Direct manipulation is commonly thought of as 'direct' actions on these physical devices. It is now very well recognized that the pilots who fly new generation commercial aircraft find their job easier than before. Their job is not only a direct manipulation steering task, but a more high-level flight management task. They need to manage a set of intertwined artificial agents that perform some of the jobs that they performed before. The development of artificial agents is a specific automation process. It is much more appropriate to investigate automation issues in terms of acceptability, maturity and emergence of new practices.

I claim that artificial agent design needs more guidance and principles. This article introduces a human-centered approach to agent design that is based on the elicitation and use of cognitive functions that are involved in the performance of tasks intended to be delegated to a computer. Software agents are used to perform a few tasks that are usually performed by people. This delegation process generates the emergence of new supervisory tasks that people need to perform. These new tasks are not necessarily easy to learn, retain and perform efficiently. The first thing to do is to identify these new tasks. They usually lead to new types of human errors and new styles of interaction that also need to be identified.

2. LESSONS LEARNED FROM AERONAUTICS

The agent-orientation of human-machine interaction is not new. Airplane autopilots have been commonly and commercially used since the 1930's. Such artificial agents perform tasks that human pilots usually perform, e.g., following a flight track or maintaining an altitude. Control theory methods and tools have handled most of such automation. In the beginning, even if computers that handled such tasks were very basic, feedback processes handled by these systems were not basic at all. If there is one thing that people who are involved in the design of agents should be aware of it is certainly the notion of feedback. It seems that computer scientists are currently (re)discovering this notion, or at least they should be! In other words, automation (that is the design of agents) is a complex process that requires particular attention. The idea of having agents designed by lazy programmers is a fallacy, and the danger is precisely there!

Becoming an airline pilot requires a long training time. This is because the airplane can be considered as an agent itself. It took a long time to integrate and validate autopilots in aircraft cockpit. Lots of research has been carried out to better understand how pilots are handling flight qualities both manually and using autopilots. Today, if autopilots are 'trivial' agents on-board, they require specific pilot training. Over the last 20 years, the development of new generation aircraft has enhanced the integration of computers into the cockpit. Software agents, such as flight management systems (FMSs), emerged. Christopher Wickens advocates the fact that this new kind of automation may cause situation awareness problems:

"While the FMS usually carries out its task silently, correctly and efficiently, there are nevertheless a non-trivial number of exceptions. In fact, a frequently quoted paraphrase of pilots' responses to many advance automated systems is: 'what did it do?, why did it do it?, and what will it do next?' (Wiener, 1989; Rudisill, 1994; Dornheim, 1995). These words are verbalizations of 'automation induced surprises', reflecting a lack of situation awareness which has been documented systematically by a series of experimental investigations carried out by Sarter and Woods (Billings, 1991; Sarter & Woods, 1992, 1994), and supported by aircraft incident analyses (Wiener, 1989; Rudisill, 1994), as well as reconstruction of several recent accidents (Dornheim, 1995)" (Wickens, 1996, page 5)

In fact, even if a pilot develops a mental model through training, that enables the anticipation of a large set of both normal and abnormal situations, this mental model may also be degraded by negative effects of system complexity (Wickens, 1996). This kind of degradation is well shown by Sarter and Woods (1994).

Here, I would like to make the point that human kind is distinguished from the other species because it has the capacity and the desire to build tools to extend its capacities. There are various kinds of tools that humans build. Let us call them artifacts. They can be more or less autonomous. They all require both intellectual and physical capacities from their users. Up to this century, most artifacts required more physical capacities than cognitive capacities from users. Today the reverse is true. From the manipulation of 'physical' tools, we have moved towards interaction with 'cognitive' systems. This is the case in aviation as in many advanced industrial sectors and our everyday private life. In addition, artifacts of the past were designed and developed over longer periods of time than now. Our main problem today is speed and thus lack of artifact maturity, i.e., we need to produce artifacts faster and faster. Users also need to adapt to new artifacts faster than before. Fast human adaptation to artifacts that demand even more, often not stabilized, cognitive resources is even more difficult. This is an excellent reason to think more about principles and criteria for a human-centered design of artificial agents. This starts by defining properly what an agent is.

3. WHAT IS AN AGENT?

An agent is an artifact or a person that/who acts. An agent produces actions that produce effects. Agents are taken in the sense of Minsky's terminology (Minsky, 1985). An agent is always associated to a cognitive function. A cognitive function can be interpreted in the mathematical sense or in the teleological sense. The former interpretation leads to the definition of an application transforming an input into an output. The input is usually a required task to be performed. The output is the result of the execution of the task. We usually say that the agent uses a cognitive function that produces an activity or an effective task. The latter interpretation leads to the definition of three attributes of a cognitive function:

- a role, e.g., the role of a postman (i.e., an agent) is to deliver letters;
- a context of validity, e.g., the context of validity of the above role is defined by a time period that is the business hours and a specific working uniform, for example;
- a set of resources, e.g., the resources necessary to execute the function are riding a bicycle, carrying a big bag and performing a delivery procedure, for example. Note that a resource is a cognitive function itself.

Some smart artifacts may not qualify for being artificial intelligence (AI) systems, but they implicitly include the use of appropriate human cognitive function resources that make intelligent the resulting user-artifact system. For example, speed bugs on airplane speed indicators are not intelligent agents in the AI sense, but they are smart artifacts. Speed bugs are set by pilots to anticipate and inform on a decision speed.

Users develop appropriate *cognitive functions* to speed up, and increase both comfort and safety of their job, i.e., the tasks that they usually perform. These cognitive functions can be *soft-coded* or *hard-coded*. When they are soft-coded, they usually appear in the form of procedures or know-how stored in their long-term memory. When they are hard-coded, they usually appear in the form of interface devices or manuals that guide users in their job. In both cases, cognitive functions can be either *implicit* or *explicit*. When they are implicit, they belong to what is usually called *expertise*. When they are explicit, they belong to what is usually called *sharable knowledge*. Sometimes, cognitive functions remain implicit for a long time before becoming explicit and easily sharable. When a cognitive function is persistent, it can be formalized into an artificial agent to improve the performance of the task. This is commonly called *automation*. The development of machine agents increases the levels of automation. Human operators are faced with machine assistants that provide a pseudo-natural interaction.

More generally, an agent can be natural or artificial (artifactual). The former type includes people, therapeutic or atmospheric agents, for example. We try to better understand how they work, and model them in order to better anticipate their actions. The latter type includes automated power plants, sophisticated vehicles, advanced computer networks or software agents, for example. Humans have built them, but it is time to better understand their usability, and model them in order to better control them. A major issue is that artificial agents cannot be studied in isolation from people who are in charge of them.

Automation has been a major concern for a long time. The clock is certainly one of the best example of an old automaton that provides time to people with great precision. People rely on clocks to manage their life. A watch is also a unique artificial agent that provides precise time information to a user. In addition, a clock may be programmed to autonomously alert its user to wake up for example. People trust clocks, but they have also learnt to know when clocks do not work properly. They have learnt to interact with such an agent. No one questions the use of such an agent today. The role of the clock agent is to provide the time to its user. Its context of validity is determined by several parameters such as the working autonomy of the internal mechanism or the lifetime of the battery. Its resources include for instance the use of a battery, the ability of its user to adjust time when necessary or to change the battery. Note that the user is also a resource for the watch artificial agent.

Thinking in terms of agents relies on a distributed-cognition view (Suchman, 1987; Vera & Simon, 1993) rather than a single-agent view (Wickens & Flach, 1988). The distributed cognition paradigm states that knowledge processing is distributed among agents that can be humans or machines (Hutchins, 1995). Sometimes designing an artificial agent that is intended to help a user may not be as appropriate as connecting this user to a real human expert; in this case, the artificial agent is a 'connector' or a 'broker' between people.

4. POSSIBLE AGENT-TO-AGENT INTERACTION

Human-centered design of artificial agents is based on the nature of interaction among both human and artificial agents. The type of interaction depends, in part, of the knowledge each agent has of the others. An agent interacting with another agent, called a partner, can belong to two classes: (class 1) the agent does not know its partner; (class 2) the agent knows its partner. The second class can be decomposed into two sub-classes: (subclass 2a) the agent knows its partner indirectly (using shared data for instance), (subclass 2b) the agent knows its partner explicitly (using interaction primitives clearly understood by the partner). This classification leads to three relations between two agents interacting:

- (A) competition (class 1);
- (B) cooperation by sharing common data (subclass 2a);
- (C) cooperation by direct communication (subclass 2b).

In the *competition* case, the agent does not understand inputs to and outputs from the other agents. This can lead to conflict for available resources. Thus, it is necessary to define a set of synchronization rules for avoiding problems of resource allocation between agents. Typically, these synchronization rules have to be handled by a supervisor, an advisor or a mediator (Figure 1). This agent can be one of the partners or an external agent. It is not necessary to explain its actions and decisions. The other agents rely on it to insure a good interaction.

In the case of *cooperation by sharing common data*, the agent understands inputs to and outputs from the other agents. Both of them use a shared data base (Figure 2). Such a shared data base can be an agent itself if it actively informs the various agents involved in the environment, or requests new information (self updating) from these agents, i.e., it is an explicit mediator. Agents use and update the state of this database. An example would be that each agent note all its actions on a blackboard to which the other agents refer before acting. Agents have to cooperate to use and manage the shared database. This paradigm leads to a data-oriented system. Such a system has to control the consistency of the shared data. Cooperative relations between agents do not exclude competitive relations, i.e., resources for which the corresponding agents may be competing generally support shared data. In this case, synchronization rules have to deal with resource allocation conflicts and corresponding data consistency checking.

In the previous cases, the interaction is indirect. In the case of *cooperating by direct communication*, agents interact directly with the others (Figure 3). They share a common goal and a common language expressed by messages, e.g., experts in the same domain cooperating to solve a problem. We say that they share a common ontology, i.e., common domain and task models. When this knowledge sharing is not clearly established, cooperation by direct communication is hardly possible: agents do not understand each other. An artificial agent that satisfy this type of relation must then include a user model (Mathé & Chen, 1996).

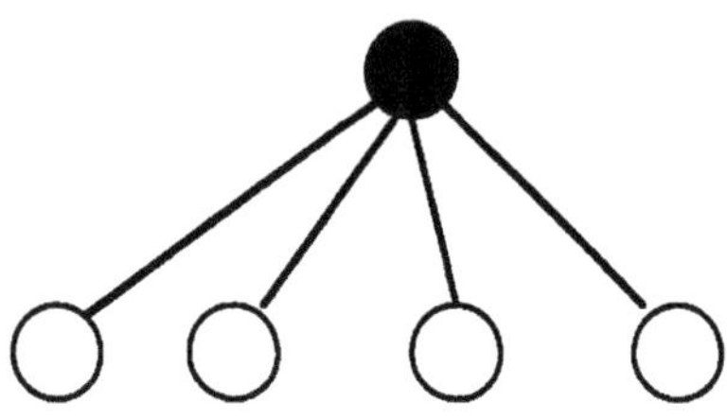

Agents

Figure 1. Competition: agents need to have a supervisor, an advisor or a mediator to help manage their interactions.

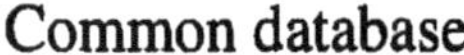

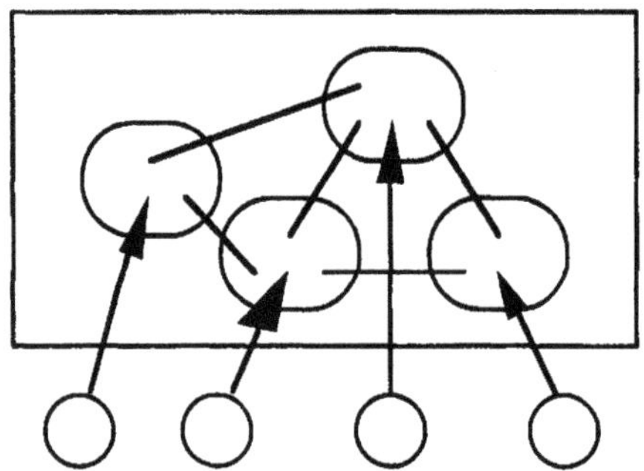

Agents

Figure 2. Cooperation by sharing common data: agents manage to communicate through a common database that is an interface between the agents.

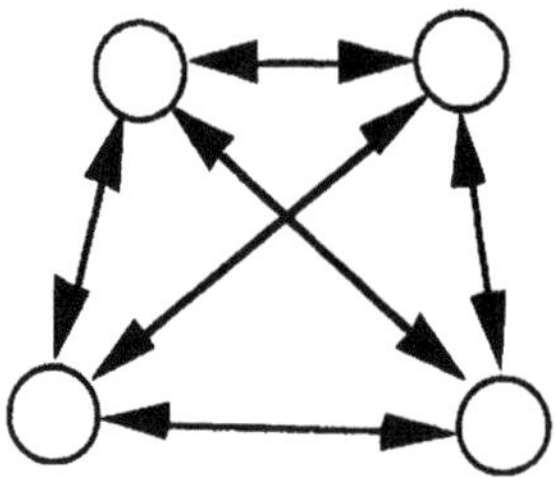

Agents

Figure 3. Cooperation by direct communication: agents interact directly with each other.

5. AN ECOLOGICAL APPROACH: LOOKING FOR MATURITY

In this section, I explain why my research agenda is not in the current main stream of the software agent community. I am not interested in the way an agent is developed from a software engineering perspective. I am interested in the way a software agent is being used, modifies current work practice, influences the environment and work results (i.e., products), and modifies ways evaluation/certification is currently performed for non-agent systems. I also try to start a theoretical discussion on what artificial agents really are or will be. I realize that I am in the same position as Jules Verne who described the way people might use a submarine one century ago long before submarines were built and operated as they are now. In other words, I am interested in exploring where we are going by developing and using software agent technology. This article takes some of the factors that Norman provided on how people might interact with agents (Norman, 1994).

6.1 Hiding unnecessary complexity while promoting necessary operations

Prior to the integration of flight management systems (FMSs) onboard aircraft, pilots planned their flights using paper and pencil technology. An FMS is a real-time database management system where flight routes are stored. It enables the pilot to program or recall a flight route and adapt it to the current flight conditions. This machine-centered flight management is programmed to define a vertical profile and a speed profile, taking into account air traffic control requirements and performance criteria. Once a flight route is programmed into the system, the FMS drives the airplane by providing setpoints to the autopilot. The FMS computes the aircraft position continually, using stored aircraft performance data and navigation data (FCOM-A320, 1997). The same kind of example was studied by Irving et al. using the GOMS approach (Irving et al., 1994), and experimentally by Sarter and Woods to study pilots' mental load model and awareness of the FMS (Sarter & Woods, 1994). "While most pilots were effective in setting up and using the FMS for normal operations, a substantial number revealed inadequate situation awareness under conditions when the system would be unexpectedly configured in an unusual, but not impossible, state. These configurations might result from an erroneous pilot input, from the need to respond to unexpected external events (e.g., a missed approach), or from a possible failure of some aspect of the automation. Under these circumstance, a substantial number of pilots simply failed to understand what the FMS was doing and why; they were surprised by its behavior in a way that would make questionable their ability to respond appropriately." (Wickens, 1996, page 5). Designers have created a large number of options to control the FMS complexity. For example, there are at least five different modes to change altitude. A software agent that would provide the right one at the right time and in the right understandable format to the pilot would be very valuable. This requires an event-driven approach to design, i.e., categories of situations where pilots would need to use an appropriate mode to change altitude, for example, should be clearly elicited and rationalized.

One of the main reasons why the event-driven approach is not frequently taken is because it is very expensive in time and money. Today engineering rules business. Engineers have a goal-driven approach to design, and they unfortunately often end up with externally complex user interfaces. Technology is evolving very fast due to smart engineers who continually improve artifacts without crossing their views with other professionals such as marketing experts, usability specialists and scientists. "Development is a series of tradeoffs, often with incompatible constraints." (Norman, 1998). This is even more true for the development of artificial agents and automation in general. If artificial agents are developed to decrease user workload or increase safety, they also tend to decrease vigilance and increase complacency (Billings, 1991). This is why cognitive function allocation is fundamental in the design process of an artificial agent: What new supervisory functions will it require from users? What situation awareness functions will it make emerge in various situations? What will be the most appropriate interaction functions that will need to be implemented in its user interface? Since such a cognitive function analysis needs to be carried out very early during the design process, the development process (and the company) should be re-organized, as Don Norman already suggested (1998).

6.2 Affordance: The ultimate maturity of an artifact

I don't want to question the main attributes of software agents provided by Pattie Maes such as personalization, proactivity, continuous activity, and adaptivity (Shneiderman & Maes, 1997). They are fine, and I am very comfortable with them as they match good technology-centered automation. However, they are not sufficient. Maturity is a key issue for automation, and high-technology in general. "... look around us at those high-technology products... ask why so many telephone help lines are required, why so many lengthy, expensive phone calls to use the product... go to a bookstore and look at how many bookshelves are filled with books trying to explain how to work the devices. We don't see shelves of books on how to use television sets, telephones, refrigerators or washing machines. Why should we for computer-based applications" (Norman, 1998). This is where the concept of affordances needs to be considered seriously. An artificial agent needs to be affordable to its user in any workable situation.

The term "affordances" was coined by James Gibson to describe the reciprocal relationship between an animal and its environment, and it subsequently became the central concept of his view of psychology, the ecological approach (Gibson, 1979). In this article, affordances are resources or support that an artificial agent offers to its user; the user in turn must process the capabilities to perceive it and use it. How do we create affordances for an artificial agent? Don't expect a simple and clear procedure for doing this. It will be an iterative cycle process of design, engineering, evaluation and analysis. However, better understanding the procedure-interface duality is key towards the incremental discovery of agent affordances. Agent affordances deal with intersubjectivity, i.e., the process in which mental activity is transferred between agents. A mental activity could be situation awareness, intentions, emotions or knowledge processing for example.

People interacting with artificial agents usually follow operational procedures in either normal or abnormal situations. Operational procedures can be learned in advance and memorized, or read during performance. Think about the operational procedure that you need to follow when you program your washing machine or your VCR. Operational procedures are supposed to help operators during the execution of prescribed tasks by enhancing an appropriate level of situation awareness and control. It is usually assumed that people tend to forget to do things or how to do things in many situations. Procedures are designed as memory aids. In abnormal situations for example, pilots need to be guided under time-pressure, high workload and critical situations that involve safety issues. Procedures are often available in the form of checklists that are intended to be used during the execution of the task (it is shallow knowledge that serves as a guideline to insure an acceptable performance), and operations rationale that needs to be learned off-line from the execution of the task (this is deep knowledge that would induce too high a workload if it was interpreted on-line.) The main problem with this approach is that people may even forget to use procedures! Or they anticipate things before the execution of a procedure. People tend to prefer to use their minds to recognize a situation instead of immediately jumping on their checklist books as they are usually required to do in aviation, for instance (Carroll et al., 1994). In other words, people are not necessarily systematic procedure followers (De Brito, Pinet & Boy, 1998). They want to be in control (Billings, 1991). Ultimately, if the user interface includes the right situation patterns that afford the recognition of and response to the right problems at the right time, then formal procedures are no longer necessary. In this case, people interact with the system in a symbiotic way. The system is affordable. The better the interface is, the less procedures are needed. Conversely, the more obscure the interface is, the more procedures are needed to insure a reasonable level of performance. This is the procedure-interface duality issue.

6.3 Discovering affordances using active design documents

By designing concurrently an artificial agent and its operational procedures from the early stages of the design process, affordances are more likely to emerge incrementally.

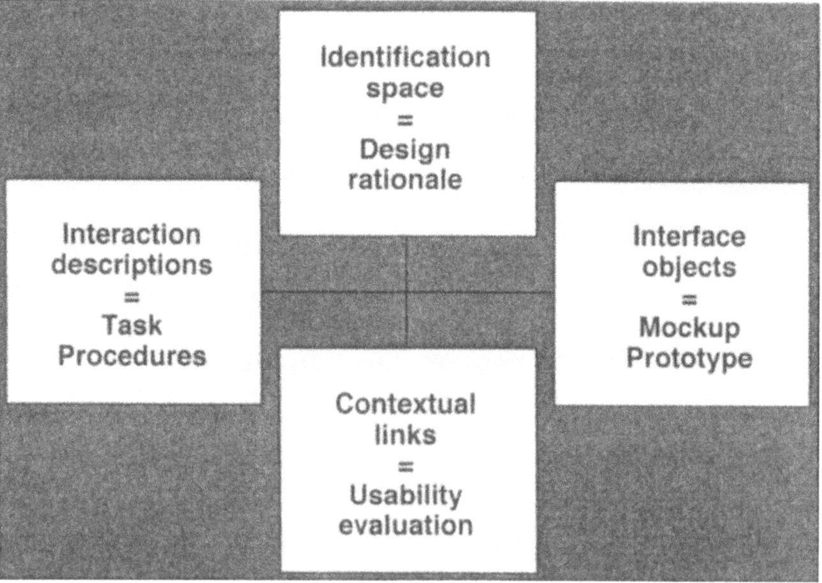

Figure 4. A generic active design document.

This is a reason why we have already proposed the active design document approach to support this process (Boy, 1998). An active design document includes four aspects (Figure 4):

- *interaction descriptions*–the symbolic aspect, which conveys ideas and information, e.g., the description of a procedure to follow; this aspect of an active design document is related to the task involved in the use of the artifact; it defines the *task space;*
- *interface objects* connected to interaction descriptions–the emotive aspect, which expresses, evokes, and elicits feelings and *attitudes*, e.g., a mockup of the interface being designed; this aspect is related to the interface of the artifact that provides interactive capabilities; it defines the *activity space*; note that interface objects are characterized by specific

cognitive functions (to be elicited incrementally by a series of usability evaluations) provided to the user to improve interaction;

- *contextual links* between the interaction descriptions and the interface objects, e.g., annotations or comments contextually generated during tests; this aspect is related to the user and the environment in which the artifact is used; it defines the *cognitive function space.*
- *an identification space*; in addition to its three definitional entities, i.e., interaction descriptions, interface objects, and contextual links, each active design document is identified by an identification space that includes a name, a list of keywords, a date of creation, a period of usability tests, a design rationale field and a set of direct hypertext links to others active design documents.

The development of active design documents is incremental and fosters participatory design. They enable the design team to minimize the required complex procedures to be learned, and maximize affordances of the artificial agent being designed. A traceability mechanism enables anyone to figure out at any time why specific affordances have emerged (Boy, 1999).

6.4 Human-centered design of artificial agents

Understanding the needs of potential users of artificial agents does not consist in asking them what they want. They usually don't know this, or even worse they think they know! Facing them with a prototype and asking them what they think of it is much better. This is what usability testing is about. This is why incremental development of active design documents is likely to generate good affordances. Users enter into the design process to provide their views on perceivable interface objects that enable them to generate an activity using the agent, and on attached interaction descriptions that enable them to guide this activity. Contextual links are filled in after each evaluation, and used to redesign the agent. Each time a design is produced, the design rationale is stored in the identification space.

Designing for simplicity is key. Artificial agents need to be simple, easily understandable, and fun to use. This does not mean that people will not have to learn new values and skills by using them. Using artificial agents looks like getting a promotion at work. You now manage a group of agents that work for you. New management skills are thus necessary. This changes work practice that needs to be addressed during the design process. The job will not be the same as before. In particular, creating artificial agents involves new cooperation and coordination processes that were not relevant before. Questions are: How different will the job be? How difficult will it be to learn it? Will it require 'new' people?

6.5 Adapting Henderson's design cycle to agents

Austin Henderson brought a very interesting distinction of design from science and engineering (Ehrlich, 1998). Science brings rationalization of current practice (Boy, 1998, page 190). Science tries to understand where we are now. Let us acknowledge that agent science is very preliminary. Design is where we would like to be. It is an exercise of imagination. For the last few decades designers have been very prolific in imagining and inventing new intelligent devices that lead to agents. Designers ask specific questions such as: "What direction can we go in? Where might that take us? What would the implications be? " (Ehrlich, 1998, page 37). Engineering addresses how do we get from here to there taking into account the available resources. Once engineers have developed new artifacts, science takes the lead again to figure out where we are according to the emergence of new practices introduced by these new artifacts (Figure 5).

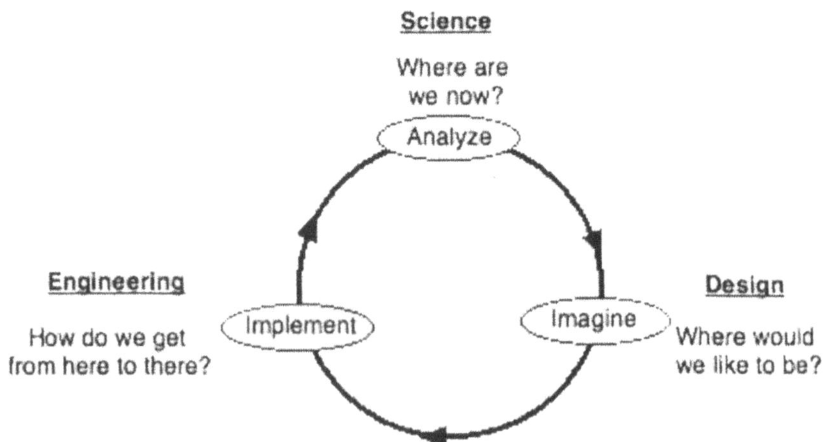

Figure 5. Henderson's cycle.

Most current software agent contributions address the engineering perspective. Since we are still very poor in agent science, it is very difficult to address properly the design perspective from a humanistic viewpoint. Although it is true that new practices that emerge from the use of artificial agents constitute very important data that science needs to analyze and rationalize. Experience feedback on the use of agents is still very preliminary. A good way to address the design perspective today is to develop participatory design (Muller, 1991) involving end-users in the design process. In addition, there will be no human-centered design of artificial agents without an appropriate set of usability principles. Several traditional human factors principles and approaches have become obsolete because the paradigm of a single agent, as an information processor, is no longer appropriate in a multi-agent world. Multi-agent models are better suited to capture the essence of today's information-intensive interaction with artificial agents. Many authors working in the domain of highly automated systems described agent-to-agent communication (Billings, 1991; Hutchins, 1995). A human agent interacting with an artificial agent must be aware of:

- what the other agent has done (history awareness);
- what the other agent is doing now and for how long (action awareness);
- why the other agent is doing what it does (action rationale awareness);
- what the other agent is going to do next and when (intention awareness).

These four situation awareness issues correspond to the most frequently asked questions in advanced cockpits (Wiener, 1995). In order to describe human-computer interaction several attributes are already widely used such as the basic usability attributes proposed by Nielsen (1993). From our experience in aeronautics, the following attributes were found important in multi-agent human-machine communication (science contribution in Henderson's sense):

- prediction, i.e., ability to anticipate consequences of actions on highly automated systems;
- feedback on activities and intentions;
- autonomy, i.e., amount of autonomous performance;
- elegance, i.e., ability not to add additional burden to human operators in critical contexts;
- trust, i.e., ability to maintain trust in its activities;
- intuitiveness, i.e., expertise-intensive versus common-sense interaction;
- programmability, i.e., ability to program and re-program highly automated systems.

6. AN EXAMPLE OF COGNITIVE FUNCTION ANALYSIS

To effectively design and use artificial agents, researchers, designers and engineers must grapple with a number of difficult questions such as: What kinds of tasks are best performed by humans or computers? What are the practical limits of system autonomy? and, Who should be in control?

The development of an artificial agent is based on an incremental process of design/evaluation. In the cognitive function analysis methodology, this process uses the Artifact-User-Task-Organizational Environment (AUTO) pyramid (Boy, 1998). In this approach to designing artificial agents, the analysis and design of cognitive systems is viewed in the light of the linked human-centered-design dimensions of *artifact* (artificial agent), *user, task* and *organizational environment*. The dimensions of user, task and artifact are the factors that are normally taken into account in system design. The dimension of organizational environment enriches the framework, encompassing as it does, roles, social issues, and resources.

Let us use an example from our everyday life, as the domain complexity of the aircraft flight deck to which the approach has been previously applied can obscure the principles of the cognitive function analysis. My point is to demonstrate, with selectively intuitive examples, that cognitive function analysis can systematically generate design alternatives based on allocation of cognitive functions (CFs). This example is given as clocks or watches are frequently used, often for very simple tasks such as setting time.

Informal enquiry revealed that many users have watches with knob-hand-display arrangements similar to that presented in Figure 6, often report confusing the selection of which knob turns on which hand or display *every time* they use their watches. Unsurprisingly users report this to be frustrating. We use this opportunity to show how different allocations of cognitive function affect design and use. Setting the minutes and hours requires the user to select the hand by pulling the knob entirely and turning it until the required time is set. Setting the week day and month day requires the user to select the right display by pulling the knob entirely, pushing it a little, and turning it right for the week days and left for the month days until the required time is set. People have difficulties finding the intermediary position, and the right direction to turn (right or left) to set weekdays and month days.

6.1 Design case 1: Allocation of cognitive functions to User

The watch in Figure 6 has a straightforward role and its affordances are clear. Even without a formal task analysis, it is reasonably clear that accomplishing the goal of setting the time, and executing the cognitive function of *setting the time to the required time* (on this watch), the user's tasks are to: *choose to change minute, hour, week day or month day, select the hands or the right display, turn the knob until the right time is set*. The resulting operation seems extremely simple. However, the user problems reported with this design case indicate that the watch does not afford the ready completion of the cognitive function *setting the time to the required time,* as performance breaks down at the task of *select the hands or the right display*.

The performance of these tasks is linked to the achievement of the goal of *setting the time to the required time* largely through the design of the watch. We can change the design and change the tasks, which is a good idea as we have task-related problems, and the goal will be met as long as the AUTO resources (artifact, user, task and organizational environment) still somehow collectively perform the required cognitive function. The watch design case in Figure 6 does not afford the task because the *knob function selection* cognitive function required of the user to find the right knob position and direction of turn is not afforded by the layout of the multi-function knob. A lack of functional retention detracts from the affordances of this watch. In this design case the user must work with the artifact (through experimentation) to accomplish the task and thus the goal. In cognitive function terms, there is a disjunction here between the prescribed task (what the designer had in mind) and the activity that is actually performed by the user. For example, some users who need to select the day display don't pull entirely the knob before finding the intermediary position, they pull the knob to the intermediary position directly and they are frustrated to observe that turning right or left does not produce any week day or month day modification. This disjunction is revealed as the performance of an added task (that of 'experimentation') to achieve the cognitive function of *knob function selection*, so that the prescribed task of performing the right sequence of *selecting* and *turning* the correct knob position can be achieved. The observed divergence between prescribed task and activity, combined with user feedback tells us that the allocation of cognitive functions amongst the AUTO resources needs redesign. The repeated 'experimental' nature of the activity informs us that it is the artifact that will benefit from redesign.

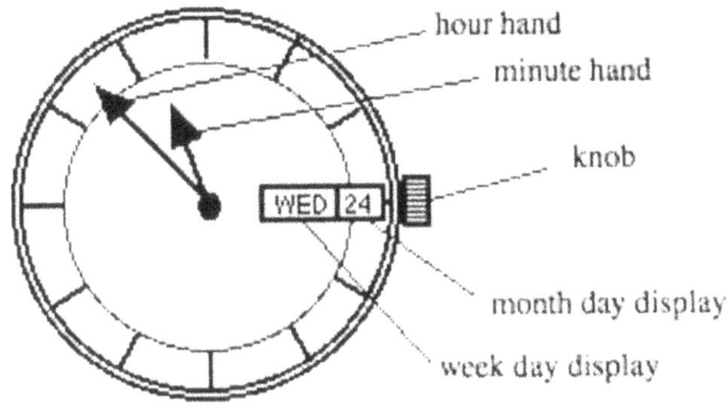

Figure 6. A 'classical' single knob watch.

This cognitive function allocation solution induces a competition process between the user and the artifact. The cognitive functions that are implemented in the watch are engineering-based. For example, the multi-function knob is a very clever piece of engineering since with a single device one can set four time parameters. The main problem is that the end-user needs to be as clever as the engineer who designed the device in order to use it successfully, or use an operation manual that will help supervise the user-watch interaction.

6.2 Design case 2: Allocation of cognitive functions to User and Artifact

In the second design case (Figure 7a), there is a knob for each function (minutes, hours, week days and month days). This alternative design removes part of the selection confusion. The user needs to know that the upper-right knob is the hour-setting knob, and so on as shown on Figure 7a. There is a pattern-matching problem. This design can be improved if the knobs are explicitly associated with the data to be set.

Figure 7a. A multi-knob setting watch.

Figure 7b presents a digital watch interface that removes the requirement for identifying *which knob operates which hand or display* from the user—and with it the cognitive function of pattern matching. The knob-display relationship has become an explicit feature of the watch that exploits existing user attributes and affords selection of the correct knob. The user's task is now simply to select the knob that is next to the time data to be set, and to turn this knob.

Figure 7b. Associative setting watch.

This cognitive function allocation solution induces cooperation by sharing common data between the user and the artifact. Each time-setting device is associated to a single function that the end-user understands immediately such as in the design case shown in Figure 7b. The small physical distance between the time-setting knob and the corresponding data display makes this possible. The end-user does not need an operational manual.

6.3 Design case 3: Allocation of cognitive functions to Artifact

In the third example (Figure 8), new technology is used to design the watch, which has the characteristic of setting time automatically in response to a voice command such as 'set the time to 23:53', 'set the week day to Wednesday', or 'set the month day to 24'. We have transferred The *select the hands or the right display, turn the knob until the right time is set* part of the cognitive function of *setting the time to the required time* is transferred to the watch. The user's task has now become that of simply pushing the voice button and talking to the watch. But, because the whole cognitive function is not transferred to the watch, the user must still perform the cognitive function of *to the required time*. This requirement results in the task of 'looking at the data being set'. Designing an artificial agent that recognizes the speech of the user is not trivial since it needs to take into account possible human errors such as inconsistencies.

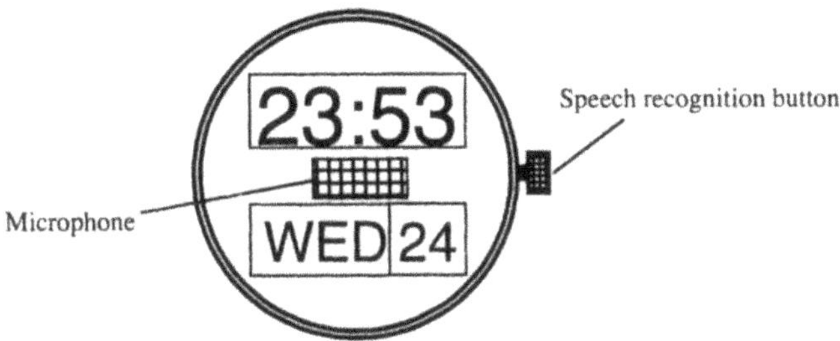

Figure 8. Automated-setting watch

This cognitive function allocation solution induces cooperation by direct communication between the user and the artifact. The watch speech recognition and natural language understanding artificial agent needs to interpret what the user is saying. It needs to filter noisy data, remove inconsistencies, ask follow-up questions in the case of misunderstanding (i.e., no pattern-matching with available patterns). This means that the corresponding artificial agent should include a user model.

We could also transfer this remaining cognitive function to the artifact by designing a radio receptor or a datalink device, which the user could trigger to get the time from a national time service, transferring authority for *the right time* to the artifact. The users task would now simply be to push the time setting button. Thus almost the entire cognitive function for achieving the goal has been transformed and transferred to the watch. Still the user may verify that the data transfer was properly done, and eventually push on the button again.

Several issues emerge from this design case, firstly that a set of inappropriate affordances has been established. This design affords being used inappropriately, for example performed in a geographical zone that is not equipped with this service.

6.4 Design case 4: Allocation of cognitive functions to Organizational Environment

Finally we consider allocating the entire cognitive function for setting the time to the AUTO environmental resource (See Figure 9). Thus, instead of providing a watch-setting device, a direct datalink connection is available on the watch, i.e., the user does not have anything to do, the watch is automatically set by taking data from the above-mentioned national service when necessary and possible.

This design case is the ultimate automation solution. User acceptance of this solution depends on the reliability of the datalink system. The user will learn what the flaws of this design solution are and adapt to them. For instance, when he or she goes on vacations in a region where the datalink connection does not work, either he or she will not care about time setting, or he or she will use another more traditional watch.

Figure 9. No time setting device (automatic datalink).

6.5 Analysis and evaluation

The nature of the interactions among the four types of design is quite different. Consequently the artifact and user cognitive functions of the systems are also different, yet they all enable the system to meet the goal. In the first design case, the user is a problem solver, in the second he or she needs only a little artifact knowledge, in the third he or she manages an artificial agent, and in the forth he or she delegates.

The AUTO pyramid helps the analyst decide which resources are relevant and important, and assists the designer in establishing appropriate design options. However, to obtain some objectivity, consistency and traceability it is important to evaluate the designs using a significant task and an appropriate set of evaluative criteria. The evaluation is performed on the *time-setting* task. Table 1 provides an evaluation of the watch design cases over attributes that were found important in multi-agent human-machine communication (Boy, 1998).

Table 1. CFA evaluation criteria ratings over watch design cases

Criteria for the Setting-time task	**Watch Design Cases**				
	1	2a	2b	3	4
Prediction	High	High	High	High	High
Feedback	Low	High	High	High	N/A
Autonomy	Low	Low	Low	High	High
Elegance	Low	Mediu	High	Mediu	High
Trust	High	High	High	Mediu	High
Intuitiveness	Low	Mediu	High	High	High
Programmability	Mediu	High	High	Mediu	N/A

Design case 1, i.e., a classical single knob watch, enables the interpretation of the first attribute (prediction) in the sense of simplicity and habit of use. In this sense, the time-setting task is very predictable,. In addition, even if several errors are possible, they are predictable. Feedback is low when the user tries to set a time and nothing happens. There is no indication of a bad mode selection for example. In addition, there is no indication on how to recover from dead-ends. Autonomy is low because the user needs to manually perform the time-setting task. Elegance is also low since the fact that human errors are very likely in any situation, they will not ease the overall process in critical contexts. Trust is high when the time-setting mechanism is working properly. The use of the single knob device is not intuitive, even if it is based on a simple design. Once the user has selected the right mode (ability to understand what to do), programming is easy (ability to perform the task efficiently).

Design case 2a, i.e., a multi-knob setting watch, is not significantly different from design case 1 as far as prediction, autonomy and trust are concerned. However, feedback is high since when the user uses any knob the result is always observable on the watch. Elegance is medium and better than in design case 1 because in critical contexts any human error can be detected rapidly for instance. Analogously, intuitiveness is medium because associations can be made between a button and a hand. Programmability is high because oce the right button is selected, it is easy to set time.

Design case 2b, i.e., associative setting watch, is a major improvement to the design case 2a since the watch is more affordable in terms of elegance and intuitiveness.

Design case 3, i.e., automated-setting watch, keeps high prediction, feedback and high intuitiveness. Its major improvement on the previous design alternatives is its high autonomy. However, it has some drawbacks. In particular, elegance is medium because in critical contexts voice could be different from the regular voice used in normal operations for instance. The complexity of the interpretation performed by the voice recognition system might induce errors that may lead to trust problems in the long term. Programmability is medium since the calibration of the voice recognition system might not work in all situations.

Design case 4, i.e., no time setting device (automatic datalink), does not require any action from the user. All evaluation criteria are rated high if the datalink system is very reliable, except the feedback and programmability attributes that are not applicable (N/A) in this case.

7. INTERPRETATION VERSUS AMPLIFICATION

A modern artifact such as the watch shown in Figure 8 can be defined as a cognitive system, i.e., it includes a software agent that constitutes a *deeper interface* between a mechanical artifact and a user. A software agent is a new tool mediating user-artifact interaction. The physical interface is only the surface of this deeper interface. A current research topic is to better understand what operators need to know of this deeper interface. Should they only know the behavior of the physical interface? Should they understand most of the internal mechanisms of the deeper interface? How should the deeper interface represent and transfer the behavior and mechanisms of the (mechanical) artifact?

From a philosophical viewpoint, the issue of user-(mechanical)artifact systems can be seen as whether the coupling is between the (mechanical) artifact and the software agent (Figure 10a) or between the software agent and the user (Figure 10b).

The distinction between *interpretation* and *amplification* is important because it entails two completely different views of the role of the user in user-artifact systems, hence also on the design principles that are used to develop new systems. In the interpretation approach, the software agent can be seen as a set of illusions re-creating relevant artifact functionalities; the user sees a single entity composed of the artifact augmented by the software agent. In the amplification approach, the software agent is seen as a tool or an assistant; the couple user/software-agent works as a team to control the artifact.

Figure 10a. Interpretation: Software agent replaces user functions.

Figure 10b. Amplification: Software agent enhances user capabilities.

Back to the direct-manipulation versus interface agents debate, interpretation induces direct manipulation, and amplification induces delegation. Let us take two examples to illustrate these two approaches:

- The file deletion function, for example, is interpreted by the manipulation of a trash icon of a desktop interface. The trash icon is the visible part of a very simple software agent that incorporates the cognitive function of deleting a file when the user drags a file icon on the trash icon. Other cognitive functions, such as highlighting the trash icon when the file is ready to be included in the trash, facilitate user manipulation by increasing accuracy and understanding. This type of reactive agent removes the burden of remembering the syntax of the delete function from the user for example. The resulting interpretation mechanism improves the affordances of the delete function for the user, and the transmission of a manipulation action of the user on the interface to the machine in the form of a machine-understandable delete function.
- Another type of artificial agent is an on-line spelling checker that informs the user of typos directly when he or she generates a text. In this case, the user delegates spelling checking to such an artificial agent. In a sense, it amplifies the spelling checking user's capability. The coordination of such an artificial agent with the user is crucial. It may result that this kind of artificial agent might be disturbing for the user if after most words it proposes a correction. In this case, the artificial agent should be taking into account the context in which a word is generated. This is very

difficult especially if a safe and mature mechanism is targeted. This is why a human-centered approach to the design of such an artificial agent is required. A very simple cognitive function analysis shows that user's cognitive functions such as interruption handling during idea generation and development (when the user is typing) is extremely disturbing for the user. Too much interruption handling may cause that the user will turn the spelling checker off, and will not use it on-line. Appropriate responses to this issue would be telling the user that the new augmented system provides a new way of generating text, and requiring that he or she follows a substantial training if necessary. The spelling checker artificial agent needs to be taken into account as an amplification mechanism that needs to be learnt and controlled. In particular, the user should be able to use it for a set of common words that he or she will use often; this needs preparation, and then involves a new way of interacting with the resulting text processor. The artificial agent must not alert the user at all times when the user makes a typo, but wait that a sentence or a whole paragraph is typed, for example.

8. CONCLUSION AND PERSPECTIVES

The watch example showed a typical evolution of current artifacts toward more integration in a technology-centered world. Watches will be automatically set using a global positioning system (GPS) via satellite. The adaptation of artifacts will be done through the use of artificial agents.

We live in an information-intensive world where one crucial issue is not information availability but access to the right information at the right time, in the right format. We usually have much more information available than we need and are able to process. Artificial agents also emerge as a necessity to handle this difficult problem of contextual access to information at the same time of a technological glue between modern artifacts and human beings. The concept of artificial agent itself needs to be thought in a broader sense than the usual software agent sense that the AI community currently proposes.

In a general sense, design is guided by the incremental definition and satisfaction of a set of constraints. An important issue is to make the constraints explicit enough to guide the decisions during the design process. These constraints may be budget-based, technology-based or human-factors-based. Budget-based constraints forces faster design and development processes. It results that current technology does not have enough time to become mature before it is replaced by new technology. In addition, I claim that human operators will experience several changes in their professional life. This is not only due to technology changes but also to job changes. It results that training is becoming a crucial issue. In particular, training is no more only a matter of an initial learning phase, but is becoming a life-time continuous education process that is based on performance support through the use of artificial agents. Even if initial training (including theoretical courses) enables the acquisition of conceptual frameworks, artificial agents could provide hands-on training with the possibility of zooming into deeper knowledge.

Artificial agents for training are not the only types of agents. As a matter of fact, a typology of artificial agents based on their use would be extremely useful. I propose an example of typology that will serve both as a starting reference and an illustration of various potential properties of agents:

- agents that enhance information access (database managers);
- agents that deal with situation awareness (secretaries, error-tolerent/error-resistent assistants or rescuers);
- agents that help users to learn (intelligent tutors);
- agents that enhance cooperative work (connectors or brokers);
- agents that perform tasks that people would not be able to perform without them (cognitive prostheses, workload relief systems);
- agents that learn from interaction experience (learning mechanisms);
- agents that require user's expertise or pure common sense for efficient and safe interaction (specialized versus public agents).

Human-factors constraints need to be more taken into account. In particular, what matters is the type of interaction that agents use to communicate among each other:

- The user does not understand what the artificial agent is doing, and it is very likely that both agent end up with competing. This is why rigid procedures are needed to coordinate agent interaction.
- The user interacts with the artificial agent through a common set of perceivable artifacts that each of them understands. A common vocabulary is used.
- Both the user and the artificial agent are able to understand the rationale of the utterances of the other. A common ontology needs to be shared. In this case, an ontology is an organized framework of cognitive artifacts that may take the form of abstract concepts or concrete devices.

These three types of interaction may be possible in various contexts using the same artificial agent. Context is truly the key issue. Context may be related to the type of user, environment, organization, task and artifact. This is why I have developed the AUTO pyramid that supports human-centered design by providing an integrated framework of these key contextual attributes. The design of an artificial agent should be based on the elicitation of the cognitive functions involved in the user-artifact interaction to execute a task in a given organizational environment. With respect to the AUTO pyramid, cognitive function resources can be user-based (e.g., physiological capabilities and limitations, knowledge and skills), task-based (e.g., checklists or procedures), artifact-based (e.g., artifact level of affordances) or organizational-environment-based (e.g., environmental disturbances, delegation to other agents). Human-centered design of artificial agents is a crucial issue that deserves more investigation and practice.

9. ACKNOWLEDGMENTS

Hubert L'Ebraly, Thierry Broignez, Meriem Chater, Mark Hicks, Christophe Solans and Krishnakumar greatly contributed to the current state of the CFA methodology at EURISCO, Aerospatiale and British Aerospace. Thank you all.

10. REFERENCES

Billings, C.E., 1991, Human-centered aircraft automation philosophy. NASA TM 103885, NASA Ames Research Center, Moffett Field, CA, USA.

Boy, G.A., 1998a, *Cognitive function analysis.* Ablex, distributed by Greenwood Publishing Group, Westport, CT.

Boy, G.A., 1998b, Cognitive Function Analysis for Human-Centered Automation of Safety-Critical Systems in Proceedings of CHI'98, ACM Press, 265-272.

Chin, D.N., 1991, Intelligent interfaces as agents. In *Intelligent User Interfaces*, J.W. Sullivan and S.W. Tyler (Eds.). ACM Press, New York, U.S.A, pp. 177-206.

De Brito, G., Pinet, J. & Boy, G.A., 1998, *About the use of written procedures in glass cockpits: Abnormal and emergency situations.* EURISCO Technical Report No. T-98-049, Toulouse, France.

Dornheim, M.A., 1995, Dramatic incidents highlight mode problems in cockpits. *Aviation Week and Space Technology*, Jan. 30, pp. 57-59.

Ehrlich, K., 1998, A Conversation with Austin Henderson. Interview. *Interactions. New visions of human-computer interaction.* November/December.

FCOM-A320, 1997, *Flight Crew Operation Manual A320.* Airbus Industrie, Toulouse-Blagnac, France.

Gibson, J., 1979, *The ecological approach to visual perception.* Boston: Houghton, Mifflin.

Hutchins, E., 1995, How a cockpit remembers its speeds. *Cognitive Science*, 19, pp. 265-288.

Irving, S., Polson, P. & Irving, J.E., 1994, A GOMS analysis of the advanced automated cockpit. *Human Factors in Computing Systems. CHI'94 Conference Proceedings.* ACM Press, 344-350.

Lanier, J., 1995, Agents of Alienation. *interactions*. July, pp. 66-72.

Mathé, N. & Chen, J.R., 1996, User-centered indexing for adaptive information access. *User Modeling and User-Adapted Interaction.* 6(2-3), pp. 225-261.

Minsky, M., 1985, *The Society of Mind.* Touchstone Books. Simon & Schuster, New York.

Muller, M., 1991, Participatory design in Britain and North America: Responding to the «Scandinavian Challenge». In *Reading Through Technology, CHI'91 Conference Proceedings.* S.P. Robertson, G.M. Ohlson and J.S. Ohlson Eds. ACM, pp. 389-392.

Norman, D.A., 1994, How might people interact with agents. *Communications of the ACM*, July, Vol.37, No. 7, pp. 68-71.

Norman, D.A., 1998, *The invisible computer*. MIT Press.

Rudisill, M., 1994, Flight crew experience with automation technologies on commercial transport flight decks. In M. Mouloua and R. Parasuraman, Eds.), *Human Performance in Automated Systems: Current Research and Trends*, Hills dale, NJ, Lawrence Erlbaum Associates, pp. 203-211.

Sarter, N.B. & Woods, D.D., 1994, Pilot interaction with cockpit automation II: An experimental study of pilots' model and awareness of the flight management system. *International Journal of Aviation Psychology*, 4, 1, pp. 1-28.

Shneiderman, B. & Maes, P., 1997, Direct manipulation versus interface agents. *interactions*. November-December issue, pp. 42-61.

Suchman, L., 1987, *Plans and situated actions: The problem of human-machine communications*. New York: Cambridge University Press.

Vera, A. & Simon, H., 1993, Situated actions: A symbolic interpretation. *Cognitive Science*, 17, pp. 7-48.

Wickens, C.D., 1996, Situation awareness: Impact of automation and display technology. *NATO AGARD Aerospace Medical Panel Symposium on Situation Awareness: Limitations and Enhancement in the Aviation Environment* (Keynote Address). AGARD Conference Proceedings 575.

Wickens, C.D. & Flach, J.M., 1988, Information processing. In E.L. Wiener & D.C. Nagel (Eds.), *Human Factors in Aviation*. San Diego, CA: Academic Press, pp. 111-155.

Wiener, E., 1989, *Human factors of advanced technology 'glas cockpit' transport aircraft*. Technical Report 117528. NASA Ames Research Center, Moffett Field, CA.

www.ingramcontent.com/pod-product-compliance
Ingram Content Group UK Ltd.
Pitfield, Milton Keynes, MK11 3LW, UK
UKHW020429200726
13857UKWH00002B/350

* 9 7 8 1 4 7 5 7 7 9 8 0 6 *